CHAMBERS

D1586880

ADULT
LEARNERS'
THESAURUS

CHAMBERS

ADULT LEARNERS' THESAURUS

CHAMBERS

CHAMBERS
An imprint of Chambers Harrap Publishers Ltd
7 Hopetoun Crescent
Edinburgh, EH7 4AY

First published by Chambers Harrap Publishers Ltd 2006

© Chambers Harrap Publishers Ltd 2006

We have made every effort to mark as such all words which we believe to be
trademarks. We should also like to make it clear that the presence of a word in this
thesaurus, whether marked or unmarked, in no way affects its legal status as a
trademark.

All rights reserved. No part of this publication may be reproduced, stored in a
retrieval system, or transmitted by any means, electronic, mechanical,
photocopying or otherwise, without the prior permission of the publisher.

A CIP catalogue record for this book is available from the British Library.

ISBN-13: 978 0550 10186 0
ISBN-10: 0550 10186 1

Designed and typeset by Chambers Harrap Publishers Ltd, Edinburgh
Printed in Italy by Legoprint

Contents

Contributors

Editors
Lucy Hollingworth
Mary O'Neill
Howard Sargeant

Publishing Manager
Patrick White

Prepress
David Reid

Preface

Chambers Adult Learners' Thesaurus is one of a series of books developed by Chambers to address the needs of adult learners.

This thesaurus aims to help adult learners develop their literacy skills and communicate effectively, whether they are filling out a job application, articulating a complaint, or composing a letter to a friend. Therefore the thesaurus has been compiled to contain alternative words and phrases of different levels of formality, but which are always relevant to the adult learner and the situations they may come across. Examples of the word in context are given for all synonyms, helping the user to identify subtle differences in meaning and usage, and to use the words themselves with confidence.

Particularly useful for adult learners is the series of *Vocabulary Choices* boxes which appear at entries such as *hide* and *poor*. These boxes have been specially written to provide discussion points about synonyms that are appropriate for particular contexts or purposes, or that hint at meanings beneath those on the surface. The boxes are intended to heighten awareness of the ways that words are used and how they can influence us, an awareness that the student can apply in daily life.

Another feature of this thesaurus is the inclusion of panels containing 'types of' (for example *accommodation* and *story*) which give learners more words at their disposal, and another way to express themselves.

To encourage ease of use, the layout is open and attractive, with entry words picked out in colour to make them immediately accessible. An identifying letter is printed at the side of the page, showing the user where they are. The typeface used has the approval of the British Dyslexia Association.

All these features make *Chambers Adult Learners' Thesaurus* an invaluable resource for adult students of literacy, for both guided work and everyday reference.

What is a thesaurus?

A thesaurus is not the same as a dictionary. A thesaurus is a book that contains lists of synonyms. Synonyms are words that have a similar meaning and might be used instead of each other.

A thesaurus allows you to look up a common word and find a range of words and phrases that have the same or nearly the same meaning, so you can choose the one that is best for your purpose.

If you have a word in your mind already, why might you want to look for a different one?

- It may be because you have used a particular word already in a piece of writing, and to use it again would make it sound boring:

    *It was really **nice** of you to have me and the girls round for dinner yesterday at your **nice** new flat. We had a really **nice** time.*

    A thesaurus can help you to find a different word when you don't want to repeat a word you have already used:

    *It was really **nice** of you to have me and the girls round for dinner yesterday at your **lovely** new flat. We had a really **enjoyable** time.*

- It may be because the word you are thinking of does not get across exactly what you are trying to say:

    *She **walked** into the room and started shouting at me.*

    A thesaurus can help you to find a word that is more exact or creates a clearer picture:

    *She **marched** into the room and started shouting at me.*

- You may be writing something quite formal, for example a job application or a letter to a head teacher, and you want to use a word or term that fits the purpose:

    *I am writing **about** your recent advertisement.*

    A thesaurus can help you to find a word or term that is more formal:

    *I am writing **with regard to** your recent advertisement.*

- On the other hand, you may be writing something quite informal, for example a letter to a friend, and you want it to have a friendly tone:

    *I'm meeting my **friends** for a meal. Do you want to come?*

A thesaurus can help you to find a word or term that is less formal, and more familiar:

*I'm meeting my **mates** for a meal. Do you want to come?*

- You may want to suggest that you like or dislike something without actually saying so:

  *Naz wears some **bright** clothes. I don't really like them.*

  A thesaurus can help you to find a word or term that hints at your feelings:

  *Naz wears some **garish** clothes.*

- You may want to make people feel a particular way about something, for example something that should make you feel pity or anger:

  *He had **asked** his kidnappers to let him go.*

  A thesaurus can help you to find a word or term that causes a response:

  *He had **pleaded** with his kidnappers to let him go.*

Finding a word in the thesaurus

There are two ways to look up words in this thesaurus. The first way is to use the thesaurus in exactly the same way as you would use a dictionary: by using alphabetical order to go to a word in the book.

However, if the word you are looking for is not there, then you can use another way to find it. Go to the **index of synonyms** at the back of the book. The index is a list, in alphabetical order, of all the synonyms in the thesaurus.

For example, you could look up the word 'abandon' in the index. You would look for it in the black column on the far left of the page.

| **abandon** | **cancel** | 39 |
| | **leave**[1] | 149 |

The words in blue are the places where you will find 'abandon' as one of the synonyms — at **cancel**, and at the first thesaurus entry for **leave**. The numbers on the far right are the numbers of the pages where these entries appear.

All you have to do is choose the entry word that is closest to the meaning of 'abandon' that you are looking for, and find it in the book. The entries will contain other words you could use instead.

Looking up the index is also a useful way of finding *all* the entries in the thesaurus where a particular word appears, so you can choose from the many different synonyms that are available.

Thesaurus entries

The entry word

The word type
To check what these are, see the glossary on page xiv.

Synonyms

Examples of the synonyms
These show you how you might use the words, and help explain the meanings even more.

Vocabulary Choices box
These tell you where and why the words are used, so that you can choose the correct one. They often tell you a little more about the meaning and tone of the words.

Different entries for the same word
There are separate entries for the different word types, shown by numbers. There are also different entries for the same word when the meanings are not connected in any way.

Technical terms
Words that are only used in certain places, for example in medicine or in the army, are shown in a separate group.

device [noun]
   appliance *kitchen appliances such as microwaves*
   contraption *a strange-looking contraption*
   gadget *clever new gadgets*
   machine *a bread-making machine*
   tool *a set of gardening tools*
  ◆ **Formal words** **implement** *spades and other garden implements*
   utensil *cooking utensils*

VOCABULARY CHOICES
• To call a device a **contraption** hints that you think it is a bit ridiculous, either because it is very shoddy or because it is more complicated than it has to be.

back[1] [noun]
He stood at the back of the room.
   end *the people at the end of the queue*
   rear *a seat at the rear of the hall*
   reverse *The picture is on the reverse of the coin.*
   tail *the emblem on the aircraft's tail*
   tail end *the people at the tail end of the queue*
  ◆ **Technical term** **stern** *She was sitting towards the stern of the boat.*

back[2] [adjective]
One of the back tyres was flat.
   hind *The dog had injured one of its hind legs.*
   rear *damage to the rear section of the vehicle*

room → roughly

Rooms:

Rooms in houses:

attic	kitchen
basement	lavatory
bathroom	living room
bedroom	loft
boxroom	lounge
cellar	playroom
conservatory	sitting room
dining room	spare room
guest room	study
hall	toilet
	utility room

> **Page headings**
> The words at the top of the page are the first and last words that appear on that page.

> **'Types of' box**
> These help you find the more exact word for something.

poor [adjective]

1 a poor country

badly off *We were badly off when we first married.*

destitute *destitute children*

hard-up *We were hard-up in those days.*

impoverished *impoverished families*

penniless *The divorce had left him penniless.*

poverty-stricken *Ethiopia and other poverty-stricken countries*

♦ **Formal words disadvantaged** *a scheme to help disadvantaged children*
underprivileged *doctors working in underprivileged areas*

♦ **Informal word broke** *Can you lend me some money? I'm broke.*

♦ **Slang word skint** *I'm skint until the weekend.*

2 a poor mark

bad *a bad score in a test*

inferior *inferior accommodation*

second-rate *companies offering a second-rate service*

shoddy *shoddy workmanship*

substandard *substandard housing*

unsatisfactory *work of an unsatisfactory standard*

> **Examples of the entry word**
> These help you to find the meaning of the entry word that you want.

> **Formal words and phrases**
> If there are formal terms that have the same meaning as the entry word, these are shown in a separate group.

> **Informal words and phrases**
> If there are informal terms that have the same meaning as the entry word, these are shown in a separate group.

> **Slang words and phrases**
> Slang terms that have the same meaning as the entry word are shown in a separate group.

Glossary

Some of the words you may come across in this thesaurus are special terms to describe language and how it is used. Some of them may be unfamiliar. This glossary explains what they mean.

adjective
An adjective is a word that tells you something about a noun. For example, *difficult, good* and *stupid* are adjectives: *a **difficult** sum* • *That film was **good**.* • *a **stupid** mistake*

adverb
An adverb is a word that tells you something about verbs, adjectives or other adverbs. For example, *badly, abroad* and *really* are adverbs: *He played **badly**.* • *I lived **abroad**.* • *I am **really** sorry.* • *He played **really** badly.*

conjunction
A conjunction is a word that links other words or parts of a sentence. For example, *and, but* and *or* are conjunctions: *salt **and** pepper* • *I like butter **but** I hate cheese.* • *do **or** die*

formal
Formal words and phrases are suitable for writing, and also for or speaking when you are being polite. For example, *reside* is a formal word meaning 'to live (somewhere)'.

informal
Informal words and phrases might be used when you are speaking to your friends, but they are not as suitable for writing. For example, *comfy* is an informal word for 'comfortable'.

interjection
An interjection is a word or phrase used to express a strong feeling like surprise, shock or anger. For example, *Oh!* and *Hooray!* are interjections.

noun
A noun is a word that refers to a person or a thing. For example, *tree, Sue,* and *idea* are nouns.

phrase
A phrase is a group of words expressing a single meaning or idea. A phrase might be used on its own or as part of a sentence. For example, *now and then* in *I go swimming **now and then*** is a phrase.

preposition
A preposition is a word put before a noun or pronoun to show how something is related or connected to it. For example, the word *in* is a preposition in the sentence *I put my shopping **in my bag***.

slang
Slang is very informal words or phrases that you use in everyday speech, but not in writing or when you are being polite. For example, *skint* is a slang word meaning 'having no money'.

verb
A verb is the word in a sentence that tells you what someone or something does. For example, *be*, *eat* and *speak* are verbs.

A

about[1] [preposition]

1 write about a subject

concerned with The report was mainly concerned with economic matters.

concerning information concerning his private life

connected with problems connected with her health

relating to documents relating to safety issues

◆ **Formal terms** **regarding** letters regarding the sale of the house

with regard to I am writing with regard to your letter.

2 walk about the town

all over The company has 200 shops all over Britain.

around travel around the world

round She showed me round the house.

throughout The band have given concerts throughout Europe.

VOCABULARY CHOICES

[meaning 1]

• **Regarding** and **with regard to** are often used in formal writing such as business letters.

about[2] [adverb]

1 about twenty

approximately a woman approximately five feet tall

around a diamond ring worth around £800

in the region of The building cost in the region of £1 million.

more or less The boys are the same age, more or less. • rooms that are more or less the same size

roughly a company employing roughly 500 people

2 run about

from place to place Coaches took them from place to place.

here and there Children were rushing here and there.

to and fro He was pacing to and fro across the room.

above[1] [preposition]

1 We flew above the clouds.

beyond The plane went up beyond the clouds.

higher than Hills are higher than the surrounding land.

over The sun shone fiercely over us.

2 Temperatures are above average for the time of year.

exceeding The crane lifts weight not exceeding 1500 kilograms.

higher than His salary was higher than the average.

in excess of driving at a speed in excess of 100 miles per hour

above[2] [adverb]

A helicopter hovered above.

overhead Birds flew overhead.

Aa

◆ **Formal word aloft** She held the trophy aloft.

abroad [adverb]
in foreign parts After service in foreign parts, he returned home.
out of the country She's out of the country at the moment.
overseas people emigrating overseas

absent [adjective]
away away from home
gone All his usual patience was gone.
lacking The evidence needed to convict the criminal was lacking.
missing missing details
not present I wasn't present at the meeting.
out She's out at the moment.
unavailable I'm afraid the manager is unavailable.

absent-minded [adjective]
distracted When he answered me, he seemed distracted.
dreamy She moved in a dreamy way, as if she was in shock.
faraway They had a faraway look in their eyes.
forgetful Mum has become confused and forgetful recently.
vacant a vacant expression on his face

abuse¹ [noun]
1 alcohol abuse • abuse of power
exploitation exploitation of cheap workers
misuse the misuse of government money
2 child abuse • abuse of animals
cruelty His treatment of his wife was sheer cruelty.
harm an organization to protect children from harm
ill-treatment There was evidence of ill-treatment by staff.
molestation Child molestation is a serious crime.
torture the threat of torture and imprisonment

◆ **Formal words maltreatment** people who suffer starvation and maltreatment
mistreatment mistreatment of prisoners by the army
3 shouting abuse at people
curses The driver started yelling curses at us.
insults an exchange of insults which escalated into violence
swear words children shouting swear words at each other

abuse² [verb]
1 abusing his power
exploit exploiting children by forcing them to work
misuse The money we collected for charity has been misused.
2 abusing animals
harm The children were terrified but had not been harmed.
molest sex offenders who have molested children
torture He was tortured by the enemy during the war.

◆ **Formal words maltreat** a shelter for cats which have been maltreated
mistreat I would arrest people who mistreat animals.

accent [noun]
brogue his deep Irish brogue
dialect The dialect of Liverpool is called 'Scouse'.
pronunciation an American pronunciation of 'tomato'
◆ **Informal word twang** The voice had a slight Australian twang.

VOCABULARY CHOICES
• The word **brogue** is usually only used about an Irish or Scottish accent.

accident [noun]
1 an accident with boiling water
misfortune She suffered bad falls and other misfortunes.

Types of accommodation:

apartment	flat	house	youth hostel
barracks	guesthouse	inn	
bed and breakfast	hostel	motel	
bedsit	hotel	villa	

mishap *He slipped once, but completed the climb without any more mishaps.*

2 a road accident
collision *a collision between two cars*
crash *Two people were injured in the train crash.*
pile-up *a ten-car motorway pile-up*
smash *Six people were killed in a horrific smash.*

◆ **Informal word** **prang** *He had a prang as he tried to reverse the car into the space.*

VOCABULARY CHOICES
[meaning 1]
• You might use the word **mishap** if you are trying to play down an accident and suggest it is not serious.
[meaning 2]
• The word **prang** suggests that the accident was slight. The word might be used to make the accident sound less serious than it really is.
• The word **smash** is used to suggest that the accident was very bad. It is often used in newspaper reports to add impact.

accidental [adjective]
chance *Tom made a chance remark and I worked out what was going on.*
unintentional *I'm sorry if I upset you — it was unintentional.*
unplanned *an unplanned pregnancy*
◆ **Formal word** **inadvertent** *an inadvertent use of the wrong word*
◆ **Informal word** **fluky** *The ball hit off his knee and he scored a fluky goal.*

accidentally [adverb]
by accident *I discovered the problem by accident.*
by chance *Some finds were made by chance.*
unintentionally *I unintentionally kicked the person sitting across from me.*
◆ **Formal word** **inadvertently** *He inadvertently scored a goal when the ball hit off his knee.*

accommodation [noun]
See the box above.

achievement [noun]
accomplishment *His most impressive accomplishment was learning French.*
deed *tales of the deeds of knights*
success *What has been your greatest success at work?*
triumph *Life is full of triumphs and failures.*

VOCABULARY CHOICES
• The word **accomplishment** and **success**, as well as the word **achievement** itself, can be used in CVs and job applications to draw attention to the important things you have done in the past.
• The word **deed** is more literary, and suggests brave acts.

active [adjective]
1 an active person • *My father is very active for his age.*
busy *I like to keep myself busy.*
energetic *His mother is an energetic eighty-year-old.*
lively *He's a happy, lively child.*
vivacious *She has a vivacious personality and loves parties.*
2 an active campaigner against the fur trade
committed *a committed Christian*
devoted *a devoted Muslim*

enthusiastic He's an enthusiastic fundraiser for charity.

VOCABULARY CHOICES
[meaning 2]
- The words **committed** and **enthusiastic**, as well as the word **active** itself, can be used in CVs and job applications to make a good impression.
- The word **devoted** gives more of an impression of being extremely keen on a cause or a belief.

admit [verb]
accept He refused to accept that he was to blame.
acknowledge She couldn't acknowledge the truth.
concede He was forced to concede that he'd made a mistake.
confess I have to confess that I wasn't paying much attention.
grant I grant that we ignored some of the rules.

adult [adjective]
full-grown a full-grown tiger
fully grown A fully grown ostrich weighs around 140 kilograms.
grown-up He is married with two grown-up children.
mature mature trees

advice [noun]
guidance a counsellor giving marriage guidance
help Can you help me with this question?
instructions The doctor can help you only if you follow her instructions.
recommendation The bank made some recommendations about taking out a loan.
suggestion My suggestion is that you just wait and see.
◆ **Formal word counsel** He was a wise man who gave good counsel to younger people.

advise [verb]
guide Let your parents guide you in life.
help I can help you with your questions.
recommend Where would you recommend for a nice, quiet holiday?
suggest I suggest you see a doctor.
warn He warned us to book early, as tickets sold fast.
◆ **Formal word counsel** We counsel couples considering divorce.

afraid [adjective]
alarmed She was alarmed at the blood coming from the wound.
fearful No child should be fearful of going to school.
frightened He was too shocked and frightened to speak.
scared I'm scared of spiders.
terrified He was shaking and looked absolutely terrified.

VOCABULARY CHOICES
- All these words could be used to create a fearful mood in a piece of text.
- The word **terrified** has a lot of impact, as it suggests that someone is very afraid.

after [preposition]
as a result of She died as a result of an accident.
following He was depressed following the death of his wife.
◆ **Formal term subsequent to** A report was published subsequent to the meetings.

VOCABULARY CHOICES
- **Subsequent to** is a term which might be used in, for example, official reports or business letters.

again [adverb]
another time I'll have to listen to the tape another time to understand what she meant.
once more He called out once more in

the hope that someone would hear.

◆ **Formal words afresh** He left the job and decided to start afresh somewhere else.

anew Tears filled her eyes anew.

against [preposition]

1 against the wall

adjacent to the street adjacent to this one

in contact with The glue hardens in contact with another surface.

on leaning on the bar

touching a trickle of blood touching his lip

2 against the plan • against our wishes

hostile to Residents are hostile to plans to open a racetrack.

in defiance of He stayed out late in defiance of his parents' wishes.

opposed to I am opposed to corporal punishment.

opposing a number of arguments opposing military action

versus Central heating was a question of expense versus comfort.

aim¹ [verb]

I aim to finish by the end of the week.

intend I intend to become a pilot.

mean He means to come home early this time.

plan She plans to be finished by the end of the year.

set your sights on They have set their sights on winning the competition.

aim² [noun]

Their only aim is to make a quick profit.

goal Happiness is my main goal in life.

intention It was never their intention to cause offence.

object The object of the game is to get rid of your cards.

objective Their objective was to overthrow the government.

purpose John's only purpose in life

◆ **Formal word design** He had dressed with the design of hiding his identity.

air¹ [noun]

1 Open the window to get a little air.

breeze She felt the cool breeze on her face.

draught There was a draught coming from the window.

2 birds flying in the air

atmosphere pollution of the atmosphere

heavens the rain which fell from the heavens

sky The balloon rose up into the sky.

3 an air of sadness

appearance He had the appearance of being very intelligent.

aura There was an aura of mystery about the place.

feeling There was a feeling of peace and calm in the building.

impression He gave the impression of a man who had a lot of money.

look There was a look of anger on her face.

quality He had an unusual quality about him.

VOCABULARY CHOICES

[meaning 2]

• The word **heavens** is quite a literary word and is usually used in stories or poems.

air² [verb]

1 air a room

ventilate Open the window to ventilate the room.

2 air an opinion

communicate He found it difficult to communicate his thoughts.

express She hasn't expressed an opinion on the matter.

give vent to He finally gave vent to the anger inside him.

make known She made known her feelings.

voice Jane voiced her concerns about the project, although few people agreed with her.

VOCABULARY CHOICES
- The phrase **give vent to** means that you are expressing negative feelings of anger or frustration. It also hints that you feel a sense of relief at saying what you think.

alike¹ [adjective]
They both look alike to me.
   akin to a quiet atmosphere akin to a library
   comparable There are no comparable courses at other colleges.
   equivalent houses that are equivalent in size, each with two bedrooms
   identical fish which are virtually identical in appearance
   similar The two boys are very similar.
   the same No two people are completely the same.

alike² [adverb]
This advice applies to men and women alike.
   equally The show appeals equally to young and old.
   similarly They had been similarly affected by the drug, as they all became drowsy.

all¹ [adjective]
All people are equal. • All Europe was at war.
   each Each person was given a gift.
   each and every Cancer can affect each and every one of us.
   every I visit her every day.
   every bit of It took every bit of control she had not to shout.
   every single I think of him every single day.
   the whole of The whole of the village was flooded.

VOCABULARY CHOICES
- The terms **each and every**, **every bit of** and **every single** are used when someone is trying to emphasize to you that they are including every person or thing or every part, and to give you a strong impression of this.

all² [noun]
This money is all I have.
   everything He listened to everything she said.
   ♦ **Informal term** **the lot** She won £1 million and gave the lot away.

allergic [adjective]
   hypersensitive people who are hypersensitive to rubber
   sensitive children who are sensitive to cow's milk

allow [verb]
1 We allowed the children to stay up late.
   approve Councillors approved the plan to build new houses.
   authorize The president had authorized the sale of the land.
   let My parents never let me go to nightclubs.
   permit People under the age of 18 are not permitted to buy alcohol.
   sanction The plan had been sanctioned by the United Nations.
2 Allow two hours for the journey.
   allocate He allocated an hour a day to housework.
   allot Every day, you should allot time to dealing with letters and bills.

VOCABULARY CHOICES
[meaning 1]
- You would be more likely to use the more formal-sounding words **approve**, **authorize** and **sanction** if someone in an official job has given permission for something to happen.

all right [adjective]
1 The film was all right, I suppose.
   acceptable an acceptable piece of work
   adequate The teaching is adequate, but could be improved.

average an average match, not very exciting

fair Her health is fair — it could be better.

not bad I'm not bad at maths.

passable Your essay was passable.

reasonable It was a reasonable performance.

satisfactory His progress in maths has been satisfactory, but he's still poor at English.

◆ **Informal words OK** Does this tie look OK?

so-so The food was so-so.

2 Are you all right?

safe It's getting dark. I hope the kids are safe.

unharmed Despite the fall, I was completely unharmed.

unhurt His leg was unhurt, but his arm was painful.

uninjured She came out of the building shocked, but uninjured.

◆ **Informal word OK** Don't worry, I'm OK.

3 I feel all right again.

healthy I feel healthier since I gave up smoking.

sound My health is quite sound for my age.

well I am pleased to say that dad feels well.

almost [adverb]

approaching It was approaching 4.30 pm.

close to Inflation was close to seven per cent.

just about I've been here just about a year.

nearing Her daughter must be nearing forty now.

nearly It was nearly dark. • I've worked here for nearly twenty years.

practically I see him practically every day.

virtually Virtually all schools are facing the same problems.

alone [adjective]

by yourself The child was all by himself in the playground.

isolated She felt isolated on the tiny island.

lonely I felt lonely when all my children left.

on your own I like to be on my own now and then.

solitary A solitary oak stood in the field.

unaccompanied Unaccompanied children must be at least twelve to see this film.

also [adverb]

as well He has a house in Italy and a house in Spain as well.

as well as They have a cat as well as two dogs.

besides I enjoy reading science fiction books and lots more besides.

in addition Each class has one teacher and, in addition, two classroom assistants.

plus He didn't want to go because he was tired, plus he didn't have enough money.

too She liked skiing and snowboarding too.

◆ **Formal words furthermore** She was skilled and it was clear, furthermore, that she took her work seriously.

moreover He was handsome and he was, moreover, a wealthy young man.

always [adverb]

consistently He has consistently denied the rumours.

constantly a couple who were constantly arguing

continually Language is continually changing.

forever He was forever trying to get attention.

invariably She was invariably polite.

perpetually a man who was perpetually drunk

Aa

unfailingly The staff were unfailingly helpful.
♦ **Informal word twenty-four-seven** I can't be around twenty-four-seven.

anger¹ [noun]
Learn to control your anger.
annoyance his annoyance at being interrupted
fury She reacted with fury at the way she'd been treated, and started shouting.
indignation her indignation at losing her job
irritation 'Of course I couldn't,' he said with irritation.
outrage Her comments provoked outrage.
rage He punched her in a fit of rage.

VOCABULARY CHOICES
• The words **annoyance** and **irritation** suggest slight anger which you sometimes try to hide, especially at something small.
• The words **fury**, **rage** and **outrage** are used of extreme anger, especially the kind that you cannot control or do not try to hide.
• **Indignation** is the anger that someone might feel because they have been insulted or their pride has been hurt.

anger² [verb]
It angers me to see them get away with it.
annoy His comments really annoyed me.
enrage The insult enraged her.
incense Her attitude incensed him even more.
infuriate He made a rude gesture that infuriated her.
irritate The mistake irritated him a little.
madden He was fond of her although she often maddened him.
rile She tried not to let him rile her.
♦ **Informal words aggravate** Her reply aggravated him.
needle The words needled her.

angry [adjective]
annoyed I was annoyed that he hadn't told me.
cross He was getting very cross.
furious She was furious that the photo had been published. • His comments provoked a furious reaction.
incensed He was so incensed that he got up and hit the man.
irate Irate customers complained about the service in the restaurant.
irritated the irritated look on his face
outraged Local people were outraged at the plans to build the road.
♦ **Informal word mad** He was mad at me for arriving late.

VOCABULARY CHOICES
• The words **annoyed**, **cross** and **irritated** suggest that someone is only slightly angry, but someone might say they are annoyed or cross if they want to hide just how angry they are.
• The words **furious**, **incensed**, **irate** and **outraged** have more impact, as they suggest that someone is extremely angry. However, sometimes they can be used to exaggerate how angry someone is, for example in a news report.

animal [noun]
beast a wild beast
creature Chimpanzees are intelligent creatures.
See also the box on the next page.

annoy [verb]
anger Her reaction angered him and he walked out.
irritate The constant delays on the roads irritated her.
rile He was calm, and nothing ever seemed to rile him.
♦ **Formal word displease** The memory of their argument displeased her.
♦ **Informal words aggravate** Her reply

Types of animal:

antelope	dolphin	koala	rabbit
ape	elephant	leopard	rat
baboon	ferret	lion	reindeer
badger	fox	llama	rhinoceros
bear	gerbil	mink	seal
beaver	gibbon	mole	sea lion
bison	giraffe	monkey	sheep
buffalo	goat	moose	squirrel
bull	gorilla	mouse	tiger
camel	hamster	orang-utan	wallaby
cat	hare	otter	walrus
cheetah	hedgehog	panda	weasel
chimpanzee	hippopotamus	panther	whale
cougar	horse	pig	wolf
cow	hyena	polar bear	yak
deer	jaguar	possum	zebra
dog	kangaroo	puma	

aggravated him.

needle *The words he used needled her.*

annoyed [adjective]

angry *She was angry that he hadn't told her.*

cross *He looked cross at the suggestion he should leave.*

irritated *an irritated look on her face*

♦ **Formal word displeased** *She was plainly displeased at the decision against her.*

annoying [adjective]

galling *It must be galling for him to fail after so many successes.*

irritating *Stop making that irritating noise!*

maddening *His behaviour could be quite maddening at times.*

tiresome *a tiresome cough*

♦ **Informal word aggravating** *The constant whistling was very aggravating.*

answer [noun]

1 *He gave them his answer.*

acknowledgement *I complained to the company three weeks ago but have had no acknowledgement yet.*

reaction *I haven't had any reaction to my news.*

reply *I'm still waiting for a reply to my letter.*

response *I left a message but haven't had any response.*

retort *an angry retort*

♦ **Formal word riposte** *a witty riposte*

2 *the answer to the riddle*

solution *a solution to the problem*

explanation *an explanation of the mystery*

VOCABULARY CHOICES

[meaning 1]

• The word **retort** itself suggests that the answer is angry, even without an adjective describing it.

answer [verb]

Why didn't you answer when I called? • *He never answers my e-mails.*

acknowledge *I wrote but he never acknowledged my letter.*

reply *I need to reply to her letter.* • *'No,' she replied.*

Aa

respond *500 people responded to the survey.* • *She responded angrily.*
retort *'Of course I'm nervous,' he retorted.*

anxious [adjective]
apprehensive *He was apprehensive about meeting her manager.*
nervous *Nervous students waited outside the exam room.*
on tenterhooks *She had been on tenterhooks waiting for the phone call.*
tense *She looked pale and tense.* • *a tense moment as he waited for the result*
uneasy *The silence made her feel uneasy.*
worried *He's been worried about the test all week.*

apply [verb]
1 apply for a job
ask for *The researchers asked for a grant of £40,000.*
claim *He's claiming compensation after the accident.*
put in for *She's put in for a transfer to another department.*
◆ **Technical term** **petition** *The husband petitioned for divorce.*
2 apply new methods
bring into play *New rules will be brought into play.*
employ *It will be a hard game, whatever tactics they employ.*
implement *attempts to implement new working methods*
use *the methods used by children to get what they want*
3 apply ointment
put on *Put some sun cream on.*
rub *She rubbed some oil on her skin.*
smear *Rob smeared ketchup all over the bacon.*
spread on *Spread the cream evenly on the cake.*

approximate [adjective]
close *It's not exactly the same colour but it's close.*

estimated *The war has left an estimated 15,000 people dead.*
loose *a loose translation of a French word*
rough *a rough estimate of £150*

area [noun]
1 a run-down area of the city
district *New York's financial district*
enclave *a Muslim enclave in Bosnia*
neighbourhood *They live in a poor neighbourhood.*
part *This is one of the oldest parts of the city.*
quarter *the city's historic quarter*
region *the Great Lakes region of North America*
zone *a factory in the industrial zone*
◆ **Formal word** **locality** *work available in the locality*
2 an area of desert
expanse *a large expanse of land*
patch *a patch of ground*
section *a dangerous section of the road*
stretch *a three-mile stretch of the river*
tract *large tracts of forest*
3 an area of study
branch *the branch of medicine dealing with childhood illnesses*
field *She's an expert in the field of psychology.*
sphere *people involved in the political sphere*
subject *French, biology and other subjects studied at school*

VOCABULARY CHOICES
[meaning 1]
• The word **enclave** is often used in the news for an area in which a particular group of people live which is different from the areas around it. It hints that the people there are rather cut off from others.

argue [verb]
1 arguing over every little detail

bicker *bickering over who was going to clear up*
fight *They were fighting about who would sleep in the bed.*
haggle *They are still haggling over the details of the contract.*
quarrel *He left home after quarrelling with his father.*
row *couples rowing over money*
squabble *two children squabbling over a toy*
wrangle *Lawyers wrangled over the judge's decision.*
2 He argued that it couldn't be so.
assert *She asserted that many improvements had been made.*
claim *The report claims that safety issues are being ignored.*
maintain *She maintained that both of them were innocent.*
reason *It was possible, he reasoned, that the crime had been committed by someone else.*
suggest *I'm not suggesting that it will be easy.*
◆ **Formal word contend** *Defence lawyers contended that he could not be guilty.*

VOCABULARY CHOICES
[meaning 1]
• Using the words **bicker** and **squabble** suggest that you do not approve of what is going on, because people are arguing about something that is not important.

argument [noun]
1 a heated argument
clash *a legal clash over the issue*
disagreement *a disagreement over who would drive*
dispute *a dispute over who owns the land*
feud *a long-running feud between the families*
quarrel *a quarrel between John and his father*

row *a political row*
tiff *He left the pub after a tiff with his girlfriend.*
wrangle *involved in a bitter legal wrangle*
◆ **Informal term slanging match** *A difference of opinion turned into a slanging match.*
2 She put forward her argument.
assertion *his assertion that they cannot be trusted*
case *the case against making the drug legal*
claim *her claim that children need a good education*
reasoning *I couldn't follow the reasoning.*
◆ **Formal word contention** *Research does not support the contention.*

VOCABULARY CHOICES
[meaning 1]
• The word **feud** suggests an argument that lasts for many years.
• The word **wrangle** is used for an argument that continues for a long time, and often involves lawyers and courts.
• The word **clash** is usually used in newspapers and news reports to add impact to the story.
• You might use the word **tiff** to play down an argument and suggest that it is not very serious. It is most often used when the people arguing are boyfriend and girlfriend, or wife and husband.

army [noun]
armed force *a country with a large armed force*
land forces *head of Germany's land forces*
military *the US military*
militia *a local militia, used only in emergencies*

around¹ [preposition]
1 all around the building

on all sides of *Rub oil on all sides of the cake tin.*
on every side of *dents on every side of the car*
round *We all sat round the table.*
2 around a dozen
about *There were about 50 people at the meeting.*
approximately *approximately 1.70 metres tall*
circa *He was born circa 1750.*
more or less *She's been here more or less 18 months.*
roughly *There were roughly 100 people at the party.*

VOCABULARY CHOICES
[meaning 2]
• The word **circa** is used in writing, before a date, to show that it is not exact.

---

around² [adverb]
1 jump around
about *The dog was leaping about.*
all over *The children were running all over.*
everywhere *I've searched everywhere.*
here and there *rushing here and there*
in all directions *people walking in all directions*
to and fro *children running to and fro*
2 stay around
at hand *I always keep my diary at hand.*
close by *Make sure the children stay close by.*
nearby *I wanted to stay nearby.*

arrange [verb]
1 arrange a meeting
co-ordinate *He had co-ordinated the group's visit.*
fix *I've fixed to go to the theatre next week.*
organize *Let's organize a surprise party for his birthday.*
plan *They are busy planning a school reunion.*

2 arranging the cards in his hand
group *He grouped the newspapers by date.*
order *The list is ordered alphabetically.*
position *He positioned the flowers carefully in the vase.*
set out *She was setting out chairs for the audience.*
sort *She sorted the clothes into two piles.*
sort out *Sort the books out by author.*

ashamed [adjective]
embarrassed *She felt embarrassed at the cruel things she'd said.*
guilty *I feel really guilty that I didn't help more.*
humiliated *He felt humiliated by his defeat.*
mortified *I was mortified that I'd hurt him.*
red-faced *Police were left red-faced after the man escaped.*
remorseful *He was deeply remorseful about his behaviour.*
sheepish *She looked a bit sheepish as she spoke.*
♦ **Formal words** **abashed** *his abashed confessions*
contrite *She was contrite and apologized.*

VOCABULARY CHOICES
• The word **mortified** suggests that someone is very ashamed.
• **Remorseful** is similar, but this word emphasizes the great regret someone feels at what they have done.
• The word **sheepish** suggests you are just slightly ashamed by something you have done.

---

ask [verb]
1 ask for help • ask for advice
appeal *Police are appealing for help in tracing the men.*
beg *I begged him not to go.*
clamour *children clamouring for attention*

plead *He pleaded for an end to the fighting.*

request *requesting help in the hunt for information*

seek *Seek advice from a solicitor.*

◆ **Formal words beseech** *No more, I beseech you!*

entreat *She entreated me to stay.*

implore *He implored her to be calm.*

solicit *soliciting donations for the charity*

2 ask awkward questions

inquire *students inquiring about courses*

interrogate *police interrogating suspects*

query *I queried whether the bill was correct.*

question *Two hundred people were questioned in the survey.*

quiz *I quizzed him about where he'd been.*

VOCABULARY CHOICES

[meaning 1]

• You might use the words **beg**, **plead**, **entreat** and **implore** when someone is asking in a desperate and urgent way. These words might be used to produce an emotional response, such as pity, in a reader.

• **Beg** and **plead** are sometimes used to suggest that someone has been forced to behave without pride or dignity in asking for something.

• The word **beseech** is a very old-fashioned word that you sometimes see in books. It also suggests that someone asks in a very urgent way.

• The words **request** and **seek** are slightly more formal than some of the others and might be used to be polite and tactful: *We politely request that you refrain from smoking.*

assistant [noun]

accomplice *The gunman had an accomplice.*

aide *the President's aides*

ancillary *specialist teachers and ancillaries*

auxiliary *nursing auxiliaries*

helper *a team of helpers*

right-hand man *the Prime Minister's trusted right-hand man*

VOCABULARY CHOICES

• The word **accomplice** would be used of someone helping another person to do something bad or even illegal.

• **Right-hand man** suggests an assistant who is particularly loyal to and trusted by the person they are helping, more so than others.

attack¹ [noun]

1 a military attack • a brutal attack on a young man

assault *the assault on Baghdad* • *a vicious assault on an elderly woman*

bombardment *the German bombardment of London in 1940*

invasion *troops involved in the Iraq invasion*

offensive *Serbian forces launched an offensive against rebels.*

onslaught *the onslaught on Russian troops*

raid *an air raid on Britain*

strike *air strikes against Afghanistan*

◆ **Formal word incursion** *They fought off an incursion by rebel soldiers.*

2 a verbal attack

abuse *verbal abuse*

assault *The MP continued his assault on the Prime Minister's policies.*

criticism *The government is facing fierce criticism.*

onslaught *a celebrity who has faced an onslaught from the newspapers*

attack² [verb]

1 attacked by Vikings • attacked by a gang

assault *She was assaulted and robbed.*

invade *Troops invaded the city.*

raid *Forces raided the city of Kojan.*

set upon *He was set upon by a gang of four men.*

storm *Troops stormed the village.*

♦ **Formal words assail** *He assailed the government for its failure to control prices.*

censure *The President deserves to be censured for his actions.*

revile *Though reviled by critics, the film was a huge success.*

♦ **Informal term lay into** *He was screaming as they laid into him with their fists.*

♦ **Slang term do over** *He was done over by a group of yobs.*

2 attacked in the newspapers

abuse *He had been threatened and verbally abused.*

criticize *Her decision has been criticized.*

denounce *The film has been denounced as offensive.*

malign *a leader who was much maligned by Republicans*

attract [verb]

appeal to *The design will appeal to young children.*

draw *It was his kindness which first drew me to him.*

entice *Buyers were enticed by low prices.*

interest *It was the location and salary which interested me.*

lure *Top players are lured by fame and money.*

seduce *seduced by a very tempting offer*

tempt *tempted by the deal on offer*

VOCABULARY CHOICES

• The words **lure** and **seduce** can hint that someone is attracted by something they should not be, or by something that appeals to emotions such as greed or selfishness.

• The words **entice**, **lure** and **seduce** are sometimes used when the thing you are attracted to might be disappointing or might not be as promising it looks.

attractive [adjective]

1 an attractive woman

beautiful *She was beautiful.*

fetching *She looked fetching in a pink dress.*

good-looking *a good-looking young man*

gorgeous *a gorgeous actress*

handsome *a handsome prince*

lovely *She looked lovely in the dress.*

pretty *a pretty woman*

♦ **Informal word stunning** *His girlfriend is absolutely stunning.*

2 an attractive offer

appealing *The idea was very appealing.*

inviting *an inviting opportunity*

seductive *seductive offers*

tempting *a tempting idea*

VOCABULARY CHOICES

[meaning 1]

• The words **gorgeous** and **stunning** suggest that you think someone is extremely attractive. They are sometimes used in newspaper and magazine articles to describe people, as the words add excitement.

average[1] [adjective]

1 an average performance, nothing special

mediocre *He gave a fairly mediocre performance.*

undistinguished *an undistinguished career as a teacher*

unexceptional *an unexceptional student*

♦ **Informal word so-so** *The concert was so-so.*

2 the average twelve-year-old • on an average day

normal *Until then, it had just been a normal day.*

ordinary *an ordinary house*

run-of-the-mill *run-of-the-mill villages*

typical *He wasn't a typical five-year-old.*

usual *the usual thing that happens*

average [noun]
  mid-point the mid-point of current salary ranges
  norm His pay was nowhere near the norm for a man of his age.
  standard below the national standard
  ◆ **Technical term mean** The mean of 4, 7 and 10 is 7.

avoid [verb]
  dodge I tried to dodge the question.
  escape You can't escape paying tax.
  evade We managed to evade capture.
  get out of get out of doing the washing up
  shirk Don't shirk your responsibilities.
  shun Neighbours shunned him after he came out of prison. • After the incident he shunned alcohol.
  sidestep try to sidestep the issue
  ◆ **Informal terms duck** duck the question
  steer clear of I try to steer clear of her.

VOCABULARY CHOICES

• The word **sidestep** is often used about cleverly avoiding difficult questions. It is often used in news stories about politicians, for example.
• You can use the phrase **get out of** when talking about getting free of an unpleasant task or duty. It might also hint that someone was lucky to do so, and there can be a note of resentment.
• **Dodge** and **shirk**, however, have a stronger sense of criticism. They suggest a person is avoiding something they really should be doing, perhaps because they are lazy or cowardly.
• **Shun** is quite a powerful word, as it conveys a strong feeling of wanting to avoid someone or something completely, sometimes because it is hated or causes harm.
• The phrase **steer clear of** would also suggest you are avoiding something in a very determined way.

awake [adjective]
  conscious It was early, and I wasn't fully conscious yet.
  wide-awake He was lying there, wide-awake.

away [adjective]
  absent absent from school
  gone When I got back he was gone.
  not present I wasn't present at the meeting.
  out She's out at the moment.
  unavailable I'm afraid the manager is unavailable.

awkward [adjective]
1 an awkward tool to use • an awkward question
  cumbersome a wedding dress that was cumbersome to wear
  difficult a difficult machine to handle
  fiddly flatpack furniture with lots of fiddly bits
  inconvenient an inconvenient time to arrive
  tricky a tricky sum • His lies have put me in a tricky situation.
  troublesome a troublesome problem to solve
  unwieldy Prams can be too unwieldy to take on to buses.
2 Stop being awkward and join in!
  obstinate an obstinate old man
  stubborn She was too stubborn to take my advice.
  unco-operative The bank manager was unco-operative when I asked for a loan.
3 I felt awkward when they started arguing in front of me.
  embarrassed When he said the wrong thing there was an embarrassed silence.
  ill at ease I felt ill at ease when she criticized me.
  uncomfortable His presence at the party made us all uncomfortable.

B

baby [noun]

child clothes for a child aged three to four
toddler a toddler wearing his first pair of shoes
- **Formal words babe** The Wise Men found the babe lying in a manger.
infant a care unit for mothers and infants
- **Informal word tot** a playgroup for mums and tots

VOCABULARY CHOICES

- **Babe** is not an everyday word. It is a literary word, usually found in stories and poems.
- The word **infant** is often used in writing about a baby's or young child's health.

back¹ [noun]

He stood at the back of the room.
end the people at the end of the queue
rear a seat at the rear of the hall
reverse The picture is on the reverse of the coin.
tail the emblem on the aircraft's tail
tail end the people at the tail end of the queue
- **Technical term stern** She was sitting towards the stern of the boat.

back² [adjective]

One of the back tyres was flat.
hind The dog had injured one of its hind legs.
rear damage to the rear section of the vehicle

back³ [verb]

1 back into the garage
back away The lion roared and we backed away.
back off We backed off from the fight before someone got hurt.
backtrack He turned round and backtracked up the hill.
go backwards How do you make the car go backwards?
recede At last the flood waters are beginning to recede.
retreat There were signs that the enemy troops were retreating.
reverse A huge truck was reversing towards us.
- **Formal word recoil** She recoiled in disgust.
2 They back the Labour candidate.
favour Which of the suggestions do you favour?
second Frank proposed the change and I seconded it.
side with If there's an argument, she always sides with her father.
support The scheme is supported by Hollywood's most powerful people.
- **Formal word endorse** The plan was endorsed by the Prime Minister.
3 the money to back a new business
finance How is the project being financed?
sponsor Soap operas were once

sponsored by soap companies.

subsidize The trip is cheaper for members because the club subsidizes them.

support The museum is supported by Lottery funding.

[meaning 3]
• The word **finance** is used when a person or company provides a lot of money to help run something big or important.
• You use the word **sponsor** especially when the company that is giving money is being advertised in return, for example at the beginning of a television programme or on the shirts of a football team.
• The word **subsidize** is used when an organization is paying only part of the cost of something.
• **Support** is a more general word you can use that means to give money to help keep something running.

bad [adjective]
1 a bad smell • a bad habit
nasty a child with very nasty habits
undesirable The drug has some undesirable effects.
unpleasant She said some very unpleasant things about me.
♦ **Formal word disagreeable** We spent a disagreeable hour in the rain.
2 a bad accident
serious Luckily, nobody suffered serious injuries.
severe Ali was complaining of severe stomach pains.
♦ **Formal word grave** The storm got worse and the boat was in grave difficulties.
3 a bad person
corrupt The problem was how to get rid of corrupt officials.
criminal He had committed a criminal act.
evil The child is occasionally naughty but not evil.

immoral Her parents regarded even the smallest lie as immoral behaviour.
sinful She said little about her sinful past.
wicked You must be punished for the wicked thing you did.
4 bad quality • bad eyesight
faulty A faulty connection could easily cause an accident.
imperfect Articles judged to be imperfect were sold at lower prices.
inferior The second hotel was of an inferior standard.
poor We complained about the poor quality of the food.
substandard I'm not paying for substandard work.
unsatisfactory Your performance this season has been unsatisfactory.
♦ **Formal word deficient** The law was deficient in this respect.
5 That meat must be bad by now.
mouldy Don't eat the bread if it's mouldy.
off Does this milk smell off?
rancid The cream had been left out of the fridge and was rancid.
rotten They are reduced to eating rotten fruit and vegetables.
sour Cheesemakers add a substance that makes the milk go sour.
spoilt Much of the fruit was rejected as spoilt.
6 a bad child
disobedient It's frustrating to be with such a disobedient child all day.
mischievous He wasn't mischievous enough to play a trick like that.
naughty Naughty children were punished.
7 a bad time to call
inconvenient They chose to visit at a very inconvenient moment.
unfortunate It was an unfortunate thing to say at that time.
unsuitable At this first stage, we reject any candidates that are clearly unsuitable.

Bb

Types of bag:

backpack	case	rucksack	shoulder bag
briefcase	duffel bag	sack	suitcase
bumbag	handbag	satchel	
carrier bag	holdall	shopping bag	

VOCABULARY CHOICES

[meaning 3]
- All of these words are very disapproving. To describe a person or action as **evil** or **wicked** is very strong, suggesting they are extremely bad and cruel for the sake of it.
- You have to be careful with the words **sinful** and **immoral** as they suggest you are making a judgement about someone's morals. **Sinful** also has a strong religious tone.
- The word **corrupt** is a very disapproving word. It is often used to describe people in power who abuse that power, or the things they do.

[meaning 7]
- You use the word **inconvenient** to describe something that causes a slight problem for you, for example because it happens at a time when you had planned to do something else. Rather than using the word 'bad', this word can be used to be polite or tactful about something that does not suit you: *Tuesday is a bit inconvenient for me. Can we arrange a different day?*
- The word **unfortunate** suggests that something causes an awkward situation, for example because people are embarrassed or offended by it.

bag¹ [noun]
See the box above.

bag² [verb] (informal)
I bag this one.
  get *Get that free table before someone else nabs it.*
  grab *I grabbed a seat by the window.*
  take *Frank took the only decent*

newspaper in the pile.

ban [verb]
  bar *He's been barred from every pub in the city.*
  exclude *Photographs like this have been excluded from our magazine.*
  forbid *Spiked shoes are forbidden in the clubhouse.*
  outlaw *The use of chemicals has been outlawed completely.*
  suppress *The government has suppressed all political meetings.*
- **Formal word prohibit** *Smoking is prohibited in the kitchens.*

bare [adjective]
1 bare skin
  exposed *Your exposed shoulders might burn in the sun.*
  naked *naked arms*
  nude *He painted nude figures.*
  uncovered *Three walls were papered, one was uncovered.*
  undressed *She barged into the room while I was undressed.*
2 The room looks bare without pictures.
  clear *a clear piece of land with no trees*
  empty *The machines were sold and the factory was left empty.*
  unfurnished *I rented an unfurnished flat.*

basic [adjective]
  central *the central theme of the story*
  elementary *She has only an elementary knowledge of the arithmetic.*
  essential *These are the essential skills needed for the job.*
  fundamental *Learn the fundamental rules of grammar before you try more complex sentences.*

key the key issues for the future of our world
primary The group's primary purpose was to overthrow the government.
root What are the root causes of the illness?

beach [noun]
sand We went for a walk along the sand.
sands The campsite is right on the sands.
seashore These are the birds you'll most likely see on the seashore.
seaside Everyone enjoys a day at the seaside.
shore The boat was a few hundred yards from the shore.

bear [verb]
1 bear pain • bear inconvenience
abide I can't abide people who complain all the time.
cope with How does she cope with that constant pain?
endure These are hardships that most of us couldn't endure.
put up with I wouldn't put up with his rudeness for very long.
stand We wonder how she stands living in the same house as her mother.
tolerate How do you tolerate all that noise?
2 bear the weight of something
carry These pillars carry the full load of the bridge.
hold I didn't think the chair would hold my weight.
support Tall buildings are supported by a steel frame.
take A good nylon rope will take that strain.

beat¹ [noun]
the steady beat of the drums
pulse The heart has regular pulses.
throbbing The noise made the throbbing in his head worse.

thump the thump of rock music from the bar below

beat² [verb]
1 a child beaten by his father
batter She would batter him if she ever found out.
hit He hit the boy across the head with his open hand.
knock The man knocked Giles to the ground.
pound He pounded on the table with his fists.
punch The other one punched me in the stomach.
strike Any teacher who struck a child would lose their job.
♦ **Informal term lay into** Three boys came from nowhere and laid into him.
2 beating faintly
pulsate The headaches come as a pulsating pain.
pulse Loud music was pulsing through the streets.
throb Her bruised arm throbbed with pain.
thump The doors opened and jazz came thumping out.
vibrate The phone vibrates when it rings.
3 beat the enemy • beat a rival team
conquer They had conquered most of the armies of Europe.
defeat Will they be defeated by their old rivals Liverpool?
outdo She was not going to be outdone by a boy.
overcome We were overcome by a more powerful force.
subdue Police quickly subdued the rioters.
surpass a performance that surpassed all previous records
trounce The favourites were trounced by the underdogs.
♦ **Informal words hammer** I think our team will hammer them.

Bb

thrash We thrashed them 10–3.

[meaning 3]
• The words **hammer**, **thrash** and **trounce** suggest that you beat someone very easily. These words are often used in newspaper sports reports to add dramatic effect.

beaten [adjective]
broken He seemed a broken man.
crushed The miners went back to work completely crushed.
defeated The troops, exhausted and defeated, stared at each other.

beautiful [adjective]
attractive It's a very attractive little town.
charming There are some charming houses on the seafront.
good-looking James was tall and good-looking.
gorgeous a gorgeous actress
handsome He was easily the most handsome man in the room.
lovely What a lovely place for a picnic!
pretty The girl is intelligent and pretty.
♦ **Informal word stunning** His girlfriend is absolutely stunning.

• The words **gorgeous** and **stunning** suggest that you think someone is very beautiful. They are sometimes used in newspaper and magazine articles to describe people, as the words add excitement.

because [conjunction]
as As we're late already, we'd better not stop.
for He didn't mention it, for now was not the time.
on account of Ma had to sit down, on account of the pain in her legs.
owing to Owing to technical problems, the software will not be released until October.
since Since you ask, I'm fine, thanks.
thanks to The company will stay in business thanks to a new order from Korea.

bed [noun]
berth a six-berth tent
bunk Each cabin has two bunks.
cot The baby was sound asleep in her cot.

before [adverb]
earlier Let's return to a subject we discussed earlier.
formerly The hotel was formerly a girls' school.
in advance The project will begin in June but I'll send out notes in advance.
previously We rented a house this time. We've previously stayed in hotels.
sooner I wish I'd known that sooner.

beg [verb]
plead We pleaded with her not to tell the manager.
♦ **Formal words entreat** He entreated Alim to overlook his mistakes.
implore Do not, I implore you, alter anything.

begin [verb]
activate This switch activates the alarm.
found The company was founded a hundred years ago.
introduce Laws were introduced to combat terrorism.
set about How will you set about finding new staff?
set in motion Emma set in motion her plans for improving the flat.
start You cannot say that a single event started the war.
♦ **Formal terms commence** Fighting could not commence until a declaration of war had been made.
embark on This is a dangerous journey we are embarking on.

beginner [noun]
  apprentice *a plumber's apprentice*
  learner *On cars, 'L' stands for 'learner'.*
  novice *I'm a novice to this business.*
  trainee *a management trainee*

behave [verb]
  act *She acts as if she's never seen food before.*
  perform *We don't know how well the car performs in these conditions.*
♦ **Formal term conduct yourself**
  Everything depends on how you conduct yourself in the interview.

behaviour [noun]
  actions *You have to learn to be responsible for your own actions.*
  conduct *The committee has found your conduct to be unacceptable.*
  habits *a man with very unpleasant habits*
  manners *She looks disgusting and her manners are very bad.*
  reaction *What will her reaction be if you turn up with a ring?*
  response *The audience's response was to remain silent.*
  ways *He's not familiar with the ways of young people.*

behind[1] [preposition]
1 *the garage behind the house*
  at the back of *the beer garden at the back of the pub*
  on the other side of *There's a lovely garden on the other side of this wall.*
  to the rear of *There are parking spaces to the rear of the office.*
2 *behind me in the queue*
  after *Your name is after mine on the list.*
  following *a car with a trailer following it*
3 *We're behind you all the way.*
  backing *Several major companies are backing Britain's bid to win the Games.*
  for *Most people are for a change to the law.*
  supporting *I'm supporting the Prince's scheme to get kids off the streets.*

4 *Who's behind all this?*
  causing *We don't know what's causing this change of heart.*
  responsible for *Who was responsible for changing the contract?*

behind[2] [adverb]
1 *an engine with six carriages following behind*
  after *the king riding at the front and the princes coming after*
2 *We've fallen behind with our payments.*
  in arrears *We were three months in arrears with the rent.*
  late *Your essay is three days late.*
  overdue *Payment is now overdue by several months.*

VOCABULARY CHOICES
[meaning 2]
• The phrase **in arrears** is often used in official documents, for example notices from a local council, as a more formal way of talking about money owed.

believe [verb]
1 *You can't believe anything they say.*
  accept *I refuse to accept that her husband knew nothing.*
  credit *If you didn't know it was true, you would never credit it.*
  rely on *Scientists should rely on firm evidence.*
  trust *Customers trust that they are getting quality goods.*
♦ **Informal word swallow** *I don't think my parents will swallow that excuse.*
2 *He believes that it may work.*
  consider *Most people consider him to be the best player of his time.*
  gather *I gather you're leaving at the end of the month.*
  guess *I guess they wanted to avoid offending you.*
  imagine *How do you imagine the thieves got in?*

presume *From what she said, I presumed she was his mother.*

reckon *I reckon they'll arrive around nine this evening.*

suppose *The woman supposed he was waiting for someone.*

think *We think the first man is telling the truth.*

below [adverb]
Look below for the answers.

beneath *They looked down into the valley beneath.*

down *The next town on the river was a few miles further down.*

under *We watched as the divers went under.*

underneath *The floorboards are laid onto the concrete underneath.*

below [preposition]
1 below the table

beneath *Nobody had swept the floor beneath the table.*

under *There's a cupboard under the sink.*

underneath *Underneath that tough exterior, he's very charming.*

2 below him in rank

junior to *These assistant managers are junior to her.*

♦ **Formal term** **subordinate to** *A colonel is subordinate to a general.*

bend [verb]
1 The reed bent but did not break. • He bent the twig till it snapped.

buckle *The front of the car buckles as it hits the wall.*

twist *The woman has twisted her wrist in the fall.*

2 I bent to look through the keyhole.

crouch *Alice crouched down behind a bush.*

lean *She leant towards him so she could hear.*

stoop *Tom has to stoop to get in through the door.*

3 The river bends to the east here.

curve *Here, the coastline curves sharply.*

veer *The road veered off to the right.*

bend [noun]
a sharp bend in the road

curve *The track follows the curve of the river.*

turn *a sharp right-hand turn*

twist *There were a few twists in the metal frame.*

beneath [adverb]
When they searched beneath, they found the body.

below *From the hilltop, they could see the town if they looked below.*

beneath [preposition]
What is beneath the surface?

below *She lives in the flat below mine.*

under *the ground under your feet*

underneath *He had a jacket on underneath his coat.*

benefit [noun]
I don't see any benefit in waiting.

advantage *Being tall can be an advantage in a crowd.*

gain *Their only interest is financial gain.*

good *Don't argue — no good will come of it.*

help *Use my dictionary if you think it will be any help.*

use *My umbrella is no use at all in this wind.*

benefit [verb]
It won't benefit us to complain.

help *It doesn't help things if you cry.*

improve *We need something that will improve our situation.*

beside [preposition]
adjacent to *The dining room was adjacent to the kitchen.*

at the side of *the table at the side of the bed*

next to *a house next to the sea*

best [adjective]
finest *staying in the finest hotel in Chicago*

greatest *She was the greatest tennis player of her generation.*
highest *Adam always gets the highest marks in the class.*
leading *one of the country's leading scientists*

bet¹ [verb]
He likes to bet on horse races.
   gamble *Her heavy gambling used up all the money.*
   stake *I'll stake five pounds that City win.*
   take a chance *I sometimes take a chance and buy a lottery ticket.*
   try your luck *Tom thought he might try his luck on the greyhounds.*
   wager *I would wager that we will hear from her again.*

bet² [noun]
Place your bets now.
   chance *I'll take a chance and play the lottery.*
   punt *I have an occasional punt on the football, but that's all.*
   stake *The minimum stake on this race is one dollar.*
   wager *He had a wager on the result of the match.*

better [adjective]
1 *a better deal • a better example*
   greater *She had never been paid a greater compliment.*
   preferable *A table in the shade would be preferable.*
   superior *Freshly-cooked food is superior to microwave meals.*
2 *getting better*
   fitter *Your dad looks a lot fitter today.*
   recovered *He hasn't completely recovered from his operation.*
   stronger *I'm feeling much stronger now I'm eating again.*
   ♦ **Informal phrase on the mend** *He's still in hospital but he's definitely on the mend.*

big [adjective]
1 *big muscles • a big change*
   colossal *A colossal truck moved up the street.*
   enormous *There's an enormous difference between them.*
   gigantic *The hotel is absolutely gigantic.*
   huge *They were greeted by huge crowds.*
   immense *an immense statue of the president*
   large *The company made a large profit.*
   mammoth *We had to load a mammoth crate onto the lorry.*
   massive *Their house is massive.*
2 *a big occasion • one of the biggest stars in football*
   important *Any wedding is an important day.*
   prominent *one of this country's most prominent athletes*
   ♦ **Formal word momentous** *The fall of the Berlin Wall was a momentous occasion.*

birth [noun]
   childbirth *The mother died during childbirth.*
   delivery *The midwife will help you during the actual delivery.*

bit [noun]
   fragment *Fragments of glass lay everywhere.*
   part *a shop selling car parts*
   particle *a particle of dust*
   piece *Cut the apple into small pieces.*
   portion *She handed me a large portion of the cake.*
   scrap *a scrap of fabric*
   segment *orange segments*
   ♦ **Formal words component** *The company supplies components for aircraft.*
   constituent *Sodium is an important constituent of salt.*

bitter [adjective]
1 *a bitter taste*
   sharp *fruit juice with a sharp taste*

Bb

sour *The sweets have a sour flavour.*
tart *Rhubarb is quite tart without sugar.*
2 a bitter remark • become old and bitter
resentful *He was resentful of his friend's success.*
◆ **Formal word embittered** *She was an old and embittered woman.*
3 a bitter wind
biting *walking into a biting north wind*
harsh *another harsh winter to come*
raw *A raw gale blew down the mountainside.*

black [adjective]
1 black hair
ebony *the animal's ebony fur*
jet-black *A shark has jet-black eyes.*
2 black clouds
dark *the dark sky*
overcast *another overcast day*
3 Your hands are black.
dirty *Get those dirty boots off my chair!*
filthy *Your trousers are absolutely filthy.*
grimy *grimy fingernails*
grubby *the boy's grubby little hands*
◆ **Formal word soiled** *He looked ill and his clothes were soiled.*

blame¹ [noun]
1 I cannot take the blame for this.
fault *The accident was the cyclist's fault.*
guilt *He admitted his guilt to his father.*
responsibility *I accept complete responsibility for the mistake.*
2 You are to blame for what happened.
at fault *The court decided the company had been at fault.*
guilty *Joan was guilty of starting the rumour in the first place.*
responsible *Who is responsible for this mess?*

blame² [verb]
I don't blame you for what happened.
accuse *The teacher accused him of lying.*
find guilty *The judge found him guilty of murder.*

hold responsible *If I fail the exam this time, I'll hold you responsible.*

blind [adjective]
1 a blind person
partially sighted *competitions for partially sighted athletes*
unsighted *How does the sighted student work best with his or her unsighted partner?*
visually impaired *help for people who are visually impaired*
2 blind faith
unquestioning *an unquestioning loyalty to his cruel master*
unreasoning *their unreasoning acceptance of everything the government says*
unthinking *an unthinking response*

blockage [noun]
block *There was a block somewhere in the pipe.*
congestion *congestion on the roads*
obstruction *Some sort of obstruction was preventing the water from flowing.*

blot [noun]
mark *a dirty mark on his white shirt*
smudge *an ink smudge*
stain *Will the liquid leave a stain?*

blow¹ [noun]
1 a blow to the head
bump *He's had a bump on the head.*
clip *Teachers used to give kids a clip round the ear.*
punch *a punch in the stomach*
slap *a slap across the face*
smack *How would you like a smack in the mouth?*
swipe *She took a swipe at him with her dishtowel.*
◆ **Informal words wallop** *The man gave him a wallop on the jaw.*
whack *She'd had a whack on the head with a blunt object.*
2 the blow of losing his job

Shades of blue:

aquamarine	cornflower	royal blue	turquoise
azure	indigo	sapphire	
cobalt	navy	sky blue	

disappointment Not getting the job was a disappointment.
setback The accident was a setback for the nuclear industry.

blow² [verb]

1 wind blowing the dry leaves around
buffet The little boat was buffeted by the wind.
drive Strong winds were driving the snow into heaps.
2 Blow on the hot soup.
breathe Don't breathe on me if you've got a cold.
pant I reached the top of the hill but was panting heavily.
3 blow a horn
play Someone in the next building was playing a trumpet.
sound The driver sounds the horn as he approaches a tunnel.
trumpet lions roaring and elephants trumpeting

blue¹ [noun]

See the box above.

blue² [adjective] (informal)

feeling blue
depressed She's been really depressed all day.
downhearted Don't be downhearted. Just try again.
gloomy the gloomy mood in the hall
low It's a good thing to do when you're feeling a bit low.
miserable You look really miserable — what's wrong?
sad the sad expression on the boy's face
unhappy a very unhappy childhood
♦ **Formal words despondent** After failing again, she was getting despondent.

melancholy a melancholy tune
♦ **Informal terms down in the dumps**
I'm a bit down in the dumps today.
fed up I'm just feeling a bit fed up.

blunt [adjective]

1 a blunt knife • a blunt pencil
dull It sharpens the dullest of blades.
worn Most of the knives were a little worn.
2 a blunt manner • a blunt statement
abrupt I disliked her abrupt manner.
curt a very curt reply
direct Angela has a direct way of talking.
frank Forgive me for being so frank.
outspoken He can be a bit outspoken at times.
plain-speaking The father was an old-fashioned, plain-speaking man.
tactless She is tactless to the point of upsetting people.
♦ **Formal words brusque** Your manner is a little too brusque.
forthright a very forthright statement

VOCABULARY CHOICES

[meaning 2]
• If you say someone is **abrupt** or **curt** with you, they are so direct it seems unfriendly, and using these words suggests you are slightly offended.
• **Direct**, **frank** and **plain-speaking** are more general terms, and these do not suggest you have taken any personal offence.
• Someone who is **outspoken** tends to give people their opinions, even if they have not been asked to, and does so in a way that might make others react.
• However, if you describe someone as

Types of boat or ship:

aircraft carrier	dinghy	hydrofoil	schooner
barge	dreadnought	kayak	speedboat
battleship	dredger	lifeboat	submarine
canoe	ferry	liner	tanker
catamaran	freighter	minesweeper	trawler
clipper	frigate	motor boat	U-boat
container ship	gondola	paddle steamer	yacht
coracle	houseboat	punt	warship
destroyer	hovercraft	rowing boat	

tactless, you mean they have not been careful enough in what they say and they have offended or upset someone. This word is more obviously disapproving than the others.

blurred [adjective]
> **fuzzy** *The picture on the screen is still fuzzy.*
> **out of focus** *If the image is out of focus, adjust the lens.*
> **unclear** *The information is pretty unclear.*
> **vague** *a vague memory of what happened*

boast [verb]
> **brag** *a man who brags about how much money he earns*
> **crow** *Avoid crowing about your success.*
> **show off** *She enjoyed praise and loved to show off.*
> ◆ **Informal term talk big** *He walked round importantly and talked big.*

VOCABULARY CHOICES
- Some of these words are very disapproving in tone. **Brag**, for example, conveys the idea of arrogance in talking about what you have done, while **crow** suggests that someone is gloating.
- **Talk big** is also disapproving, but hints that you find the person's behaviour silly, perhaps because they have little to boast about.
- **Show off** is a less critical word to use, and

might even be used affectionately sometimes.

boat [noun]
See the box above.

body [noun]
1 a muscular body
> **build** *clothes for a man with a bigger build*
> **figure** *She has a very slim figure.*
> **physique** *an athletic physique*

2 a dead body
> **carcass** *an elephant carcass lying by the side of the road*
> **corpse** *Police divers fished a corpse out of the river.*
> ◆ **Slang word stiff** *Two guys were carrying a stiff down the stairs.*
> ◆ **Technical term cadaver** *Medical students are given a cadaver to practise on.*

bold [adjective]
1 take bold action
> **brave** *Rescuing them was a very brave thing to do.*
> **courageous** *a courageous act*
> **daring** *They carried out daring raids into enemy land.*
> **fearless** *The child was completely fearless around animals.*
> **spirited** *a spirited defence of the championship*
> ◆ **Formal words audacious** *It was an audacious plan to take control.*

Bb

Types of book:

audio book	**children:**	encyclopedia	jotter
bestseller	annual	gazetteer	journal
hardback	picture book	guidebook	notebook
paperback	**Books of**	handbook	pad
Story books:	**information:**	manual	sketchbook
horror	almanac	thesaurus	textbook
novel	atlas	**Books for writing**	**Books for putting**
romance	A to Z	**or drawing in:**	**things in:**
thriller	cookbook	diary	album
Books for	dictionary	exercise book	scrapbook

intrepid *an intrepid explorer*
valiant *The team made a valiant effort.*
2 bold behaviour
brazen *the brazen way he asked me my age*
forward *She didn't like strangers who were so forward.*
◆ **Formal words impertinent** *impertinent remarks*
impudent *I wouldn't tolerate his impudent remarks.*
insolent *The child's tone was insolent.*
◆ **Informal word cheeky** *It was a cheeky thing to say.*
3 a bold pattern
bright *a lovely bright design*
eye-catching *You've used very eye-catching colours.*
flamboyant *He always dressed in a very flamboyant style.*
loud *That shirt's a bit loud.*
showy *Most of the flowers were a little too showy.*
vivid *vivid colours*
◆ **Informal word flashy** *She arrived in a flashy sports car.*

VOCABULARY CHOICES

[meaning 3]
• If you describe something as **eye-catching**, it is so bright that people notice it easily. This word also usually gives the impression that something looks good.

• However, to give the impression that something is so bright that it is unpleasant to look at, it could be described as **loud**, **flashy** or **showy**.

---

book[1] [noun]
borrow a book from the library
publication *No part of this publication should be copied.*
volume *the third volume in the Lord of the Rings trilogy*
work *the collected works of Shakespeare*
◆ **Formal word tome** *shelves full of impressive tomes*
See also the box above.

book[2] [verb]
We'd better book our seats early.
arrange *Don't worry — I'll arrange the flights.*
organize *You can organize the theatre tickets.*
reserve *I'll reserve front row seats for you.*

bore [noun]
bother *It's a bit of a bother having to do it twice.*
nuisance *She avoided tasks that were a nuisance.*
◆ **Informal words drag** *Most of us find housework a drag.*
headache *Would it be a headache to fix?*

pain *Walking all the way into town was a real pain.*

boring [adjective]

dull *a pretty dull film*

monotonous *I was given the most monotonous jobs.*

routine *We lived a fairly routine life at the time.*

tedious *The first chapter is a bit tedious.*

uneventful *It was an uneventful match.*

unexciting *an unexciting journey*

uninteresting *Their children's books are drab and uninteresting.*

borrow [verb]

1 *Can I borrow your pen?*

have a loan of *I let her have a loan of my umbrella.*

use *Do you mind if I use your rubber?*

♦ **Informal words   cadge** *She cadges books off the other students.*

scrounge *I'll be able to scrounge the bus fare off someone.*

sponge *Jack was always sponging off his friends.*

2 *He borrowed another writer's ideas.*

copy *The story is copied from a Stephen King book.*

lift *This entire episode is lifted from 'Casablanca'.*

take *This is a quotation taken from the Bible.*

♦ **Formal word   plagiarize** *Several students were accused of plagiarizing.*

VOCABULARY CHOICES

[meaning 1]

• The informal terms **cadge**, **scrounge** and **sponge** are all rather insulting terms. They suggest that the person doing the borrowing is simply being a nuisance and is not behaving with any dignity. However, they are sometimes used in a humorous way, suggesting you are sorry for the trouble you are causing someone: *Can I cadge a lift home?*

[meaning 2]

• All these words are more direct and less tactful than 'borrow', and are more likely to suggest that using someone else's work is dishonest.

boss [noun]

director *Will he give up his position as company director?*

employer *Employers are angry at being forced to pay higher wages.*

head *Maggie is the head of the sales department.*

leader *Police have tracked down the gang's leader.*

manager *The assistant has gone to ask the manager.*

supervisor *If workers need the toilet, they have to ask one of the supervisors.*

♦ **Informal words   gaffer** *He told the gaffer that one of the workers had left early.*

supremo *The rebels made him their supremo.*

bossy [adjective]

assertive *She was very assertive and always got what she wanted.*

demanding *the most demanding boss I know*

domineering *Her domineering older sister told her what to wear.*

overbearing *He liked to be in control and could be overbearing.*

♦ **Formal words   authoritarian** *I didn't like my teacher's authoritarian tone.*

dictatorial *She gave her instructions in a dictatorial manner.*

bother[1] [verb]

Stop bothering me while I'm working.

annoy *Don't annoy your dad when he's trying to concentrate.*

disturb *I'm sorry to disturb you, but there's an urgent call.*

harass *The couple are constantly harassed by photographers.*

inconvenience We hope the delay doesn't inconvenience passengers too much.
plague The project has been plagued by setbacks.

bother² [noun]
It's no bother for me to check those details.
difficulty We had no difficulty getting in touch with her.
fuss I don't want a system that involves a lot of fuss.
inconvenience The company hopes that customers will not be caused any inconvenience.
nuisance The wet weather is a bit of a nuisance.
problem Have you had any problems with the new motor?
trouble I never imagined him having trouble with the police.
♦ **Informal words aggravation** I don't need this aggravation.
hassle She's had a bit of hassle with bullies.

bottom [noun]
1 the bottom of the ladder
base a silver trophy on a wooden base
foot There's a side table at the foot of the stairs.
2 Look at the bottom of the cup.
underside Tiles had fallen away from the Shuttle's underside.
3 sitting on his bottom
behind Someone kicked me on the behind.
buttocks Fat can gather on the buttocks and thighs.
rump He slapped the horse's rump and off they went.
♦ **Informal words backside** He slipped and fell on his backside.
bum Does my bum look big in these trousers?

box [noun]
carton Milk is sold in plastic bottles or cartons.
case a warehouse full of packing cases
chest He stored his clothes in a large wooden chest.
crate Crates of fruit were standing at the dockside.
trunk Suitcases and trunks were being loaded onto the train.

boy [noun]
son My youngest son is nine.
youth She was stopped by a gang of youths.
♦ **Informal word lad** The assistant was just a young lad.

brainy [adjective] (informal)
bright one of the brightest students in the class
brilliant a brilliant scientist
clever Teachers were paying more attention to the clever pupils.
intelligent Amanda was a pretty and intelligent young woman.
smart She's much too smart to fall for a trick like that.

brave [adjective]
bold The company is making a bold attempt to win back public confidence.
brave as a lion The king was brave as a lion in the battle.
courageous Congratulations on taking this courageous first step.
daring The lifeboat crew carried out a daring rescue on the coast.
fearless Journalists in war zones appear to be fearless.
unafraid They continued to work, unafraid of the danger.
♦ **Formal words intrepid** Intrepid reporter Jason Burt travelled across the border.
valiant It was a valiant effort by everyone on the team.

Bb

- **Brave as a lion** is a **simile**. It is also a phrase that has been used so often that it has very little impact — a **cliché**.
- **Valiant** is a word which lends an air of dignity and is used, for example, when writing about bravery in battle.

break¹ [verb]

1 break a bone • break a window
crack *The movement of passing trains causes the plaster to crack.*
fracture *She fractured her hip in the fall.*
shatter *The windscreen is designed to shatter when hit by a stone.*
smash *The plates fell on the floor and smashed.*
snap *The branch looked like it was going to snap.*
splinter *The wood splintered when the axe struck the door again.*
split *The handle of her racket had split.*

2 break the law
disobey *You have disobeyed my instructions.*
flout *These players are openly flouting the rules.*
♦ **Formal words** **breach** *The company had breached the terms of its contract.*
contravene *The court can fine governments that contravene European laws.*
infringe *The man's human rights had clearly been infringed.*
violate *The action you are taking violates international law.*

3 break for lunch
pause *We'll pause now for coffee.*
stop *The game stops for five minutes to allow players to get a drink.*

4 break the news
announce *They have announced that they intend to marry.*
inform *We are writing to inform you of a change to the law.*

reveal *The newspaper revealed that the actor will leave the show next month.*
tell *Have you told your children yet?*
♦ **Formal words** **disclose** *The exact amount has not been disclosed.*
divulge *She was not willing to divulge that information.*
impart *A teacher's job is not only to impart knowledge.*

5 break a record
beat *If we really try, I think we could beat their total.*
better *His score of 303 has never been bettered.*
surpass *That figure is unlikely to be surpassed this year.*

break² [noun]

1 a break in the pipe
breach *Workers are repairing the breach in the wall.*
crack *Oil was escaping through this crack in the tank.*
fracture *He was kept in hospital with a suspected skull fracture.*
hole *We taped up the hole in the cable.*

2 have a break for coffee
interlude *a ten-minute interlude between sessions*
intermission *an intermission halfway through the film*
interval *After an interval of five minutes, the Sri Lankans will come out to bat.*
pause *There was a pause to allow players to get a drink.*
♦ **Formal word** **respite** *It seems there is no respite from the terrible conditions.*
♦ **Informal words** **breather** *We all felt it was time for a breather.*
let-up *There was no let-up in the rain for three days.*

breathe [verb]

gasp *The diver came up gasping for air.*
pant *By the time we reached the top, I was panting heavily.*

puff *He was puffing and out of breath.*
♦ **Technical term respire** *This is how the plant respires.*

breeze [noun]
  draught *She could feel a draught round her ankles.*
  gust *A sudden gust of wind ripped the paper from his hand.*
  wind *The sailing was off – there was no wind at all.*

brief [adjective]
1 a brief description
  concise *a concise statement of our policy*
  pithy *She summed the day up in a single pithy comment.*
  short *Their reply was short – 'Sell it!'*
  succinct *Don't write notes in whole sentences. A few succinct phrases are much better.*
2 a brief interruption • a brief stay
  fleeting *a fleeting visit to Paris*
  momentary *It was a momentary lapse of concentration.*
  passing *Don't worry – it's just a passing teenage phase.*
  quick *That was a quick conversation.*
  short-lived *Luckily, his anger was only short-lived.*
  temporary *Any loss of memory will be temporary.*

VOCABULARY CHOICES
[meaning 2]
• The word **fleeting** can describe something that lasts for an extremely short time, and it sometimes suggests that you feel sad that it lasted such a short time.
• You can use the word **passing** simply to mean that something will end at some time in the future, but it can also suggest that you are quite glad it will not last for ever.

bright [adjective]
1 bright lights • bright sunshine
  blazing *We shelter from the blazing sun.*

dazzling *the dazzling headlights of the cars*
  luminous *The walls were painted a horrible luminous green.*
  shining *her shining eyes bright with excitement*
  sparkling *a string of sparkling diamonds*
2 a bright smile
  cheerful *A cheerful grin spread across his face.*
  happy *the children with their happy expressions*
  vivacious *She's a pretty girl with a vivacious personality.*
♦ **Formal word joyful** *A party should be a joyful occasion.*
3 The future looks bright.
  encouraging *encouraging signs for the future of the sport*
  favourable *Would the weather conditions be favourable?*
  hopeful *I was in a hopeful mood as we approached the end of the job.*
  promising *He has a very promising career in front of him.*
  rosy *The future looks rosy for the industry.*
♦ **Formal word auspicious** *Today's win is an auspicious start to the season.*
4 a very bright child
  clever *Is Michael the cleverest boy in the class?*
  intelligent *She's always been an intelligent player.*
  smart *Alan was smart enough not to be fooled by that.*
♦ **Informal word brainy** *You expect the brainy kids to do well.*
5 dressed in bright clothes
  flamboyant *His flamboyant outfits always get him noticed.*
  loud *Frank looked ridiculous in another of his loud shirts.*
  showy *Most of the flowers were a little too showy.*
  vivid *vivid colours*

Bb

Shades of brown:

auburn	chocolate	fawn	sepia
beige	coffee	hazel	tan
bronze	copper	mahogany	
chestnut	earth	russet	

6 a bright day

cloudless *We're hoping for another cloudless day.*

fine *And there's more fine weather on the way.*

sunny *It was the sunniest weekend on record.*

VOCABULARY CHOICES

[meaning 5]

• **Flamboyant** is generally used in a positive way about something that is intended to catch the eye, but occasionally it might be used by someone who wants to suggest that something is over the top, but does not want to say so.

• If you want to give the impression that something is so bright that it is unpleasant to look at, you might describe it as **loud** or **showy**.

brilliant [adjective]

1 a brilliant pianist

exceptional *Vaughan is also an exceptional player.*

gifted *At age eleven, she was already a gifted painter.*

outstanding *She is an outstanding talent and a thoroughly nice person.*

skilful *He was clearly the more skilful boxer.*

talented *Both parents are talented musicians.*

2 a brilliant star

bright *the bright lights of Las Vegas*

dazzling *the dazzling beam of the lighthouse*

shining *The horses, too, had their shining armour.*

sparkling *beautiful sandy beaches and a sparkling sea*

3 a brilliant idea

clever *It was a particularly clever plan.*

intelligent *Mentioning it now would not be an intelligent move.*

bring [verb]

cause *The storms caused damage along the coast.*

create *These recent wins have created an atmosphere of hope.*

draw *The Games continue to draw huge crowds.*

produce *What has produced this reaction?*

provoke *The news provoked an angry response from consumers.*

broad [adjective]

1 broad shoulders • a broad river

large *He beat his large chest with his fists.*

vast *the vast plains of North Dakota*

wide *a long wide avenue*

2 a broad category

general *It's a very general term.*

wide-ranging *There's been a wide-ranging discussion of the issue in schools.*

♦ **Formal word comprehensive** *The book is a comprehensive survey of British history.*

broken [adjective]

1 a broken leg • a broken window

fractured *We were hoping the arm was only bruised, not fractured.*

shattered *twisted metal and shattered glass*

2 This machine is broken.

damaged *Damaged goods should be returned to the shop.*

faulty The device was clearly faulty.
out of order Like most payphones, it was out of order.
◆ **Slang word kaput** The engine was completely kaput.

brown[1] [noun]
See the box on the previous page.

brown[2] [adjective]
skin getting brown in the sun
  bronzed his bronzed forearms
  sunburnt Her face was weather-beaten and sunburnt.
  tanned dark hair and a tanned complexion

bug[1] [noun]
1 (informal) a tummy bug
  bacterium How does the bacterium get into the blood?
  disease It's a kind of liver disease.
  germ Household cleaners kill only a fraction of these germs.
  infection He was off work with a chest infection.
  micro-organism A new type of micro-organism has been discovered in the water.
  virus The virus is very good at protecting itself.
2 bugs in the system
  error There must have been an error in the computer program.
  failing This was a failing in the applications system.
  fault The problem was caused by a fault in the painting process.
  flaw I can see a flaw in this argument.
◆ **Informal word gremlin** It sounds like there's a gremlin in the system.

bug[2] [verb]
1 bug their offices
  listen in on The device allows you to listen in on conversations over a mile away.
  spy on The government had been spying on them for months.
  tap Morris knew his phone was being tapped.
2 (informal) Don't bug me with questions!
  annoy Doesn't that constant noise annoy you?
  badger He's been badgering me to see a doctor.
  bother I don't want to bother you with constant phone calls.
  disturb Their sleep had been disturbed by rowdy teenagers.
  harass She was regularly harassed by reporters.
  irritate The way he chewed his food irritated me.
◆ **Informal word needle** The Australian players had been needling him all day.

build[1] [noun]
a slim build
  body a handsome face and a beautiful body
  figure She has a slim, athletic figure.
  physique a man with a muscular physique
  shape You have a lovely shape!

build[2] [verb]
1 build a house • build a wall
  construct New flood defences will be constructed.
  erect A statue of him was erected in the main square.
  make They're making an artificial lake next to the hotel.
◆ **Informal word knock up** We'll knock up some sort of shelter.
2 Pressure is building up.
  increase The temperature inside the room increased.
  intensify Attacks intensified and the airport closed again.
  rise Prices continued to rise.
  strengthen The wind had strengthened overnight.

building [noun]
  structure The tower is an impressive

Types of building:

Buildings to live in:	gurdwara	theatre	barracks
block of flats	mandir	**Buildings where**	fort
bungalow	monastery	**people learn:**	fortress
cabin	mosque	college	**Other buildings:**
cottage	pagoda	school	factory
farmhouse	synagogue	university	hospital
house	temple	**Small buildings:**	hotel
mansion	**Buildings for**	beach hut	observatory
palace	**leisure:**	gazebo	office
tower block	café	outhouse	office block
villa	cinema	shed	power station
Religious	gym	summerhouse	prison
buildings:	library	**Farm buildings:**	shop
abbey	multiplex	barn	skyscraper
cathedral	museum	farmhouse	warehouse
chapel	pub	stable	windmill
church	restaurant	**Military**	
	sports centre	**buildings:**	

structure.

♦ **Formal words   construction** The platform is a lightweight wooden construction.
edifice The Colosseum is a magnificent edifice.
See also the box above.

bully [verb]
browbeat The manager had browbeaten him into resigning.
persecute Jews in Europe had been persecuted by the Nazis.
terrorize Young thugs were terrorizing the neighbourhood.
torment He was tormented by the gang throughout his school days.
♦ **Formal words   coerce** Janice was coerced into taking the job.
intimidate He wasn't going to be intimidated by them.
tyrannize the military group which tyrannized our country
♦ **Informal term   push around** If you don't fight back, they'll carry on pushing you around.

bump [verb]
1 bump your head against the door
bang He banged his elbow on the wardrobe door.
crash A second car crashed into us from the side.
hit You're scared your kids will hit their heads on something.
knock I knocked my knee against the seat in front.
strike The horse struck a rail with his hind leg.
2 bumping along on the uneven surface
bounce We bounced down the lane for about half a mile.
jerk The sudden stop jerked me awake.
jostle She was jostled by other, bigger passengers.
rattle The little white van rattled along the track.

bump [noun]
1 We hit the other car with a bump.
bang a bang on the head

blow a heavy blow to the chest
collision Their car was in collision with a tram.
crash the crash of plates on the kitchen floor
impact She was thrown forward by the force of the impact.
jolt The horse landed with a jolt.
thud The sack hit the cellar floor with a thud.
thump the thump of boots on the stairs
2 bumps on the surface
bulge the bulges around your hips
hump Which camel has two humps?
lump There was a hard lump on his neck.
swelling Put a cold cloth on it to reduce the swelling.
◆ **Formal word** **protuberance** This small protuberance develops into the animal's head.

bumpy [adjective]
choppy It was a rough crossing on choppy seas.
knobbly Sleeping wouldn't be easy on such a knobbly mattress.
lumpy a lumpy bed
uneven The floors were very uneven.

bunch [noun]
1 a bunch of keys
bundle She produced a bundle of dirty washing.
cluster a thick cluster of apple trees
collection an odd collection of books in her bag
2 a bunch of flowers
bouquet The florist had delivered a beautiful bouquet.
posy She presented the Princess with a posy.
spray The bouquet contained a small spray of pansies.
3 a bunch of thugs
band Trains were regularly attacked by bands of robbers.
crowd A crowd of protesters had gathered outside the office.

gang He had been part of a criminal gang for years.
mob A violent mob was looting shops and houses.
party How many children are in your party?
team The review was carried out by a team of experts.

burglar [noun]
housebreaker an iron bar used by a housebreaker
robber the van driven by the bank robbers
thief The thieves had entered through a side door.

burn [verb]
1 A fire is burning. • burn the rubbish
blaze The fire continued to blaze into the night.
cremate a short service, after which the body will be cremated
ignite If the wood is damp, it will not ignite.
incinerate The waste is usually incinerated.
light He spent ten minutes trying to light the barbecue.
smoulder The wreckage was still smouldering.
2 burn your finger • burn the food
scald Steam can scald you badly.
scorch The grass was scorched by months of hot sun.
singe Her hair had been singed by the bonfire.

burst [verb]
crack If the wall cracks, there could be a landslide.
explode It was the sound of a tyre exploding.
puncture The impact of the steering wheel had punctured a lung.
rupture One of the pipes had ruptured.
shatter The glass shattered in the blast.
split As he bent over, his trousers split.

business [noun]
1 the business sector

commerce *the government department responsible for commerce*
trade *rates for trade customers*

2 *a successful business*
company *a national bus company*
corporation *one of America's major oil corporations*
enterprise *a multinational enterprise*
firm *a local plumbing firm*
operation *an international mining operation*
organization *the money made by private organizations*

3 *What business are you in?*
job *He asked me what my job was.*
line *What line of work would you like to be in?*
occupation *Have you thought about any particular occupation?*
profession *Medicine is the most popular profession.*
vocation *For some people, teaching is a vocation.*
work *What sort of work does the company do?*

4 *That's not our business.*
affair *I don't get involved in other people's affairs.*
issue *She has some personal issues to deal with.*
matter *It sounded like a private matter.*
question *We discussed the question of the rent.*
subject *The subject of marriage never comes up.*

busy [adjective]
1 *I've had a busy day.*
eventful *It's been an eventful summer.*
full *We've had a very full two weeks.*
hectic *It's a good way to unwind after a hectic day.*
2 *keep yourself busy • a busy woman*
active *She has been active all her life.*
energetic *an energetic eighty-year-old*

lively *He's a happy, lively child.*
3 *a busy street*
bustling *a bustling town famous for its fountain*
crowded *the crowded market square*
swarming *Like most beaches, it was swarming with bathers.*
teeming *Oxford was teeming with tourists.*
4 *All the lines are busy.*
engaged *I called them again but they were still engaged.*
occupied *Several of the cubicles were already occupied.*
♦ **Informal term** **tied up** *She's been tied up in meetings all day.*

buy [verb]
get *Mum got me one from the same shop.*
pay for *You choose a jacket and I'll pay for it.*
♦ **Formal word** **purchase** *It must be returned to the shop where it was purchased.*

buzz [verb]
1 *bees buzzing*
drone *High up, an aeroplane droned.*
hum *The boat hummed on down the river.*
whirr *I could hear its blades whirring before I saw the helicopter.*
2 *buzz with excitement*
bustle *The village was bustling with anticipation.*
pulse *The girls' youthful excitement pulsed through the house.*
throb *The town is not exactly throbbing with nightlife.*

by accident [adverb]
by chance *Some finds were made by chance.*
unintentionally *I hurt her feelings unintentionally.*
♦ **Formal word** **inadvertently** *I inadvertently stood on a child's foot.*
♦ **Informal phrase** **by a fluke** *He scored by a fluke when the ball hit off his knee.*

C

cake[1] [noun]

a cream cake
  bun cream buns
  fancy a plate of iced fancies
  gateau a chocolate gateau
  pastry coffee and pastries
  sponge a sponge filled with jam and cream
  tart a plate of strawberry tarts

cake[2] [verb]

an oven caked with grease
  coat shoes coated with mud
  cover His face was covered in blood.
  encrust potatoes encrusted with dirt

call[1] [noun]

1 a call for assistance
  cry Rescuers heard desperate cries for help.
  exclamation He gave an exclamation of pain.
  scream Neighbours heard her screams for help.
  shout There were shouts from the crowd.
  yell He let out a yell of fright.
2 The doctor has several calls to make.
  visit He began to look forward to her visits.
3 I'll give you a call later.
  ring You promised to give me a ring.
◆ **Informal words** **bell** Give me a bell when you're free.

  buzz He'll give you a buzz later.
  tinkle I'll give you a tinkle and let you know.
4 calls for his resignation
  appeal Police have made an appeal for information.
  plea Her parents made an emotional plea for her to come home.
  request requests for information

VOCABULARY CHOICES
[meaning 4]
• The word **plea** is usually used to suggest that someone is desperate for something to happen, and so it might be used to appeal to your emotions.

call[2] [verb]

1 They called the baby Ann. • a book called 'The Final Journey'
  christen They christened him John Adam.
  entitle a report entitled 'Teaching in Schools'
  name They named her Madhura.
2 They called him a hero.
  dub a man who has been dubbed 'the worst husband in Britain'
  label He was labelled 'a cheat' by his ex-wife.
3 He called her name.
  cry 'Come here, Jen!' he cried.
  exclaim 'How beautiful!' she exclaimed.
  shout He shouted up the stairs to his father.

Cc

yell *She yelled for him to come and help.*
4 She called us all in for a meeting.
order *He ordered me over to his desk.*
send for *The head teacher sent for her.*
summon *The manager summoned me to her office.*
5 I'll call you later.
call up *Just call me up if you need me.*
dial *She grabbed the phone and dialled for an ambulance.*
phone *I'll phone you tomorrow.*
ring *John rang me last night.*
ring up *She rang me up to tell me.*
telephone *We'll telephone you with the results.*
♦ **Informal phrases give a buzz** *I'll give you a buzz tomorrow.*
give a tinkle *Give me a tinkle when you're ready.*

calm[1] [adjective]

1 The police told us to remain calm. • He is calm under pressure.
composed *He looked composed and confident.*
cool *She tried to remain cool.*
level-headed *She's level-headed enough to cope with the pressure.*
placid *a very sweet, placid little baby*
relaxed *He appeared relaxed and confident.*
unemotional *She was unemotional during the funeral.*
unflustered *The waiters were smiling and unflustered.*
unruffled *He remained unruffled despite the chaos around him.*
♦ **Informal words laid-back** *He's so laid-back about everything.*
unflappable *He was normally cool and unflappable.*
2 calm waters
smooth *the smooth water of the pool*
still *Still water is perfect for swimming.*
tranquil *a tranquil lake*

VOCABULARY CHOICES
[meaning 1]
• The words **level-headed, placid, laid-back** and **unflappable** suggest that someone is calm as a part of their personality. **Level-headed** and **laid-back** in particular are quite complimentary, and suggest you admire this aspect of a someone's personality.
• **Unemotional**, however, is less complimentary in that it hints that being cool is not natural in the situation.
• The word **unruffled** is usually used in writing rather than speaking. It suggests you stay cool in a particular situation.

calm[2] [verb]

He's calmed a bit since this morning.
compose yourself *He lit a cigarette and composed himself.*
pacify *attempts to pacify angry customers*
quieten *Try to relax your body and quieten your mind.*
relax *A week's holiday would really relax me.*
sedate *She was given a drug to sedate her.*
soothe *He was soothed by the sound of the water.*
♦ **Formal word placate** *He tried to placate her by talking in a softer voice.*

calm[3] [noun]

1 Her usual calm had gone.
calmness *his calmness in a difficult situation*
composure *She showed great composure under pressure.*
♦ **Formal word serenity** *She had the same quietness and serenity as his wife.*
2 the calm of the mountain village
peace *the peace of the countryside*
quiet *the quiet of the church*
stillness *the stillness of the early morning*
tranquillity *The gardens had an*

atmosphere of tranquillity.

◆ **Formal word** **serenity** the serenity of the garden

cancel [verb]
abandon I had to abandon plans to join him.
call off The meeting has been called off because he's ill.
drop They dropped plans to open up a shop.

car [noun]
automobile We went back to where the automobile was parked.
motor car the effect of motor cars on the environment
◆ **Informal word** **motor** He's bought a new motor.

VOCABULARY CHOICES
• The word **automobile** is usually used in American English.

care¹ [noun]
1 drive without the necessary care
attention The problem hadn't received the attention it needed.
carefulness In spite of her carefulness, she had lost the money.
caution Use caution when handling dangerous chemicals.
regard He jumped in without any regard for his own safety.
◆ **Formal word** **prudence** balance risk and prudence
2 in their care
charge pupils left in the charge of a teacher
control The business was under the control of his son.
custody The files are in the custody of the police.
keeping He has the jewels in his keeping.
supervision children under the supervision of an adult

care² [verb]
Don't you care about me at all?
bother He didn't bother about how silly he looked.
mind I don't mind whether you come or not.
worry He didn't worry what she thought.

career [noun]
job jobs in the steel industry
occupation Please give your name, address, and occupation.
profession Medicine is different from many other professions.
trade Get yourself a good trade, like plumbing.
vocation He took his vocation as a priest very seriously.
◆ **Formal word** **calling** a doctor truly dedicated to his calling

care for [verb]
look after My husband looks after the baby while I go to work.
nurse She nursed her father in the last years of his life.
provide for I need my job so I can provide for my family.
take care of They take good care of their children.
tend They volunteered to tend the sick and the poor.

careful [adjective]
1 Be careful, please!
cautious You should be cautious about walking alone at night.
wary Be wary as there is a lot of forged money around.
◆ **Formal word** **prudent** A prudent doctor would test for the disease.
2 a careful study
detailed a detailed survey of UK businesses
meticulous meticulous planning
painstaking a painstaking search for evidence

Cc

39

Breeds of cat:

Abyssinian	Burmese	Manx	silver tabby
British longhair	chinchilla	Persian	Tortoiseshell
British shorthair	domestic tabby	Siamese	

scrupulous scrupulous attention to detail
thorough a thorough police investigation

careless [adjective]
1 a careless remark
inconsiderate inconsiderate comments
thoughtless her own thoughtless words
unguarded He made an unguarded reply to a journalist.
unthinking an unthinking response
2 careless work
slapdash slapdash work by builders
slipshod A slipshod performance by his team mates meant they lost.
sloppy a sloppy piece of writing

carry [verb]
1 lorries carrying goods • We carried the bags upstairs.
bring We brought the books into the hall.
move We need to move the chairs into another room.
take He took the papers to his office.
transfer She was transferring glasses from the tray to the table.
transport lorries transporting dangerous loads
♦ **Formal word convey** The coffin was conveyed through the streets by a horse and carriage.
2 carried the entire weight
bear The chair isn't strong enough to bear an adult's weight.
stand The bookshelf won't stand the weight of so many books.
support The posts support a large canopy.
♦ **Formal word sustain** There are concerns that the balcony cannot sustain much weight.

cash [noun]
banknotes money in the form of banknotes
change Do you have any change for the coffee machine?
coins She put the coins into the parking meter.
money Do you have any money on you?
notes notes and coins

casual [adjective]
1 a casual meeting
accidental The meeting was planned rather than accidental.
chance a chance discovery
random random happenings
2 a casual remark
offhand I made an offhand reply.
spontaneous spontaneous comments shouted from the audience
throwaway A throwaway remark almost ended his career.
♦ **Formal word impromptu** give an impromptu performance
3 a casual attitude
apathetic people's apathetic attitude towards the environment
blasé blasé about the dangers of the sun
lackadaisical He was lazy and lackadaisical.
relaxed a relaxed attitude to life
♦ **Formal word nonchalant** nonchalant about the risks he was taking
♦ **Informal words couldn't-care-less** a couldn't-care-less attitude towards work
laid-back He is more laid-back about things.
4 casual work
irregular The work she had was irregular.
occasional occasional work

short-term *a short-term job to help with the cost of Christmas*
temporary *people in temporary jobs*
5 casual clothes
comfortable *Change into something more comfortable.*
informal *informal wear*
leisure *Sales of leisure clothing rose last year.*
relaxed *For a more relaxed look, swap your skirt for jeans.*

VOCABULARY CHOICES

[meaning 3]
- The words **apathetic, couldn't-care-less** and **lackadaisical** usually suggest that you do not approve, because you think someone cannot be bothered to take care.
- The word **laid-back** is more approving, and suggests that you rather admire someone's casual attitude.

---

cat [noun]
  kitten *The old cat was playful as a young kitten.*
  tabby *a tabby with dark stripes*
  tomcat *tomcats making a din outside*
◆ **Informal words** **kitty** *We are taking the poor kitty to the vet.*
  moggy *She's not a pedigree cat, just a moggy.*
  pussy-cat *the old song about the owl and the pussy-cat*
See also the box on the previous page.

cause [verb]
  bring about *The people of a country can bring about change.*
  involve *The task doesn't involve much work.*
  lead to *Poor housing leads to other social problems.*
  mean *Less grant money will mean severe cutbacks.*
  result in *The decision will result in anger among the workers.*

cautious [adjective]
  careful *You must be careful about accepting lifts from strangers.*
  wary *Be wary as there is a lot of forged money around.*
◆ **Formal word** **tentative** *They were very tentative about the relationship.*

central [adjective]
1 *a central role in the film* • *the central points of the debate*
  chief *Keeping taxes down is our chief concern.*
  essential *Parents have an essential role to play in education.*
  important *an important part of our work*
  key *a key issue that needs discussing*
  main *the main subject on the agenda*
  principal *the principal aim of the project*
  vital *his vital role in the business*
2 *a central courtyard* • *central Paris*
  inner *inner London*
  middle *the middle section of the book*

centre [noun]
  core *The core of the town is the Town Hall.*
  heart *a beautiful house in the heart of Amsterdam*
  hub *the hub of Britain's motorway network*
  middle *walking through the middle of the village*
  nucleus *Manchester is the nucleus of the region.*

certain [adjective]
1 *I'm certain he's telling the truth.*
  confident *I'm confident he knows what he's talking about.*
  convinced *I was convinced I wouldn't win.*
  positive *I'm positive I saw her.*
  sure *Are you sure that's what he said?*
2 *It was certain to happen sometime.*
  bound *The relationship was bound to end.*
  destined *a project that was destined to fail*

Cc

fated They were fated to meet sooner or later.
inevitable The results were inevitable.
sure It was sure to be a success.

3 a certain person we both know • below a certain point
particular The parts are all arranged in a particular way.
specific references to specific people

VOCABULARY CHOICES
[meaning 2]
• The words **destined** and **fated** suggest that you think there is a mysterious power that is controlling what happens and you cannot change it.

chance¹ [noun]

1 come across it by chance
accident I found the place by accident.
coincidence By coincidence, he was in Chicago when I was.
fate Fate brought us together.
luck It was pure luck that I met her.
♦ **Informal word fluke** You don't win a tennis championship by fluke.
2 take a chance
gamble I took a gamble when I bought the business.
risk He took a risk but was successful.
3 a chance of winning millions
likelihood There was little likelihood of success.
possibility There was a possibility she might be there.
probability The probability of winning was not very high.
prospect The prospect of failing frightened her.
4 a second chance
occasion There will be other occasions, I'm sure.
opening Winning the game was the opening she needed.
opportunity an opportunity to travel

chance² [adjective]

a chance remark
accidental I don't think his being there was accidental.
casual a casual meeting in the street
random random happenings
♦ **Formal word fortuitous** a fortuitous encounter

VOCABULARY CHOICES
• The formal word **fortuitous** suggests that there is an element of luck and that the result is good.

change¹ [verb]

1 Prices keep changing. • We need to change the law.
alter The town has altered a lot over the years. • It doesn't alter the way I feel.
fluctuate Temperatures fluctuate throughout the year.
modify The system has been modified to improve it.
reform The law needs to be reformed.
shift Attitudes towards marriage have shifted.
transform Her life has been transformed by the operation.
vary The menu varies from day to day. • Try to vary your diet.
2 changing into a butterfly
convert ways of converting waste into fuel
transform The hall has been transformed into a games room. • She has transformed from schoolgirl to model.
♦ **Formal word metamorphose** a happy little boy who had metamorphosed into an awkward teenager
3 change one thing for another • change a light bulb
exchange I'd like to exchange this red sweater for a green one.
replace We replaced the broken lock with a new one.
substitute You could substitute low-fat

margarine for butter.
swap I'll swap two of my sweets for one of your chocolates.
switch Someone had switched the labels on the boxes.

VOCABULARY CHOICES

[meaning 1]
- The word **fluctuate** suggests that something changes very often from a higher to a lower amount and back.
- The word **modify** suggests that someone has made a small change to something in order to make it better.
- The word **shift** often suggests that a situation or feeling changes gradually over a long period of time.
- The word **transform** suggests that something changes very greatly and becomes better.

change² [noun]
A change is on the way.
alteration make alterations to our plans
fluctuation a fluctuation in temperature
modification make modifications to the equipment
shift a shift in attitudes
transformation the transformation in his behaviour

charge¹ [verb]
1 charge a high price
ask They're asking a lot of money for it.
want They want £5,000 for the car.
2 charge him with theft
accuse He was accused of murder.
prosecute She was prosecuted for failing to pay a fine.
♦ **Technical term indict** He was indicted for war crimes.
3 charged into the crowd
rush Everyone rushed to the door.
storm Troops stormed the city. • He stormed out of the house.

charge² [noun]
1 high charges
cost Housing costs are rising.
fee He charges a fee of £20 per session.
price a rise in oil prices
2 a charge of murder
accusation an accusation of rape
allegation allegations of assault
3 in your charge
care children in your care
custody files in the custody of the police
keeping The jewels are in his keeping.

chart [noun]
diagram a diagram showing the parts of the eye
graph His progress was plotted on the graph.
table information presented in a table

chat¹ [noun]
Have you time for a chat?
conversation having a conversation about the weather
gossip neighbours enjoying a gossip over the garden wall
heart-to-heart a heart-to-heart about the state of their marriage
talk I had a talk with her teacher yesterday.
♦ **Formal word tête-à-tête** the Prime Minister's tête-à-tête with the President
♦ **Informal words chinwag** We went down the pub for a good chinwag.
natter having a natter over a cup of tea

VOCABULARY CHOICES

- The word **gossip** suggests that people are talking about other people's private lives and things that are not any of their business.
- The word **heart-to-heart** suggests that only two people are involved and they are being very honest about their private feelings.
- The word **tête-à-tête** means that only two people are involved and they want to keep the conversation secret.

Cc

Cc

chat² [verb]
I can't stand here chatting all day.
>**chatter** *chattering about what they did last night*
>**gossip** *gossiping about someone else's business*
>**talk** *talking about the weather*
>◆ **Informal words** **natter** *two people nattering on the street corner*
>**rabbit** *What's she rabbiting about now?*
>**rabbit on** *He was rabbiting on about all his problems.*

VOCABULARY CHOICES
• You would use **rabbit** or **rabbit on** only to suggest that someone is talking so much that it is boring.

cheap [adjective]
>**bargain** *bargain breaks in the sun*
>**budget** *budget hotels*
>**economy** *economy flights*
>**inexpensive** *inexpensive places to stay*
>◆ **Informal words** **cut-price** *cut-price deals on new cars*
>**dirt-cheap** *The drinks were dirt-cheap.*
>**knock-down** *clothes at knock-down prices*

cheat¹ [verb]
cheated out of her inheritance
>**deceive** *He was deceived into giving them all his money.*
>**defraud** *She had defrauded the bank of £30,000.*
>**dupe** *A thief duped his way into the woman's house.*
>**fool** *I had been fooled into handing over my money.*
>**hoodwink** *women hoodwinked into spending money on skin products that don't work*
>**swindle** *He'd been swindled out of his life savings.*
>**trick** *She was tricked into giving her bank details to the thief.*

>◆ **Informal terms** **con** *He had conned her out of her life savings.*
>**diddle** *He was diddled out of £300.*
>**do** *Check your change — they often try to do you in that shop.*
>**fleece** *how to avoid being fleeced by bad builders*
>**rip off** *People are ripped off by companies who charge too much for phone calls.*

cheat² [noun]
nothing but a rotten cheat
>**fraud** *The man's a fraud and not to be trusted.*
>**fraudster** *a convicted fraudster*
>**swindler** *swindlers who claim benefits they shouldn't*
>**trickster** *By getting your bank details, the tricksters can take money from you.*
>◆ **Formal word** **charlatan** *charlatans with no medical training who claim they can cure illness*
>◆ **Informal terms** **con man** *A con man had tricked her out of her life savings.*
>**shark** *a shark who took money form elderly people*

check¹ [verb]
checking her bank statement
>**examine** *Mechanics examined the car's brakes.*
>**inspect** *He went to inspect the damage.*
>**scrutinize** *She scrutinized the documents, looking for mistakes.*
>◆ **Informal phrase** **give the once-over** *Would you mind giving my essay the once-over?*

check² [noun]
regular health checks
>**check-up** *a check-up at the dentist*
>**examination** *an examination of his heart*
>**inspection** *an inspection of the brakes*
>**test** *blood tests*

cheeky [adjective]
>**brazen** *brazen jokes*

chief → cinema

Cc

disrespectful He was drunk and disrespectful towards staff.

forward She didn't like strangers who were so forward.

◆ **Formal words impertinent** impertinent remarks
impudent impudent young boys
insolent The child's tone was insolent.

chief¹ [adjective]
our chief concern
central the central aims of the project
key the key issue to be discussed
main the main problem
predominant My predominant feeling was one of anger.
primary Smoking is the primary cause of lung cancer.
prime one of the prime reasons why the system failed
principal the principal aim of the project
◆ **Formal word paramount** Good behaviour is of paramount importance.

chief² [noun]
the chief of the research team
boss bosses of various industries
commander the commander of the troops
director company directors
head the head of the bank
leader business leaders
manager company managers

child [noun]
minor the offence of selling alcohol to minors
youngster There's nothing for youngsters to do in the evenings.
◆ **Formal word infant** Infants are particularly at risk from the illness.
juvenile juveniles who have committed crimes
◆ **Informal word kid** I hated school when I was a kid.

VOCABULARY CHOICES
• The words **juvenile** and **minor** are words used in law.

• The word **infant** is quite a formal word, and it is often used in writing about a baby's or young child's health.

choice [noun]
1 You don't have any choice.
alternative I had no alternative but to leave.
option You have the option of staying.
say He had no say in the matter.
2 a restaurant offering a wide choice of meals and snacks
selection There was a selection of desserts on offer.
variety a variety of things you can do

choose [verb]
opt for In the end we opted for a church wedding.
pick He was trying to pick something suitable to wear.
select information that will help you select a holiday
settle on We finally settled on a cottage in Dorset.
◆ **Formal word elect** He had elected to stay at home.
◆ **Informal word plump for** She plumped for a long silk dress.

cinema [noun]
1 the world of cinema
films interested in films
◆ **Informal word movies** I wanted to work in movies.
2 go to the local cinema
multiplex What's on at the multiplex?
picture house Find out what is showing at the local picture house.
the pictures My dad used to take me to the pictures a lot.
◆ **Slang term the flicks** The three of us went to the flicks.

VOCABULARY CHOICES
[meaning 2]
• The terms **picture house** and **flicks** sound

45

Cc

old-fashioned. They might be used if someone is thinking fondly about the past.

claim [verb]

1 It was claimed he had been cheating.
allege It was alleged she'd lied in court.
assert He asserted that he was not involved in the decision.
insist He insists he's doing everything he can.
maintain She maintains she has done nothing wrong.
♦ **Formal word profess** He professed to be 80 but he didn't look it.
2 claim a refund
ask for Ask for your money back.
demand I demand a refund.
request Request a replacement if the goods are faulty.

VOCABULARY CHOICES

[meaning 1]
• The words **insist** and **maintain** suggest that you are saying something even though other people may not believe you.
• You might use the word **profess** to suggest that someone is saying something that is not true.
[meaning 2]
• The word **demand** suggests that you ask for something in a very forceful way.

class¹ [noun]

1 a class of people • a class of plants
category These songs come into the category of 'love songs'.
group whales belonging to the group known as 'toothed whales'
type What type of dog is it?
2 a geography class
lesson a French lesson
seminar I have a seminar this afternoon.
tutorial We'll discuss this in the tutorial.

class² [verb]

People under 16 are classed as juniors.
categorize The town has been classified

as a high-risk area.
classify some information classified as secret
grade The eggs are graded according to size.
group The books are grouped by subject.

clean¹ [adjective]

1 clean laundry
immaculate His house is immaculate — not a speck of dirt anywhere.
spotless a spotless white shirt
washed a pile of washed clothes
2 clean air • clean water
pure the pure mountain air
uncontaminated uncontaminated water
unpolluted unpolluted rivers

clean² [verb]

Clean your teeth before you go to bed.
cleanse Cleanse your skin.
mop He mopped the floor.
rinse rinsing the dishes
wash She washed the cups in the sink.
wipe He was wiping the table with a cloth.

clear [adjective]

1 The meaning is not clear.
apparent It was apparent that things were not right between them.
distinct There is a distinct possibility you are wrong.
evident His lack of interest was evident.
obvious He made his feelings very obvious.
plain She made it plain that we weren't wanted.
understandable The meaning of the words is not understandable.
♦ **Formal word explicit** I gave you explicit instructions to keep quiet about this.
2 clear water
translucent beautiful translucent seas
transparent transparent glass
see-through a see-through blouse

clever [adjective]
bright one of the brightest students in the class
brilliant a brilliant scientist
intelligent Amanda was a pretty and intelligent young woman.
quick-witted He is great fun and very quick-witted.
smart She's much too smart to fall for a trick like that.
• **Informal word brainy** You have to be brainy to be a doctor.

climb [verb]
clamber Children clambered onto the roof of the building.
mount She mounted the stairs to her room.
scale He scaled a wall to get into the garden.
• **Formal word ascend** We ascended the stairs.
• **Informal term shin up** Tom shinned up the pole and stole the flag.

close¹ [verb]
1 close the gate
fasten Fasten the windows.
shut Shut the door.
• **Formal word secure** Make sure all doors and windows are secured.
2 closing the meeting
end I'd like to end my speech by thanking everyone.
finish Before we finish the session, I'd like to say something.
wind up We need to wind up the discussion now.
• **Formal word conclude** To conclude the meeting, I'd like to arrange the date for the next one.

close² [noun]
at the close of the day
end the end of the meeting
finish at the finish of school
• **Formal word conclusion** the conclusion of the talks

close³ [adjective]
1 a close neighbour
adjacent the house and adjacent garage
near I walked to the nearest town.
nearby nearby towns
neighbouring France and neighbouring countries
2 Christmas is very close.
imminent the imminent arrival of her second baby • War seemed imminent.
impending She was dreading the impending visit of her mother.
3 a close friend • We're very close.
dear one of my dearest friends
devoted They were a devoted couple.
intimate an intimate friend of his mother's

VOCABULARY CHOICES
[meaning 2]
• The word **impending** often suggests that the thing that is about to happen is bad. It can be used to create a feeling of suspense.

clothes [noun]
clothing children's clothing
dress dancers in traditional Russian dress
garb women in riding garb
outfit a new outfit for the party
wear leisure wear
• **Formal words attire** wedding attire
garments a collection of designer garments
• **Informal words gear** She was dressed in cycling gear.
get-up He looks silly in that get-up.
togs designer togs
See also the box on the next page.

VOCABULARY CHOICES
• The word **get-up** suggests you think someone has tried too hard, and looks a bit ridiculous.

clue [noun]
evidence We are looking for evidence that he's been here.

Cc

Cc

Clothes:

Types of dress:
ballgown
caftan
cocktail dress
evening dress
kimono
pinafore dress
shirtwaister

Types of skirt:
dirndl
kilt
mini skirt
pencil skirt
sarong

Types of trousers:
bell-bottoms
Bermuda shorts
breeches
Capri pants
cargo pants
combat trousers
cords
culottes
drainpipes
dungarees
hipsters
jeans
jodhpurs
leggings
pedal-pushers
plus-fours
shorts
slacks

Types of top:
blouse

cardigan
dress shirt
fleece
jersey
jumper
polo neck
polo shirt
pullover
shirt
sweater
sweatshirt
tank top
T-shirt
twinset
waistcoat

Types of coat or jacket:
anorak
biker jacket
blazer
bomber jacket
cagoule
duffel coat
fleece
overcoat
mac
parka
raincoat

Types of suit:
boiler suit
catsuit
coveralls
dress suit
jumpsuit
leisure suit

lounge suit
morning suit
shell suit
three-piece suit
tracksuit
trouser suit
wet suit

Types of underwear:
basque
body stocking
boxer shorts
bra
briefs
camiknickers
camisole
corset
garter
girdle
G-string
panties
pants
petticoat
shift
slip
stockings
suspender belt
suspenders
teddy
thong
tights
singlet
string vest
underpants
vest

Y-fronts

Clothes for bedtime:
bed-jacket
bedsocks
dressing-gown
housecoat
negligee
nightdress
nightie
nightshirt
pyjamas

Accessories:
belt
bow tie
braces
cap
cravat
cummerbund
earmuffs
gloves
hat
leg warmers
mittens
muffler
necktie
pashmina
scarf
shawl
socks
stole
tie
veil

hint *hints as to what she's thinking*
indication *an indication that he may change his mind*
pointer *The big house and car were pointers to his wealth.*
sign *looking for signs that she was unhappy*

clumsy [adjective]
   awkward *an overweight, awkward child*
   unco-ordinated *Her movements were unco-ordinated.*
 ♦ **Formal word ungainly** *an ungainly teenager*
 ♦ **Informal word ham-fisted** *ham-fisted*

Cc

attempts to catch the ball

cold¹ [adjective]

1 cold weather
- **biting** *a biting wind*
- **bitter** *It's bitter outside.*
- **chilly** *a chilly night*
- **cold as ice** *Your hands are cold as ice!*
- **cool** *the cool mountain air*
- **freezing** *It's freezing in this room.*
- **icy** *an icy wind*
- **nippy** *It's a bit nippy outside.*
- **raw** *a raw December day*
- ◆ **Informal word parky** *It's a bit parky today, isn't it?*

2 He was cold with me.
- **aloof** *She came across as being aloof.*
- **cool** *Her tone was cool when she spoke to him.*
- **distant** *I found him a bit distant.*
- **reserved** *a reserved man who didn't go out much*
- **standoffish** *He can be quite standoffish sometimes.*

VOCABULARY CHOICES

[meaning 1]
- The words **biting**, **bitter**, **chilly**, **icy** and **raw** suggest that something is unpleasantly cold.
- However, the word **cool** suggests that something is pleasantly cold.
- **Cold as ice** is a **simile**. It is also a phrase that has been used so often that it has lost its impact — a **cliché**.

cold² [noun]

shivering from the cold
- **chill** *the chill of winter*
- **chilliness** *the chilliness of a December night*
- **coldness** *the icy coldness of the water*
- **coolness** *the coolness of the breeze*

colour¹ [noun]

1 all the colours of the rainbow
- **shade** *The shirts come in a variety of shades.*
- **tint** *papers in a large range of tints*
- **tone** *the carpet's rich orange tones*
- ◆ **Formal word hue** *the beautiful red hues of the sunset*

2 put colour in her cheeks
- **glow** *skin with a healthy glow*
- **rosiness** *the rosiness of her face*
- **ruddiness** *the ruddiness of someone who works outdoors*

colour² [verb]

cloth coloured with natural dyes
- **dye** *She had dyed her hair.*
- **stain** *You can stain the wood.*
- **tint** *The black and white photo had been tinted with colours.*

colourful [adjective]
- **bright** *tubs of bright flowers*
- **multicoloured** *multicoloured shirts*
- **vivid** *a vivid red and orange scarf*

come [verb]

1 He was coming along the road towards me. • The train is coming.
- **approach** *The dog barked when anyone approached.*
- **move towards** *The car was moving towards me.*
- **near** *as we neared the town*
- ◆ **Formal terms advance** *The man was advancing towards her.*
- **draw near** *He felt nervous as he drew near.*

2 They came yesterday.
- **arrive** *The letter arrived this morning.*

3 The attack came without warning.
- **happen** *Accidents often happen when you're least expecting them.*
- **occur** *The problem occurred as we were leaving.*

comfortable [adjective]

1 I like a comfortable bed. • I need a comfortable pair of shoes.
- **cosy** *his warm, cosy bed*
- **snug** *snug boots with a fur lining*
- ◆ **Informal word comfy** *a comfy chair*

Cc

2 comfortable with the decision
at ease *He was not at ease with his mother-in-law.*
happy *I'm not happy with the idea of letting him do it.*
relaxed *She seemed very relaxed with the situation.*

common [adjective]
commonplace *Violence is commonplace on many city centre streets at night.*
everyday *solutions to everyday problems*
familiar *a flower that is a familiar sight in many gardens*
frequent *In the winter, snow is frequent.*
regular *Crime is a regular occurrence round here.*
usual *It's quite usual to feel like that.*
widespread *an illness that is widespread among children*
♦ **Formal word prevalent** *a disease that is prevalent in parts of Africa*

company [noun]
1 Let me know if you need company.
companionship *A pet provides companionship for older people.*
friendship *I enjoy the friendship of my sister.*
presence *Your presence at the party will be very welcome.*
2 a national bus company
business *She runs a successful business.*
corporation *one of America's major oil corporations*
firm *a local plumbing firm*
operation *a large mining operation*
organization *the money made by private organizations*

compensation [noun]
damages *He won £100,000 in damages after an operation went wrong.*
♦ **Formal word recompense** *As recompense for the delay, he was given free plane tickets.*

competition [noun]
1 a swimming competition
championship *They won the football championship.*
contest *a contest to find Britain's best hotel*
game *She won the money in a poker game.*
match *a match between two teams*
race *run in the 800 metres race*
tournament *a tennis tournament*
2 competition between the brothers
competitiveness *competitiveness between the teams*
rivalry *There's a lot of rivalry among the children.*

complain [verb]
1 I will complain to the manager about the bad service.
file a complaint *Many customers filed complaints with the company.*
lodge a complaint *The country lodged a complaint with the United Nations.*
object *Residents have objected strongly to the plans.*
protest *I must protest at the way I have been treated.*
2 You're always complaining!
grumble *What are you grumbling about now?*
moan *The children kept moaning that they were cold.*
whine *He's always whining about something.*
♦ **Formal word bemoan** *He was bemoaning the fact that he didn't have a girlfriend.*
♦ **Informal words carp** *She was carping about the way he'd been treated.*
gripe *She's been griping about that all day.*

VOCABULARY CHOICES
[meaning 1]
• All of these synonyms are formal enough to be used in letters of complaint.

[meaning 2]
- If you use the word **whine**, you are suggesting that the person is annoying you with their complaining. Along with **moan**, it hints at self-pity.
- **Carp** gives the impression that someone is continuously complaining about something fairly unimportant, and is being annoying.

complaint [noun]
1 I've received several complaints about his behaviour.
  criticism criticisms of the way the problem had been handled
  grievance Do you have any grievances about the company you work for?
  grumble There were a few grumbles about the price.
  moan the moans about life in this country
  objection They received fifty objections to the building plans.
  protest protests about noise from the airport
- **Informal word gripe** reps who deal with people's gripes about their holiday
2 a chest complaint
  condition people with heart conditions
  disease liver disease
  disorder a kidney disorder
  illness minor illnesses such as colds
  trouble He has heart trouble.
- **Formal word ailment** minor ailments such as tummy bugs

VOCABULARY CHOICES
[meaning 1]
- The word **grievance** is used when you are complaining that you have been treated unfairly, and is often used in the context of work.

complete¹ [adjective]
1 The work is complete.
  done That's the washing done.
  finished The extension to the house is finished.

over The race is over.
2 a complete set of cards
  entire a photograph of the entire squad
  full the full range of colours
  whole I heard the whole story.
- **Formal words comprehensive** The book is a comprehensive survey of history.
  exhaustive I made an exhaustive list of every item of furniture.
3 I feel a complete fool.
  absolute The party was an absolute disaster.
  downright I knew it was a downright lie.
  sheer That's sheer nonsense!
  total We were left in total shock.
  utter a look of utter amazement on her face

complete² [verb]
They have completed the work.
  finish We'll finish the job next month.
- **Formal word conclude** Are there any questions before we conclude the meeting?
- **Informal term round off** We rounded off the afternoon with an ice cream.

completely [adverb]
  absolutely The film was absolutely brilliant.
  quite The day was quite awful.
  thoroughly We were thoroughly shocked.
  totally The bottle is totally empty.
  utterly Most of the children looked utterly bored.

compliment [noun]
  tribute Tributes were paid to him on his retirement.
- **Formal word accolade** He doesn't get the accolades he deserves.

compulsory [adjective]
  forced the forced sale of the company
- **Formal words mandatory** Every prisoner will face mandatory drug testing.
  obligatory The training is optional, not obligatory.

Cc

computer → concerned

Cc

Computer terms:

Types of computer:
Apple Mac®
desktop
handheld
iMac®
laptop
Mac®
mainframe
microcomputer
minicomputer
notebook
palmtop
PC (personal
  computer)

Hardware:
cable modem
chip
circuit board
CPU (central
  processing unit)
disk drive
floppy drive
graphics card
hard drive
joypad
joystick
keyboard
light pen
microprocessor
modem
monitor
motherboard

mouse
printer
scanner
screen
sound card
touchpad
trackball
VDU (visual display
  unit)
video card

Software:
application
freeware
program
shareware

Memory:
CD-R (Compact
  Disc Recordable)
CD-ROM
  (Compact Disc
  Read Only
  Memory)
DVD-ROM (Digital
  Versatile Disc Read
  Only Memory)
RAM (Random
  Access Memory)
ROM (Read Only
  Memory)

Disks:
CD (Compact Disc)
DVD (Digital
  Versatile Disc)

floppy disk
hard disk
magnetic disk
optical disk
zip disk

Web:
e-mail or email
hit
hyperlink
Internet
intranet
ISDN (international
  services digital
  network)
link
URL (uniform
  resource locator)
World Wide Web
  (WWW)

Other computing words:
backup
boot
bug
byte
cursor
data
database
debugging
directory
editor
file
format

gigabyte
graphics
icon
installation
interface
kilobyte
login
log off
log on
megabyte
menu
message box
mouse mat
network
output
package
password
port
reboot
scroll bar
spellchecker
spreadsheet
toolbar
upgrade
virus
virus checker
window
Windows®
word processing
workstation

computer [noun]
  PC *working on a PC*
  processor *a 200 megahertz Pentium processor*
♦ **Informal word machine** *My machine is refusing to let me log in.*
See also the box above.

concentrate [verb]
  pay attention *You need to pay attention*

to what you're doing.
  think *I can't think with all this noise.*
♦ **Formal term apply yourself** *He applied himself to his work.*

concerned [adjective]
1 concerned parents
  anxious *Anxious relatives waited for news.*
  troubled *a troubled expression on his face*

uneasy *A man was walking close behind her and she felt uneasy.*
worried *She was worried about the future on her own.*
2 the people concerned
affected *I will contact the people affected.*
involved *the politicians involved in the scandal*

confidence [noun]
1 Some young children lack confidence and need encouragement.
courage *He needed courage to ask her for a date.*
self-assurance *She was cocky and full of self-assurance.*
self-confidence *a shy man, lacking in self-confidence*
2 She had little confidence in my ability.
faith *He had little faith in the system.*
trust *She had a lot of trust in her teachers.*

confident [adjective]
1 a confident young woman
self-assured *She looked very self-assured.*
self-confident *a game for older and more self-confident children*
2 We are confident that everything will be ready on time.
certain *I feel certain that business will improve.*
convinced *I'm convinced that we'll be successful.*
sure *We're sure that we can handle more work.*

confuse [verb]
1 confusing her further
baffle *Tax forms baffle many people.*
mystify *His reply mystified me.*
puzzle *The final paragraph of the letter puzzled him.*
◆ **Formal words** **bewilder** *Her reaction bewildered me.*
perplex *Unclear road signs have*

perplexed visitors to the city.
2 Don't confuse the blue and the brown wires in the plug.
mistake *People often mistake me for my sister.*
mix up *I always mix him up with his brother.*
muddle *I always muddle their names.*
muddle up *He's muddled your birthday up with mine.*

confused [adjective]
1 looking confused • a confused old lady
baffled *He looked baffled at her comments.*
bewildered *He looked bewildered, as if he wasn't sure what to say.*
disoriented *She was sleepy and disoriented after a bump on the head.*
puzzled *a puzzled look on his face*
◆ **Formal word** **perplexed** *a perplexed frown on his face*
◆ **Informal word** **flummoxed** *She was flummoxed by the question.*
2 a confused mess of dirty plates
chaotic *a chaotic scene with people running everywhere*
disorderly *the disorderly state of the papers on his desk*
disorganized *disorganized ways of working*
untidy *an untidy mess of leaves and rubbish*

confusing [adjective]
baffling *a baffling number puzzle*
complicated *Application forms can be very complicated.*
unclear *The captain's instructions were unclear.*
◆ **Formal word** **bewildering** *a bewildering choice of shampoos and conditioners*

connect [verb]
attach *The doctor attached the heart monitor to his chest.*

Cc

Cc

fasten The bicycle was fastened to the railings with a chain.
join Join the two wires together.
link He linked the cable to the machine.

considerate [adjective]

caring a very caring young man
kind It was kind of her to give us a lift.
thoughtful It was very thoughtful of you to help.
unselfish an unselfish decision
◆ **Formal word** **attentive** The hotel staff are friendly and attentive.

contact¹ [noun]

Do you still have contact with your brother?
association his past association with criminals
communication There is no communication between the sisters.

contact² [verb]

Don't try to contact him.
call I'll call you tomorrow and we can discuss details.
get in touch with I should get in touch with John.
phone I'll phone you next week.
ring He rang me to ask if I could help.
◆ **Formal word** **approach** He was approached by someone who offered him a job.
◆ **Informal phrase** **get hold of** You can get hold of me on my mobile.

contest¹ [noun]

a hard-fought contest
battle Saturday's battle between the two players
competition She won a competition to design a new building.
fight a fight between the two clubs for the title
game the game that will decide the result
match The players are ready for Saturday's match.

VOCABULARY CHOICES
• The words **battle** and **fight** are often used to add impact to newspaper reports about, for example, a sports contest.

contest² [verb]

contesting the will
argue against people wanting to argue against the ruling
challenge They challenged the court's decision.
dispute The result was disputed by many people.
oppose people opposing the decision

contraception [noun]

birth control modern methods of birth control
family planning free advice about family planning

control¹ [verb]

1 The policeman controlled the traffic.
direct He was asked to direct the project.
govern The country is governed by the Labour Party.
lead Who's leading the project?
manage a business managed by three women
rule a country ruled by a King
run a project run by the Catholic Church
2 control the temperature
adjust You can adjust the temperature with this knob.
regulate a dial used to regulate the heat
3 control one's temper
contain He couldn't contain his rage.
curb She needs to learn to curb her anger.
hold back He was trying to hold back his tears.
◆ **Formal word** **restrain** He was unable to restrain his annoyance any longer.

control² [noun]

1 have full control
authority He was given full authority to make changes.

charge *She has charge of the money side of the business.*
command *the squadron in his command*
direction *the organization under her direction*
management *a business under new management*
2 controls on spending
curb *curbs on smoking in public places*
restraint *strict budget restraints*
3 fiddle with the controls
button *press a button to start the machine*
dial *He twiddled the dials.*
knob *the control knobs on the cooker*
lever *the machine's control levers*
switch *light switches*

cook [verb]
concoct *She concocted a meal from things she found in the fridge.*
make *He was in the kitchen making a snack.*
prepare *She was preparing dinner.*

VOCABULARY CHOICES
• The word **concoct** suggests you have cooked something unusual using a lot of different things.

cool¹ [adjective]
1 a cool breeze • a cool climate
chilly *a chilly day*
cold *a cold wind*
fresh *a nice fresh breeze*
refreshing *a refreshing breeze*
2 his ability to stay cool in a difficult situation
calm *He managed to stay calm.*
composed *She tried hard to look composed.*
level-headed *She's level-headed enough to cope with the pressure.*
unruffled *He stayed unruffled in all situations.*
♦ **Informal word** **laid-back** *She's always so laid-back about everything.*

cool² [verb]
Cool the dish before serving.
chill *Chill the meat after cooking it.*
refrigerate *Refrigerate the sauce after opening.*

cope [verb]
get by *How do single parents get by?*
manage *I don't know how we'll manage without you.*
survive *I couldn't survive without his help.*

copy¹ [noun]
1 A copy of the letter will be sent to all parents of children at the school.
carbon copy *Make carbon copies of all the documents.*
photocopy *a photocopy of his birth certificate*
♦ **Formal word** **duplicate** *Keep duplicates of all bills.*
2 a copy of an original painting
fake *fakes of designer clothes*
forgery *Her passport was a forgery.*
imitation *His expensive watch was an imitation, but it looked real.*
replica *a steel replica of an old passenger plane*
reproduction *a reproduction of a famous painting*

VOCABULARY CHOICES
[meaning 2]
• **Fake** often carries the idea of cheap imitations, and is sometimes used to hint that someone has bad taste.
• The word **forgery** conveys the idea of wrongdoing, and often tells you that something is an illegal copy.

copy² [verb]
1 Children often copy what you do.
ape *young people aping the actions of their heroes*
imitate *imitating the way he speaks*
impersonate *She impersonates her aunt to make us laugh.*

Cc

mimic *children behind him mimicking his walk*

2 copy the documents
photocopy *Photocopy the letter.*
♦ **Formal word duplicate** *Menus have to be typed and duplicated.*

correct[1] [verb]
I had to correct his faulty spelling.
put right *mistakes that are easily put right*
right *promises to right past wrongs*
♦ **Formal words amend** *Obvious errors can be amended.*
rectify *attempts to rectify faults*
remedy *He tried to remedy the mistake.*

correct[2] [adjective]
1 *the correct answer • correct in every detail*
accurate *accurate information*
right *She gave the right answer.*
true *a true picture of what was happening*
2 *the correct way to address the queen*
appropriate *the appropriate way to deal with the problem*
proper *the proper way to do it*
right *the right way to address your teacher*

cost [noun]
charge *the charge for petrol*
price *the price of coal*

cosy [adjective]
comfortable *the hotel's comfortable rooms*
homely *The restaurant was warm and homely.*
intimate *a pub with an intimate atmosphere*
snug *He felt snug under the duvet.*
♦ **Informal word comfy** *his warm comfy bed*

count[1] [verb]
1 *counting sheep • count up to 100*
add up *He's adding up what he's spent.*
calculate *I calculated the number of people in the room.*
♦ **Informal term tot up** *totting up how much money she'd got*
2 *that doesn't count*
matter *Her feelings didn't matter.*
3 *count yourself lucky*
consider *He considered himself hard done by.*
regard *She regarded herself as a failure.*
think *I never thought him good enough for you.*

count[2] [noun]
Make a count of your earnings.
calculation *His calculation was that he had £500.*
reckoning *By my reckoning, we should have made a lot of money.*

country[1] [noun]
1 *a foreign country • several European countries*
kingdom *the kingdom of Brunei*
nation *European nations*
principality *the principality of Monaco*
state *France and other European states*
2 *a walk in the country*
countryside *rambling in the countryside*
farmland *lovely views overlooking farmland and hills*

country[2] [adjective]
City people don't understand country ways.
rural *rural living*
rustic *The house was in a rustic setting among trees.*

VOCABULARY CHOICES
• The word **rustic** is often used in a positive way to describe something from the countryside as attractive, or pleasantly old-fashioned.

couple [noun]
duo *the famous comedy duo, Laurel and Hardy*
pair *He gave the pair a lift to the station.*
twosome *Spend more time as a twosome.*

courage [noun]
boldness She was surprised at her own boldness.
bravery the bravery of the soldiers
daring acts of amazing daring
fearlessness I admire her fearlessness.
mettle The men showed true mettle.
nerve I didn't have the nerve to say anything.
pluck a boy full of pluck and determination
♦ **Formal words audacity** He was amazed at her audacity.
valour soldiers' acts of valour
♦ **Informal word guts** He didn't have the guts to go and speak to her.

VOCABULARY CHOICES
• The words **mettle** and **pluck** are rather old-fashioned words, and they are usually used in an admiring way. You may come across these words in stories.
• **Valour** is a word which lends an air of dignity and is used, for example, in awards for military bravery.

course [noun]
1 I'm doing a computer course.
classes going to maths classes
lessons having French lessons
2 the course of events
progress the progress of time
progression the progression of the disease
sequence a sequence of events
3 along the river's course
direction The wind has changed direction.
path the path of an oncoming car
route following the route of the old road

cover¹ [verb]
1 A sheet covered the body.
conceal A heavy cloth concealed the box.
hide Piles of dirty plates hid the work surface.

mask A green shawl masked her features.
obscure a veil that obscured most of her face
2 covered with mud
cake His face was caked with blood.
coat books coated with dust
daub His car had been daubed with paint by vandals.
plaster Her face is plastered in make-up.
3 cover a topic
deal with Chapter 3 deals with the subject of crime.
include The leaflet includes details of what to do in an emergency.
♦ **Formal word embrace** a course that embraces many subjects

cover² [noun]
1 a protective cover
case Put the camera back in its case.
jacket the jacket that protects a book
lid a sandpit with a lid
wrapper a sweet wrapper
2 take cover from the weather
protection looking for protection from the rain
refuge We took refuge inside an old building.
shelter We found shelter under a tree.

coward [noun]
♦ **Informal words chicken** Go on jump, you chicken!
scaredy-cat Don't be such a scaredy-cat!
wimp He won't argue — he's a right little wimp.

cowardly [adjective]
spineless a spineless little man
weak-kneed He stood there like a weak-kneed schoolboy.
♦ **Formal word timorous** a shy, timorous boy
♦ **Informal words chicken** I'm too chicken to have a tattoo done.

Cc

57

wimpy *He was a wimpy man and too close to his mother.*

Cc

crash¹ [noun]

1 a car crash

accident *an accident on the motorway*

bump *I've had a few bumps in the car but nothing serious.*

collision *a collision involving a car and a van*

pile-up *a motorway pile-up involving ten cars*

smash *Four people were killed in the smash.*

♦ **Informal word** **prang** *I had a prang in the car park.*

2 The glass fell to the ground with a crash.

bang *She hit the floor with a bang.*

clatter *the clatter of plates being dropped*

thud *a thud as the book hit the floor*

thump *His head hit the door with a thump.*

VOCABULARY CHOICES

[meaning 1]

• The word **bump** suggests that the crash is not serious, and that no one was injured. **Prang** also suggests that the crash is slight, for example if you hit another car while trying to get into a parking space. Both these words might be used to make an accident sound less serious than it really is.

• The word **smash** suggests that the crash is very serious. It is a word often used in newspaper reports to add impact.

crash² [verb]

A van crashed into the bridge.

bang *His knee banged into the edge of the table.*

bump *She bumped into me and knocked my hat off.*

collide *The two vans collided. • He stopped so suddenly I almost collided with him.*

hit *The car hit a wall.*

crazy [adjective]

1 a crazy idea • a crazy man

idiotic *idiotic questions • acting like idiotic schoolboys*

insane *The idea is completely insane. • You're driving me insane!*

mad *full of mad ideas • You must be mad travelling with a two-week-old baby.*

ridiculous *a ridiculous suggestion • Don't be so ridiculous!*

silly *a silly idea • Don't be so silly!*

stupid *a stupid thing to do • He must be stupid to do something like that.*

♦ **Formal word** **ludicrous** *a ludicrous decision • He looks utterly ludicrous in that hat.*

♦ **Informal words** **barmy** *barmy plans to close the hospital • She obviously thought I was barmy.*

daft *daft questions • Is there someone daft enough to give him a job?*

potty *potty ideas • The noise was driving her potty.*

2 (informal) crazy about her

mad *He's mad about Jane and keeps talking about her.*

wild *She admitted she was wild about Ramesh.*

♦ **Formal words** **infatuated** *He was infatuated with his wife's sister.*

smitten *He seems really smitten with her.*

♦ **Informal word** **potty** *They were obviously potty about each other.*

crime [noun]

1 an increase in crime

lawbreaking *There are harder attitudes to lawbreaking.*

♦ **Formal word** **wrongdoing** *He has pleaded not guilty to any wrongdoing.*

2 a serious crime

offence *drug offences*

♦ **Formal word** **misdemeanour** *sexual misdemeanours*

criminal[1] [noun]
a hardened criminal
  lawbreaker *the punishment of lawbreakers*
  offender *young offenders*
◆ **Informal word** **crook** *a known crook and drug addict*

criminal[2] [adjective]
a criminal act
  illegal *illegal drug use*
  illicit *the illicit trade in alcohol*
  unlawful *unlawful behaviour*
◆ **Informal words** **bent** *bent business deals*
  crooked *crooked dealings*

VOCABULARY CHOICES
• The word **unlawful** is a word used in law, and often appears in writing about the law or crime.

crisp [adjective]
  crispy *crispy pastry*
  crunchy *a crunchy apple*

criticize [verb]
  attack *a speech attacking the Prime Minister*
  find fault with *She finds fault with everything I do.*
  pick holes in *Everyone picked holes in my plan.*
◆ **Formal word** **condemn** *a decision that has been condemned by police officers*
◆ **Informal words** **knock** *He's always knocking people who don't work.*
  slam *The advert has been slammed by teachers.*
  slate *The vicar was slated for his decision to miss the funeral.*

VOCABULARY CHOICES
• The phrase **find fault with** suggests that someone is criticizing someone for something small and unimportant.
• The word **knock** might be used to hint that the criticism is not fair, or that you feel some sympathy for the person being criticized.
• The words **condemn**, **slam** and **slate** suggest that someone is criticizing someone or something very strongly and in public. The words **slam** and **slate** are usually used in newspaper reports to add interest.

cross[1] [adjective]
I hope you are not cross with me.
  angry *He was angry because we were late.*
  annoyed *She was annoyed that I didn't phone.*
  irritated *He was getting irritated at the delay.*
◆ **Informal word** **shirty** *Don't get shirty with me!*

cross[2] [verb]
1 cross the road
  go across *He went across the road.*
2 Our paths cross now and again.
  meet *the place where the path and road meet*
◆ **Formal word** **intersect** *the place where the lines intersect*
3 crossing French cattle with British ones
  crossbreed *attempts to crossbreed lions with tigers*

cross[3] [noun]
a cross between a horse and a zebra
  crossbreed *an eight-month-old crossbreed*
  mongrel *a black and white mongrel puppy*
◆ **Formal word** **hybrid** *A loganberry is a hybrid between a blackberry and a raspberry.*

crowd[1] [noun]
crowds of fans
  group *A group of protesters gathered outside.*
  horde *the hordes of tourists who visit the area*
  mob *a mob of angry customers*

Cc

rabble *a rabble of drunken men*
swarm *A swarm of photographers followed the princess.*
◆ **Formal word throng** *She pushed her way through the throng.*

VOCABULARY CHOICES
• Describing a crowd as a **horde** or a **swarm** gives a fairly negative impression. The words suggest that the crowd is annoying and gets in the way.
• The word **rabble** is also a disapproving word to refer to a crowd that is disorganized and noisy.
• The word **mob** is often used to refer to a group of people doing bad things. It is sometimes used in newspapers to describe a group of people behaving in a violent or criminal way, to suggest disapproval.

crowd² [verb]
people crowding round the entrance
congregate *Fans congregated outside his hotel.*
flock *Groups of adoring women flocked around him.*
gather *Fans gathered around her.*
mass *About 15,000 people massed around the cathedral.*
swarm *Players swarmed around the referee.*
◆ **Formal word throng** *His supporters thronged around him.*

crowded [adjective]
busy *London's busy streets*
congested *congested city centres*
packed *a train packed with commuters*
swarming *a city swarming with tourists*
teeming *a teeming city of 18 million people*
◆ **Informal word jam-packed** *The pub was jam-packed.*

cruel [adjective]
callous *callous remarks*
hard-hearted *a hard-hearted woman*

harsh *harsh treatment of prisoners*
heartless *the heartless people who attacked an old lady*
merciless *the merciless killing of an old man*
ruthless *a violent and ruthless thug*
savage *a savage murder*
◆ **Formal words barbaric** *Keeping bears in small cages is barbaric.*
inhumane *inhumane treatment of animals*
sadistic *a sadistic man who took pleasure in hurting people*

crush [verb]
1 *Crush the garlic cloves.*
grind *Grind the peppercorns.*
press *juice from freshly pressed grapes*
pulp *apples pulped to make cider*
◆ **Formal word pulverize** *seeds pulverized into flour*
2 *Her dress got crushed in the case.*
crumple *Sitting for so long crumpled her skirt.*
squash *She squashed her hat when she sat on it.*

cry¹ [verb]
1 *cry pitifully*
bawl *a toddler bawling because his Mum wouldn't buy sweets*
snivel *She looked sad and started to snivel.*
sob *He sobbed for hours after she left.*
wail *She was wailing like an animal in pain.*
weep *She wept when she heard the news.*
whimper *He whimpered with fear.*
◆ **Informal word blubber** *He was blubbering like a child.*
2 *crying for help*
call *He called for his mother to come.*
exclaim *'I don't know,' he exclaimed.*
shout *She shouted for help.*
yell *'What shall we do now?' he yelled.*

VOCABULARY CHOICES
[meaning 1]
• The word **bawl** is usually used about children and suggests they are crying in a

loud and perhaps annoying way.
- **Blubber** is a word that suggests more strongly that you feel impatient with someone because they are crying loudly in an annoying way.
- The word **snivel** also suggests that you feel some contempt, this time for someone who is crying quietly in a complaining way.
- The word **weep** is not disapproving and is more likely to make you feel sympathy for the person crying. It is often used in stories and poems rather than in everyday speech.

cry[2] [noun]
1 have a good cry
  sob He had a good sob when he heard the news.
  weep She went outside and had a quiet weep.
2 a cry for help
  call a call from upstairs
  shout a shout for help
  yell a yell from outside

cuddle [verb]
  hug He picked the girl up and hugged her.
  ◆ **Formal word** **embrace** She embraced him.

cure[1] [verb]
cure a disease
  help things you can do to help depression
  relieve a cream that relieves itching
  ◆ **Formal word** **alleviate** a herb that can alleviate colds

cure[2] [noun]
a cure for eczema
  medicine medicines for coughs and colds
  remedy a remedy for a hangover
  treatment treatments for cancer

curious [adjective]
1 Children are very curious about many different things.
  inquisitive an inquisitive young girl
  interested He was interested to find out all he could.

questioning She had a questioning mind.
2 a curious sight
  bizarre a bizarre arrangement
  extraordinary the extraordinary sight of an elephant in the road
  funny It was funny to meet our neighbours on holiday.
  odd an odd feeling that I'd been here before
  peculiar the peculiar sight of a man on top of a train
  strange It's strange the way he never talks to us.
  unusual He has an unusual way of walking.

custody [noun]
1 He was granted custody of the children.
  care We were given care of his pets while he was away.
  charge the pupils in his charge
  protection the children under her protection
2 in police custody
  detention The protesters are being held in detention.
  imprisonment overnight imprisonment

custom [noun]
  practice religious practices
  tradition Spanish traditions
  way He didn't understand their ways.
  ◆ **Formal word** **convention** social conventions

customer [noun]
  client a lawyer who visits clients in their own homes
  consumer Consumers want more choice.
  shopper special offers to encourage shoppers
  ◆ **Formal word** **patron** The car park is reserved for patrons only.
  ◆ **Informal word** **punter** a barmaid talking to punters at the bar

VOCABULARY CHOICES
- The word **consumer** is usually used in the

Cc

61

context of writing or speaking about business and the economy.

• The word **patron** is often used on polite notices to people who are using a hotel, restaurant, etc.

Cc

___

cut[1] [verb]

1 Cut the carrot into slices.
chop Chop the vegetables.
divide Divide the cake into six pieces.
hack He hacked the meat into chunks.
slice Slice the onions.

2 cut the hedge • cut your hair
lop I lopped a bit off the end.
mow She mowed the lawn.
prune He was pruning the apple tree.
shave Shave the hair off your legs.
trim She trimmed her hair.

3 cut his finger
gash She gashed her hand on some glass.
nick He nicked his thumb on the can.
slash The attacker had slashed her face.
♦ **Formal word lacerate** The glass had lacerated his arm.

4 cutting prices
decrease decrease costs to the employer
lower Many supermarkets have lowered their prices.

reduce They were forced to reduce the price of petrol.

cut[2] [noun]

1 a deep cut
gash a gash on his leg
nick He got a nick on his finger from the sheet of paper.
slash a deep slash on her arm
♦ **Formal word laceration** deep lacerations on his arm
♦ **Technical term incision** We'll make a small incision in your stomach.

2 spending cuts
cutback cutbacks in grants
decrease a decrease in taxes
reduction price reductions

VOCABULARY CHOICES
[meaning 1]
• The words **gash**, **slash** and **laceration** are used for deep cuts and serious injuries, and can be used to add impact to a news story or text.
• The word **nick** is used for a slight cut, but might also be used to make the cut seem less serious than it really is.
• The word **incision** is usually used when a doctor cuts into skin as part of a medical operation.

D

daft [adjective]
   absurd *The idea is absurd.*
   crazy *a crazy idea*
   foolish *a foolish thing to say*
   idiotic *his idiotic comments*
   silly *What a silly thing to do!*
   stupid *stupid ideas*
♦ **Formal word** **inane** *inane comments*

damage[1] [noun]
damage to the ozone layer
   destruction *insects that cause destruction of crops*
   devastation *The storm caused widespread devastation.*
   harm *Tourists can cause a lot of harm to the countryside.*
♦ **Formal word** **impairment** *deafness or hearing impairment*

damage[2] [verb]
Try not to damage the cover.
   harm *Sunbathing can harm your skin.*
   hurt *Looking at the sun can hurt your eyes.*
   weaken *Chemicals will weaken the material.*
♦ **Formal word** **impair** *Age had not impaired her beauty.*

damp[1] [adjective]
My hair's still damp.
   dank *a dank November morning*
   humid *humid air*
   misty *a misty morning in December*
   moist *moist soil*

VOCABULARY CHOICES
• The word **dank** is usually used in writing, and creates an unpleasant, gloomy atmosphere.

damp[2] [noun]
protection against damp
   dampness *a smell of mould and dampness*
   humidity *conditions of high humidity*
   moisture *moisture in the air*

dance[1] [verb]
They were dancing in the streets.
   prance *prancing around like a ballet dancer*
   sway *The whole audience swayed to the rhythm.*
   whirl *The dancers whirled round to a waltz.*
♦ **Informal terms** **bop** *bopping around to pop music*
   hoof it *hoof it at the local disco*
   jig *Ian was jigging about, enjoying himself.*
   shake a leg *Come on, granny! Let's shake a leg!*

VOCABULARY CHOICES
• Informal terms such as **bop**, **hoof it**, **jig** and **shake a leg** are quite humorous in tone. They give a strong impression of people not dancing in a very skilled or formal way, but having a lot of fun.

63

Dd

dance² [noun]
The company holds a dance every year.
ball a student ball
social We booked a band for the company social this year.

danger [noun]
hazard the health hazards of mobile phones
risk the health risks of high blood pressure
threat the threat to health from drinking too much
◆ **Formal word peril** the perils of being married to a pop star

VOCABULARY CHOICES
• The word **peril** is sometimes used when you want to be funny and suggest that something has more dangers than it really does.

dangerous [adjective]
hazardous hazardous driving conditions
risky a risky operation with little chance of success
treacherous the treacherous waters of the lake
unsafe The river is unsafe for swimming.
◆ **Formal words perilous** a perilous journey
precarious the precarious nature of a roofer's job

dark¹ [adjective]
It is too dark to see anything.
black It was completely black outside.
dim The room was very dim.
dingy a dingy corridor
unlit an unlit hallway

VOCABULARY CHOICES
• The word **dingy** suggests that a place is dark in an unpleasant way, and often suggests that it is slightly dirty too.

dark² [noun]
afraid of the dark
blackness the blackness of the night

darkness He was lost in the darkness of the tunnel.
dimness The dimness of the room meant he could hardly see.
gloom Her eyes shone in the gloom.

VOCABULARY CHOICES
• The words **dimness** and **gloom** are usually used in stories to create a dark, slightly threatening atmosphere.

day [noun]
1 during the day
daylight The attacks all happened in daylight.
daytime He's at home in the daytime.
2 in the days of King John
age in the age of steam trains
era a new era in British politics
generation the best writer of her generation
period a famous painter of that period
time in the time of Queen Victoria

dead [adjective]
1 dead on arrival at hospital
late her late husband
lifeless His lifeless body was dragged from the water.
◆ **Formal word deceased** the graves of deceased relatives
departed the ghost of his departed wife
2 My fingers went dead.
numb My arms were numb from leaning on them.

VOCABULARY CHOICES
[meaning 1]
• The words **lifeless** and **departed** are often used in books and stories rather than everyday speech.
• **Departed** and **deceased** are sometimes used to be tactful when someone has died, rather than say the word 'dead'.

deaf [adjective]
hard of hearing You'll have to speak up,

I'm a bit hard of hearing.
stone-deaf He was stone-deaf and was lip-reading.

dear¹ [adjective]

1 my dear friend
beloved her beloved dog
cherished a cherished friend
darling her darling daughter, Jane
precious the loss of their precious son
treasured treasured photos of her grandfather

2 A car was too dear so I bought a bike.
costly a costly divorce from his wife
expensive Houses are very expensive round here.
high-priced stores selling high-priced clothes and shoes
♦ **Informal word pricey** The meal was good but a bit pricey.

dear² [noun]

Be a dear and get me a coffee.
darling Have you had a good day, darling?
treasure He's a real treasure.
♦ **Formal word beloved** He had gone to visit his beloved.

death [noun]

end He met with an unpleasant end.
loss She never recovered from the loss of her husband.
passing Her passing is a great loss to this country.
♦ **Formal words demise** He inherited the land on his father's demise.
fatality an increase in fatalities on Britain's roads

VOCABULARY CHOICES

• The words **loss** and **passing** are often used to be tactful, and to avoid upsetting people by saying the word 'death'.
• The word **fatality** is used for deaths which happen because of accidents, wars, or disease, and is used in official reports.

debt [noun]

arrears rent arrears
bill She couldn't afford to pay her bills.

deceive [verb]

cheat He had been cheated out of all his money.
dupe She had been duped into buying a stolen car.
fool He was fooled into giving all his bank details.
hoax hoaxed by a man claiming to be a police officer
hoodwink She's too clever to be hoodwinked by anyone.
mislead Women are misled into believing the cream will get rid of wrinkles.
trick He had been tricked into signing the papers.
♦ **Informal terms con** People have been conned into sending money to fake charities.
take for a ride Customers are being taken for a ride by dodgy garages.
take in I feel stupid to have been taken in by him.

decent [adjective]

1 It's not decent to marry again so soon.
appropriate She didn't feel it was appropriate to say anything.
proper the proper thing to do
respectable a respectable family
♦ **Formal word seemly** It's not seemly to say bad things about people who've died.

2 That's very decent of you.
generous It was really generous of you to help.
kind It's kind of you to offer.
thoughtful It was thoughtful of her to give us a lift.
♦ **Formal word courteous** It was courteous of him to let us know.

3 a decent salary • a decent effort
acceptable an acceptable standard
adequate an adequate supply

Dd

Dd

fair *a fair attempt to solve the problem*
reasonable *a reasonable amount of money*
satisfactory *a satisfactory effort*

decide [verb]
1 She decided to become a police officer.
choose *He chose to stay at home that morning.*
opt *He opted to take early retirement.*
reach a decision *We hope to reach a decision soon.*
2 The case will be decided in court.
settle *The matter can be settled later.*
♦ **Formal word determine** *The decision will determine the future of the company.*

decorate [verb]
1 decorate the tree
deck *a boat decked with flags*
trim *silk trimmed with gold beads*
♦ **Formal words adorn** *Flowers adorned the entrance to the hotel.*
embellish *material embellished with gold*
2 decorating the bedroom
paint *What colour are you going to paint the room?*
paper *the decorator who papered the lounge*

decoration [noun]
1 a style with little decoration
adornment *The room was bare and without adornment.*
ornamentation *the tower with its magnificent gold ornamentation*
♦ **Formal word embellishment** *the embellishment of church interiors*
2 Christmas decorations
bauble *gold and silver baubles on a Christmas tree*
ornament *garden ornaments*

decrease[1] [verb]
The frequency of the attacks has decreased.
decline *The number of people living in the countryside has declined.*

diminish *Ice in the Arctic has diminished by a huge amount.*
drop *Sales dropped by fifteen per cent.*
dwindle *The number of people going to church has dwindled.*
fall *The number of crimes fell sharply.*
shrink *The number of babies born in the UK has shrunk each year.*
slide *The company's profits are sliding steadily.*

decrease[2] [noun]
a decrease in membership
decline *a decline in the number of people out of work*
downturn *a downturn in sales*
drop *a drop in profits*
fall *a fall in the number of people claiming benefits*
reduction *a reduction in the birth rate*
slide *There was a slide in the band's popularity.*

deep [adjective]
1 a deep gorge
bottomless *a bottomless lake*
2 deep sadness
deep-seated *deep-seated jealousy*
heartfelt *heartfelt sympathy*
intense *intense anger*
3 a deep groan • a deep voice
booming *his booming laugh*
low *a low moan*
4 a deep sleep
heavy *waking from a heavy sleep*
sound *He fell into a sound slumber.*
5 a deep red carpet
dark *dark blue eyes*
rich *material in rich reds and browns*

defeat[1] [verb]
1 The team were defeated 17–12.
beat *Liverpool were beaten by Manchester United.*
conquer *They had conquered most of the armies of Europe.*

outdo *She was not going to be outdone by a boy.*
overcome *We were overcome by a more powerful force.*
overpower *She overpowered the Italian player 6–1, 6–3.*
trounce *The team were trounced 6–0.*
♦ **Informal words** **hammer** *I think our team will hammer them.*
thrash *They were thrashed 8–0.*
2 *a lock that will defeat any thief*
foil *Police have foiled a robbery attempt.*
get the better of *I won't allow the situation to get the better of me.*
thwart *My plans were thwarted by a lack of money.*

VOCABULARY CHOICES
[meaning 1]
• The words **hammer, thrash** and **trounce** suggest that you defeat someone very easily. These words are often used in newspaper sports reports to add dramatic effect.

defeat[2] [noun]
1 *a 4–1 defeat against France*
beating *a 3–0 beating by Chelsea*
loss *The team has had four wins and three losses.*
♦ **Informal words** **thrashing** *an 8–0 thrashing*
trouncing *a trouncing in the finals*
2 *defeat on a specific issue*
failure *the failure of her plans*

defend [verb]
1 *guards defending the country's borders*
guard *soldiers guarding the building*
protect *He wasn't able to protect himself from attack.*
safeguard *software to safeguard against computer viruses*
shield *actors shielded by bodyguards*
2 *She defended her husband when he was criticized in the press.*

back *I will back him all the way.*
stand up for *He stood up for her when everyone else criticized her.*
stick up for *Why do you always stick up for him?*
support *She carried on supporting him throughout the scandal.*

Dd

definite [adjective]
certain *It's certain that he will turn up.*
decided *The chocolate pudding is a decided favourite.*
guaranteed *This athlete is a guaranteed winner.*
settled *The date of the wedding is settled.*
sure *It's sure to rain later.*

definitely [adverb]
certainly *I'll certainly think about coming.*
undoubtedly *He is undoubtedly one of the best players.*
unquestionably *She is unquestionably one of the best writers around.*

delay[1] [noun]
unnecessary delays
hold-up *hold-ups on the motorway*
wait *After a short wait we were on our way.*

delay[2] [verb]
1 *delay progress*
hinder *Bad weather hindered the search.*
hold up *hold up the process of change*
obstruct *Lack of money will obstruct research.*
set back *a problem which set back his recovery*
♦ **Formal word** **impede** *a decision that will impede progress*
2 *delay the wedding*
postpone *postpone the meeting until next week*
put off *We decided to put the party off for a while.*
♦ **Formal word** **defer** *It is possible to defer entry to college for a year.*

Dd

deliberate [adjective]
conscious *a conscious attempt to improve the situation*
intentional *Sorry I upset you. It wasn't intentional.*
planned *innocent victims of a planned attack*

delicate [adjective]
1 delicate lace
dainty *dainty glass cups*
fine *fine china*
◆ **Formal word exquisite** *exquisite diamond jewellery*
2 a delicate child
frail *a frail woman*
weak *a weak young boy*

delicious [adjective]
appetizing *a large, appetizing meal*
luscious *a bowl of luscious strawberries*
mouthwatering *a range of mouthwatering desserts*
tasty *tasty pies*
succulent *a succulent pear*
◆ **Formal word flavoursome** *flavoursome tomatoes*
◆ **Informal words moreish** *I picked a bag of moreish-looking chocolates.*
scrumptious *a scrumptious meal*
yummy *all kinds of yummy snacks*

VOCABULARY CHOICES
• The word **yummy** is quite childish in tone, and is often used about the foods children like.

delighted [adjective]
happy *I'm really happy with my new car.*
overjoyed *We're overjoyed at the decision.*
pleased *I'm pleased to announce that John and Millie are getting married.*
thrilled *We were thrilled to hear your news.*

deliver [verb]
1 deliver a parcel

bring *He brought the box to the door.*
carry *She carried the bag into the house.*
2 deliver a speech
give *Liam gave an interesting talk.*
speak *Anna spoke a few words.*
utter *He uttered a strange spell.*
3 deliver a blow
inflict *inflicted a punishment*
◆ **Formal word administer** *He administered a slap to her face.*

delivery [noun]
1 a delivery of goods
◆ **Formal word consignment** *consignments of books*
2 an easy delivery
birth *a difficult birth*
labour *a long and difficult labour*

demolish [verb]
1 demolishing the building
bulldoze *plans to bulldoze the houses*
knock down *They knocked the block of flats down.*
pull down *The house has been pulled down.*
tear down *Beautiful old houses are being torn down.*
2 an experience that demolished her self-confidence
destroy *He had destroyed her happiness.*
ruin *an injury that ruined his career*
wreck *Bad luck had wrecked her hopes.*

VOCABULARY CHOICES
[meaning 1]
• The term **tear down** has a lot of impact and is usually used in newspaper reports. It is used especially to suggest that it is the wrong thing to do.

dense [adjective]
1 dense woods
thick *lost in the thick forest*
◆ **Formal word impenetrable** *impenetrable jungles*
2 dense fog

heavy *heavy clouds*
thick *thick smoke*

deny [verb]

1 deny the accusation
dispute *He angrily disputed claims that he'd lied.*
◆ **Formal word refute** *He refuted allegations that money had been wasted.*
2 deny them basic human rights
refuse *Staff refused her access to the club.*
withhold *Vital documents were withheld.*

department [noun]

1 a government department
branch *a branch of the organization*
division *the company's sales division*
office *government offices*
unit *the hospital's intensive care unit*
2 That's not my department.
domain *Housework used to be a woman's domain.*
responsibility *Filing the papers is my responsibility.*
sphere *Politics was outside his sphere.*

depend on [verb]

1 We depend on his income.
count on *He's not the sort of person you can count on.*
rely on *people who rely on state benefits*
◆ **Informal term bank on** *We're banking on some help from friends.*
2 That depends on several factors.
hang on *The policy all hangs on who wins the election.*
hinge on *A lot hinges on whether he gets the job or not.*
rest on *The strength of a school rests on its staff.*

depressed [adjective]

down *I'm feeling a bit down at the moment.*
downhearted *He refused to be downhearted after losing the game.*
glum *He looked glum.*

low *She's been feeling low recently.*
miserable *Many people feel miserable in winter.*
sad *I was sad for a long time after my mother died.*
unhappy *people who feel unhappy*
◆ **Formal word melancholy** *teenage melancholy*
◆ **Informal terms down in the dumps** *She's down in the dumps.*
fed up *I'm just feeling fed up at the moment.*

VOCABULARY CHOICES

• If someone is **depressed** in the strict sense of the word, then they have a medical condition, and are not simply unhappy because of things that happen to them. If this is what you mean, then it is better not to use the above words, which only mean that someone is feeling down.

depression [noun]

1 go into a deep depression
gloom *He wasn't sure what had caused his gloom.*
hopelessness *a sense of hopelessness about the future*
low spirits *his low spirits since his brother's death*
sadness *the sense of sadness she felt*
◆ **Formal words despondency** *His mood sunk into despondency.*
melancholy *Melancholy struck him as he got older.*
◆ **Informal term the blues** *people suffering from the blues*
2 economic depression
hard times *The country is facing hard times.*
recession *Many businesses closed as a result of the recession.*
slump *a slump in the economy*
3 a depression in the rock
cavity *a cavity in the rockface*
dip *a dip in the surface*

Dd

Dd

hollow *a little hollow in the floor*
indentation *a deep indentation in the wall*
pit *pits in his skin*

VOCABULARY CHOICES
[meaning 1]
• In the strict sense of the word, **depression** is a medical condition. If this is what you mean, then it is better not to use the above words, which only mean a feeling of unhappiness because of things that have happened.

describe [verb]
detail *He detailed the reasons behind the decision.*
explain *He explained what had happened.*
outline *She outlined what we would cover in the course.*
report *Witnesses reported seeing a man leaving the building.*
♦ **Formal words recount** *She recounted her experiences.*
relate *He related the details of the accident.*

deserve [verb]
merit *That boy has merited a place in the team.*
rate *The pub definitely rates a mention in the guide.*
warrant *The cathedral warrants a visit.*
♦ **Formal phrase be worthy of** *a song that is worthy of a place in the charts*

design¹ [noun]
1 a design for the garden
blueprint *the blueprint for a new stand at the football ground*
drawing *a drawing of the new office blocks*
plan *You can see plans for the houses.*
sketch *a sketch of the proposed building*
2 the design of the car
shape *The shape of the toy makes it good*

for young children.
structure *the structure of a flower*
style *the style of the furniture*
3 cups with a blue and gold design on them
motif *a heart motif on her bag*
pattern *the pattern on the curtains*

design² [verb]
1 classes designed to help you prepare for the birth
intend *a drug intended to help people with asthma*
plan *The book was planned to appeal to students.*
2 designing a computer program
create *creating the latest products*
develop *developing new software*
invent *inventing low-fat recipes*
think up *thinking up games for the children to play*

VOCABULARY CHOICES
[meaning 2]
• The word **develop** gives a strong impression of working through stages to produce something worthwhile. It is a word that can be used to good effect in CVs and job applications.

desperate [adjective]
1 a desperate look
despairing *a despairing cry*
hopeless *a hopeless situation*
2 a desperate attempt to escape
do-or-die *a do-or-die attempt to beat his fear of flying*
frantic *her frantic efforts to find her passport*
frenzied *frenzied attempts to free himself*
3 a building in desperate need of repair • a desperate shortage of nurses
acute *an acute shortfall in funding*
critical *a critical lack of money*
serious *in serious need of supplies*
severe *severe droughts*
urgent *He was in urgent need of a drink.*

VOCABULARY CHOICES
[meaning 2]
• **Do-or-die** is quite a dramatic word, usually used in newspaper stories and reports.

destroy [verb]
1 Bombs destroyed the city.
devastate The library was devastated by the blaze.
ravage a country ravaged by war
raze the school that was razed by fire
wreck Our house was wrecked by the flood water.
2 The scandal destroyed his career. • Her lies destroyed their trust in her.
ruin The experience ruined his confidence.
undermine The noise undermined our enjoyment of the holiday.
wreck Fresh fighting has wrecked hopes of peace.
3 The animal had to be destroyed.
kill The dog had to be killed because it attacked a child.
put down The cat had to be put down because it was so old.

VOCABULARY CHOICES
[meaning 1]
• The words **devastate** and **ravage** create strong images of complete ruin, and are usually used in writing because of their dramatic effect.
[meaning 3]
• The term **put down** is less strong than **kill** or **destroy**, and can be used to avoid upsetting people.

determined [adjective]
1 She was determined to succeed.
insistent on Despite the injury, he was insistent on playing.
intent on She seems intent on causing trouble.
2 a determined young woman
persistent He was very persistent and

wouldn't take no for an answer.
single-minded She's very single-minded.
strong-willed a strong-willed child
♦ **Formal word   resolute** Her voice was calm and resolute.

VOCABULARY CHOICES
[meaning 1]
• If you describe someone as being **intent on** something, it suggests that they plan to do something bad and you do not approve.

develop [verb]
1 Babies develop quickly.
advance Technology advances every day.
evolve The story evolved into a tragedy.
grow It is exciting to watch your children grow.
mature Colin is maturing into a handsome young man.
progress My spelling is progressing well.
2 The company is developing rapidly.
branch out The business has branched out into other countries.
expand My job is expanding to include new duties.
spread The illness is spreading quickly.
3 We are developing new business ideas. • I developed a better system.
create creating new products
design designing software
improve ways of improving the way we work
invent He invents his own recipes.
plan The book was planned to appeal to students.
think up thinking up games for the children to play

VOCABULARY CHOICES
[meaning 3]
• The words **create** and **plan**, as well as the word **develop** itself, can be used in CVs and job applications to make a good

impression. They suggest working methodically through different stages to produce a worthwhile result.

device [noun]

appliance *kitchen appliances such as microwaves*
contraption *a strange-looking contraption*
gadget *clever new gadgets*
machine *a bread-making machine*
tool *a set of gardening tools*
♦ **Formal words implement** *spades and other garden implements*
utensil *cooking utensils*

VOCABULARY CHOICES

• To call a device a **contraption** hints that you think it is a bit ridiculous, either because it is very shoddy or because it is more complicated than it has to be.

diagram [noun]

chart *a chart showing information*
drawing *a drawing of the human body*
plan *a plan showing where everyone would sit*
sketch *a sketch of where the house was*

diary [noun]

1 Write the date in your diary.
appointment book *I've put the date in the appointment book.*

2 She keeps a diary hidden in a drawer.
journal *He kept a journal of his travels.*

die [verb]

1 die young
breathe your last *Poor old Ted has finally breathed his last.*
pass away *She passed away peacefully in her sleep.*
♦ **Formal word perish** *Hundreds perished in the terrorist attacks.*
♦ **Slang terms kick the bucket** *I'm not about to kick the bucket just yet.*
peg out *Who's going to help me if you peg out?*

snuff it *I read in the paper that he'd snuffed it.*

2 The sound of their voices died away.
disappear *The noise of the lorry gradually disappeared.*
fade *The sound of the footsteps faded.*
peter out *The clapping petered out.*
♦ **Formal word subside** *I waited until the cheers had subsided.*

3 (informal) dying for an ice cream
long for *I'm longing for a chance to see the baby.*
yearn *He was yearning to kiss her.*

VOCABULARY CHOICES

[meaning 1]
• The phrase **breathe your last** is quite literary, and is usually used in texts such as poems and stories.
• The word **perish** is also used in writing when people die suddenly, for example in an accident or war.
• The term **pass away** is often used to be tactful, and to avoid upsetting someone by saying the word 'die'.

[meaning 3]
• You usually see the word **yearn** in poems and stories rather than everyday writing, as it is quite literary.

diet [verb]

cut down *I'm going to cut down because I've been eating too much.*
slim *foods for people who are slimming*
♦ **Informal word weight-watch** *The pudding is not suitable for people who are weight-watching.*

difference [noun]

1 There's no difference between them.
contrast *There was a marked contrast between him and his brother.*
distinction *the distinction between banks and building societies*
variation *a great deal of variation between schools*

2 settle their differences
disagreement *disagreements with the neighbours*
dispute *a dispute over who owns the land*
♦ **Formal word conflict** *It's about time they resolved the conflict.*

different [adjective]
1 Your bike is different from mine.
unalike *The sisters were so unalike.*
♦ **Formal word dissimilar** *two very dissimilar people*
2 different colours
assorted *clothes in assorted sizes*
diverse *people from diverse backgrounds*
various *towels in various colours*
3 He has always felt different.
unconventional *She's a bit unconventional.*
unique *She's quite unique.*
unusual *an unusual but interesting person*

difficult [adjective]
1 a difficult journey
demanding *a demanding job*
hard *She'd had a hard day at work.*
strenuous *You've a strenuous day ahead.*
tough *a tough assignment*
♦ **Formal word arduous** *an arduous journey to Australia*
2 a difficult problem
complex *It's a complex issue.*
complicated *The situation is a bit complicated.*
thorny *the thorny problem of what to do about his mother*
tricky *These are tricky questions to answer.*
3 a difficult child
awkward *She's always been awkward and stubborn.*
demanding *a demanding little boy*
troublesome *troublesome children*
trying *He can be very trying at times.*

difficulty [noun]
1 He has difficulty in walking.

problem *Did you have any problem finding the house?*
trouble *He had trouble finding somewhere to park.*
2 encounter many difficulties
complication *There were a few complications on the way.*
obstacle *how to overcome obstacles*
pitfall *the pitfalls in buying a house*
problem *the problems we face*
stumbling block *Lack of time is a major stumbling block in trying to get fit.*
♦ **Formal word hindrance** *Her lack of height wasn't a hindrance to her.*

VOCABULARY CHOICES
[meaning 2]
• The word **pitfall** is used most often about the difficulties people may have in a situation unless they're careful.

dig [verb]
1 dig a hole
burrow *animals burrowing into the ground*
♦ **Formal word excavate** *excavating a narrow tunnel*
2 digging me in the ribs
poke *He poked me with his elbow.*
prod *She prodded my arm.*

dignified [adjective]
majestic *a majestic ceremony*
solemn *a solemn occasion*
stately *the stately elegance of the town*

dinner [noun]
1 a formal dinner in honour of the President
banquet *a banquet for the Queen*
feast *a wedding feast*
meal *a meal to raise money for charity*
2 What are we having for dinner?
lunch *Would you like to come for lunch?*
supper *We're having supper at the moment.*
tea *We had fish and chips for tea.*

Dd

dirt [noun]
1 dig in the dirt
earth *picking worms out of the earth*
mud *walking in the mud*
soil *children playing in the soil*
2 covered in dirt
filth *the noise and filth of the factory*
grime *windows covered in a layer of grime*
muck *the muck on his boots*

dirty [adjective]
filthy *The room was filthy.*
grimy *grimy windows*
grubby *grubby hands*
mucky *a baby's mucky bib*
◆ **Formal word soiled** *soiled clothes*

disabled [adjective]
crippled *a crippled man with one arm*
handicapped *She works with handicapped people.*
impaired *people who are hearing impaired*

VOCABULARY CHOICES
• The words **crippled** and **handicapped** are old-fashioned and many people do not use them now, as they can sound offensive.

disagree [verb]
1 disagree about which method to use
argue *We argue over money quite a lot.*
differ *They differ over issues such as physical punishment.*
2 The two sets of readings disagree.
conflict *The new findings which conflict with earlier evidence.*
contradict *The reports contradict each other.*
differ *Their accounts of what happened differed.*

disagreement [noun]
1 We had a disagreement over who should drive to the party.
argument *They are having an argument about what to do.*

quarrel *Sue and John had a quarrel over money.*
squabble *a squabble between two brothers*
2 The disagreement in the figures is quite significant.
difference *There's a difference in their stories.*
◆ **Formal word discrepancy** *discrepancies in the accounts*

disappear [verb]
1 Spots will disappear gradually.
fade away *The bruises had faded away now.*
vanish *The mark had vanished.*
2 The thieves disappeared as soon as the police arrived.
go *He went when he realized what was happening.*
leave *He left as soon as we arrived.*
◆ **Formal word flee** *She fled upstairs when she saw him.*
◆ **Informal word scarper** *The man had scarpered by the time I got there.*
3 Dinosaurs disappeared millions of years ago.
become extinct *a bird which is in danger of becoming extinct*
die out *More than 50 types of fish have died out.*

disappointed [adjective]
let down *He felt let down when his date didn't turn up.*
sad *I'm sad that I didn't do better in the test.*
upset *I'm a little upset that we didn't win.*
◆ **Formal word discouraged** *He was discouraged by the news that he'd failed again.*
◆ **Informal word miffed** *She was slightly miffed at not being invited.*

disappointment [noun]
1 Meera couldn't hide her disappointment.
regret *He was full of regret that he hadn't*

done what he wanted.
sadness our sadness at losing
2 The match was a bit of a disappointment.
anticlimax The New Year celebrations were rather an anticlimax.
let-down The event was a let-down because so few people turned up.
♦ **Informal terms damp squib** The final turned out to be a damp squib.
washout The protest had been a washout as less than 50 people were there.

disaster [noun]
1 a rail disaster which killed 25 people
accident Accidents on the railway are becoming more frequent.
calamity natural calamities such as floods and earthquakes
catastrophe floods that are the worst natural catastrophe the country has seen
tragedy Ten people died in the tragedy.
2 The project was a disaster.
failure The plan was a complete failure.
fiasco It was an embarrassing fiasco for the government.
♦ **Formal word catastrophe** The decision was a catastrophe for the company.
♦ **Informal word flop** The show was a flop and lost money.

VOCABULARY CHOICES
[meaning 2]
• Using the word **fiasco** conveys a criticism of the people involved, and suggests that they have done things completely wrong.
• A **flop** is a person or thing that is not successful, and using the word mocks them a little.

discover [verb]
1 discover a hidden valley
find Drugs were found in his house.
uncover A search uncovered illegal weapons.
unearth Police have unearthed a huge

bomb-making factory.
♦ **Formal word locate** I've been trying to locate a copy of the book.
2 discover the truth
find out Find out what has been going on.
learn It was a long time before I learned the truth.
realize I didn't realize what was happening until later.
see Go and see what she wants.
♦ **Formal word ascertain** The fire brigade had to ascertain the cause of the fire.
3 Who discovered penicillin?
invent Edison invented the light bulb.
pioneer a treatment that was pioneered in America

disease [noun]
illness the treatment of illnesses
infection childhood infections such as chickenpox
♦ **Formal word ailment** ailments such as colds and tummy bugs

disgusted [adjective]
appalled I was appalled at the way they treated the animals.
outraged People are outraged at his murder.
revolted He was revolted at the idea of eating horse meat.

disgusting [adjective]
1 a disgusting smell
foul a foul stench
nasty He had a nasty taste in his mouth.
nauseating a nauseating odour
revolting The meal looked revolting.
vile a vile green colour
2 It's disgusting, the amount of food that is wasted in this country.
obscene the obscene amounts of money that some footballers earn
outrageous It's outrageous that people are treated so badly.
scandalous a scandalous waste of money

Dd

dishonest [adjective]
  corrupt *corrupt government officials*
  lying *lying salesmen*
  untrustworthy *She was completely untrustworthy.*
♦ **Formal words** **deceitful** *a deceitful man*
  disreputable *disreputable car dealers*
♦ **Informal word** **shady** *shady business deals*

Dd

VOCABULARY CHOICES
• The word **corrupt** is often used as a strong criticism of people in powerful jobs who are dishonest in the way they do their job.

dislike[1] [verb]
I don't dislike him.
  hate *I hate bananas.*
  object to *He strongly objected to having his Sunday evening disturbed.*

VOCABULARY CHOICES
• The words **hate** has a lot of impact, as you would use it if you disliked someone or something very much.
• **Object to** is not as strong a term to use.

dislike[2] [noun]
a strong dislike of cheats
  hatred *their hatred for each other*
♦ **Formal words** **antipathy** *her antipathy towards experiments on animals*
  distaste *his distaste for children*

disobey [verb]
  break *people who break the law*
  flout *Drivers are still flouting the ban on mobile phone use in the car.*
  ignore *Too many people ignore speed limits.*
♦ **Formal words** **contravene** *This food contravenes public health laws.*
  defy *He defied his parents and went out.*

VOCABULARY CHOICES
• The words **flout** and **ignore** are used when someone disobeys a law or rule because they think it is unnecessary or stupid.

distant [adjective]
  faraway *stories of faraway countries*
  far-flung *trips to far-flung corners of the world*
  out-of-the-way *people living in out-of-the-way places*
  remote *remote mountain villages*

VOCABULARY CHOICES
• **Faraway** and **far-flung** can make a place sound exotic, that is, attractive because it is very different and unfamiliar.

disturb [verb]
1 *disturbing his rest*
  disrupt *The holiday was disrupted by building work at the hotel.*
  interrupt *The call interrupted his work.*
2 *disturbed by the news*
  distress *We are all distressed by pictures of starving children.*
  unsettle *The news had unsettled her.*
  upset *The decision has upset many people.*
  worry *You shouldn't let it worry you.*
3 *disturbing the neat piles of books*
  upset *The dog ran into the room, upsetting the papers on the floor.*
♦ **Formal word** **disarrange** *Everything in the room had been disarranged.*

divide [verb]
1 *Divide the orange into segments.*
  break up *Break the chocolate up into pieces.*
  cut *Cut the cake into slices.*
  separate *Separate the two halves.*
  split *Split the class into three groups.*
2 *dividing the money equally*
  distribute *There are ways to distribute food more fairly.*
  share *The inheritance was shared equally between the brothers.*
  split *They split the cash between them.*

Breeds of dog:

Afghan hound	dachshund	Labrador	setter
alsatian	Dalmatian	lurcher	shih tzu
basset hound	Doberman pinscher	Old English	springer spaniel
beagle	fox terrier	sheepdog	St Bernard
Border collie	German Shepherd	Pekingese	terrier
bulldog	golden retriever	pit bull terrier	West Highland
bull mastiff	Great Dane	pointer	terrier
bull terrier	greyhound	poodle	whippet
chihuahua	husky	pug	wolfhound
cocker spaniel	Irish wolfhound	Rottweiler	Yorkshire terrier
collie	Jack Russell	schnauzer	
corgi	King Charles spaniel	Scottish terrier	

3 dividing families
   separate *Divorce can often separate families.*
   split *an issue that has split the Conservative Party*
4 divide the men from the boys
   sort *Sort the decent clothes from the ones to be thrown away.*
♦ **Formal word segregate** *segregate men from women*

divorce[1] [noun]
One in three marriages ends in divorce.
   break-up *the break-up of his marriage*
   separation *Separation often affects children.*

divorce[2] [verb]
We got divorced fifteen years ago.
   separate *The couple separated in 2002.*
   split up *She split up with her husband last year.*

do [verb]
1 do the repairs
   achieve *We've achieved a lot today.*
   carry out *builders carrying out work on the house*
   look after *She looks after the cooking while I do the cleaning.*
   perform *I had to perform various tasks.*
   prepare *preparing a meal*
♦ **Formal words accomplish** *We've accomplished all we set out to do.*
   undertake *the skills needed to undertake these jobs*
2 That'll do nicely.
   be enough *One pint will be enough.*
   be fine *These shoes will be fine for the wedding.*
♦ **Formal word suffice** *I'd like tea, but coffee will suffice.*

VOCABULARY CHOICES
[meaning 1]
• **Accomplish** and **achieve** give a strong impression of having done something well.
• **Achieve** in particular is a good word to use in job applications when writing about things you have done.

dog [noun]
   hound *a black hound*
   mongrel *a scruffy looking mongrel*
   puppy *a young puppy*
♦ **Informal words mutt** *my girlfriend and her mutt*
   pooch *the most pampered pooch in Britain*
See also the box above.

door [noun]
   doorway *a box sat in the doorway*
   entrance *He was standing by the entrance.*

Dd

doubt [verb]
be unsure *She was unsure of her own ability to cope.*
question *He questioned his doctor's diagnosis.*
suspect *I don't suspect the truth of what he says.*

draw¹ [verb]
1 draw a diagram
sketch *She sketched a map of where she lived.*
trace *He traced his name in the sand.*
2 draw a crowd
attract *The concert attracted a lot of people.*
bring in *an event that brought in hundreds of fans*
entice *A good window display will entice customers into the shop.*
3 a caravan drawn by two horses
haul *trains hauled by steam engines*
pull *a plough pulled by oxen*
tow *a caravan towed by a car*
4 The teams drew.
be even *The two sides were even at the end.*
tie *The teams tied in the first round.*

draw² [noun]
The match was a draw.
dead heat *The race was a dead heat.*
tie *The game ended in a tie.*

dream¹ [noun]
1 have a bad dream • *He could see them in his dreams.*
daydream *In his daydreams he was a famous man.*
nightmare *children's nightmares about monsters*
vision *She claimed she had seen God in a vision.*
2 achieve a dream
ambition *achieve his ambition of becoming a footballer*
desire *her desire to be successful*

goal *He talked about what his goals were.*
hope *his hopes of becoming an actor*
♦ **Formal word aspiration** *their aspirations for the future*

dream² [verb]
I dream of winning the lottery.
fantasize *He fantasized about starting a new life in Australia.*
imagine *He imagined himself sitting on the beach.*
visualize *She visualized herself in the manager's office.*

dreaming [adjective]
distracted *When he answered me, he seemed distracted.*
faraway *They had a faraway look in their eyes.*
inattentive *It is dangerous to be inattentive while driving.*
preoccupied *She was preoccupied and didn't notice me.*

dress [verb]
1 She dressed quickly.
get dressed *She got dressed and went downstairs.*
put on *He put on his clothes.*
2 dressing his wounds
bandage *He bandaged the cut on his leg.*

drink¹ [noun]
1 a cool drink
♦ **Formal word beverage** *We serve a range of hot and cold beverages.*
2 He turned to drink after his wife died.
alcohol *restaurants serving alcohol*
♦ **Formal word liquor** *restrictions on the sale of liquor*
♦ **Informal word booze** *We need some booze for the party.*

VOCABULARY CHOICES
[meaning 2]
• In Britain, the word **liquor** is usually used

when writing about the laws relating to alcohol. In American English, the word is used more generally.

drink² [verb]

1 She drinks only water.

down He downed a bottle of champagne.

gulp He gulped his coffee and rushed out.

quaff quaffing champagne on her yacht

sip She was sipping a cup of tea.

sup supping a pint of beer

♦ **Informal terms** **knock back** He knocked back three whiskies before leaving.

swig He was swigging from a bottle of beer.

2 She sometimes drinks after work.

♦ **Informal terms** **booze** going boozing tonight

hit the bottle We hit the bottle last night.

tipple tippling in the bar

VOCABULARY CHOICES

[meaning 1]

• The terms **down** and **knock back** suggest you drink a lot of something very quickly, and might be used if you want to suggest this is a bad or silly thing to do.

• The word **quaff** suggests that people are enjoying themselves while they are drinking something. The word is usually used in writing rather than speaking.

drive¹ [verb]

1 driving home

motor He motored south towards the coast.

ride I walked but the others rode in the car.

travel travelling in the van

2 I'll drive you to the station.

ferry ferrying the children to and from school

run I'll run you to the airport.

take Can you take me to the station?

3 drive a tractor

handle learn how to handle a motorbike

operate You are not licensed to operate the vehicle.

4 Floods had driven them out of their homes.

force War forced many people to leave the area.

♦ **Formal word** **compel** She felt compelled to look.

5 driven by steam

operate trains operated by electricity

power powered by solar energy

propel old boats propelled by oars

drive² [noun]

1 You will need plenty of drive and enthusiasm for this job.

ambition a woman full of ambition to succeed

determination his determination and dedication

energy You need energy and enthusiasm to be a teacher.

motivation This team has the motivation to win the game.

♦ **Informal word** **get-up-and-go** He's lost his get-up-and-go.

2 a drive to improve standards

campaign a campaign to change people's attitudes to drink driving

crusade a crusade to raise awareness of the problem

effort an effort to change the way things are done

3 a long drive

jaunt a jaunt to the seaside

journey a long journey to the coast

ride He went for a ride in his new car.

spin go for a spin in the country

trip a trip in the van

VOCABULARY CHOICES

[meaning 3]

• The words **jaunt** and **spin** suggest a trip in a car for pleasure, one that you enjoy.

Dd

Dd

drop[1] [noun]

1 a drop of water
bead beads of sweat
drip drips of blood on the table
droplet water droplets
♦ **Formal word** globules of grease
2 a drop in exports
decrease a decrease in the number of murders
fall a fall in the number of people out of work
plunge a plunge in oil prices
reduction a reduction in taxes
slide a slide in profits

drop[2] [verb]

1 dropped to the ground
descend The balloon descended slowly.
fall The vase fell to the floor.
plummet He plummeted 100 feet down a hole.
plunge Her car plunged down a mountain.
sink He sank to his knees.
slide I slid down the bank, into the water.
2 Prices are dropping.
fall Share prices fell again.
plummet Revenues have plummeted.
plunge Sales have plunged by fifteen per cent.
slide The value of the pound slid recently.
tumble Profits have tumbled by nearly two thirds.
3 He dropped the ball.
let go of She let go of her bag.

VOCABULARY CHOICES

[meanings 1 and 2]
• The words **plummet** and **plunge** are dramatic in tone, as they that suggest the drop is very quick and very far.

drug [noun]

medicine Keep medicines out of the reach of children.
potion Pills and potions aren't the only way to cure ills.
remedy remedies for coughs and colds
♦ **Formal word** **medication** Are you taking any medication for your illness?

VOCABULARY CHOICES

• The word **potion** is used in stories, and the word suggests that it works in a magic way that no one really understands. However, when the word is used in other writing, it is in a slightly mocking way, and suggests that you do not trust it to work.

dry [adjective]

arid an arid desert
parched the parched landscape of the dust bowl

dull [adjective]

1 I found the film very dull.
boring a boring book
dreary a dreary little town
humdrum his humdrum life
monotonous people in monotonous jobs
tedious a tedious task
uneventful It was an uneventful match.
unexciting an unexciting journey
unimaginative a room decorated in an unimaginative way
2 dull weather
cloudy grey, cloudy skies
dreary a dreary winter's day
gloomy The weather was damp and gloomy.
grey a grey November morning
overcast It was overcast and drizzling.

earlier [adjective]
preceding a point made the preceding paragraph
previous Turn back and look at the previous page.
prior He had made friends on a prior visit to the town.

early[1] [adjective]
1 an early response
prompt Thank you for your prompt delivery.
quick They were very quick in replying.
speedy We were impressed by the speedy service.
2 early civilizations
ancient We learned about the ancient Egyptians.
primitive These rules didn't exist in primitive cultures.
◆ **Formal word primeval** one of Europe's last areas of primeval forest

early[2] [adverb]
We arrived early.
ahead of time The ship docked in New York a day ahead of time.
beforehand The instructor will speak to each of you beforehand.
in advance You'll receive the documents a couple of weeks in advance.
in good time We wanted to arrive in good time.
prematurely Alan was prematurely bald.

earn [verb]
1 earn a good salary
bring in We weren't bringing enough in between us.
get How much does he get a month?
make Nina probably makes more than I do.
◆ **Formal word realize** We don't expect to realize a profit in the first year.
◆ **Informal term pull in** He'll be pulling in about three thousand a month.
2 You have earned your success.
deserve I think I deserve a day off.
merit Is all this praise merited?
rate A manager like that doesn't rate respect.
warrant This certainly warrants further investigation.

earth [noun]
1 all over the Earth
globe all four corners of the globe
planet the destruction of our planet
world one of the best players in the world
2 planted in the earth
ground The ground is baked hard by the sun.
land The men joined the army and the women worked on the land.
soil This tool breaks up the soil ready for planting.
◆ **Formal word sod** His body lies under the sod.

Ee

Places of education:

Schools for very young children:	middle school	sixth-form college	**Schools for adults:**
kindergarten	primary school	**Schools that you pay fees for:**	adult-education centre
nursery school	**Schools for older children:**	boarding school	business school
Schools for children aged between 5 and 12:	city technical college (CTC)	finishing school	college
	high school	prep school	secretarial college
	grammar school	public school	technical college
infant school	secondary school	private school	university

easy [adjective]
1 an easy task
simple I had to answer a couple of simple questions.
straightforward It's a fairly straightforward problem to solve.
uncomplicated We came up with an uncomplicated system.
undemanding Most of these tasks are pretty undemanding.
◆ **Informal word cushy** He was expecting a cushy job in an office somewhere.
2 an easy pace
calm the calm mood inside the meeting room
carefree Sarah has a carefree life now she's retired.
comfortable The horse set off at a comfortable trot.
leisurely a leisurely stroll along the beach
relaxed We continued jogging at a fairly relaxed pace.

VOCABULARY CHOICES
[meaning 1]
• If you say something is **undemanding**, then you can do it without trying very hard or thinking very hard. However, this might hint that it is a bad thing, as it might not be very interesting or challenging.
• If you describe something as **straightforward** or **uncomplicated**, you mean that it does not have a lot of different parts that make it difficult to deal with. These words suggest a positive point of view.

eat [verb]
1 eating toast
chew Chew your food properly.
consume Imagine how much fatty food he consumes.
devour The children were devouring a pizza.
munch The dog was munching a biscuit.
swallow You have to swallow the tablet whole.
◆ **Formal word ingest** The tests proved he had ingested arsenic.
◆ **Informal word scoff** The kids had scoffed the lot!
2 We eat at eight o'clock.
◆ **Formal word dine** We're dining out this evening.
◆ **Slang word trough** I didn't want to watch them troughing.

edge [noun]
1 the edge of the table • the edge of the sea
border a green tablecloth with an embroidered border
boundary A white line marks the boundaries of the pitch.
margin lots of white space at the margins of the page
rim a crack in the rim of the cup
◆ **Formal words perimeter** a 20 foot

fence around the perimeter of the prison
periphery the countries on the periphery
of Europe
2 The athlete had the edge over the other
competitors.
advantage Neither team had a clear
advantage.
upper hand a situation in which the buyer
has the upper hand

education [noun]
instruction She gave instruction in art.
schooling Her schooling had been very
thorough.
teaching a career in teaching
training The children also receive training
in practical subjects.
tuition Do students have to pay tuition
fees?
See also the box on the previous page.

effect [noun]
1 the effect of the disease on children
impact The storms had a terrible impact
on the town. • The changes we made had
great impact.
impression His words had a great
impression on me.
influence War has a great influence on
art.
2 the effects of a long plane journey
consequence the consequence of eating
too much
outcome the outcome of the investigation
result the results of our efforts
upshot What was the upshot of the
meeting?

VOCABULARY CHOICES
[meaning 1]
• The word **impact** can make a good
impression in job applications if you are
answering a question about something you
did and the effect it had.

efficient [adjective]
1 an efficient worker

able a very able student
capable Does your employer regard you
as a capable joiner?
competent a very competent young
lawyer
skilful one of France's most skilful
players
2 an efficient office
well-organized It's a well-organized
operation.
well-run Any well-run company should
make a profit.

VOCABULARY CHOICES
[meaning 1]
• If you describe someone as **competent**,
you mean that they have all the knowledge
and skill that they should have and will not
make silly mistakes. People use this word
especially when they are talking about how
well someone does their job.

effort [noun]
1 There's too much effort involved.
energy We've all put a lot of energy into
the project.
pains She's gone to great pains to avoid
upsetting you.
trouble after all the trouble you've taken
to finish the job on time
2 make a good effort
attempt They made a heroic attempt to
save the ship.
try Don't worry. That's only your first
try.
♦ **Formal word endeavour** the bravest
endeavour of the twentieth century
♦ **Informal words go** Let me have a go.
shot Give everybody a shot at hitting it.
stab We all had a stab at calming the
animal down.

elderly [adjective]
aged the birthday of an aged aunt
ageing the woman's ageing parents
old Is your father very old?

Ee

embarrassed [adjective]
> **awkward** There was a moment of awkward silence.
> **bashful** He tried to overcome his bashful nature.
> **humiliated** I felt humiliated at being beaten by a child.
> **mortified** I was mortified at being offered money for my advice.
> **self-conscious** Janice was too self-conscious to make the speech in public.

VOCABULARY CHOICES
- If you say someone is **humiliated** then they feel extremely embarrassed and ashamed about something that has happened to them.

employ [verb]
1 employing school-leavers
> **enlist** Many companies are enlisting workers from overseas.
> **hire** His uncle was hired to protect the Prime Minister.
> **recruit** We'll be recruiting new staff for our kitchen.
> **take on** Malcolm had taken on an assistant.
- ◆ **Formal words commission** She was once commissioned to paint the Queen.
> **engage** I engaged workmen to do the jobs I couldn't manage.
2 employing new techniques
> **make use of** The artist makes good use of colour.
> **use** Which method did you use?
> **utilize** the materials that were utilized for the casing

employment [noun]
> **job** Does he have a job at the moment?
> **line** What line was he in, this businessman?
> **occupation** He tried to think of a more interesting occupation.

> **profession** Dentistry was her chosen profession.
> **trade** Young people get a chance to learn a trade.
> **work** What sort of work are you interested in doing?

encourage [verb]
1 We encouraged them to continue.
> **hearten** We were heartened by this good news.
> **inspire** Young people feel inspired to produce good work.
> **rally** A good leader will always know how to rally supporters.
> **reassure** You see teachers reassuring pupils that they're on the right lines.
> **spur on** Spurred on by the crowd, she came back to take the silver medal.
> **urge** My parents were urging me to take the job.
- ◆ **Informal term egg on** He had been egged on by the other boys.
2 a scheme to encourage tourism in the area
> **boost** The trip is planned to boost trade with Britain.
> **further** The talks are aimed at furthering relations between the two countries.
> **promote** The government is trying to promote healthy eating in schools.
> **stimulate** We want to stimulate interest in learning.
> **support** We do everything we can to support local businesses.
- ◆ **Formal word foster** These centres exist to foster talent.

VOCABULARY CHOICES
[meaning 1]
- You say someone has been **egged on** if they have been encouraged by others to do something bad or silly. You might be suggesting that the person was not completely responsible for what they did, because someone else tried to make them do it.

end[1] [noun]

1 the end of the war
close *the score at the close of play*
finish *He still looked fresh at the finish of the race.*
◆ **Formal words** **cessation** *the cessation of violence between the two groups*
conclusion *an exciting conclusion to a thrilling season*
termination *the legal termination of their marriage*
2 the ends of the table
boundary *a village on the region's northern boundary*
edge *the plants growing round the edge of the pond*
limit *the limits of French territory*
tip *the tip of your little finger*

end[2] [verb]

End the fighting now.
close *This session is officially closed.*
finish *Each service finishes with a prayer.*
stop *Work on the bridge will stop at the weekend.*
wind up *She leaned over and asked the speaker to wind up.*
◆ **Formal words** **conclude** *That concludes the case for the defence.*
culminate *The event culminates in a firework display.*

enemy [noun]

opponent *Don't let your opponent see your weaknesses.*
other side *Now she was playing for the other side.*
rival *Cutler was one of his greatest rivals.*
the opposition *We tried to avoid giving the opposition an advantage.*
◆ **Formal words** **adversary** *They had been courtroom adversaries on many occasions.*
foe *You need to know if they are friend or foe.*

VOCABULARY CHOICES

• The formal words **adversary** and **foe** are used in stories and sometimes in newspapers. These words suggest strongly that someone feels hostile towards another person, and dislikes, or even hates, them.
• The words **opponent** and **rival** are often used about people in an arranged competition, or people with different views or aims, for example in politics. These words do not suggest dislike and aggression as strongly.

energy [noun]

1 the energy to succeed
drive *The student must have the drive to learn.*
liveliness *We were charmed by the liveliness of her personality.*
stamina *Will he have the stamina to complete the course?*
strength *Her encouragement gave me the strength to carry on.*
zest *His recent performances have had great zest.*
◆ **Formal words** **dynamism** *a leader with great dynamism*
vitality *The younger children are bursting with vitality.*
◆ **Informal words** **get-up-and-go** *We need workers with a lot of get-up-and-go.*
zip *I woke up full of zip.*
2 cleaner forms of energy
force *This motion provides the force that works the pump.*
power *People still have concerns about nuclear power.*

enjoy [verb]

like *I like a good detective story.*
relish *I relished the opportunity of seeing her again.*
revel in *The younger ones revelled in all the excitement.*
savour *It was a day to savour for years to come.*

Ee

Ee

Forms of entertainment:

Equipment for entertainment:			
CD player	cinema	concert	magic show
DVD player	music hall	dance	musical
radio	night club	disco	pageant
television	opera	fair	pantomime
video recorder	theatre	festival	Punch-and-Judy
	waxworks	fete	show
Places of	zoo	firework party	puppet show
entertainment:	**Events:**	gig	recital
cabaret	barbecue	gymkhana	revue
casino	carnival	karaoke	rodeo
	circus	laser show	variety show

◆ **Formal terms delight in** *He delights in women's company.*
take pleasure in *They took pleasure in teasing me.*

enough [1] [adjective]
enough money to live on
  adequate *Make sure you have adequate food for the journey.*
  ample *There is ample parking space outside the house.*
  plenty of *There's plenty of time to get there.*
◆ **Formal word sufficient** *There won't be sufficient time for a discussion.*

enough [2] [adverb]
He seems happy enough.
  fairly *The room was fairly comfortable.*
  reasonably *She looked fitter and ate reasonably well.*
◆ **Formal words adequately** *The rules were not explained adequately.*
  sufficiently *The oven wasn't at a sufficiently high temperature.*

entertain [verb]
  amuse *These stories amused us all.*
  delight *She delighted the children with her magic tricks.*

entertainment [noun]
  amusement *There were little shows for the amusement of visitors.*
  enjoyment *Children get a lot of enjoyment out of simple games.*

fun *What do you do for fun in such a small town?*
play *Adults need time for play too.*
pleasure *They get a lot of pleasure out of walking.*
◆ **Formal words diversion** *The place offered little in the way of diversion.*
  recreation *For recreation, he goes out into the garden.*
See also the box above.

enthusiastic [adjective]
  avid *The children are avid readers.*
  eager *We were eager to have a go.*
  keen *a keen follower of cricket*
  passionate *She is passionate about folk music.*
◆ **Formal words ardent** *an ardent football supporter*
  fervent *The family are fervent Christians.*

entry [noun]
1 an entry at the back
  access *There's no access to the building from this side.*
  door *Is there a side door?*
  doorway *A narrow doorway led into the room.*
  entrance *He stands at the front entrance.*
  way in *First we needed to find the way in.*
2 He was refused entry to the club.
  admission *There's no admission to children under 12.*

entrance *Entrance is free.*
◆ **Formal word admittance** *A sign on the gate said 'No Admittance'.*
3 an entry in his diary
item *the last item in the first column*
note *Look over the notes in your jotter.*
4 a late entry into the race
candidate *All candidates will be interviewed twice.*
competitor *over fifty competitors in the championship*
contestant *Will the next contestant step forward, please.*
entrant *A letter was sent to all entrants.*

envy [noun]
jealousy *I admit I acted out of jealousy.*
resentment *She felt resentment towards her more talented sister.*

equipment [noun]
accessories *a shop selling computer accessories*
apparatus *shelves full of scientific apparatus*
gear *Climbing gear is very expensive.*
kit *We packed flasks of hot tea with our kit.*
tackle *a box of fishing tackle*
things *Have you got your school things ready?*
tools *Did you bring your welding tools?*
◆ **Formal word paraphernalia** *The film crew packed up its paraphernalia and left.*
◆ **Informal word stuff** *Don't forget to take your swimming stuff.*

escape [verb]
1 escape from prison
bolt *The prisoner had bolted.*
break free *We waited for a chance to break free from the building.*
break loose *One of the hostages broke loose from the chains.*
break out *The guys in the next cell were planning to break out.*
get away *Did any of the thieves get away?*

run away *When he opened the gate, the animal ran away.*
◆ **Formal words abscond** *A dozen inmates have absconded.*
flee *With their lives in grave danger, they decided to flee across the border.*
2 escape serious injury
avoid *I managed to avoid the more unpleasant jobs.*
elude *A female thief sometimes eludes detection.*
evade *The first two have so far evaded capture.*
3 gas escaping into the atmosphere
leak *Water was leaking from a crack in the pipe.*

even [adjective]
1 an even surface
flat *flat ground*
flush *Make sure the hob is flush with the worktop.*
horizontal *Every horizontal surface was covered with books.*
level *That shelf is not quite level.*
smooth *a smooth flight*
2 The scores are even.
balanced *a balanced score of 15–15*
equal *We will all receive an equal share of the money.*
fifty-fifty *a fifty-fifty share of the profits*
level *The runners were level after the first lap.*
neck and neck *The competitors are neck and neck at the halfway stage.*

evening [noun]
dusk *The garden looked pleasant in the dusk.*
nightfall *She was sleeping an hour before nightfall.*
sundown *I must get home before sundown.*
sunset *In midsummer, sunset is after ten o'clock.*

Ee

twilight *We could barely see each other in the twilight.*

event [noun]

1 events in history

affair *recent political affairs*

episode *It was a sad episode in British history.*

happening *Her story is based on a strange happening in her family.*

incident *The incident is being investigated.*

occurrence *Crashes were a regular occurrence in the area.*

2 organize a special event

ceremony *a ceremony to remember the dead*

function *a royal function hosted by the Queen*

occasion *Her wedding dress is ready for the big occasion.*

party *We're having a party to mark your birthday.*

3 a sports event

competition *The competition is sponsored by a local business.*

contest *a contest involving Europe's top players*

tournament *the first round of the tournament*

evil¹ [adjective]

1 an evil murderer

cruel *a leader who was not just harsh, but cruel*

vile *It was a vile thing to do!*

wicked *They believed that wicked people were sent to hell.*

◆ **Formal word malevolent** *Black magic makes use of malevolent forces.*

2 an evil influence

destructive *The affair had a destructive effect on their marriage.*

harmful *Is the substance harmful to plants?*

◆ **Formal word detrimental** *Violence has a detrimental impact on the community.*

evil² [noun]

the lesser of two evils

corruption *an example of corruption in society*

immorality *the immorality of stealing from a friend*

sin *Some people regard casinos as places of sin.*

wickedness *the wickedness of the country's rulers*

wrongdoing *Any wrongdoing was severely punished.*

◆ **Formal word depravity** *Children would be upset at seeing such depravity.*

exact [adjective]

1 an exact amount • the exact meaning

accurate *an accurate description of the situation*

precise *I can't tell you the precise number of complaints.*

right *Can you tell me the right time?*

specific *Was it this specific house, or just one like it?*

true *Make sure the measurement is true.*

2 She's very exact in all she does.

careful *a careful worker*

methodical *You have to be methodical when you're keeping records.*

meticulous *years of meticulous planning*

orderly *Simon has a very orderly way of working.*

rigorous *a rigorous system for keeping accounts*

scrupulous *Scrupulous cleanliness is needed in the kitchen.*

examination [noun]

1 examination of the evidence

analysis *analysis of the results of the experiment*

inspection *a thorough inspection of the crime scene*

investigation *We carried out an investigation into the accident.*

♦ **Formal word** **appraisal** *Her work will be given a thorough appraisal.*
2 a French examination
  assessment *There will be five written assessments during the course.*
  exam *a geography exam*
  test *school tests*

excellent [adjective]

1 an excellent player
  fine *a fine singer*
  first-rate *As a boy, he was a first-rate swimmer.*
  good *She's always been really good at her job.*
  outstanding *Alan has been an outstanding manager.*
  remarkable *a remarkable cricketer*
  wonderful *a wonderful chef*
♦ **Formal word** **distinguished** *one of the club's most distinguished captains*
2 excellent hotels
  fine *fine wines*
  first-class *first-class accommodation*
  first-rate *a first-rate hotel*
  prime *prime beef*
  splendid *What a splendid shot!*
  superb *the superb food*
  wonderful *It's a wonderful book.*
♦ **Informal words** **great** *The service in the place was great.*
  top-notch *a top-notch meal*

excited [adjective]

  elated *They were elated at the prospect of seeing him again.*
  thrilled *We're thrilled to be here.*
  wild *When he came on stage, the audience went wild.*
♦ **Informal word** **high** *The children have been high as kites all day.*

exciting [adjective]

  electrifying *an electrifying performance from the champion*
  exhilarating *It was exhilarating to be travelling at high speed.*

  rousing *Kinnock made some rousing speeches.*
  stirring *I think it's a very stirring piece of music.*
  thrilling *a thrilling finish to an excellent game*
♦ **Informal word** **nail-biting** *The chapter ends in nail-biting fashion.*

VOCABULARY CHOICES
- All of these words can be used to create a mood of excitement in a piece of text.
- If you describe something as **thrilling**, you think it is very exciting, perhaps in a slightly frightening way.
- You usually use the word **exhilarating** about physical experiences that are exciting, for example riding on a rollercoaster or jumping off a diving board.
- The word **electrifying** is usually used to describe something exciting that you are watching, rather than experiencing yourself. It is sometimes used in newspapers to describe the great skill shown by a sportsperson, actor or other performer.
- You use the words **rousing** and **stirring** to describe things that excite you in a way that makes you feel strong emotion, perhaps so strong that you feel like crying.

excuse[1] [verb]

1 I can't excuse such behaviour.
  forgive *I can't forgive her cruelty.*
  pardon *These criminals were officially pardoned by the government.*
2 He was excused from games.
  let off *We asked if she could be let off homework for a few days.*
♦ **Formal word** **exempt** *His poor health exempts him from these duties.*

VOCABULARY CHOICES
[meaning 2]
- **Let off** is quite an informal term, so you would be more likely to use the words

Ee

excuse or **exempt** in, for example, a letter to your child's teacher.

---

excuse [2] [noun]
There's no excuse for what you did.

explanation *What explanation did she give for her behaviour?*

◆ **Formal words   grounds** *You have no grounds for making a complaint.*

justification *Can there be any justification for his attitude?*

pretext *He spends hours watching films, under the pretext of doing research.*

◆ **Informal word   cop-out** *She says she's tired, but that's just a cop-out.*

VOCABULARY CHOICES
- To describe an excuse as a **cop-out** suggests that you do not believe the excuse, and you are not pleased with the person who has used it.
- The word **pretext** is also used to suggest that an excuse is not true, or that it is covering up what a person is really doing. Using this word would also suggest that you do not approve of this.

---

exhausted [adjective]
tired out *We were tired out after our long walk.*

weak *By the evening, I was weak with hunger.*

worn out *What have you been doing? You look worn out.*

◆ **Informal terms   done in** *I felt done in about half way through the race.*

shattered *Katy felt shattered after swimming three lengths.*

washed-out *She had a washed-out look for a while after she was ill.*

expect [verb]
1 Expect the money soon.

anticipate *We're anticipating a reply any day now.*

bargain for *We hadn't bargained for bad weather.*

hope for *How big an audience are you hoping for?*

look for *Don't look for any thanks.*

◆ **Formal word   envisage** *I'd envisaged finishing the work by the summer.*

2 We expect you to comply.

count on *When you take a penalty, the whole team is counting on you to score.*

rely on *Parents rely on teachers to look after their children well.*

◆ **Informal term   bank on** *We hope she wins, but we're not banking on it.*

---

expensive [adjective]
costly *a costly piece of equipment*

dear *Of course, I preferred the dear jacket.*

high-priced *a shop selling high-priced furniture*

◆ **Formal words   exorbitant** *a fancy shop charging exorbitant prices*

extortionate *Some solicitors charge an extortionate amount to write a letter.*

◆ **Informal word   steep** *£60 seems a bit steep for a pair of trainers.*

VOCABULARY CHOICES
- If something simply has a high price, you can describe it as **costly**, **dear** or **high-priced**.
- However, you can use the stronger word **exorbitant** to describe a price that you think is extremely high.
- If you think that a price is so high it is unreasonable, you can say that it is **extortionate**.

---

experience [1] [noun]
1 She has a lot of experience of working with children.

familiarity *You rely on your guide's familiarity with the area.*

involvement *He has involvement in all levels of the sport.*

practice *People improve as they get more practice.*

2 an interesting experience

episode It was a curious episode in her life.

event the political events of the last few weeks

happening a TV series about strange happenings

incident Police are already investigating the incident.

occurrence Was this an unusual occurrence?

VOCABULARY CHOICES

[meaning 1]

• Words that put across the idea that you have experience, including the word **experience** itself, are very useful for CVs and job applications.

experience [2] [verb]

You may experience some side effects.

endure The family would endure another harsh winter.

go through We understand what you're going through.

live through These are people who lived through two wars.

suffer The team suffered another defeat at the weekend.

◆ **Formal word undergo** Lee has undergone an operation.

experienced [adjective]

accomplished an accomplished veteran of motor racing

expert expert opinion • someone who is expert in family law

practised He is a practised professional who doesn't lose his temper on the field.

skilled a skilled teacher

well-versed well-versed in the ways of the world

expert [noun]

authority She's an authority on history.

specialist The doctor referred me to a heart specialist.

◆ **Formal words connoisseur** Hugh is a connoisseur of fine wines.

virtuoso His days as a virtuoso in ballet seem to be over.

◆ **Informal term dab hand** Andrew is a dab hand at putting shelves up.

VOCABULARY CHOICES

• Someone who is an **authority** knows a lot about a particular subject and other people involved in that subject admire them.

• If someone is a **specialist**, they have a lot of skill and knowledge in one particular area of a subject.

• You usually use the word **connoisseur** about someone who can use their knowledge of a subject to judge what is good and what is bad.

• A **virtuoso** is someone who has great skill and talent, especially in music, dancing or art.

explode [verb]

blow up The second bomb blew up on a bus.

go off The device was timed to go off during the rush hour.

explore [verb]

1 exploring the island

tour We toured the region on bikes.

travel round Sarah spent the summer travelling round Germany.

2 Explore the options you have.

consider We considered the problem from every angle.

examine Let's examine the facts again.

look into The course looks into all aspects of English.

study Doctors studied the effects of the drug.

extra [1] [adjective]

1 an extra room

additional We needed an additional two weeks to finish the job.

further They've asked us to pay a further £50.

Ee

other *Are there any other questions?*
◆ **Formal word supplementary** *There are no hidden supplementary costs to the holiday.*

2 We have no extra time to spare.
excess *Wipe off the excess cement.*
leftover *Put any leftover paper back in the drawer.*
spare *All our spare cash went on the holiday.*
surplus *What happens to any surplus food we produce?*

extra[2] [noun]
hidden extras on the DVD
accessory *You get all these accessories free with the bike.*
bonus *As a bonus, they give you a year's free insurance.*

extra[3] [adverb]
I am extra fond of plain crisps.
especially *Be especially careful on the main road.*
particularly *Helen was looking particularly lovely.*

eye up [verb] (informal)
look at *Colin was looking at the girls at the other table.*
watch *Two men in the doorway were watching him.*

Ee

face¹ [noun]

She has a nice face.
features his rugged features
profile a young man with a handsome profile
♦ **Informal word** **mug** I hate my ugly mug!

face² [verb]

1 facing the river
look on to The kitchen looks on to the garden.
overlook My bedroom overlooks the park.
2 face danger bravely
confront You have to confront the problem, not run away from it.
face up to The government isn't facing up to these challenges.
tackle This is a difficult issue to tackle.

fact [noun]

1 a list of facts
detail a note of your personal details
item Look at the second item on the list.
piece of information This would be a useful piece of information to have.
point Let's discuss that first point.
2 a story based on fact
reality That was the plan, but the reality was very different.
truth The truth is, I don't like him very much.

fail [verb]

1 His business failed.

collapse The whole industry seemed likely to collapse.
fall through The deal has fallen through.
go under A lot of smaller businesses are going under.
go wrong Where had the plan gone wrong?
♦ **Formal word** **founder** Peace talks have foundered.
♦ **Informal terms** **flop** What will you do if the scheme flops?
fold Soon afterwards, the business folded.
go bust The company has since gone bust.
2 fail to pay the bill
♦ **Formal words** **neglect** The doctor neglected to warn them of the dangers.
omit She omitted to tell me that part of the story.
3 failed her parents
disappoint Peter has disappointed a lot of people who trusted him.
let down Don't feel that you have let anybody down.

faint¹ [adjective]

a faint cry • faint colours
dim a dim light
feeble a feeble whisper
pale I prefer bright to pale colours.
slight a slight breeze
soft a soft speaking voice
weak a weak signal

faint² [verb]

I fainted when I heard the news.

black out *I blacked out and woke up on the floor.*

collapse *Mum collapsed in the hospital.*

lose consciousness *A severe shock can make you lose consciousness.*

pass out *He passes out at the sight of blood.*

fair [adjective]

1 a fair judge • a fair decision

even-handed *an even-handed attitude*

impartial *We need someone who is impartial.*

objective *You have to take an objective view of the situation.*

unbiased *unbiased reporting*

unprejudiced *an unprejudiced observer*

2 a fair way to treat people

just *We want to build a just society.*

proper *That's not a proper way to behave.*

right *It's not right to take the child's money.*

3 He's not dark, he's fair.

blond, blonde *a blond youth • His wife is tall and blonde.*

fair-haired *rows of fair-haired children*

4 fair weather

bright *a beautiful bright morning*

clear *On a clear day, you can see the bridge.*

cloudless *a cloudless sky*

dry *We hope it's dry, at least.*

fine *more fine weather to come*

sunny *a picnic on a sunny afternoon*

5 It's not great, but it's fair.

acceptable *an acceptable piece of work*

all right *The film was all right, but not brilliant.*

average *a very average student*

middling *a middling golfer*

not bad *I'm not bad at maths.*

passable *His Spanish accent is passable.*

reasonable *It was a reasonable performance.*

satisfactory *a satisfactory essay*

♦ **Informal terms OK** *We had an OK time.*

so-so *The food was so-so.*

fake¹ [adjective]

1 fake diamonds

bogus *a bogus insurance claim*

counterfeit *counterfeit banknotes*

forged *forged documents*

imitation *imitation pearls*

2 fake emotion

affected *Her smile seemed affected.*

false *false enthusiasm*

mock *Alan jumped back in mock surprise.*

sham *She cried, but they were sham tears.*

♦ **Formal word simulated** *a look of simulated interest on his face*

♦ **Informal word phoney** *the phoney romance between the two stars*

fake² [verb]

faking an injury

pretend *She pretended to be happy for Albert's sake.*

put on *Nancy looked upset, but she was clearly putting it on.*

♦ **Formal words affect** *Karl affected a look of surprise.*

feign *Professional players are good at feigning injuries.*

simulate *As an actor, you're simulating emotion every day.*

fall¹ [verb]

1 fall from a great height

drop *Chunks of hot rock were dropping from the sky.*

plunge *the place where Holmes plunged to his death*

sink *The building seemed to be sinking into the ground.*

2 She fell and broke her wrist.

stumble *Frances stumbled and hit her head.*

trip *I must have tripped on a stone.*

3 The crime rate is falling.

decline *The government's popularity is declining.*

drop *Sales dropped by ten per cent.*

dwindle *The value of the currency was dwindling.*

go down *We were expecting prices to go down.*

plummet *The following day, temperatures plummeted.*

slide *The company's profits were sliding steadily.*

◆ **Formal word subside** *Wait until her anger has subsided.*

VOCABULARY CHOICES

[meaning 3]

• If you want to emphasize the bad result of something falling, you can use the word **decline**. Newspapers often use this word to give a negative opinion about something.

• If something is falling slowly and steadily, you can use the word **dwindle**.

• You can use the word **plummet** to suggest that something falls very quickly from a high level to a much lower level. This word is also often used in newspapers, to talk about things such as prices or values, to add drama.

fall² [noun]

a fall in profits

decline *Most shops complain of a decline in sales.*

decrease *a decrease in the amount of oxygen in the atmosphere*

drop *a drop in temperature*

reduction *price reductions*

slide *a slide in the value of the pound*

false [adjective]

1 false information

inaccurate *inaccurate readings on the monitor*

incorrect *What he said is incorrect.*

mistaken *mistaken beliefs*

untrue *We know the story is untrue.*

wrong *The government report was wrong.*

2 false diamonds

bogus *a bogus insurance claim*

counterfeit *counterfeit banknotes*

fake *fake fur*

forged *forged documents*

imitation *imitation pearls*

3 false enthusiasm

affected *Her smile seemed affected.*

fake *fake emotions*

mock *Alan jumped back in mock surprise.*

sham *She cried, but they were sham tears.*

◆ **Formal word simulated** *a look of simulated interest on his face*

◆ **Informal word phoney** *the phoney romance between the two stars*

Ff

family [noun]

people *Her people come from Skye.*

relations *Michael has hundreds of relations.*

relatives *a party for relatives and close friends*

◆ **Informal word folks** *I'm spending the weekend with my folks.*

famous [adjective]

famed *Rome is famed for its ancient monuments.*

legendary *legendary footballers such as Pele*

noted *a town noted for its scenery*

notorious *the notorious cruelty of their prison system*

prominent *a prominent member of the golf club*

well-known *The book contains recipes from well-known chefs.*

◆ **Formal words celebrated** *an article by a celebrated journalist*

distinguished *the country's most distinguished actors*

eminent *They hired an eminent London lawyer.*

Ff

renowned *The city is renowned for its exciting bars.*

VOCABULARY CHOICES

• To emphasize that something or someone is famous all over the world, you can describe them as **legendary**, especially when people admire them very much.
• If something or someone is famous for their bad qualities, you can describe them as **notorious**. This word is often used in newspapers to describe well-known criminals.

fan [noun]
  admirer *I'm a great admirer of the Harry Potter books.*
  enthusiast *a quiz for science fiction enthusiasts*
  follower *Followers of the band will be delighted by the news that they're touring.*
  lover *It's a programme for music lovers of all kinds.*
  supporter *Many of the club's supporters can't afford these ticket prices.*
• **Formal word devotee** *His wife is a devotee of alternative medicine.*
• **Informal words buff** *a film buff*
  freak *fitness freaks who jog every day*

fancy [verb]
1 *I fancy going to the cinema.*
  desire *the money to buy everything you've ever desired*
  feel like *I feel like a cup of tea.*
2 (informal) *My friend fancies you.*
  be attracted to *I'm attracted to strong, silent people.*
  be interested in *My friend tried to set me up with his cousin, but I wasn't interested in her.*
  find attractive *I find your brother really attractive.*
• **Informal phrases be mad about** *I was mad about David Cassidy when I was young.*

  have a crush on *I think my son has a crush on your daughter.*
• **Slang phrase have the hots for** *He has the hots for every woman he meets.*

fancy [adjective]
fancy shops
  decorative *paintings and other decorative objects*
  elaborate *elaborate swirling patterns*
  ornamental *This is an ornamental sword, not a practical one.*
  ornate *an ornate crown decorated with diamonds*
  showy *showy clothes*
• **Informal word flashy** *She has a flashy new car.*

far [adverb]
1 *I have driven far in my time.*
  extensively *He has travelled extensively in Africa.*
  widely *She has journeyed widely.*
2 *This is far better work than your last effort.*
  considerably *She's considerably taller than her sister.*
  much *Andy seemed much happier in his new job.*
• **Formal word decidedly** *He had put on weight and looked decidedly older.*

far [adjective]
far countries
  distant *a distant corner of the world*
  faraway *a holiday on some faraway island*
  far-flung *Her job takes her to far-flung places like Singapore.*
  far-off *young soldiers buried in a far-off land*
  out-of-the-way *Why would anyone live in such an out-of-the-way place?*
  remote *They live in a remote village on the edge of the desert.*

VOCABULARY CHOICES

• The words **out-of-the-way** and **remote** suggest that a place is a long way from anywhere else, whereas **faraway** and **far-flung** suggest that the place is a long way from where you are.

• **Faraway** and **far-flung** can make a place sound exotic, that is, attractive because it is very different and unfamiliar.

fashion [noun]
craze Salsa became the latest craze.
fad Perhaps MP3 players are just a fad.
trend the trend for driving huge cars in towns
vogue Sports bags with brand names are in vogue.

fast¹ [adjective]
a fast run
brisk walking at a brisk pace
hasty Boris made a hasty grab for the glass.
hurried a hurried journey north
quick We made a few quick repairs.
rapid The change was too rapid.
speedy We hope she makes a speedy recovery.
swift The supermarket is hoping for a swift response from customers.
♦ **Informal word nippy** He was a nippy little footballer.

VOCABULARY CHOICES
• You use the word **brisk** especially about the fast way someone is doing something, often walking.
• If something is done quickly because you are in a hurry, you can describe it using the word **hasty** or **hurried**, and these words sometimes suggest that something is poor because it is not done in a careful or organized way.

fast² [adverb]
run fast
hastily She hastily pushed the book back into her bag.
hurriedly We dashed back to the hotel and packed hurriedly.

quickly I quickly tidied up the mess.
rapidly The talk moved rapidly from one topic to another.
speedily We hope the problem is dealt with speedily.
swiftly The group moved swiftly on to the next place on the list.
♦ **Formal word apace** Her confidence is growing apace.
♦ **Informal phrases like a flash** The answer came to me like a flash.
like a shot The boy ran out like a shot.

fat [adjective]
chubby He looked too chubby to be so fit.
flabby flabby cheeks
heavy Her husband is quite a heavy man.
obese A lot of people in the streets are obese.
overweight the number of overweight children
plump She had a pretty but rather plump face.
tubby a tubby young boy

VOCABULARY CHOICES
• **Plump** is often used to suggest roundness and softness, and this word is usually used in a positive way. The term **chubby** also conveys the idea of being round and soft.
• **Flabby** is a more critical word, as it suggests unattractive fat.
• The terms **overweight** and **obese** are more technical, but **obese** is stronger as it describes a fatness that could damage your health.

father [noun]
♦ **Formal word patriarch** He was the patriarch ruling the family.
♦ **Informal words da** I'll tell my da!
dad I have to call my dad.
daddy Give the sweets to daddy.

VOCABULARY CHOICES
• **Patriarch** particularly suggests the power a father can have, especially if he is in

Ff

charge of the home.
• The word **daddy** can suggest childish dependency on your father when it is used in the context of adults.

---

fault [noun]
1 We like her despite her faults.
 failing He was happy to admit to his past failings.
 flaw There are no serious flaws in his character.
 shortcoming Laziness is Angela's only shortcoming.
 weakness If he has one weakness, it's pride.
 foible Be polite and patient about their foibles.
2 a fault in the system
 error no errors in your spelling
 mistake A single mistake could cost us the championship.
 slip Don't worry about the odd little slip.
3 It's your fault.
 liability The company accepts no liability for damage to cars.
 responsibility Kennedy was unwilling to take the responsibility.

faulty [adjective]
 broken Our washing machine is broken again.
 damaged Damaged goods should be returned to the shop.
 imperfect Reduced-price items may be slightly imperfect.
 out of order The coffee machine is out of order.
 ◆ **Formal words defective** repairing a defective boiler
 flawed I think the plan is deeply flawed.
 impaired Your hearing is slightly impaired.

favour [noun]
1 He did me a favour.
 good turn She's done me many good turns over the years.
 ◆ **Formal word kindness** Many thanks

for your numerous kindnesses.
2 find favour with some powerful people
 approval Will the scheme win the approval of local people?
 support My MP is giving the plan his wholehearted support.

favourite [1] [adjective]
my favourite film
 best-loved This tatty old bear is her best-loved toy.
 dearest my dearest friend
 ◆ **Formal word preferred** What would your preferred choice be?

favourite [2] [noun]
He is a favourite with older women.
 darling He was the darling of the Conservative Party for years.
 idol posters of the latest teen idols
 ◆ **Informal term blue-eyed boy** or **blue-eyed girl** Karen was the blue-eyed girl of the sixth year.

fear [1] [noun]
a fear of flying
 apprehension I thought about the test with apprehension.
 dread I had the usual sense of dread at being asked a question.
 fright The cat ran away in fright.
 horror I stared at the blood in horror.
 panic A feeling of panic spread through the crowd.
 phobia The older child had a phobia about insects.
 terror the terror of being shut in a small space
 worry Debt was the main cause of worry.

VOCABULARY CHOICES
• All these words can be used to create a mood of suspense or fear in a piece of text.
• The words **horror** and **terror** in particular suggest extreme fear, and are used for more impact.

fear² [verb]

They fear the consequences of such an action.

> **dread** *I dreaded telling them the bad news.*
>
> **shudder at** *Maggie shuddered at the thought of being stranded here.*

feel¹ [verb]

1 feel pain

> **experience** *Are you experiencing any dizziness?*
>
> **go through** *It was a terrible experience to go through.*
>
> **suffer** *She suffered bad headaches as a young child.*

2 felt the texture

> **handle** *We got to handle those beautiful fabrics.*
>
> **touch** *Please don't touch the displays.*

3 It feels different.

> **appear** *She appears to have grown.*
>
> **seem** *It seems like a long time since I saw him.*

4 feel it is too soon

> **believe** *I believe she's the right person for the job.*
>
> **consider** *Do you consider her a good friend?*
>
> **reckon** *Janice reckons this job will pay more.*
>
> **think** *I think you're wise not to trust him.*

feel² [noun]

the soft feel of wool

> **texture** *wood with a rough texture*
>
> **touch** *the touch of her skin*

feeling [noun]

1 a feeling of freedom

> **sensation** *the sensation of flying through the air*
>
> **sense** *The house gives you the sense of being completely private.*

2 I have a feeling he's lying.

> **hunch** *I had a hunch she would change her mind.*

> **idea** *Where did you get the idea that you were coming too?*
>
> **impression** *I got the impression she didn't like me.*
>
> **inkling** *We had no inkling she was unhappy.*
>
> **instinct** *My instinct told me not to trust him.*
>
> **suspicion** *Marie had a slight suspicion the whole thing was a lie.*

3 show their feelings • hurt her feelings

> **emotion** *He's not used to expressing his emotions.*
>
> **sentiment** *the sentiments expressed in the letter*
>
> ◆ **Formal word** **sensibility** *You have to take other people's sensibilities into account.*

4 a feeling of space and light

> **air** *The place has an air of luxury about it.*
>
> **atmosphere** *the violent atmosphere on the streets*
>
> **mood** *the serious mood in the meeting-room*
>
> **quality** *The man had a slightly dangerous quality.*

fierce [adjective]

1 a fierce tiger

> **ferocious** *ferocious beasts of the forest*
>
> **savage** *a savage dog*

2 fierce heat • fierce anger

> **biting** *biting winds • biting remarks*
>
> **intense** *intense feelings of hate • intense cold*
>
> **powerful** *powerful emotions • a powerful bomb blast*
>
> **strong** *her strong determination to lead a normal life*
>
> **violent** *a violent struggle*

fight¹ [noun]

1 a hard fight • a street fight

> **brawl** *a pub brawl*
>
> **clash** *clashes between police and protesters*
>
> **struggle** *A man was knifed in the struggle.*

tussle *a tussle on the pavement outside the bar*

◆ **Formal words bout** *a heavyweight bout*

encounter *the first encounter between the two opponents*

fracas *Two elderly women were injured in the fracas.*

◆ **Informal words fisticuffs** *Are you ready for a spot of fisticuffs?*

scrap *another scrap in the playground*

scuffle *The two men had a brief scuffle.*

set-to *The boys had a bit of a set-to.*

2 have a fight with the boss

argument *We had an argument about something unimportant.*

dispute *disputes between management and workers*

quarrel *It was a silly quarrel about nothing at all.*

row *They were always rowing in those days.*

3 the fight for freedom

campaign *a campaign for women's rights in the workplace*

crusade *the government's crusade against drugs*

struggle *People thought Mandela had abandoned the struggle.*

VOCABULARY CHOICES

[meaning 1]

• **Bout** is used to refer to an organized match in boxing or wrestling.

• **Encounter** is a very mild term which can be also be used for an organized match. It does not say whether the fight was very violent or not.

• The terms **scrap** and **scuffle** are best used for minor fights.

• The word **clash**, however, suggests a more violent struggle. It is often used in news reports to add impact.

fight ² [verb]

1 fight an opponent

brawl *grown men brawling in the street*

clash *Rival supporters clashed outside the stadium.*

2 The brothers seem to fight continuously.

argue *I'm always arguing with the children.*

bicker *I could hear them bickering in the next room.*

quarrel *What did you two quarrel about?*

squabble *a couple of schoolkids squabbling over conkers*

◆ **Formal terms cross swords** *She'd crossed swords with the manager before.*

joust *The minister and I have frequently jousted with each other.*

3 fight the proposals

campaign against *We're campaigning against animal testing.*

oppose *The union will oppose the decision.*

◆ **Formal words contest** *The decision was contested in court.*

resist *Passengers will resist attempts to put fares up.*

film [noun]

1 a black-and-white film

feature film *Disney's first full-length feature film*

motion picture *starring in a major motion picture*

movie *I feel like watching a good movie.*

2 a thin film of dust

coating *a biscuit with a coating of chocolate*

covering *The chicks have a covering of yellow down.*

layer *the layer of red dust that covers everything in the dry season*

filthy [adjective]

dirty *dirty marks on his shirt*

foul *breathing in foul air*

grimy *the grimy windows of the deserted house*

grubby *the little boy's grubby hands*
mucky *Why are your shoes so mucky?*
♦ **Formal word soiled** *His trousers looked soiled.*

find [verb]
come across *I came across these old photos in the basement.*
discover *Scientists have discovered the cause of the disease.*
stumble on *I stumbled on the shop on my way to the station.*
trace *Officers traced the van to a warehouse in Croydon.*
track down *Police tracked him down in Spain.*
uncover *They uncovered a plot to kill the president.*
unearth *The weapons were unearthed in a house in Birmingham.*
♦ **Formal word locate** *We haven't located the stolen vehicle yet.*

fine [adjective]
1 fine thread • fine stitching
delicate *the delicate petals of a flower*
flimsy *The fabric is quite flimsy.*
fragile *A butterfly's wings are fragile.*
thin *This material is very thin.*
2 It all seems fine.
acceptable *an acceptable standard*
all right *Are you feeling all right?*
good *It's good that they arrived on time.*
great *'I've brought the book you wanted.' 'Great. Thanks.'*
satisfactory *She asked the guests if everything was satisfactory.*
♦ **Informal word OK** *I'm OK, thanks.*
3 fine weather
bright *a lovely bright morning*
clear *a clear day*
cloudless *cloudless skies*
dry *more dry weather on the way*
sunny *Tuesday was nice and sunny.*

finish¹ [verb]
1 finishing the job

complete *The work will be completed next month.*
2 What time does the film finish?
close *The meeting closed around noon.*
end *The season ended with a exciting game.*
stop *At last, the rain stopped.*
wind up *The party wound up around midnight.*
♦ **Formal words conclude** *Let's conclude the meeting there.*
terminate *the station where this service terminates*
3 We've finished the milk.
drink up *Drink up your juice, boys.*
eat up *She keeps telling me to eat up my vegetables.*
use up *We've used up all the spare paper.*
♦ **Formal word exhaust** *They were tired and their supplies were exhausted.*
4 We finished off the meal with a coffee.
♦ **Informal terms round off** *We rounded off the afternoon with an ice cream.*
top off *Scholes topped off his season with two goals against Arsenal.*

finish² [noun]
the finish of business
close *the value of shares at the close of trading*
end *exhausted at the end of the race*
♦ **Formal words conclusion** *a thrilling conclusion to the season*
finale *the grand finale of the Mountain Bike Championships*

finished [adjective]
1 The painting is finished.
complete *The extension to the house is complete.*
done *That's the washing done.*
over *The race is over.*
2 We'll have to drink wine — the beer is finished.
exhausted *Our oil supplies are exhausted.*

Ff

101

used up I was missing an engine and my fuel supply was used up.

fire¹ [noun]
A fire destroyed the house.
> **blaze** Over twenty firefighters tackled the blaze.
> **flames** The flames had already reached the bedroom.
> ◆ **Formal word** **inferno** He made six journeys into the blazing inferno to help save lives.

fire² [verb]
He was fired from yet another job.
> ◆ **Formal words** **discharge** She was discharged after only a week.
> **dismiss** Ben was dismissed from his job three months later.
> ◆ **Informal word** **sack** You could be sacked if they catch you.

first [adjective]
1 the first day at school
> **introductory** the book's introductory section
> **opening** the opening scene of the film
> **primary** Americans call primary schools elementary schools.
> ◆ **Formal words** **initial** I didn't like her initial remarks.
> **preliminary** the preliminary stages of the competition

2 the first humans
> **earliest** the earliest civilizations
> **original** the car's original owner

3 Scotland's first minister
> **chief** the department's chief secretary
> **head** Astrid is the club's head coach.
> **leading** the leading actor of his generation
> **main** These are our main concerns.
> **prime** The city was the bombers' prime target.
> **principal** Our principal objection was the cost.
> ◆ **Formal word** **paramount** This issue is of paramount importance.

firstly [adverb]
> **at first** I didn't say much at first.
> **initially** We initially had only 22 members.
> **originally** He was originally a miner.
> **to begin with** To begin with, I thought she was very shy.
> **to start with** To start with, why don't we introduce ourselves?

fit¹ [adjective]
1 fit for use • fit to drive
> **able** Will I be able to carry on working?
> **competent** Is the patient competent to answer questions?
> **qualified** I'm not qualified to give an opinion.
> **suitable** The water wasn't even suitable for washing in.

2 fit and well
> **healthy** I'm feeling much healthier nowadays.
> **in good shape** He should complete the course. He's in pretty good shape.
> **strong** Luckily, she was strong enough to survive the fall.
> **well** You're looking well today.

fit² [verb]
1 fits the description
> **agree with** These new facts didn't agree with the information we already had.
> **match** The suspect didn't match the description the police had.
> **tally with** The signatures should tally with the names on the list.
> ◆ **Formal term** **correspond to** The numbers correspond to the amounts of money we have received.

2 fit a new kitchen
> **install** They've had a satellite dish installed.
> **put in** My husband's putting a new bathroom in.

fit[3] [noun]
a fit of sneezing
    attack an attack of nerves
    bout a bout of violent coughing
    spasm a spasm of nervous excitement

fix [verb]
1 fix a shelf to the wall
    attach How do you attach the bracket to the post?
    fasten He showed us how to fasten the sail to the mast.
    nail The boards are nailed together.
    pin A photo was pinned to the noticeboard.
    stick The tiles had been stuck onto the ceiling.
    ♦ **Formal word secure** Each pole is firmly secured in place.
2 fix a date
    agree on Have we agreed on a time for the meeting?
    decide on We need to decide on a good place to meet.
    set A date has been set for the wedding.
    settle on The hardest thing is settling on a price.
3 fix the broken chair
    mend The hole was too big to mend with thread.
    repair Once it's repaired, the chair will look like new.
    restore She restores old furniture.

flash[1] [noun]
a flash of light
    beam the beam from the car's headlights
    burst a burst of sunshine
    ray rays of sunlight streaming in though the window
    shaft A shaft of moonlight slanted through the shutters.
    spark a spark of starlight
    sparkle the blue sparkle of the pool

flash[2] [verb]
flashing headlamps

    flare hundreds of flaring candles
    gleam The car's paintwork gleamed in the sun.
    light up The sky lit up with hundreds of fireworks.
    shimmer The glow of the lanterns shimmered on the water.
    shine The sun was shining and there wasn't a cloud in the sky.
    sparkle Her eyes sparkled with excitement.
    twinkle A million stars twinkled overhead.

Ff

flat[1] [adjective]
1 a flat surface
    horizontal My back doesn't hurt when I'm horizontal.
    level You need a playing surface that is level.
2 The game was a bit flat.
    boring a boring film
    dead The town is dead at the weekend.
    dull a dull match
    lacklustre a lacklustre performance from the champion
    unexciting a fairly unexciting party
    uninteresting The first chapter is pretty uninteresting.
3 a flat refusal
    absolute an absolute rule
    straight It's difficult not to answer such a straight question.
    total a total rejection of everything her parents stand for
    ♦ **Formal word categorical** a categorical denial of the charge
4 a flat tyre
    burst The airbed was burst.
    punctured a punctured lung

flat[2] [noun]
He lives in the flat above mine.
    apartment a small development of apartments
    rooms She was given rooms in the college.

suite He lived for years in a suite in a hotel.

flavour[1] [noun]

1 a sweet flavour • a fruity flavour

tang a cake with a lemony tang

taste We all like the taste of chocolate.

2 It has something of the flavour of an old cowboy movie.

character It has the character of a seaside town.

feel This machine has a feel of class.

feeling There's a feeling of luxury about the place.

quality There's an eerie quality about the castle.

flavour[2] [verb]

rice flavoured with herbs

season Season the fish with pepper.

spice rhubarb jam spiced with ginger

float [verb]

bob Our little boat bobbed into the harbour.

drift A boy on a lilo drifted past me.

sail I watched my hat go sailing down the river.

flood[1] [verb]

1 The river burst its banks and flooded the farmland.

swamp Several villages were swamped by the water.

♦ **Formal words engulf** The river had engulfed huge areas of land.

submerge Entire streets had been submerged.

2 water flooding into the lock

flow The blood continued to flow freely.

gush Thick black oil was gushing out of the ground.

pour Rainwater was pouring down the walls.

rush From here, the river rushes on down to Hartford.

stream Tears were streaming down his face.

surge Water came surging into the channel.

flood[2] [noun]

a flood of inquiries

deluge A deluge of complaints followed the show.

rush There's been a recent rush of applications.

spate a spate of accidents in recent months

stream a stream of calls for the minister to resign

floor [noun]

deck on the ship's upper deck

level We parked on level 6.

storey the third storey of a ten-storey building

flow[1] [verb]

lava flowing down the hill

pour White water poured over the rocks.

run The river runs out into the North Sea.

rush the noise of water rushing along gutters

spill Soup was spilling over the edge of the pan.

spurt Blood was spurting from the cut.

flow[2] [noun]

a steady flow of requests

deluge Viewers sent a deluge of complaints.

flood a flood of letters from angry customers

spate a recent spate of violent attacks

stream a stream of abuse from the youth's mouth

flower[1] [noun]

a bunch of flowers

bloom The flowers are not yet fully in bloom.

blossom the pink blossom on the cherry trees

See also the box on the next page.

flower[2] [verb]

late-flowering tulips

bloom The lilacs haven't bloomed at all this year.

Ff

Types of flower:

aster	forget-me-not	lily-of-the-valley	primrose
azalea	foxglove	lupin	rose
begonia	freesia	marigold	snapdragon
bluebell	fuchsia	nasturtium	snowdrop
carnation	gardenia	orchid	stock
chrysanthemum	geranium	pansy	sunflower
cornflower	gladiolus	petunia	sweet pea
crocus	hollyhock	phlox	sweet william
daffodil	hyacinth	pink	tulip
dahlia	iris	poinsettia	violet
daisy	lily	poppy	wallflower

Ff

blossom *The flowers blossom in March.*

fluffy [adjective]
feathery *the feathery hair on the boy's cheeks*
furry *a little furry caterpillar*
velvety *the plant's soft velvety leaves*

fly [verb]
1 *I fly from tree to tree*
flit *A few small birds flitted away from the roadside.*
glide *An enormous vulture glided across the plain.*
hover *Watch the kestrel hover above its prey.*
soar *A buzzard was soaring overhead.*
2 *We flew down the road.*
dart *A squirrel darted up a tree.*
dash *Two boys dashed past me.*
race *A man was racing across the car park towards me.*
rush *I rushed into the street to see them.*
shoot *A police car shot past with its lights flashing.*
streak *A bullet streaked past his ear.*
tear *We were tearing along the road at a frightening speed.*
zoom *RAF jets zoom around in the sky above the town.*

foggy [adjective]
hazy *Conditions can be hazy in the sun.*
misty *a misty autumn morning*

murky *It was a grey, murky evening.*

follow [verb]
1 *Night follows day.*
come after *What day comes after Tuesday?*
come next *You have to work out what number comes next.*
replace *Hawke replaced him as Deputy Prime Minister.*
succeed *He succeeded Shankly as Liverpool manager.*
2 *a dog following the car*
chase *The cows chased her across the field.*
go after *I went after her to apologize.*
hound *They're hounded by reporters wherever they go.*
shadow *He knew he was being shadowed.*
tail *The police tailed them for a couple of miles.*
♦ **Formal word pursue** *The couple were pursued by photographers.*
3 *follow the rules*
obey *These instructions must be obeyed.*
♦ **Formal terms adhere to** *The government hasn't adhered to this policy.*
comply with *Does the equipment comply with safety regulations?*
heed *She never heeds my advice.*
observe *You must observe the Highway Code at all times.*

4 I can't follow these instructions.
grasp Maths was something I could never grasp.
understand Do you understand this diagram?
♦ **Formal words comprehend** for reasons I couldn't comprehend
fathom We couldn't fathom it either.

food [noun]
cooking He's missing his mother's cooking.
diet a bird's diet of insects and berries
meals She cooks really fancy meals.
nourishment Nuts and seeds are good nourishment.
♦ **Formal words cuisine** French cuisine
fare We wanted traditional British fare.
nutrition a nutrition expert at the hospital
♦ **Informal words grub** The rooms were dingy but the grub was okay.
nosh The nosh is tinned but better than nothing.

fool¹ [noun]
I was a fool to trust her.
idiot Which idiot didn't close the freezer door?
moron Not like that, you moron!
♦ **Formal word imbecile** The man was clearly an imbecile.
♦ **Informal words clown** Some clown parked across our drive.
mug I felt like a right mug.

fool² [verb]
She was fooled into parting with her money.
cheat Hundreds of people were cheated out of their savings.
deceive We feel the government has deceived us.
delude If you believe that, you are deluding yourself.
dupe I'd been duped into taking him with me.
have on Anne suspected he was having her on.

mislead Their solicitor was deliberately misleading them.
swindle We were angry at having been swindled.
take in She's too clever to be taken in by that.
♦ **Informal term con** I had a feeling I was being conned.

force¹ [verb]
I was forced to go along with the scheme.
drive What drove him to act that way?
make Nobody is making you do it.
press-gang I had been press-ganged into helping them out.
pressurize He had been pressurized into making an apology.
push Arthur had been pushed into retiring.
♦ **Formal words coerce** They had been coerced into making their statements.
compel She felt compelled to take action of some kind.
oblige The law obliges you to pay tax.

force² [noun]
1 They use force to get what they want.
aggression Aggression was the only weapon they had.
pressure We hope to put pressure on the council.
violence They had used violence to take control of the country.
2 the force of the waves
power the terrifying power of the storm
strength We were thrown to the ground by the strength of the blast.

foreign [adjective]
1 a foreign country • The situation seemed foreign to him.
alien alien cultures
imported imported attitudes and beliefs
strange living in a strange country
unfamiliar These were very unfamiliar surroundings.
2 foreign travel
external external trade

international international politics
overseas overseas influences

forever [adverb]
1 Nobody lives forever.
  for all time Prices have been frozen for all time.
  permanently It changed our lives permanently.
  perpetually Nature perpetually renews itself.
◆ **Formal words eternally** We are eternally grateful.
  evermore It has always existed and shall exist evermore.
2 I'm forever reminding him of that.
  always The teachers are always telling us off.
  constantly The sky is constantly changing colour.
  continually The rules are continually being updated.
◆ **Formal words endlessly** Brian talks endlessly about engines.
  incessantly She complains incessantly.
  persistently His blood pressure is persistently high.

forget [verb]
  lose sight of I had lost sight of what life was about.
  overlook You lost marks because you overlooked the first question.
◆ **Formal words neglect** I neglected to tell her my address.
  omit The office omitted to inform us.

forgive [verb]
  excuse That doesn't excuse your bad behaviour.
  let off We'll let you off this time.
  overlook We can overlook a small mistake like that.
  pardon Have my sins been pardoned?
◆ **Formal word condone** He doesn't condone the terrorists' actions.

foul [adjective]
  evil an evil smell
  filthy The bathroom was in a filthy state.
  noxious noxious fumes
  offensive The medicine has an offensive taste.

fragile [adjective]
  breakable Wrap any breakable objects well.
  delicate She had very delicate skin.
  flimsy The tent looked pretty flimsy to me.
◆ **Formal word insubstantial** Insubstantial buildings are easily blown over in a storm.

frail [adjective]
  delicate the delicate state of the patient's health
  feeble I pulled the letter from his feeble grasp.
  slight Andrews was a slight figure.
  weak He looked tired and weak.
◆ **Formal word infirm** medical care for elderly and infirm patients

free[1] [adjective]
1 free time • Is this seat free?
  available How much available time do you have?
  empty We found an empty compartment.
  spare I needed half a dozen spare seats.
  vacant The toilet was now vacant.
◆ **Formal word unoccupied** A table by the window was unoccupied.
2 free tickets
  free of charge These activities are free of charge.
  on the house The last round of drinks was on the house.
◆ **Formal words complimentary** They sent me two complimentary tickets.
  gratis The shop gave us three gratis copies of the book.
3 a free run to the coast
  clear a clear view of the stage
  open The road was open again.

Ff

Ff

◆ **Formal word unimpeded** *Police riders ensure the car's progress is unimpeded.*

free² [verb]
freeing himself from her grasp
> **release** *We couldn't release him from the animal's grip.*
> **rescue** *Three fishermen were rescued from the sinking boat.*
> **save** *Who could save us from this terrible fate?*
◆ **Formal words deliver** *Deliver us from evil.*
> **disentangle** *I managed to disentangle my jacket from the thorns.*
> **extricate** *People tried to extricate the boy's head from the railings.*
> **liberate** *He aimed to liberate all people from slavery.*

freeze¹ [verb]
1 *the sea froze*
> **ice over** *the year the lake iced over*
> **ice up** *The windscreen was already icing up.*
> **solidify** *What would happen if the juice solidified?*
2 *freeze wages*
> **fix** *Rates have been fixed at six per cent.*
> **hold** *We're holding prices at their current level.*
> **suspend** *Trade with China was suspended for 48 hours.*

freeze² [noun]
1 *a sudden freeze*
> **cold snap** *A lot of plants died in the sudden cold snap.*
> **freeze-up** *the usual January freeze-up*
2 *a freeze on production*
> **halt** *There is a halt on new members at the moment.*
◆ **Formal words embargo** *embargoes on trade with South Africa*
> **suspension** *the suspension of aid to developing countries*

freezing [adjective]
> **biting** *a biting easterly wind*
> **bitter** *wrapped up against the bitter cold*
> **cutting** *a cutting breeze from the north*
> **frosty** *frosty conditions in the early morning*
> **icy** *Her hands were icy.*
> **raw** *the raw March wind*
> **wintry** *more wintry weather to come*

frequent [adjective]
> **numerous** *our numerous visits to the area*
> **recurring** *This is a recurring problem.*
> **regular** *She makes regular trips to France.*
> **repeated** *We've made repeated requests.*

fresh [adjective]
1 *fresh supplies*
> **additional** *We need an additional four tables.*
> **extra** *I've ordered some extra boxes.*
> **further** *Are there any further questions?*
> **more** *We need more volunteers.*
2 *Take a fresh look at the problem.*
> **different** *a fresh approach*
> **new** *She's got lots of new ideas.*
◆ **Formal word novel** *That's a novel way of looking at it.*
3 *a fresh breeze*
> **bracing** *a bracing walk along the seafront*
> **brisk** *flags snapping in the brisk wind*
> **crisp** *the crisp winter air*
> **refreshing** *a refreshing swim in the sea*
◆ **Formal word invigorating** *an invigorating climb up the hill*

friend [noun]
> **companion** *She became a close companion of mine.*
> **playmate** *my young son's playmates*
◆ **Formal word comrade** *Bob is an old comrade from my army days.*
◆ **Informal words buddy** *one of his navy buddies*
> **mate** *He's meeting some mates in the pub.*
> **pal** *her pals from school*

friendly [adjective]

1 friendly neighbours

approachable *The new manager seems very approachable.*

neighbourly *a very neighbourly thing to do*

sociable *Don't bother inviting her. She's not a very sociable person.*

◆ **Formal words affable** *Her husband seems like an affable chap.*

amiable *Frank was an amiable soul, and everyone liked him.*

amicable *We have a fairly amicable relationship now.*

2 a friendly atmosphere

warm *Thank you for your warm welcome.*

welcoming *a welcoming smile*

◆ **Formal word cordial** *a cordial invitation*

VOCABULARY CHOICES

[meaning 1]

• You can use the word **approachable** about someone who is friendly and willing to listen to people, especially someone such as a boss who might be too busy, or might think they are too important, to talk to you.

• You usually use the word **neighbourly** about kind things that people do, rather than about people themselves.

• You use the word **sociable** to describe someone who enjoys other people's company and likes going out with friends to places like pubs and restaurants.

fright [noun]

alarm *The horse reared up in alarm.*

dread *I was filled with dread at the thought of the exam.*

fear *Children don't have a fear of death.*

horror *Jane remembered with horror that she had not switched the iron off.*

panic *A feeling of panic seized me.*

terror *Horne heard a sound and jumped up in terror.*

VOCABULARY CHOICES

• All these words can be used to create a mood of suspense or fear in a piece of text.

• The words **dread**, **horror** and **terror** in particular suggest extreme fear, and are used for more impact.

frighten [verb]

scare *Don't let them scare you into agreeing.*

shock *We were all shocked by the news.*

startle *Something must have startled the horse.*

terrify *The sight of the animal terrified us.*

terrorize *These gangs terrorize our neighbourhood.*

◆ **Formal words alarm** *I didn't mean to alarm you.*

intimidate *They'd been intimidated into paying the money.*

unnerve *The strange sound completely unnerved me.*

frightening [adjective]

chilling *There was a chilling silence in the hotel.*

creepy *a room at the end of a creepy corridor*

eerie *eerie shadows*

scary *Getting stuck in a lift was a scary thought.*

hair-raising *a hair-raising scream*

spine-chilling *a spine-chilling ghost story*

terrifying *the terrifying violence of the wind*

◆ **Informal word spooky** *The room was dark and spooky.*

VOCABULARY CHOICES

• All these words can be used to create a mood of suspense or fear in a piece of text.

• The words **chilling**, **hair-raising**, **spine-chilling** and **terrifying** in particular suggest something is extremely frightening, and are used for more impact.

Ff

Types of fruit:

Types of apple:	tangerine	redcurrant	kumquat
Bramley	**Types of melon:**	strawberry	lemon
Cox's Orange Pippin	cantaloupe	**Other fruits:**	lime
crab apple	Galia	apricot	lychee
Gala	honeydew	avocado	mango
Golden Delicious	watermelon	banana	nectarine
Granny Smith	**Types of berry:**	cherry	papaya
Types of pear:	bilberry	damson	pawpaw
Conference	blackberry	date	peach
William	blackcurrant	fig	pineapple
Types of orange:	blueberry	gooseberry	plum
clementine	boysenberry	grape	pomegranate
Jaffa	cranberry	grapefruit	rhubarb
mandarin	elderberry	greengage	sloe
satsuma	loganberry	guava	star fruit
Seville	raspberry	kiwi fruit	Ugli® fruit

---

front [noun]
façade the house's elegant façade
head the people at the end of the queue
lead the competitors in the lead
nose the nose of the aeroplane
◆ **Technical term bow** She was sitting towards the bow of the boat.

frown¹ [noun]
a disapproving frown
grimace a grimace of disgust
scowl She stamped into the room with a scowl on her face.
◆ **Informal term dirty look** Why is Sheena giving me dirty looks?

frown² [verb]
She frowned at me as I came in.
glare The sergeant glared at me over his glasses.
glower George sat there glowering at everyone.
grimace Muller grimaced at the thought of the long journey.
scowl When I mentioned boyfriends, she scowled and walked off.

fruit [noun]
See the box above.

full [adjective]
1 full of water • full of people
crammed buses crammed with tourists
crowded a crowded street
jammed The roads would be jammed with holiday traffic.
packed The place was packed with schoolchildren.
stuffed a suitcase stuffed with pound notes
2 the full range of colours
complete the complete short stories of James Joyce
entire a photograph of the entire squad
whole Searchlights lit up the whole sky.
3 a full report
thorough a thorough investigation
◆ **Formal words comprehensive** The book is a comprehensive survey of history.
exhaustive I made an exhaustive list of every item of furniture.
extensive We keep extensive business records.
4 at full speed
highest She achieved the highest score possible.

maximum The oven has reached its maximum temperature.

top a top speed of 200 kilometres an hour

un [noun]

amusement They danced and sang for our amusement.

enjoyment You can get a lot of enjoyment out of walking in the countryside.

entertainment The islanders made their own entertainment.

pleasure The children depend on these toys for their pleasure.

• **Formal word recreation** It gave working people some time for recreation.

unny [adjective]

1 a funny story

amusing an amusing film

comical a comical expression on his face

entertaining The performance was very entertaining.

hilarious Some of her stories are hilarious.

humorous He's best known for his humorous poems.

witty He's a very witty speaker.

2 funny behaviour

curious It was a curious thing to ask.

mysterious the mysterious circumstances of his death

odd People at the camp wore very odd clothes.

peculiar I heard a peculiar noise in the bathroom.

strange The strange thing was that I never knew his name.

unusual a bird with unusual markings

weird the weird sounds coming from these instruments

VOCABULARY CHOICES

meaning 1]

• If something is both interesting and funny, you could say that it is **entertaining**, especially if it is something that you are watching or listening to.

• You use the word **comical** to describe something that is funny because it is slightly strange or silly.

• **Witty** is used to describe people, or the things they say, when they are funny in a clever way.

• If you describe something as **hilarious**, then you are saying it is extremely funny and it makes you laugh a lot.

Ff

furious [adjective]

1 He was furious with us.

fuming She was still fuming after her row with Sandra.

incensed The family are absolutely incensed about it.

infuriated a charge by an infuriated bull

livid He was livid at being left out.

raging He hadn't apologized and I was raging.

♦ **Informal terms mad** I was still mad with the kids for forgetting.

up in arms The whole neighbourhood was up in arms about the decision.

2 a furious wind

fierce a fierce storm

violent A violent explosion rattled the windows.

wild out on the moors on a wild night

fuss [noun]

Don't make such a fuss.

commotion There was a huge commotion in the ticket office.

palaver the usual palaver over money

trouble I expect there will be trouble when they find out.

upset She didn't want to cause any more upset.

♦ **Formal word furore** the furore around the manager's resignation

♦ **Informal words flap** He's in a bit of a flap about the wedding.

hassle Dad doesn't need this hassle at his age.

hoo-ha *the hoo-ha over an affair she had with a younger man*

to-do *There was a real to-do when he left.*

fuss^2 [verb]

She keeps fussing about the arrangements.

bother *Don't bother yourself about it too much.*

fret *Stop fretting and try to relax.*

grumble *Patients were grumbling about the time they'd been kept waiting.*

worry *I keep telling him to stop worrying.*

fussy [adjective]

finicky *children who are finicky eaters*

hard to please *When it comes to wine, he's pretty hard to please.*

particular *Is the child particular about what she wears?*

pernickety *Our pernickety neighbours objected to the mess.*

scrupulous *She is absolutely scrupulous about cleanliness.*

◆ **Informal word choosy** *At my age, I can't afford to be choosy.*

G

gamble [verb]
You shouldn't gamble with your future.
  bet I bet she would pass her driving test this time.
  risk Will you risk your job by going on strike?
  take a chance I sometimes take a chance and buy a lottery ticket.
  try your luck Tom thought he might try his luck on the horses.

gamble [noun]
She's taking a gamble by lying on her CV.
  bet This horse looks like a good bet.
  chance I'll take a chance and play the lottery.
  risk You are taking a risk with your life if you swim in this river.

game [noun]
1 I enjoy sports and games.
  amusement A fairground has lots of amusements.
  entertainment Their entertainment was singing.
  sport Tennis is the sport I enjoy most.
  ◆ **Formal word recreation** The guests are here for rest and recreation.
2 the Olympic Games
  competition She won a badminton competition.
  contest an exciting contest between two former champions
  event a major athletics event

  tournament an international tennis tournament
3 a game of football
  match our last match of the season
  tie an exciting tie between two great teams

gang [noun]
  band Robin Hood and his band of men
  circle She's not part of Alan's circle of friends.
  crowd She didn't belong to the school's skater crowd.
  group a group of schoolchildren walking round the museum
  party We led a party of friends round the village.
  set The second play features the same set of actors.
  ◆ **Informal words crew** The usual crew are travelling up from Coventry.
  lot My lot decided to go to the pub.
  mob There's some of our mob, outside the shop.

gather [verb]
1 people gathering outside the hall • Gather your things together.
  assemble Guests assemble here.
  congregate Youths congregated outside the motorbike shop.
  crowd Teenage fans crowded round the pop stars.
  group Group all the leaflets together in a single place.

113

◆ **Formal word convene** *The clubs convene here tonight for a special meeting.*
2 gather information
collect *I collected the names of people who were interested.*
◆ **Formal word amass** *She had amassed a huge fortune.*
3 I gather he's leaving.
believe *I believe his wife's French.*
hear *I hear you've moved house.*
understand *We understand you've been complaining.*

generous [adjective]
1 a generous person • a generous gesture
charitable *not a very charitable thing to say*
good *Their daughter had married a good man.*
kind *It's kind of you to help.*
unselfish *We admired her unselfish attitude.*
◆ **Formal word benevolent** *money given to her by a benevolent old uncle*
2 a generous helping
abundant *The region has abundant wildlife.*
ample *an ample supply of fuel*
big *a big piece of cake*
large *a large amount of money*
◆ **Formal words copious** *She drank copious amounts of water.*
plentiful *Plentiful supplies of wood were available.*

gentle [adjective]
1 a gentle person
calm *He is a very calm presence in the team.*
gentle as a lamb *He looks tough, but he's gentle as a lamb.*
mild *We need someone with a mild temperament.*
placid *the dog's placid nature*
tender *a tender caress*

2 a gentle breeze
light *light winds*
moderate *a moderate increase in temperature*
slight *a very slight dip in the road*
soft *soft lighting*

VOCABULARY CHOICES
[meaning 1]
• **Gentle as a lamb** is a **simile**. It is also a phrase that has been used so often that it has lost impact – a **cliché**.

get [verb]
1 I got lots of presents.
come by *How did he come by all that money?*
gain *I gained a lot from the experience.*
receive *How many cards did you receive this year?*
secure *secure a deal*
win *win a big contract*
◆ **Formal words acquire** *He acquired the business in 1995.*
obtain *help with obtaining employment*
2 It's getting light outside.
become *I was becoming more angry by the minute.*
grow *We are all growing older.*
turn *It turned colder at night.*
3 Get me my coat.
bring *He brought us some food.*
collect *Can you collect my dry-cleaning?*
fetch *Fetch me a hammer.*
4 I've got the cold.
catch *I catch all the illnesses that are going around.*
come down with *Mum came down with flu last winter.*
pick up *I've picked up a tummy bug.*
◆ **Formal word contract** *The child contracted measles.*

gift [noun]
1 birthday gifts
donation *regular donations to charity*

present *Christmas presents*
tip *If the waiter is rude, I leave no tip at all.*
♦ **Formal word offering** *We accepted her offering of flowers and fruit.*
♦ **Informal word freebie** *She took every freebie on offer.*
♦ **Technical term legacy** *She inherited a legacy from her wealthy parents.*
2 You have a real gift for getting people to do what you want.
ability *He had a natural ability to entertain others.*
flair *Gina had a flair for solving other people's problems.*
genius *The champion shows his genius in the second game.*
knack *He seemed to have a knack for making money.*
talent *You have to admire her talent.*
♦ **Formal word aptitude** *a child's aptitude for learning*

give [verb]
1 *She gave him the pencil.*
hand *I handed Geoff the letter.*
hand over *We had to hand over our passports.*
offer *She offered me another biscuit.*
pass *Would you pass me the butter?*
present *The staff presented her with a watch.*
2 *Give us more time.*
allow *They allowed us a few minutes alone.*
♦ **Formal word grant** *The council granted the centre more money.*
3 *Don't give me trouble.*
cause *The injury is still causing her some pain.*
create *Her attitude is creating problems.*
make *I don't want to make any trouble for you.*
4 *The chair gave under his weight.*
break *I thought the table was going to break.*

collapse *The bridge seemed close to collapsing.*
give way *The second floor of the building gave way.*

give up [verb]
1 *She found it easy to give up junk food.*
quit *quit drinking*
stop *I managed to stop eating chocolate altogether.*
♦ **Informal term pack in** *It's hard to pack in smoking.*
2 *Just give up and do something else.*
admit defeat *He won't admit defeat easily.*
give in *I am getting tired, but I won't give in.*
surrender *They were determined not to surrender, despite losing the battle.*
♦ **Formal term concede defeat** *The Conservatives conceded defeat as the votes were counted.*
♦ **Informal phrase throw in the towel** *The other team were too strong, and we threw in the towel.*

glad [adjective]
1 *I'm glad to hear you are better.*
delighted *We're delighted she's accepted our invitation.*
happy *I'm happy to say that the operation was a success.*
pleased *She's just pleased to know you're all safe.*
2 *I'll be glad to help.*
ready *I'm ready to do whatever you ask.*
willing *She was very willing to accept that risk.*

go[1] [verb]
1 *We go to school by bus.*
make for *We made for the nearest town.*
travel *She travels to work by train.*
♦ **Formal word journey** *The family journeyed across the desert on camels.*
2 *We go to the cinema every week.*
attend *She attends school daily.*

Gg

Gg

often go to *We often go to the park at the weekend.*

visit often *Tanya visited them often in those days.*

3 The engine was still going.

function *Oil keeps everything functioning smoothly.*

run *Keep the motor running.*

work *The pump was working at full power.*

4 a bridge going across the river

extend *The new centre will extend from the bus station to the park.*

reach *The road doesn't reach as far as the school.*

stretch *farmland that stretches all the way to the river*

5 Time goes quickly.

pass *The summer holidays passed slowly.*

◆ **Formal word elapse** *Weeks elapsed before they heard more news.*

◆ **Informal term roll on** *The years rolled on and nothing changed.*

6 It's time I was going.

leave *We left just after midnight.*

set off *After lunch, Albert set off for Oxford.*

◆ **Formal word depart** *The train departed on time.*

go^2 [noun]

1 (informal) have a go

attempt *my second attempt at passing my driving test*

try *Will I get another try?*

turn *It's the other team's turn to bat.*

◆ **Informal words bash** *I'll have a bash at most household jobs.*

shot *You could have another shot at persuading your parents.*

stab *If she fails this week, she'll have another stab at it next week.*

2 (informal) full of go

energy *Does Denise have the energy for a job like this?*

life *We need young people with a lot of life in them.*

spirit *He didn't have the spirit to fight back.*

◆ **Formal words dynamism** *leaders with dynamism*

vitality *Faye was bursting with intelligence and vitality.*

◆ **Informal word get-up-and-go** *She was full of get-up-and-go.*

good^1 [adjective]

1 a good worker • good at maths

able *a very able member of the team*

accomplished *The girl was an accomplished singer.*

capable *a very capable performer*

excellent *John turned out to be an excellent storyteller.*

expert *She became expert at drawing animals.*

first-class *Mandy was a first-class player.*

first-rate *She's a first-rate teacher.*

gifted *The boy was a gifted musician.*

talented *a talented chess player*

2 It was good of you to come.

charitable *a charitable thing to do*

kind *You're very kind to help me so much.*

3 a good man

honest *Mr Matekoni was an honest man.*

moral *We expected somebody more moral.*

trustworthy *James wasn't trustworthy enough to be given the keys.*

◆ **Formal words righteous** *He said only righteous people would get into heaven.*

upright *an upright member of the community*

virtuous *She was far too virtuous to tell a lie.*

4 You've been a good boy today.

obedient *a very obedient dog*

well-behaved *What well-behaved children!*

well-mannered *his well-mannered daughter*

good² [noun]
I'm doing this for your good.
  benefit *For his own benefit, he should start learning to drive now.*
  sake *We're doing all this for your sake, not mine.*
  welfare *I have the children's welfare to think about.*

gradually [adverb]
  bit by bit *She tidied the garden bit by bit.*
  little by little *Little by little the truth emerged.*
  progressively *The weather got progressively worse.*
  slowly *The traffic is moving slowly.*
  step by step *You can improve your writing skills step by step.*

grateful [adjective]
  thankful *We're thankful to you for that.*
  ♦ **Formal word appreciative** *I hoped for a more appreciative audience.*

great [adjective]
1 *a great house • the Great Plains*
  colossal *The explosion rocked the colossal tower.*
  enormous *an enormous castle overlooking the beach*
  gigantic *There's a gigantic statue in the town square.*
  huge *They have a huge garden at the back.*
  immense *An immense ocean liner docked in the harbour.*
  large *a very large breed of dog*
  mammoth *Mammoth waves roared over the beach.*
  massive *The animal had a massive head and shoulders.*
  vast *a vast expanse of jungle*
2 *with great care*
  extreme *The job requires extreme concentration.*

  ♦ **Formal word considerable** *This was a considerable amount of money.*
3 *a great actor*
  famous *one of the most famous players of the decade*
  fine *a fine musician*
  outstanding *outstanding pupils*
  ♦ **Formal words celebrated** *the celebrated artist, Francis Bacon*
  distinguished *The speaker was a distinguished lawyer.*
  eminent *one of the most eminent surgeons in the country*
  renowned *the renowned Shakespearean actor, Sir John Gielgud*
4 (informal) *That's great!*
  excellent *excellent news*
  terrific *We all had a terrific time.*
  tremendous *The day was a tremendous success.*
  wonderful *What a wonderful idea.*
  ♦ **Informal words brilliant** *She's brilliant at writing stories.*
  cool *You're coming too? Cool!*
  fantastic *These photos are fantastic.*
  wicked *That hat is wicked.*

greedy [adjective]
1 *greedy for food*
  gluttonous *Gluttonous rats ate the remains of the bread.*
  ♦ **Formal word insatiable** *an insatiable appetite for alcohol*
2 *greedy for wealth*
  grasping *He was a selfish, grasping man.*
  self-interested *a self-interested company chairman, only concerned with profits*
  ♦ **Formal word avaricious** *an avaricious money lender who charged high interest*

green¹ [adjective]
1 *a green field*
  grassy *the many grassy areas in Belfast*
  leafy *a very leafy part of the town*
2 *green issues*

Gg

Shades of green:

aquamarine	emerald	sage
avocado	jade	turquoise
bottle	khaki	

Shades of grey:

charcoal	silver

eco-friendly *We're developing more eco-friendly systems.*
ecological *articles on ecological issues*
environmental *the party's environmental policies*
environmentally aware *We need more environmentally aware politicians.*

green² [noun]
the bowling green
  grass *Your grass is looking very healthy.*
  lawn *She's mowing the lawn before the rain comes on.*
See also the box above.

grey [noun]
See the box above.

grief [noun]
  anguish *the anguish caused by the accident*
  distress *They apologized for the distress they had caused.*
  misery *I cannot imagine the misery she suffered.*
  pain *I don't want to cause you any more pain.*
  sadness *feelings of deep sadness*
  sorrow *great sorrow at the death of a child*
  suffering *the suffering of these desperate people*

grip¹ [noun]
The cup slipped out of her grip.
  clutches *I snatched the letter from his clutches.*
  grasp *Nathan pulled his leg free from the man's grasp.*
  hold *Keep a tight hold on the rope.*

grip² [verb]
He gripped her hand tightly.
  clasp *She clasped the kitten to her bosom.*
  clutch *He was clutching my wrist painfully.*
  grasp *I managed to grasp a branch and steady myself.*
  hold *Hold the line with one hand.*

gripping [adjective]
  absorbing *an absorbing story*
  compelling *a compelling story of their love*
  enthralling *The dancing display was enthralling.*
  fascinating *a fascinating performance by the actor*
  mesmerizing *The scene was both revolting and mesmerizing.*
  riveting *a riveting TV drama*
  spellbinding *People in the crowd admired his spellbinding skill.*

groan¹ [noun]
a groan of pain
  moan *a moan of hunger*
  sigh *sighs of despair*

groan² [verb]
The audience groaned as he fell.
  moan *I moaned as the weight hit my chest.*
  sigh *The children sighed at the thought of another day stuck indoors.*

group¹ [noun]
1 a group of friends
  band *We were a band of brothers.*
  circle *a different circle of friends*
  crowd *They belong to a different crowd.*
  gang *gangs of teenagers outside the shop*

party How many children are in your party?

squad A squad of hooligans were pushing people around.

team Another team of workers took their place at midnight.

→ **Formal word faction** We didn't want the party to split into warring factions.

→ **Informal word crew** one of the girls in Jason's crew

2 Sort the toys into groups.

bunch We counted the nails into bunches of five dozen.

category What category of word does 'you' belong to?

class There are three classes of hotel in the resort.

classification We merged these different classifications.

grouping We don't belong to any political grouping.

set different sets of stamps

♦ **Technical term species** There are nine different species of bird on the island.

group² [verb]

1 grouped around their parents

assemble Forces had assembled on a hill.

congregate Dozens of fans had congregated around the stage door.

gather People had already started to gather outside the shop.

2 Group them according to size.

arrange The information is arranged in columns.

classify The Tourist Board has to classify hotels.

organize The books had been organized into 'fiction' and 'other'.

sort Sort these toys into groups.

grow [verb]

1 grow in size

develop The animal developed into a healthy adult.

expand Her business is expanding.

increase The popularity of the toys increased.

mushroom Our debts mushroomed into thousands of pounds.

spread His fame has spread across the world.

2 grow crops

farm The ponds are used to farm prawns and crayfish.

raise He's retiring to raise cattle.

♦ **Formal word cultivate** Maize is the main crop cultivated in the area.

3 grow cold

become She quickly became bored with the job.

get I could tell he was getting angry.

go It's gone much colder this week.

turn The weather was turning wintry.

grumpy [adjective]

bad-tempered The boss can be a bit bad-tempered.

cantankerous a cantankerous old man

irritable She gets a bit irritable when she's hungry.

surly The manager was a surly middle-aged man.

♦ **Informal word crotchety** He was tired and crotchety.

guarantee¹ [noun]

a guarantee of quality

assurance The teacher gave us an assurance that this would be done.

pledge a pledge to get rid of nuclear weapons

promise You made a promise to your friends.

word of honour I give you my word of honour that this will not happen again.

guarantee² [verb]

I can guarantee a profit.

assure I can assure you that I received no money.

ensure Can you ensure the safety of the children?

promise *We promise that no animals will be harmed.*

guard[1] [verb]

He was left to guard the post.

defend *The castle was defended on all sides.*

mind *I'll mind the bags while you're away.*

patrol *Troops would be patrolling the border.*

protect *Every entrance is protected.*

guard[2] [noun]

1 an armed guard

bodyguard *Her uncle was one of the Prince's bodyguards.*

lookout *Lookouts had been posted all along the wall.*

sentry *A sentry controls the main entrance.*

◆ **Informal word** **minder** *The star travels with three or four minders.*

2 a guard against infection

buffer *They take the medicine as a buffer against stress.*

defence *A healthy lifestyle is your defence against illness.*

protection *Your doctor cannot give you protection from some common diseases.*

safeguard *The money gave us a safeguard against redundancy.*

guess[1] [verb]

1 I wasn't sure so I guessed.

estimate *They estimated the amount of cement needed.*

judge *We had to judge the importance of this information.*

2 I guess they've already left.

assume *I assume you'll be coming too.*

imagine *Stella imagined he'd be pleased.*

reckon *I reckon it's time we told you the truth.*

suppose *She supposed there would be no money left by now.*

suspect *I suspected something had gone wrong.*

think *We think you're old enough to do this by yourself.*

guess[2] [noun]

If you don't know, have a guess.

estimate *a rough estimate of the cost*

feeling *I had the feeling it was a lie.*

suspicion *I had the suspicion that something was wrong.*

guide[1] [verb]

He guided us to the camp.

direct *A man directed me to the nearest police station.*

lead *She led us up the hill to her house.*

manoeuvre *She managed to manoeuvre her arm out of the seatbelt.*

steer *Will I be able to steer the car through that tight space?*

usher *We were ushered to our seats.*

◆ **Formal words** **conduct** *An official conducted us into the minister's office.*

pilot *Sally piloted the boat skilfully into a mooring.*

guide[2] [noun]

1 a tour guide

adviser *Each student has an adviser of studies appointed to them.*

courier *The courier travels on the same bus as the tourists.*

escort *We joined our escort outside the church.*

leader *The police officer wants to speak to the leader of your group.*

◆ **Formal word** **mentor** *He had been both a friend and a mentor.*

2 a guide to the Lake District

guidebook *She had a number of guidebooks on the region.*

handbook *a motorists' handbook*

manual *Unfortunately, we had lost the instruction manual.*

VOCABULARY CHOICES

[meaning 1]

• An **adviser** is someone who gives advice and information, for example to a politician

Types of gun:

bazooka	howitzer	revolver	shotgun
cannon	pistol	rifle	

or a pupil, to help them make a decision.
- A **courier** is someone who gives help and advice to people on holiday and usually goes with them as a guide on trips.
- An **escort** is a person who goes somewhere with someone, either to show them around or to protect them.

guilty [adjective]

1 the people guilty of this offence
offending *Offending youngsters usually receive lighter sentences.*
responsible *We'll find the person responsible for this crime.*

◆ **Formal word culpable** *The fact that he'd helped made him culpable.*
2 I feel guilty.
ashamed *He's clearly ashamed of what he's done.*
regretful *It's no use feeling regretful.*
remorseful *The court decides if an offender is remorseful.*
sorry *Don't you feel sorry at all?*
◆ **Formal words repentant** *She could not make herself feel repentant.*

gun [noun]

See the box above.

Gg

H

habit [noun]
>**custom** Was it his custom to stay out late?
>**practice** I unplugged the TV, as is my usual practice.
>**routine** Shower, breakfast, newspaper was his usual morning routine.
>**tendency** Sarah had a tendency to nod off in the afternoon.
>♦ **Formal word wont** She reached for the whisky, as was her wont at this time of the day.

hairy [adjective]
>**bearded** Her husband was a tall, bearded man.
>**bushy** The vicar had bushy eyebrows.
>**furry** The hawk eats anything small and furry.
>**shaggy** a dog with a very shaggy coat
>♦ **Formal word hirsute** the hirsute duo of John Lennon and Yoko Ono

half[1] [noun]
Save half for later.
>**portion** She cut the apple in half and gave me one portion.
>**section** the two sections of the pipe
>**share** Leon and I took a share of the profit.

half[2] [adverb]
The glass was half full.
>**partially** The meat was only partially cooked.
>**partly** I was partly relieved and partly disappointed.

handsome [adjective]
>**attractive** Her husband is really attractive.
>**good-looking** I was served by a good-looking young man.

handy [adjective]
1 Keep it handy.
>**at hand** She always keeps a dictionary at hand.
>**convenient** The flat is convenient for the train station.
>**to hand** I didn't have my mobile to hand.
2 a handy guide
>**helpful** Your advice was very helpful.
>**useful** Did you find the instructions useful?

VOCABULARY CHOICES
[meaning 1]
• If you say that something is **convenient**, you are saying that it makes life easier. Estate agents often use these words when they describe the location of a house, to make it sound appealing.

hang [verb]
1 hang from a branch • long hair hanging down over his eyes
>**dangle** Her legs dangled in the stream.
>**drape** A blanket drapes over the back of the chair.
>**flop** His red hair flopped down in front of his face.
>**trail** You don't want the dress trailing along the ground.

2 hang in the air
float *A few wispy clouds floated past.*
hover *High above his head, a buzzard was hovering.*

happen [verb]
occur *strange things occurring*
take place *When did the accident take place?*
◆ **Formal word arise** *One or two problems have arisen since then.*

happiness [noun]
cheerfulness *His cheerfulness made others feel better.*
contentment *Her new life filled her with contentment.*
delight *To his delight, he realized he was in the lead.*
optimism *a mood of optimism about the future*
◆ **Formal word joy** *We bring news of great joy.*

happy [adjective]
1 We were very happy to see her.
content *I feel content with what I've achieved.*
delighted *We're delighted you've come.*
elated *She was elated when she won.*
glad *I'm glad everyone's safe.*
pleased *I was pleased to hear you're feeling better.*
thrilled *They were thrilled at the news.*
2 in a happy mood
cheerful *You look very cheerful today.*
light-hearted *He started the day in a light-hearted mood.*
optimistic *I am optimistic by nature, and see the best in things.*
positive *Gran has a positive outlook on life.*
◆ **Formal word joyful** *We bring joyful news.*
◆ **Informal phrase happy as Larry** *The children looked happy as Larry, playing in the sand.*

VOCABULARY CHOICES
[meaning 1]
• The word **glad** is associated with feelings of gratitude or relief, while **content** suggests an inward feeling of satisfaction.
[meaning 2]
• The informal phrase **happy as Larry** is a phrase that has been used so often that it has lost impact — a **cliché**.

hard¹ [adjective]

Hh

1 a hard surface
firm *The ground was firmer at the edge.*
solid *We had to cut through solid stone.*
stiff *The body was quite stiff.*
tough *The surface is tough enough to withstand heat.*
2 I found the exam quite hard.
baffling *The last question was completely baffling.*
complex *complex maths problems*
difficult *a difficult situation to deal with*
tricky *a tricky sum*
3 a hard day's work in the garden
backbreaking *Lifting slabs is a backbreaking job.*
exhausting *It was an exhausting walk into town.*
strenuous *The doctor says I mustn't do any strenuous lifting.*
tiring *It's been a tiring day for the children.*
◆ **Formal words arduous** *the arduous task of moving the wardrobe*
laborious *the laborious process of collecting firewood*
4 a hard taskmaster
callous *He could be quite callous with the children.*
cruel *a cruel and evil dictator*
harsh *Don't you think you're being harsh?*
heartless *a heartless decision*
severe *She was unsmiling and severe.*
strict *Teachers need to be strict sometimes.*

hard² [adverb]
You have studied hard this term.
strongly The team fought strongly to retain their title.
♦ **Formal words diligently** Officers searched diligently for clues.
industriously Some of the children work very industriously.

hard-working [adjective]
energetic She's an energetic supporter of the club.
♦ **Formal words conscientious** a conscientious worker
diligent one of my most diligent pupils
industrious Sarah is a very industrious child.

harm¹ [verb]
1 It's wrong to harm animals.
hurt What kind of monster could hurt a child?
injure The fall injured his arm.
2 We don't want anything to harm your future career.
damage Cigarettes can damage your health.
hurt His behaviour will hurt his chances of promotion.
ruin The injury ruined my hopes of winning.
spoil Any mention of money would spoil the atmosphere.

harm² [noun]
causing harm to the environment
damage His drinking caused damage to his health.
hurt Lying could cause a lot of hurt.
injury We escaped serious injury.

harmful [adjective]
damaging It had a damaging effect on his health.
destructive the destructive force of the storm
♦ **Formal word detrimental** A move now would be detrimental to her career.

harmless [adjective]
safe These substances are quite safe to use.
♦ **Formal words innocuous** an innocuous comment
inoffensive We think of rabbits as inoffensive creatures.

harsh [adjective]
1 a harsh punishment
cruel a cruel system of government
severe severe treatment of the prisoners
strict Some of the teachers are very strict.
2 a harsh sound
grating a grating voice
jarring a jarring sound on the guitar
rasping Danny had a rasping cough.
♦ **Formal word strident** the strident noise of a truck's horn
3 harsh colour
garish clowns in garish costumes
gaudy gaudy feather hats
loud Your shirt's a bit loud.
♦ **Formal word lurid** walls painted a lurid shade of orange

hate [verb]
despise I despise people who tell lies.
detest She was a manager whom everyone detested.
loathe Anna loathed being called 'Miss'.
♦ **Formal word abhor** We abhor racism.

VOCABULARY CHOICES
• Words such as **detest**, **loathe** and **abhor** are very powerful words which suggest very deep hate, and they should be used with some care. However, in some less serious contexts these words can lose their force, for example I detest weak tea.
• **Despise** conveys a feeling of contempt as well as dislike.

have [verb]
1 They have a nice house.
own Brian owned three cars.
♦ **Formal word possess** They robbed me

of everything I possess.
2 The house has a wonderful view of the beach.
enjoy I enjoy good health.
♦ **Formal phrase be endowed with**
Lilian was endowed with a wicked sense of humour.
3 He had a difficult time.
endure Maya endured the pain bravely.
experience I had never experienced such rudeness.
suffer We still had to suffer the terrible heat of summer.
♦ **Formal word undergo** Our lives have undergone many changes.
4 have a baby
give birth to She's given birth to a beautiful baby girl.

head [noun]
boss Company bosses will like the decision.
director the director of a local football club
leader Party leaders are meeting in Westminster.
manager the manager of a building society
ruler the rulers of ancient China

VOCABULARY CHOICES
• The words **director** and **manager** are slightly more formal and are usually used about people in charge of things such as businesses and organizations.
• The word **leader** is often used about people in charge of a political party and it can also be used about people in charge of a group, for example a group of tourists or boy scouts.
• A **ruler** is a person in charge of a country. You usually use this word to refer to someone with a lot of power who lived in the past. People don't normally use this word to refer to modern political leaders.

heal [verb]
cure Can she be cured, doctor?
remedy A lack of calcium can be remedied easily.
soothe This lotion should soothe the skin slightly.
treat We treat such complaints with antibiotics.

health [noun]
condition His lungs are still in good condition.
shape She keeps herself in good shape.
state Everything depends on the state of her heart.
wellbeing A warm home is essential to the wellbeing of older people.

healthy [adjective]
1 a healthy child • stay healthy
fit Joanne came back from her holiday looking fit and healthy.
in good shape He's in good shape for his age.
sound a sound liver
strong He has a good strong heart.
well Aren't you feeling very well?
2 healthy food
nourishing a nourishing bowl of soup
nutritious Burgers are not very nutritious.
wholesome Tap water is safe and wholesome to drink.

VOCABULARY CHOICES
[meaning 1]
• **Well** suggests only that your health is satisfactory for the time being, and the word tends to be used in polite inquiries or their answers.
• The words **sound** and **strong**, on the other hand, give the impression of constant good health.
• **Fit** is slightly different in that it means being in good condition and able to take on physical exercise.

Hh

hear [verb]

1 I hear him calling.
>**catch** I didn't catch his name.
>**overhear** She overheard Stan say he was retiring.
>**pick up** I managed to pick up the street name but not the house number.

2 I heard she's going to Australia.
>**find out** We found out she'd been lying all along.
>**gather** I gather you're getting married.
>**learn** I learned of the disaster on the radio.
>**understand** We understand you're being investigated by the police.

heat[1] [noun]

the heat of the stove
>**hotness** He could feel the hotness of tears in his eyes.
>**warmth** We lay on the beach and enjoyed the sun's warmth.

heat[2] [verb]

Heat the stew before serving.
>**reheat** She reheated soup left over from lunchtime.
>**warm** I usually warm their pyjamas on a radiator.
>**warm up** Warm up the pie in the microwave.

heavy [adjective]
>**hefty** She looks heftier than she used to.
>**substantial** You need a substantial coat in this weather.
>**weighty** He blocked the door with his weighty bulk.

help[1] [verb]

1 Can you help me, please?
>**aid** His advice has aided me in my job.
>**assist** Just a minute. I'll find someone to assist you.
>**give a hand** Could you give me a hand with this box?
>**lend a hand** I'll be there to lend a hand if you need me.

2 Shouting won't help the situation.
>**improve** That attitude won't improve matters.
>**relieve** The cough mixture relieved my throat a little.

help[2] [noun]

in urgent need of help
>**aid** Two other drivers came to her aid.
>**assistance** Can I be of any assistance?
>**benefit** The drug brought no benefit at all.
>**helping hand** ready to lend a helping hand
>**use** Telling lies won't be any use.

helper [noun]
>**accomplice** A girl of seventeen was the thief's accomplice.
>**assistant** My assistant deals with the paperwork.
>◆ **Formal word collaborator** Douglas was my collaborator on the project.

helpful [adjective]

1 She made some helpful comments.
>**practical** The book gives practical tips on cooking.
>**useful** There's more useful information at the back of the book.
>**valuable** That's very valuable advice.
>**worthwhile** We feel it's a worthwhile thing to do.
>◆ **Formal words beneficial** the beneficial effects of eating healthy foods
>**constructive** Please make your comments more constructive.

2 a helpful person
>**kind** It's kind of you to spend so much time with me.
>**neighbourly** That was a very neighbourly thing to do.
>**supportive** Jim has always been a supportive friend.

hero [noun]
>**champion** She's a champion of the women's rights movement.
>**idol** The fans wanted a glimpse of their idol.

Hh

star *Gemmill was the star of the team.*
superstar *He was a superstar in the world of cricket.*

hidden [adjective]
1 a hidden door
camouflaged *The tanks were camouflaged with netting and branches.*
concealed *The jewels were concealed behind a false panel in the wall.*
disguised *The agent carries a sword disguised as a walking stick.*
secret *The gang had a secret store of weapons.*
2 a hidden meaning
cryptic *a crossword with cryptic clues*
mysterious *She had some mysterious reason for asking that question.*
obscure *The song had an obscure meaning that we didn't grasp.*
secret *Nobody knew the secret password.*

hide [verb]
1 hiding the key • hid the truth
conceal *The police are concealing the man's identity.*
cover up *The government tried to cover up the scandal.*
disguise *It was the truth disguised as a joke.*
mask *Her husband masked his real feelings.*
obscure *His face was partly obscured by sunglasses.*
shroud *The whole affair is shrouded in mystery.*
suppress *He accused the Prime Minister of suppressing the facts.*
2 The boys hid behind some rocks.
go to ground *The robbers had already gone to ground.*
lie low *With the police sniffing round, Bates decided to lie low for a while.*
take cover *Our men took cover behind some bushes.*

◆ **Informal term hole up** *The terrorists were holed up in the hills.*

VOCABULARY CHOICES
[meaning 1]
• **Mask** and **disguise** suggest that something has being changed so as not to stand out or be recognized for what it is, so these terms might be used of hiding unpleasant things.
• **Cover up** can simply mean putting a cover over something, but on another level it is often used when someone, especially someone in politics, has hidden the truth because it would be shameful or embarrassing.
• **Suppress** is also used for the deliberate hiding of information or facts, especially things it would be in people's interest to know.

high [adjective]
1 a high tower
tall *These birds nest in the tallest trees.*
towering *the hard rock face of the towering cliffs*
◆ **Formal word lofty** *the lofty peaks of the mountains*
2 a high wind
extreme *The creature can survive extreme temperatures.*
intense *I was feeling sick in this intense heat.*
strong *strong winds and driving rain*
3 a high official
important *She has an important job in the Foreign Office.*
powerful *the most powerful position in the British legal system*
senior *These decisions are made by senior civil servants.*
4 a high voice
high-pitched *The whistle produces a high-pitched sound.*
piercing *We heard a piercing scream.*
shrill *She has one of those annoyingly shrill voices.*

Hh

hire¹ [verb]

1 hire a house • We hired a boat.
charter They chartered a plane to take them to the island.
lease The offices are leased for six months.
rent We rented a cottage by the sea.
2 hire a lawyer
appoint The committee have appointed a new chairman.
employ They employ someone to do housework.
take on We'll need to take on more staff.
♦ **Formal word commission** Stewart was commissioned to paint the Queen.

hire² [noun]

a company specializing in boat hire
rent We pay nearly three hundred pounds a month in rent.
rental Car rental will be about a hundred pounds a week.

history [noun]

former times the people who lived here in former times
the olden days What was it like in the olden days, Mum?
the past In the past, people didn't have luxuries.

hit¹ [verb]

1 She hit the man on the chin.
beat The teachers weren't allowed to beat you.
punch The second man punched him in the stomach.
slap I'd like to slap him across the face!
smack You still see parents smacking their children.
thump I'll thump you if you do that again!
♦ **Formal word strike** He was struck on the head with a baseball bat.
♦ **Informal word clout** If you misbehaved, your dad clouted you.
2 He fell and hit his head on the table.

bang I banged my elbow on the doorframe.
bump She bumped her knee in the fall.

hit² [noun]

This song will be a hit.
success The film was a box-office success.
triumph The show will be a triumph.

hoarse [adjective]

croaky an old man with a croaky voice
gravelly People loved Armstrong's gravelly singing style.
husky Actresses developed a husky voice to sound sexy.
rough He had a deep, rough voice.
throaty a throaty cough

hobby [noun]

pastime One of the most popular pastimes is yoga.
relaxation What do you do for relaxation?
♦ **Formal word pursuit** outdoor pursuits such as hillwalking

hold¹ [verb]

1 hold her hand
clutch The girl was clutching a teddy bear.
grasp I managed to grasp a branch.
grip She put out a hand and gripped his forearm.
♦ **Formal word embrace** Old friends were embracing each other fondly.
2 hold a meeting
♦ **Formal word conduct** The interviews will be conducted in my office.
3 hold fifty passengers
carry Our car can only carry five people.
♦ **Formal word accommodate** How many people does each apartment accommodate?
4 holding him for questioning
♦ **Formal terms detain** The suspect is being detained at Paddington Green police station.
keep in custody She was kept in police

custody for over five hours.

hold² [noun]

1 keep a tight hold

grasp If she released her grasp, she would fall.

grip My grip on the rope was loosening.

◆ **Formal word** **embrace** a lovers' fond embrace

2 His parents have a hold over him.

control The blackmailer gets control over his victim.

influence I have no influence over the decision.

power We felt we were completely in her power.

hole [noun]

1 a hole in the pipe

breach A breach in the flood wall weakened the structure.

crack Water was getting in through cracks in the brickwork.

gap The man escaped through a gap in the hedge.

puncture There were several punctures in the skin.

tear His face was badly cut and he had a tear in his shirt.

2 a hole in the ground

burrow rabbits in their burrows

hollow Walking in the woods, she had fallen into a hollow.

pit Rubbish was dumped into an old gravel pit.

holiday [noun]

break We had another short break at Easter.

day off She hasn't had a day off for months.

leave I get 25 days' annual leave.

time off I think you need some time off.

VOCABULARY CHOICES

• **Leave** is a slightly formal word that people use to refer to the amount of time they are allowed to have off work as holidays. This

word is also used by soldiers and other people in the armed forces.

holy [adjective]

1 holy ground

sacred The city is a sacred site for Muslims.

◆ **Formal words** **consecrated** Sinners were not allowed to be buried in consecrated ground.

hallowed Tibet's most hallowed Buddhist shrine

2 a holy man

devout She comes from a very devout family.

faithful Alan was a very faithful Christian.

God-fearing The people in the village were a God-fearing bunch.

religious He wasn't a very religious man.

home¹ [noun]

a guest in my home

house I invited him to live in my house for a while.

◆ **Formal words** **dwelling** The cave made a warm and comfortable dwelling.

residence the more impressive residences on Belmont Street

home² [adjective]

a happy home life

family I had a few family matters to deal with.

household He worked through a list of household jobs.

◆ **Formal word** **domestic** domestic problems

homeless [adjective]

down-and-out The streets of London were full of down-and-out miners.

vagrant vagrant children living on the streets

◆ **Formal phrase** **of no fixed abode** The court heard that the suspect was of no fixed abode.

Hh

honest [adjective]

1 an honest answer

blunt *I asked what she thought of me, and got a blunt reply.*

candid *a candid interview*

frank *To be frank, I don't like him much.*

genuine *She's always so genuine when she speaks to you.*

open *I want you to be very open with me.*

sincere *a sincere expression of thanks*

straight *Give me a straight answer.*

truthful *a truthful account of the war*

♦ **Formal word forthright** *a forthright statement of his opinion*

2 an honest citizen

honourable *Jackson was too honourable to lie.*

law-abiding *law-abiding folk who live in fear of crime*

trustworthy *I know you like him, but is he trustworthy?*

♦ **Formal words upright** *an upright member of the community*

virtuous *Some children think it's boring to be virtuous.*

VOCABULARY CHOICES

[meaning 1]

• You use the words **frank** and **straight** to emphasize that someone is telling the truth even though it might offend or upset other people. If you want to suggest you disapprove of this, you might use the word **blunt**.

• If you say someone, or someone's words or feelings, are **sincere** or **genuine**, you are suggesting that you approve of them as they really mean what they say or show.

[meaning 2]

• If someone is described as **law-abiding**, it means they are unlikely to cause trouble, and might even be a little afraid of doing so.

• If you describe someone as **virtuous**, you mean that they are good in general, but you might be hinting that they are rather self-righteous about it and therefore not pleasant to be with.

hope[1] [noun]

1 We were full of hope for peace.

confidence *their confidence in their chance of success*

faith *You have to have faith in your own ability.*

optimism *a mood of optimism in the dressing room*

2 It's my hope to play for my country.

ambition *Learning to read music was one of her ambitions.*

dream *It was my dream to visit her in Africa.*

wish *These people share my wish for peace.*

♦ **Formal word aspiration** *He has no aspirations to become a teacher.*

hope[2] [verb]

I hope you're all well.

wish *We wish that you'll have a long and happy life together.*

♦ **Formal word aspire** *He aspires to become an instructor.*

hopeful [adjective]

1 I'm hopeful that it will turn out well.

confident *We're confident the day will be a success.*

optimistic *Are you optimistic about the outcome?*

2 a hopeful sign

bright *The future looks bright.*

encouraging *A win would be an encouraging result.*

promising *She had a promising career ahead of her.*

reassuring *It's reassuring to know that we can't lose any money.*

♦ **Informal word rosy** *It's not a rosy picture for people who have borrowed a lot of money.*

hopeless [adjective]
1 I felt hopeless about the future.
 defeatist Don't take such a defeatist attitude.
 dejected After a third defeat, the team looked dejected.
 demoralized Demoralized young people are worrying about the future.
 downhearted Try not to be downhearted — there's still hope.
 negative He has a very negative view of the world.
 ◆ **Formal words despondent** With this latest failure, she had become even more despondent.
 pessimistic Charles took a pessimistic view of our chances.
2 a hopeless dream
 impossible It was an impossible task.
 ◆ **Formal words futile** a futile attempt to make him change his mind
 vain Parents make a vain search for affordable toys.

horrible [adjective]
 appalling an appalling lack of food
 awful The weather was too awful for a walk.
 disgusting The hotel rooms were disgusting.
 dreadful We had a dreadful flight.
 shocking The standard of service was shocking.
 terrible I've had a terrible day at work.

horrify [verb]
 appal We were appalled by the dirty conditions.
 disgust The lack of fairness disgusts me.
 shock I was shocked to hear that a child had been injured.
 terrify The thought of all that responsibility terrifies me.

hot [adjective]
1 a hot day
 baking It was baking inside the classroom.

 blistering the blistering midday heat
 boiling It's boiling with the heating on.
 roasting Can we open a window? It's roasting.
 scorching The weather is usually scorching.
 sweltering a sweltering day
2 a hot plate
 burning hot The sand was too burning hot to walk on.
 heated a heated oven
 red-hot red-hot metal
 roasting These potatoes are roasting.
 scalding Don't shave using scalding water.
3 a hot curry
 fiery the fiery taste of chilli
 nippy a nippy sauce
 spicy Nigel loves spicy food.
 strong a herb with a very strong taste

VOCABULARY CHOICES
[meaning 1]
 • **Sweltering** suggests it is so hot that it is extremely uncomfortable.
 • The words **blistering** and **scorching** are even stronger, and suggest it is so hot that it could cause danger or damage, for example to your skin.
[meaning 2]
 • The terms **burning hot** and **scalding** suggest something is so hot that it could cause danger or damage.

house¹ [noun]
a house in the country
 home You have a beautiful home.
 ◆ **Formal word residence** the Prime Minister's official residence
See also the box on the next page.

house² [verb]
1 plans to house the refugees
 lodge The child was lodged with foster parents.
 put up Can you put me up for a few days?

Hh

Types of house:

	Homes in larger buildings:	Large houses:	
bungalow			log cabin
cottage		hall	shack
council house	apartment	lodge	shanty
detached house	bedsit	manor	tepee
semi–detached house	flat	mansion	treehouse
	granny flat	villa	wigwam
terraced house	maisonette	Simple houses:	
thatched cottage	penthouse	hut	
town house	studio	igloo	

---

take in *People in the village took in children who'd lost their parents.*

◆ **Formal word accommodate** *How many students are accommodated on campus?*

2 (formal) *The Tower of London houses the crown jewels.*

contain *The engine is contained in this compartment.*

hold *This building holds the nation's most valuable treasures.*

keep *Where are the spare blankets kept?*

store *Fitness equipment is stored in these cupboards.*

hug [superscript 1] [verb]

He hugged the baby.

clutch *She clutched the teddy to her chest.*

cuddle *He was cuddling his girlfriend on the sofa.*

hold *I need someone to hold me tight.*

◆ **Formal word embrace** *lovers embracing on a public bench*

hug [superscript 2] [noun]

I need a hug.

clinch *young lovers in a passionate clinch*

cuddle *Give me a cuddle.*

◆ **Formal word embrace** *a fond embrace*

huge [adjective]

1 *a huge mansion*

colossal *A colossal truck moved up the street.*

enormous *There's an enormous*

difference between them.

gigantic *The hotel is absolutely gigantic.*

immense *an immense statue of the president*

mammoth *We had to load a mammoth crate onto the lorry.*

massive *Their house is massive.*

2 *a huge occasion*

important *Any wedding is an important day.*

◆ **Formal word momentous** *The fall of the Berlin Wall was a momentous occasion.*

human [superscript 1] [noun]

The drug has not been tested on humans.

human being *Film stars are ordinary human beings too.*

individual *He's a nasty individual.*

person *His wife's a lovely person.*

soul *Frank is a kind soul.*

human [superscript 2] [adjective]

Of course I'm upset. I'm only human.

◆ **Formal words fallible** *Don't be angry with him. We're all fallible, after all.*

mortal *We know that all people are mortal.*

humble [adjective]

1 *Try to be humble.*

modest *He's very modest about his achievements.*

◆ **Formal words self-effacing** *Most of the people were quiet and self-effacing.*

unassuming *The director was a very unassuming man.*

unpretentious I like his unpretentious style.

2 their humble home
ordinary She lives in a very ordinary house.
plain plain cooking
simple a flat with simple furniture
◆ **Formal word lowly** a lowly cattle shed

humour [noun]
comedy a lot of comedy in the film
jokes You need more jokes in the speech.
wit I liked his wit.

hunger [noun]
1 die from hunger
famine another winter of famine
lack of food People shouldn't be dying for lack of food.
starvation Thousands had died of starvation.
◆ **Technical term malnutrition** Doctors treated many children suffering from malnutrition.
2 hunger for power
craving a craving to be loved
desire Clarke's desire to be party leader
longing a longing to hear his voice
thirst These kids have a real thirst for knowledge.
yearning my yearning to see her again

hungry [adjective]
1 feel hungry
famished Is dinner ready? I'm famished.
starving millions of starving children round the world
◆ **Formal word ravenous** By lunchtime, I was ravenous again.
◆ **Informal word peckish** She feels peckish around mid–morning.
2 hungry for knowledge
eager By Friday, I was eager to see Jack again.
longing I am longing to mix with people like me.
thirsty His wife was thirsty for power.

hunt[1] [verb]
1 Police are hunting the killer.
chase Officers chased him into a train station.
hound She is constantly hounded by photographers.
track Police tracked him to a disused warehouse.
trail Sharpe suspected they had been trailing him.
◆ **Formal word pursue** I was pursued by three guard dogs.
2 hunt for her umbrella
look for We looked everywhere for the keys.
rummage He rummaged around in his briefcase for a pen.
search Jackie searched for the photos.

Hh

VOCABULARY CHOICES
[meaning 1]
• If someone **hounds** you, they follow you wherever you go, in a way that causes you trouble.

hunt[2] [noun]
the hunt for the lost child
search Local people carried out a search for the missing man.
◆ **Formal words pursuit** Three officers set off in pursuit.
quest the quest to find a new British champion

hurry[1] [verb]
We'll have to hurry or we'll be late.
dash I dashed into the nearest shop.
fly A boy came flying up the street on a bike.
rush There's no need to rush — we've got plenty of time.
◆ **Informal phrase get a move on** We'll have to get a move on if we want to catch that train.

hurry[2] [noun]
Don't be in such a hurry to leave.

haste You know what they say — more haste, less speed.
rush I'm in a bit of a rush this morning.
♦ **Formal word urgency** Send the form off whenever you're ready — there's no urgency.

hurt[1] [verb]
1 My leg hurts.
ache This tooth has been aching all day.
smart My eyes were still smarting from the onions.
sting This might sting a bit.
throb Janice's ankle was throbbing with pain.
2 hurt her head
injure She injured her elbow in the fall.
wound Luckily, the leg hadn't been badly wounded.
3 It hurts me when he behaves like that.

offend I was offended by his lack of concern.
upset Her comments had clearly upset John.
♦ **Formal word sadden** We were saddened by her casual attitude.

hurt[2] [adjective]
His leg is hurt.
injured Five people are dead and thirteen injured.
wounded a badly wounded soldier

hygienic [adjective]
clean These people need clean water to drink.
germ-free A hospital should be a germ-free environment.
sterile Put a sterile dressing on the wound.
♦ **Formal word sanitary** People are living in conditions that are not sanitary.

Hh

idea [noun]

1 He wasn't happy with the idea of my going to France.

thought The thought of dying terrified her.

◆ **Formal words concept** Many people aren't happy with the concept of change.
notion She couldn't get used to the notion of living without him.

2 Her ideas about education are very different from mine.

belief the mistaken belief that the drug was safe
opinion She has strong opinions on many subjects.
thought What are your thoughts on the matter?
view people with strong views on abortion

3 a good idea

plan The plan is to expand the business.
scheme a money-making scheme
suggestion Going out for a meal is an excellent suggestion.

◆ **Formal word proposal** Officials welcomed the proposal.

ideal [adjective]

best That would be the best solution.
dream My dream holiday would be a world cruise.
perfect It would be the perfect Christmas present for my daughter.

◆ **Formal word optimum** Childhood is the optimum time to learn a language.

idiot [noun]

dimwit What a dimwit!
dunce He was the dunce of the gang.
fool You stupid fool! What did you do that for?
halfwit His brother had called him a halfwit.
moron Which moron left the cooker on?
simpleton He looked at her as if she was a simpleton.

◆ **Formal word imbecile** She was behaving like a complete imbecile.

◆ **Informal words chump** 'Not in the road, you chump!' he shouted.
nitwit He's a bit of a nitwit.
twit What are you doing, you twit?

ignore [verb]

overlook We can't just overlook past problems.
shut your eyes to The government can no longer shut its eyes to the problem.
take no notice of She took no notice of the question.

◆ **Formal word disregard** people who disregard health warnings about drinking

ill [adjective]

ailing her ailing mother
laid up He was laid up with flu.
off-colour He's been a bit off-colour recently.
poorly I've been poorly a lot this winter.
sick She was off sick for two weeks.

unwell *feeling unwell*
♦ **Informal phrases out of sorts** *I've been really out of sorts lately.*
under the weather *He's a bit under the weather at the moment.*

VOCABULARY CHOICES
• The words and phrases **off-colour, out of sorts** and **under the weather** suggest someone is feeling slightly ill, and they make an illness sound less serious.
• The word **ailing** is mainly used in books rather than in everyday speech.

illegal [adjective]
criminal *criminal activities*
illicit *illicit drugs*
unlawful *unlawful possession of drugs*
wrongful *sue the police for wrongful arrest*

VOCABULARY CHOICES
• The word **unlawful** is usually used in writing about law rather than in everyday speech.

illness [noun]
complaint *in hospital with a stomach complaint*
disease *childhood diseases such as measles and chickenpox*
disorder *a liver disorder*
♦ **Formal words affliction** *a crippling affliction of the nervous system*
ailment *minor ailments such as coughs and colds*
♦ **Informal word bug** *I picked up a tummy bug while I was on holiday.*

VOCABULARY CHOICES
• The word **bug** is used for illnesses you can catch that are not very serious. Using this word helps to make light of the illness.

imagine [verb]
1 *He was imagining what his holiday would be like.*
picture *I can just picture him lying on the beach.*

visualize *I tried to visualize what it must have been like.*
♦ **Formal word envisage** *I can't envisage her as Prime Minister.*
2 *I imagine so.*
assume *I assume he'll want to eat when he gets here.*
guess *I guess she's not very happy about the situation.*
suppose *I don't suppose you've had time to do it yet.*
think *I think things will get better.*

immediate [adjective]
instant *This kind of behaviour results in instant dismissal.*
instantaneous *Her death must have been instantaneous in the crash.*
prompt *We would appreciate prompt payment.*
swift *a swift response to the problem*

immediately [adverb]
at once *I could tell at once that he was dead.*
instantly *I recognized him instantly.*
now *I'll go and do it now.*
right away *She didn't come back right away because the phone rang.*
straight away *I'll come and fetch him straight away.*
without delay *He set off without delay.*

impatient [adjective]
fidgety *She was growing fidgety.*
restless *The children were getting restless.*

important [adjective]
key *a key role in the discussions*
major *Sport is a major part of my life.*
serious *an extremely serious matter*
significant *a very significant development*
valuable *a valuable piece of information*
vital *He had a vital role in organizing the event.*

impossible [adjective]
hopeless *the hopeless task of persuading*

li

him to give up smoking
out of the question *We have no savings, so buying a car is out of the question.*

impress [verb]
excite *a discovery that has excited scientists*
strike *I was struck by how well she coped.*
◆ **Informal terms bowl over** *We were bowled over by their generosity.*
grab *The idea didn't really grab me.*

improve [verb]
1 *I'm sure things will improve.*
get better *The situation has got a lot better.*
look up *Things are starting to look up.*
pick up *Sales have picked up.*
2 *plans to improve the bus service*
boost *The result has boosted his confidence.*
enhance *The room could be enhanced by a new carpet.*
upgrade *money needed to upgrade the London Underground*

increase¹ [verb]
The number of unemployed people has increased.
climb *The price of oil continues to climb.*
go up *The cost of petrol is going up.*
jump *The death toll has jumped to 40.*
mount *Pressure is mounting on the Prime Minister.*
rise *Temperatures are rising.*
◆ **Formal word intensify** *The wind intensified.*

VOCABULARY CLUES
• The word **jump** indicates a sudden and dramatic rise, and is used in news reports.

increase² [noun]
an increase in the temperature
jump *a jump in house prices*
rise *local tax rises*

inexperienced [adjective]
green *The girl was too green to know better.*
immature *He's just a boy and he's too immature to deal with this.*
naive *a naive young woman*

infection [noun]
disease *It's a kind of liver disease.*
virus *He must have some sort of virus.*
◆ **Informal word bug** *I picked up a tummy bug while I was on holiday.*

information [noun]
data *Computers can store a lot of data.*
details *Please send me further details of the course.*
facts *facts about the disease*
◆ **Informal words bumf** *piles of bumf about the election*
info *For more info, visit the website.*

VOCABULARY CHOICES
• The word **bumf** is used about leaflets and printed adverts, especially to suggest they are not any use and just a nuisance.

injure [verb]
damage *His brain was damaged in the accident.*
hurt *She hurt her elbow in the fall.*
wound *He wounded his leg.*

injury [noun]
bruise *a large bruise on the arm*
cut *a bad cut on his leg*
damage *damage to the internal organs*
wound *A first-aider can treat minor wounds.*

innocent [adjective]
1 *She is innocent of the crime.*
blameless *He is not totally blameless for what has happened.*
◆ **Formal word guiltless** *He is not altogether guiltless.*
2 *too innocent to understand adult ways*
childlike *a childlike delight in simple things*

li

Types of insect:

bee	earwig	ladybird	stick insect
beetle	flea	locust	termite
butterfly	fly	louse	wasp
cockroach	gnat	mayfly	weevil
crane fly	grasshopper	midge	woodlouse
cricket	greenfly	mosquito	woodworm
daddy longlegs	hornet	moth	
dragonfly	horsefly	nit	

naive *She was too naive to be aware of the dangers.*

unsophisticated *an unsophisticated man*

unworldly *She was a shy and unworldly girl.*

VOCABULARY CHOICES

[meaning 2]

• If you describe someone as **naive**, you are suggesting they are a bit too innocent, and that they tend to believe false things that other people tell them.

insect [noun]

See the box above.

inside¹ [noun]

It's bigger on the inside than it looks.

interior *the interior of the house*

inside² [adverb]

1 We went inside.

indoors *It's cold. Let's go indoors.*

◆ **Formal word** **within** *A voice called from within.*

2 He seems positive but inside he must be very worried.

inwardly *He was inwardly wondering what he would do next.*

privately *He privately doubted she would survive.*

secretly *Secretly I think he's annoyed about it.*

inside³ [adjective]

an inside wall

inner *the inner leaves of a lettuce*

interior *the interior doors of the house*

internal *the internal walls of a building*

instructions [plural noun]

brief *I was given a brief to take some photos for the magazine.*

directions *Read the directions on the tin before you heat the soup.*

guidelines *guidelines on using fireworks*

orders *Your commanding officer will give you your orders.*

instrument [noun]

device *devices for measuring speed*

gadget *kitchen gadgets*

tool *a tool for undoing screws*

◆ **Formal words** **implement** *implements used by surgeons*

utensil *cooking utensils*

insult¹ [verb]

I felt insulted when he said I looked my age.

abuse *He was drunk and abusing everyone around him.*

call someone names *children who call each other names*

offend *He had offended her by saying she was fat.*

slight *He felt slighted because he hadn't been invited.*

VOCABULARY CHOICES

• The phrase **call someone names** suggests someone is making very childish insults.

insult² [noun]

a heckler shouting insults from the back

abuse *He began to scream abuse at her.*

slight *Her comment was not meant as a slight.*

snub *His refusal to come was a deliberate snub.*

→ **Formal word** **affront** *His comments are an affront to people who work hard.*

intelligent [adjective]

bright *She's very bright.*

clever *a very clever child*

quick-witted *He is great fun and very quick-witted.*

smart *He's a smart kid.*

→ **Informal word** **brainy** *You have to be brainy to be a doctor.*

interested [adjective]

curious *She is curious about science.*

fascinated *I was fascinated by all the animals.*

keen *He is very keen on history.*

interesting [adjective]

compelling *a compelling story of their love*

entertaining *an entertaining speech*

fascinating *a fascinating book about Japan*

gripping *a gripping story*

intriguing *an intriguing contest*

stimulating *I want a stimulating and challenging job.*

VOCABULARY CHOICES

• **Fascinating**, **gripping**, **intriguing** and **compelling** convey a much stronger sense of interest than the word 'interesting'.

interfere [verb]

1 It is best not to interfere with someone else's business.

intrude *She's always intruding where she's not wanted.*

meddle *meddling in other people's affairs*

pry *I don't mean to pry, but is something wrong?*

→ **Informal phrase** **poke your nose in** *She shouldn't come poking her nose in where it isn't wanted.*

2 interfere with the proceedings

hamper *A lack of money is hampering our work.*

hinder *hindering progress*

obstruct *He had been fined for obstructing a police search.*

→ **Formal words** **impede** *Darkness and poor weather impeded the search.*

inhibit *Lack of sunlight inhibits plant growth.*

interrupt [verb]

disturb *Don't disturb me while I'm working!*

intrude *Jones intruded on the meeting.*

→ **Informal term** **butt in** *You always butt in when I'm telling a joke.*

intrude [verb]

butt in *I hope you don't think I'm butting in.*

interfere *I wish you'd stop interfering.*

meddle *You are meddling in things that are none of your business.*

invalid [noun]

suitable food for invalids

patient *Patients should be given plenty to drink.*

invalid [adjective]

an elderly, invalid aunt

ailing *her ailing parents*

frail *his frail mother*

ill *She left her ill husband in bed.*

invalid [adjective]

an invalid passport

expired *an expired bus ticket*

out of date *Your tax disc is out of date.*

void *The contract was declared void.*

invent [verb]

create *We are creating new products.*

develop *The company is developing new software.*

devise *He enjoys devising new recipes.*

think up *thinking up games for the children to play*

involve [verb]

1 The extension will involve a lot of work.

entail *What does being a firefighter entail?*

mean *Less grant money will mean*

139

severe cutbacks.

necessitate *The job necessitates a lot of lifting.*

require *The test requires great concentration.*

2 Try to get involved in a hobby.

engage *I was engaged in many projects at work.*

participate *She participated in a project to clean up the park.*

take part *I like to take part in team sports.*

VOCABULARY CHOICES

[meaning 2]

• The word **involve** and its synonyms can make a good impression in CVs and job applications. They emphasize that you are willing to take part in working life.

itch [verb]

Soap makes her itch all over.

irritate *My skin is irritated by nylon clothes.*

prickle *His woollen socks were prickling his feet.*

tingle *His skin was tingling.*

itch [noun]

a maddening itch on my back

irritation *an irritation caused by soap powder*

itchiness *The itchiness might be caused by allergies.*

prickling *He felt a prickling in the skin of his hands.*

tickle *She felt a tickle on the back of her neck.*

J

jail[1] [noun]
You could go to jail for what you've done.
  prison She was sent to prison for five years.
  ◆ **Informal word** **nick** He's just out of the nick.
  ◆ **Slang word** **clink** I've spent seven years in the clink.

jail[2] [verb]
He was jailed for six years for the robbery.
  imprison You could be fined or imprisoned.
  ◆ **Formal words** **detain** She has been detained for questioning.
  intern During World War II, many Italians were interned as enemies.
  ◆ **Informal terms** **lock up** Local people are saying he should be locked up.
  put away They could put him away for years.
  send down He pleaded guilty and was sent down for life.

jealous [adjective]
1 She is jealous of her sister.
  envious Anna was clearly envious of her friend's success.
  resentful If they do better than you, you might feel resentful.
2 a jealous husband
  possessive She married a very possessive man.
  ◆ **Informal word** **green-eyed** a suspicious look from the green-eyed wife

job [noun]
1 She has a very good job.
  career The girls didn't want a career in nursing.
  employment He had found employment as a waiter.
  occupation Aim for a more interesting occupation.
  position Ameena had a good position in a local law firm.
  post I had a post abroad for five years.
  profession Medicine is my profession.
  situation the 'situations vacant' columns of the newspaper
  trade Get yourself a good trade, like plumbing.
  vocation Being in the army was a vocation, not a hobby.
  work You'll soon find work.
2 household jobs such as ironing
  activity Cleaning the tools is the last activity of the day.
  project He's working on several projects at the moment.
  task Catching a bull is a difficult task.
  ◆ **Formal words** **enterprise** Crossing the ocean was a dangerous enterprise.
  undertaking Building a new centre was a costly undertaking.

VOCABULARY CHOICES
[meaning 1]
• The word **employment** means the same as

Jj

work, but it is slightly more formal.

- The word **occupation** is also quite formal, and is often used on forms that you have to fill in.
- If you have a **trade**, you do a job that involves knowledge and practical skill, for example as a plumber or a car mechanic.
- Someone who has a **career** does the kind of work in which you can get promotions to more senior jobs.
- A **profession** is a job that involves a lot of studying and training, usually at university, for example the job of a teacher, a doctor or a lawyer.
- The word **vocation** suggests that the person has a strong feeling that they want to do the job, especially when the work involves helping other people.

join [verb]

1 Join the two pieces together.
attach *Attach piece A to piece F.*
combine *You could combine the two jobs.*
connect *You have to connect one tube to the other.*
couple *The train's carriages are coupled together.*
fasten *We have to find a way of fastening the board to the wall.*
tie *Tie one end of the rope to this loop.*
2 The two motorways join at Perth.
come together *The two rivers come together a few miles further south.*
connect *This is where the tubes connect.*
meet *Here is where the river meets the sea.*
◆ **Formal word converge** *The two motorways then converge.*
3 join a club
enlist *Boys as young as 15 were trying to enlist in the army.*
enrol *I've enrolled for a pottery class.*
sign up *Which courses have you signed up for?*

joint [adjective]

collective *Don't thank just me. This has been a collective effort.*
combined *The two groups raised a combined total of £3,600.*
common *There are three rooms with a single common bathroom.*
shared *We have a shared love of good food.*
◆ **Formal words communal** *There's a communal toilet on the landing.*
mutual *It seems we have a mutual friend.*

joke¹ [noun]

1 He often cracks a few jokes.
quip *She smiled and made another quip.*
◆ **Informal words crack** *She made some crack about my lack of hair.*
gag *He tells the usual gags about mothers-in-law.*
one-liner *a series of rapid one-liners*
wisecrack *The cab-driver couldn't resist one last wisecrack.*
2 They played a joke on him.
practical joke *She tied his laces together as a practical joke.*
prank *The boys played silly pranks on each other.*
trick *Don't believe her. It's a trick.*

VOCABULARY CHOICES

[meaning 1]

- The word **quip** is used about a short, clever remark, and is often used with a hint of admiration.
- **Wisecrack**, on the other hand, hints that you feel impatient or annoyed with the person making the jokes, either because they seem to think they are funnier than they really are, or because they are being a bit offensive.

joke² [verb]

You shouldn't joke about things like that.
clown around *He was the kind of dad who clowned around in public.*

fool *When he fell to the ground, everyone thought he was fooling.*
tease *Don't get upset. He's only teasing.*

journey [noun]
expedition *an expedition to Antarctica*
jaunt *a jaunt to London*
pilgrimage *the pilgrimage to Mecca*
trek *a trek across India • It's a long trek to the shops from here.*
trip *a trip in the car*
voyage *a voyage around the world*

VOCABULARY CHOICES
- An **expedition** is a long journey, usually made to find something out. It can also be used jokingly of a journey that could be long and tiring: *the weekly shopping expedition.*
- The word **pilgrimage** is used about journeys made in the name of religion. Sometimes it is used to convey the idea of devotion in any journey: *the regular pilgrimage to the local football ground.*
- **Trek** also suggests a long and difficult journey, but **voyage** suggests a long journey that is quite an adventure.

jumble¹ [verb]
The bits were all jumbled together.
disorganize *Don't disorganize my papers!*
mix up *He mixes up the cups and you guess which one the ball is under.*
muddle *The dirty clothes were muddled with the clean ones.*
tangle *clothes all tangled together in washing machine*

jumble² [noun]
a jumble of broken toys
clutter *a clutter of glasses and empty bottles from the party*
mix-up *a mix-up of sweets and chocolates in a bag*
muddle *a muddle of dirty clothes*

jump [verb]
1 *The cow jumped over the moon.*
clear *The dog could easily clear that wall.*
leap *He leapt into the air and caught the ball.*
spring *The soldier sprang to his feet and stood to attention.*
♦ **Formal word vault** *John vaulted the hedge as if it wasn't there.*
2 *The noise made me jump.*
flinch *The man pulled out a knife but Tom didn't even flinch.*
start *A loud noise made the horses start.*
wince *Geeta winced as the antiseptic touched the wound.*
3 *You jumped a few lines there.*
miss out *You can miss out question 5.*
skip *I normally skip the introduction.*
♦ **Formal word omit** *You can omit breakfast if there isn't time.*

Jj

K

Kk

keen [adjective]
1 a keen gardener
avid an avid collector of stamps
devoted a devoted fan of Manchester United
enthusiastic an enthusiastic golfer
2 He was very keen to help.
eager eager to be involved with the project
motivated I am highly motivated and I enjoy being busy.
willing a very willing worker

VOCABULARY CHOICES
[meaning 2]
• All these words can be used in CVs and job applications to convey that you are a keen worker.

keep [verb]
1 Keep the receipt.
hang on to You ought to hang onto it. It might be worth something.
hold on to Hold on to your ticket because you can use it again.
save Save the food in case you want it later.
♦ **Formal word retain** You should retain your receipt.
2 I keep the scissors in the drawer.
store You should store medicines out of children's reach.
3 keep walking
carry on He carried on talking.

continue They continued jogging for another mile.
keep on He keeps on complaining that he's bored.
♦ **Formal word persist in** She persisted in being rude.
4 He keeps pigs and chickens.
care for how to care for rabbits
look after Looking after animals takes a lot of time.
rear rearing pigs on farms
5 I won't keep you long.
delay I won't delay you any longer.
hold up I don't want to hold you up.
♦ **Formal word detain** I'll only detain you for a few minutes.
6 keep to the rules
fulfil fulfil your promise to help
obey obeying school rules
♦ **Formal terms adhere to** adhere to the terms of the contract
comply with comply with health and safety laws

VOCABULARY CHOICES
[meaning 3]
• The term **keep on** often suggests that someone keeps doing something and you find it annoying.

kick [verb]
boot He booted me in the leg.
hoof hoof the ball up the field
strike He struck the ball well but it went wide.

kidnap [verb]
  abduct He was abducted at knifepoint.
  snatch The child was snatched from the street.

kill [verb]
  assassinate an attempt to assassinate the President
  massacre They had massacred 20 children in the village.
  murder He murdered his wife.
  slaughter About a hundred people were slaughtered by troops.
  ◆ **Informal terms** **bump off** He was bumped off by another gang member.
  do away with She did away with her husband.
  do in They threatened to do him in.

VOCABULARY CHOICES
• The word **assassinate** is used when someone kills a famous person, especially a politician or leader.
• The words **massacre** and **slaughter** are used when someone kills a lot of people on one occasion. These words have a lot of impact and are often used in newspaper reports.

kind [noun]
What kind of person would do such a thing?
  brand What brand of washing powder do you use?
  breed a new breed of mobile phone
  sort a different sort of problem
  type She isn't the type of person to get angry.
  variety a new variety of rose

kind [adjective]
I like people who are kind to animals.
  generous It's very generous of you to help.
  good-natured He was cheerful and good-natured.
  kind-hearted a kind-hearted woman who would help anyone

kindly a gentle kindly man
  sympathetic He's very sympathetic when you've got a problem.
  thoughtful She's a very thoughtful person.
  unselfish a very unselfish gesture

kindness [noun]
1 I'll thank them for their kindness.
  generosity her generosity in helping
  kindliness I was grateful for his kindliness when I was ill.
  unselfishness unselfishness towards the poor
2 You did me a kindness.
  favour He did my a favour by taking my library book back.
  good turn You'll be doing me a good turn by eating the cake.
  service I thought I was doing him a service.

kiss [verb]
She kissed the baby's head.
  peck He pecked her on the cheek.
  ◆ **Informal words** **neck** They were necking in the back of the car.
  smooch couples smooching on the dance floor
  snog I've snogged him a couple of times but nothing more.

kiss [noun]
a quick kiss on the cheek
  peck a peck on the lips
  ◆ **Informal words** **smacker** He gave me a huge smacker on the lips.
  snog Any chance of a snog?

VOCABULARY CHOICES
• **Smacker** is quite humorous in tone, especially when it refers to a kiss you're not expecting.

kit [noun]
  apparatus shelves full of scientific apparatus
  set I bought my daughter a chemistry set.

Kk

tackle *a box of fishing tackle*
tools *Did you bring your welding tools?*
♦ **Informal words gear** *Climbing gear is very expensive.*
stuff *Don't forget to take your swimming stuff.*

knife [noun]
blade *a steel blade in his hand*
penknife *She cut the box open with a penknife.*

knock[1] [verb]
She knocked her knee against the desk.
bump *He bumped his elbow on the table.*
hit *I hit my head on something.*
♦ **Formal word strike** *The stone struck me on the leg.*

knock[2] [noun]
a knock on the door
rap *They were interrupted by a rap on the door.*

tap *There was a tap at the window.*

know [verb]
1 *I didn't know he was here.*
be aware *I wasn't aware there was a problem.*
realize *I didn't realize you were going to be here.*
2 *I know George.*
be familiar with *people who are familiar with the rules of the game*
recognize *I recognize that man from the tennis club.*

knowledge [noun]
intelligence *The army had the intelligence that an enemy attack was planned.*
understanding *The teacher has great understanding of the subject.*
wisdom *Old age does not always bring wisdom.*

Kk

146

L

land¹ [noun]

1 We'll reach land in an hour.
   ground *The plane hit the ground at high speed.*
   solid ground *I'll be glad to get back on solid ground again.*
2 work on the land
   earth *planting seeds in the earth*
   soil *digging the soil*
3 buy land
   countryside *the countryside around the town*
   farmland *acres of farmland*
   grounds *the grounds around the house*
4 a foreign land
   country *countries such as Spain and Portugal*
   nation *the world's poorest nations*

VOCABULARY CHOICES

[meaning 1]
• The phrase **solid ground** sets up a contrast between the land and the air or the sea, and suggests in particular how much safer land feels.

land² [verb]

1 The plane landed on the runway.
   touch down *The plane touched down around midnight.*
2 The bird landed on a branch • The car landed in a ditch.
   come to rest *The van came to rest upside down.*
   end up *The ball went high into the air and ended up on the roof.*
   settle *The pigeon settled on a wall.*
3 land a big contract
   get *He's just got a new job.*
   secure *secure a deal*
   win *win a big contract*
   ◆ **Formal words acquire** *He acquired the business in 1995.*
   obtain *How was the money obtained?*

large [adjective]

big *a big house*
enormous *an enormous amount of money*
great *a great improvement in his behaviour*
huge *a huge slice of cake*
immense *There have been immense changes.*
massive *They have a massive swimming pool in their garden.*
substantial *a substantial increase in costs*
vast *Russia is a vast country.*
◆ **Informal words mega** *She earns mega amounts of money.*
whopping *The ring cost a whopping £27,000.*

VOCABULARY CHOICES

• The word **whopping** is often used in newspaper stories to emphasize how big something is, especially when it involves a sum of money or other figure.

Ll

147

last [adjective]

the last page of the novel
> **end** the end part of the film
> **final** It's the final programme in the TV series.

♦ **Formal word concluding** the concluding chapter of the book

last [verb]

This strike could last for weeks.
> **carry on** The situation carried on for over a year.
> **continue** Their affair continued for six months.
> **go on** The trial went on for five weeks.

late [adjective]

> **delayed** The train was delayed.
> **overdue** Her baby is a week overdue.

laugh [verb]

I laughed when he told me what he'd done.
> **chortle** He chortled when he read her letter.
> **chuckle** She chuckled to herself as she drove.
> **giggle** children giggling all the way through the film
> **guffaw** He guffawed at his own joke.
> **snigger** Boys sniggering when the teacher mentioned the word 'bottom'.
> **titter** Jane tittered, unsure whether it was a joke.

♦ **Informal terms crease up** I just creased up when I saw him slip.
> **fall about** Everyone was falling about when they heard what had happened.

VOCABULARY CHOICES

- The word **giggle** suggests the laugh of a child or young girl, and can hint that people are being silly or childish by laughing.
- **Titter** suggests someone is laughing quietly because they are nervous or embarrassed.
- **Snigger** suggests quiet, unpleasant laughing, perhaps in an unkind way, at something that is not supposed to be funny.
- The word **guffaw** means someone is laughing very loudly, but it also hints that the laughter is annoying or unnecessary.

laugh [noun]

My brother has a very loud laugh.
> **chortle** Tom gave a sudden chortle.
> **chuckle** I bet he had a chuckle when he wrote that.
> **giggle** giggles from the back of the classroom
> **guffaw** The joke raised a few guffaws.
> **snigger** Her bright yellow hat was greeted with sniggers from the children.
> **titter** The joke drew a few titters from the audience.

lazy [adjective]

> **idle** Like most lads of that age, he was idle.
> **workshy** workshy people who claim too many benefits

lead [verb]

1 lead him by the hand
> **escort** He escorted her down the corridor.
> **guide** She guided him through the crowded room.
> **steer** He took her arm and steered her into the kitchen.
> **usher** He ushered them into the office.

2 lead the country
> **govern** the people who govern this country
> **head** She heads a team of scientists.
> **rule** rule the country

3 leading by three lengths
> **be ahead** Spurs were ahead by two goals.
> **be in front** We were in front at half time.
> **winning** Murray was winning by two sets.

lead [noun]

1 have a five-point lead
> **advantage** a two-goal advantage at half time
> **edge** They had a slight edge over their competitors.

LI

2 follow the lead of the United States
example *follow the example of his older brother*
model *Our education system is a model for other countries.*
3 give the police a lead
clue *We are following up several clues.*
tip *A tip from a member of the public led to the arrest.*

leader [noun]
captain *captain of the football team*
chief *business chiefs*
commander *commander of the troops*
director *the director of the gallery*
head *She's head of the organization.*
principal *the principal of a college*
◆ **Informal word boss** *company bosses*

lean¹ [verb]
1 leaning to the left
list *The ship started to list.*
tilt *His head was tilted to one side.*
2 a ladder leaning against the wall
prop *A bicycle was propped against a tree.*
rest *His head was resting against the back of the seat.*

lean² [adjective]
a lean body
skinny *skinny legs*
slim *You are much slimmer than you used to be.*
thin *You are too thin for your own good.*
toned *a toned, athletic body*
trim *She is always trim and well-dressed.*

VOCABULARY CHOICES
• The words **slim**, **toned** and **trim** are approving words which suggest someone is lean in an attractive way.
• The word **skinny** is a more negative word and it could offend someone, as it suggests that they are too thin and do not look healthy.

learn [verb]
1 She learns things quickly.
grasp *trying to grasp the basics of Spanish*
master *The language is quite difficult to master.*
pick up *Using a computer isn't difficult to pick up.*
2 learn a poem
learn by heart *She had learned the speech by heart.*
memorize *He was trying to memorize the list.*
3 I learned later about his accident.
discover *I discovered the truth last week.*
find out *I found out about the affair from a friend.*
hear *He heard about her death when he got to work.*

learner [noun]
apprentice *The hairdressing salon takes on three apprentices each year.*
beginner *The golf club welcomes beginners.*
novice *windsurfing novices*
pupil *He wasn't a very good pupil.*
student *photography students*
trainee *management trainees*

leave¹ [verb]
1 He left around midnight.
disappear *She'd disappeared before I got there.*
go *What time do we need to go?*
◆ **Formal word depart** *He departed after lunch.*
◆ **Informal terms clear off** *He cleared off before the police came.*
take off *She took off as soon as she saw me.*
2 She left the job after two years.
give up *I decided to give up work after I had a baby.*
pull out *I pulled out of the course at the end of the first term.*

LI

resign from *She resigned from her post.*
3 He left his wife.
abandon *He had abandoned his wife
and children.*
desert *Her husband had deserted her for
another woman.*
walk out *She walked out on her husband.*
◆ **Informal word dump** *She dumped him
and moved in with another man.*
4 leave him money in her will
hand down *the jewellery which had
been handed down to her*
◆ **Formal word bequeath** *He
bequeathed his paintings to a museum.*

VOCABULARY CHOICES
[meaning 1]
• The terms **disappear**, **clear off** and **take
off** suggest that someone leaves a place
very suddenly or quickly because they do
not want to be found there.

leave² [noun]
1 get leave to go
authorization *Changes cannot be made
without authorization.*
consent *The operation cannot be done
without the patient's consent.*
permission *She had permission to take
photographs in the school.*
◆ **Formal word dispensation** *He had
been given special dispensation to join the
course.*
2 take a few days' leave
holiday *How much holiday do you get?*
time off *I'm taking some time off next
week.*

leg [noun]
1 She broke her leg.
limb *broken limbs*
◆ **Informal word pin** *You need a decent
pair of pins to be a model.*
2 the legs of the table
prop *Props were used to stop the roof
collapsing.*

support *the bridge supports*
3 the last leg of the journey
lap *the first lap of the tour*
part *This was the most difficult part of the
course.*
portion *We did a portion of the journey
by train.*
section *the uphill section of the race*
stage *The last stage of the journey was
the train north.*
stretch *the easiest stretch of the run*

legal [adjective]
1 Is it legal?
above board *I can assure you it's all
above board.*
lawful *lawful protests*
◆ **Formal word legitimate** *a legitimate
business*
2 a legal inquiry
judicial *judicial decisions*

VOCABULARY CHOICES
[meaning 1]
• The word **lawful** is used in writing about the
law rather than in everyday talk.

lesson [noun]
class *He teaches a photography class on
Thursdays.*
seminar *The tutor will take a seminar on
grammar.*
tutorial *weekly music tutorials*

let [verb]
1 Let him go out.
agree to *I agreed to her putting my name
on the list.*
allow *She doesn't allow her children to
play outside.*
give permission *Who gave you
permission to park here?*
permit *School rules didn't permit children
to wear jewellery.*
2 I have let my old flat.
hire out *They hire out the room for big
events.*

LI

lease *She's leased the house to a Japanese couple.*
rent out *He rents out his apartment.*

let down [verb]
Don't feel that you have let anybody down.
  disappoint *Peter has disappointed a lot of people who trusted him.*
  fail *Donna has failed her parents with her behaviour.*
• **Informal phrase leave in the lurch** *I expected him to help with the cleaning, but he left me in the lurch.*

VOCABULARY CHOICES
• **Fail** is a slightly more formal-sounding word than the others here. It might be used, for example, in school reports.

letter [noun]
1 *I sent her a letter.*
  message *I wrote a message and posted it.*
  note *He sent me a note saying he'd arrive on Saturday.*
2 *a capital letter*
  character *The password should not be more than eight characters long.*

level¹ [adjective]
1 *Make sure it's level.*
  even *an even surface*
  flat *Trim the cake to give a flat surface.*
  flush *Make sure the hob is flush with the worktop.*
  horizontal *Every horizontal surface was covered with books.*
2 *The teams were level at half-time.*
  balanced *a balanced score of 15–15*
  equal *The scores were equal.*
  even *The teams were even after the first half.*
  neck and neck *The election polls put the Conservatives neck and neck with Labour.*

level² [verb]
1 *levelling the buildings*
  demolish *Several houses were demolished by the hurricane.*

destroy *Floods have destroyed thousands of homes.*
  flatten *an area which was flattened by the earthquake*
  knock down *a building which has been knocked down by bulldozers*
  raze *homes razed to the ground by fire*
2 *level the score*
  equalize *Leeds equalized early in the second half.*
  even *Smith evened the score at 1–1.*
3 *level the ground*
  flatten *flatten the surface*

level³ [noun]
1 *at the same level*
  height *The height of the water is rising.*
2 *the next level up*
  degree *a job that needs a high degree of skill*
  grade *promotion to management grade*
  position *people in a more senior position*
  rank *officers of higher ranks*

liar [noun]
  fibber *You fibber! He didn't say that at all.*

lie¹ [verb]
I lie about my age.
  fib *He had fibbed about where he had been.*
  tell lies *Children often tell lies to get attention.*

lie² [noun]
I cannot tell a lie.
  fabrication *The story was a complete fabrication.*
  fib *Children often tell fibs.*
  white lie *I told a white lie and said I liked her new haircut.*
• **Formal words invention** *His explanation was an invention to make himself look better.*
  untruth *the untruths told my some politicians*
• **Informal word porky** *I think you're telling porkies!*

LI

VOCABULARY CHOICES
• The word **white lie** suggests you are telling a lie that does not harm anyone, and you may have done it to avoid upsetting someone.

lie³ [verb]
Lie on the sofa.
> **stretch out** He stretched out on the bed with his eyes closed.

life [noun]
1 a long and happy life
> **existence** It was a hard existence for many people.

2 full of life
> **energy** She's full of energy and enthusiasm.
> **liveliness** He brought liveliness to the party.
> **sparkle** All her sparkle had gone.
> **vigour** Although he was old, he had a certain vigour.
> ♦ **Formal words vitality** She had the vitality of a younger woman.
> **vivacity** Her vivacity and wit made her very popular.

lift [verb]
1 She lifted the chair.
> **hoist** He hoisted the boy onto his shoulders.
> **raise** She raised the glass to her lips.

2 It lifted their spirits.
> **boost** His hopes had been boosted.
> **buoy up** His mood had been buoyed up by a glass of whisky.
> ♦ **Formal word uplift** a massage oil that can help uplift your spirits

3 The ban was lifted.
> **cancel** The President cancelled the ruling.
> **remove** They are taking action to remove sanctions.

light¹ [noun]
1 the light from the candles
> **glare** the glare of the car's headlights
> **glow** the soft glow of the fire

2 He switched the light on.
> **lamp** a bedside lamp

3 at first light
> **dawn** They set off at dawn.
> **daybreak** He worked from daybreak to dusk.
> **sunrise** shortly before sunrise

VOCABULARY CHOICES
[meaning 3]
• The word **daybreak** is quite literary, and usually used in stories.

light² [verb]
1 light the fire
> **ignite** The gas was ignited by a spark.
> **set fire to** He set fire to the papers.

2 lighting the sky
> **brighten** the sunlight which brightened the room
> **light up** Fireworks lit up the night.
> ♦ **Formal word illuminate** The car's lights illuminated the car park.

light³ [adjective]
1 a light corner
> **bright** a lovely bright room
> **sunny** a sunny part of the garden
> **well-lit** You should park in well-lit areas.

2 light skin • light hair
> **blond, blonde** He dyed his hair blond. • She had long blonde hair.
> **fair** a woman with fair hair and fair skin
> **pale** people with pale complexions

3 light blue
> **pale** a pale blue T-shirt
> **pastel** a pastel pink colour

light⁴ [adjective]
1 light as a feather
> **lightweight** a lightweight jacket

2 a light breeze
> **gentle** a gentle draught
> **soft** the trees rustling in the soft wind

3 light entertainment
> **entertaining** The book is an entertaining read.

LI

frivolous *He enjoyed reading frivolous and childish things.*
light-hearted *a light-hearted look at the news*

VOCABULARY CHOICES
[meaning 3]
• The word **frivolous** suggests that you are criticizing someone or something for not being serious enough.

like [adjective]
1 I've got a jacket just like that.
identical *a car identical to the one he had before*
same *Our curtains are the same as those.*
similar *an animal similar to a rat*
2 countries like Spain and Italy
such as *small animals such as hamsters and gerbils*

like [verb]
1 I like reading.
be fond of *I'm very fond of that chair.*
enjoy *I enjoy gardening.*
love *He loves playing the piano.*
relish *I relish a challenge.*
2 I like her very much.
be fond of *I'm very fond of Ann. She's been a good friend.*
care for *I really care for him.*
3 Eat as much as you like.
want *Take as much time as you want.*
♦ **Formal word wish** *Do as you wish.*

likely [adjective]
1 It is likely to rain.
expected *the expected date of the next election*
♦ **Formal word probable** *Pilot error was the probable cause of the crash.*
2 a likely candidate for the job
appropriate *looking for an appropriate place to park*
hopeful *This hotel looks quite hopeful if we want a meal.*
promising *This one looks quite promising,*

suitable *This looks a suitable place for a picnic.*

likely [adverb]
He'll most likely be there already.
doubtlessly *You'll doubtlessly have to wait a while.*
likely as not *She'll be in bed by now, likely as not.*
no doubt *a comment you'll no doubt agree with*
probably *They'll probably ask you to get there early.*

limit [noun]
1 the outer limits of the galaxy
border *the borders of the fields*
boundary *Mark the boundaries of the area to be paved.*
confines *She rarely left the confines of her house.*
2 a limit on spending • a time limit
ceiling *a ceiling of two per cent on pay increases*
curb *curbs on taxes*
limitation *limitations on the range of items*
maximum *a maximum of four free tickets per person*
restraint *restraints on imports*
restriction *restrictions on the numbers of people*

VOCABULARY CHOICES
[meaning 1]
• The word **confines** suggests that you think the limits are very small, and too restricting.
[meaning 2]
• The word **ceiling** is often used in writing about the economy.

limit [verb]
Limit yourself to two units of alcohol.
curb *petrol taxes to curb car use*
restrict *plans to restrict the sale of knives*

limp [verb]
The horse was limping.
hobble *He hobbled towards the door.*

LI

limp² [adjective]

limp, lifeless hair

drooping drooping leaves

floppy His body was all floppy.

slack His slack mouth was half-open.

line [noun]

1 draw a line

dash Put a dash next to each thing on the list.

2 a line of people • a line of cars

column a column of soldiers

procession a long procession of bikes heading to the coast

queue a queue of people outside the post office

row a row of chairs

3 lines on his face

crease creases at the corners of his eyes

wrinkle a skin cream that claims to get rid of wrinkles

♦ **Formal word furrow** deep furrows between her eyebrows

listen [verb]

eavesdrop He was eavesdropping outside the door.

lend an ear He's always willing to lend an ear if you've got a problem.

pay attention You need to pay attention to what he's saying.

prick up your ears I pricked up my ears when I heard her name.

VOCABULARY CHOICES

• **Eavesdrop** is used when you are secretly listening to someone else's conversation.

• **Lend an ear** is used when you are listening to someone's problems, but **prick up your ears** is used when you start to listen because something is interesting.

little¹ [adjective]

1 a little man • a little car

mini mini chocolate bars

miniature a miniature version of the ship

minute minute amounts of chemicals

short At 163cm, he's very short for a man.

small small animals

tiny a tiny room at the top of the house

♦ **Informal word wee** a lovely wee boy

2 a little pause

brief a brief pause

fleeting For a fleeting moment I thought he was going to hit me.

short There will be a short break between the two lessons.

♦ **Informal word wee** We may have to wait a wee while.

3 too little water • We have little money.

meagre meagre amounts of food

scant the days of scant supplies during the war

sparse The furniture was sparse — just a table and chair.

4 a few little details

minor one or two minor problems

petty He is making a fuss about petty matters.

small She can remember every small detail of the day.

trivial trivial concerns

unimportant It's not worth losing your temper over unimportant things.

♦ **Formal word insignificant** insignificant facts

VOCABULARY CHOICES

[meaning 4]

• The word **petty** is often used as a criticism. It suggests that something is so small and unimportant that you think it is silly that someone is concerned about it.

little² [adverb]

a little-known writer

barely I barely know her.

hardly I hardly slept last night for worrying.

not much He didn't say much.

rarely I rarely go out in the evenings.

scarcely There was scarcely any traffic at that time of night.

LI

seldom *Scarlet fever is a disease that is seldom seen these days.*

little ³ [noun]
Take a little care.

bit *Just give me a bit of time.*

dab *She put a dab of perfume on her wrists.*

dash *Add just a dash of lemon juice.*

drop *Just a drop of milk in my coffee, please.*

spot *We're having a spot of trouble.*

touch *There will be a touch of frost tonight.*

trace *Traces of chemicals were found in the milk.*

live ¹ [verb]
1 live for seventy years

exist *the largest animal that has ever existed*

2 live in a tent

inhabit *polar bears who inhabit icy regions*

♦ **Formal word reside** *Applicants must reside and work in the UK.*

3 live a quiet life

lead *He led a very interesting life.*

spend *I don't want to spend my life working.*

live ² [adjective]
1 live births

alive *people who are alive*

living *living creatures*

2 live electric cable

charged *charged wires*

electrified *an electrified wire fence*

lively [adjective]
1 He's a happy, lively child.

active *She has been active all her life.*

alert *I'm not very alert first thing in the morning.*

energetic *His mother is an energetic eighty-year-old.*

vivacious *She's a pretty girl with a vivacious personality.*

2 a lively city

bustling *a bustling town famous for its fountain*

busy *the busy market square*

vibrant *a city with vibrant nightlife*

loan ¹ [noun]
a bank loan

credit *a company that offers credit*

♦ **Technical term mortgage** *take out a mortgage*

VOCABULARY CHOICES

• A **mortgage** is specifically a loan to buy a house.

loan ² [verb]
Can you loan me a fiver?

lend *He lent me some money.*

lonely [adjective]
1 a lonely old woman

alone *She felt completely alone.*

isolated *Mothers with young children often feel isolated.*

lonesome *He was lonesome and unhappy.*

2 a lonely farmhouse

isolated *isolated beaches*

out-of-the-way *out-of-the-way villages*

remote *a remote mountain retreat*

VOCABULARY CHOICES

[meaning 1]

• The word **lonesome** is usually used in American English.

long [adjective]
lengthy *lengthy discussions*

long-drawn-out *a long-drawn-out legal case*

♦ **Formal word prolonged** *a prolonged period of cold weather*

look ¹ [verb]
1 She looked at her watch.

examine *He examined his face in the mirror.*

gaze *He gazed at her lovingly.*

LI

glance *She glanced out of the window to see what was happening.*

inspect *Make sure you inspect things closely before you buy them.*

peep *She opened the box and peeped inside.*

scan *I scanned the newspaper of the man next to me.*

stare *I stared at him in amazement.*

watch *She watched him intently.*

• **Informal word gawp** *What are you gawping at?*

2 He is looking very smart.

appear *He appeared to be a little nervous.*

seem *She seemed surprised at the news.*

VOCABULARY CHOICES
[meaning 1]
• The words **examine** and **inspect** suggest you look at something carefully, especially in order to find faults.
• The word **gaze** suggests that you look at someone or something for a long time because you find them attractive or interesting.
• The word **peep** suggests you look at something secretly.
• The word **gawp** is a critical word, as it suggests that someone is looking at someone or something in a way that seems rude or stupid.

look² [noun]
1 Take a good look.

gaze *She was trying to avoid his gaze.*

glance *a quick glance at his watch*

peek *She took a peek inside the room.*

2 The man has a frightening look.

appearance *a man with a youthful appearance*

face *the changing face of farming*

3 He gave me a warning look.

expression *There was a strange expression on his face.*

look after [verb]
care for *Some elderly people can be cared for at home.*

maintain *The groundsman maintains the grass well.*

nurse *She nursed her father in the last years of his life.*

protect *Our instinct is to protect our children.*

provide for *I need my job so I can provide for my family.*

take care of *They take good care of their pets.*

tend *They tend the sick and the poor.* • *We should tend the garden better.*

watch over *He says God watches over us while we sleep.*

loose [adjective]
1 a loose tooth

wobbly *Her tooth was wobbly.*

2 loose clothing

baggy *a baggy sweater*

loose-fitting *a pair of loose-fitting trousers*

3 a loose description

vague *vague promises*

• **Formal words imprecise** *an imprecise estimate*

inexact *an inexact explanation*

lose [verb]
1 He lost his pen.

mislay *I've mislaid my passport.*

• **Formal word misplace** *The airline had misplaced his luggage.*

2 lose a race

suffer defeat *The team suffered defeat for the second time this season.*

lost [adjective]
1 lost property

mislaid *mislaid items*

missing *She found her missing shoe.*

• **Formal word misplaced** *misplaced luggage*

2 look lost

bewildered *She felt bewildered and confused.*
disoriented *He felt disoriented and tired.*
3 lost time
    squandered *There have been many squandered chances.*
    wasted *wasted time and money*

lot [noun]
1 lots of food • a lot of people
    a good deal *Being a mum takes a good deal of patience.*
    a great deal *They put a great deal of effort into organizing things.*
    great number *a great number of people*
    large amount *a large amount of money*
    many *Many parents feel like this.*
    numerous *The same thing has happened on numerous occasions.*
◆ **Informal words heaps** *We've got heaps of time.*
    loads *There's loads of milk in the fridge.*
    masses *There is masses of space.*
    shedload *He gets paid a shedload of money.*
2 They are an interesting lot.
    crowd *They're an unusual crowd.*
    group *a strange group*
    set *a new set of friends*

loud [adjective]
1 a loud voice
    blaring *blaring music*
    booming *a booming laugh*
    deafening *There was a deafening crash.*
    ear-splitting *the ear-splitting roar of the plane's engines*
    noisy *The music from next door was noisy.*
    piercing *a piercing scream*
2 a loud tie
    brash *a room painted in brash colours*
    garish *a garish orange and purple shirt*
    gaudy *women dressed in gaudy colours*

VOCABULARY CHOICES
[meaning 1]
• The words **deafening** and **ear-splitting**
are particularly associated with very high-pitched loud noises.

love [verb]
1 He loves his children.
    adore *She absolutely adores her sons.*
    dote on *She dotes on her grandchildren.*
    worship *She worships her older sister.*
2 I love dancing.
    enjoy *She enjoys gardening.*
    like *I like chocolate.*
    passion *his passion for painting*

VOCABULARY CHOICES
[meaning 1]
• The term **dote on** is usually used when someone loves someone who is younger than themselves, and they show their love by the things they do.

love² [noun]
1 the love she had for her children
    affection *I shall remember him with affection.*
    devotion *Their devotion to each other was obvious.*
    fondness *her fondness for him*
2 his love of music
    enjoyment *her enjoyment of outdoor activities*
    liking *his liking for whisky*
    passion *her passion for painting*

lovely [adjective]
    attractive *an attractive little town*
    beautiful *a beautiful part of the country*
    charming *a charming cottage*
    delightful *a delightful view*
    pleasant *We spent a very pleasant evening with them.*
    pretty *pretty flowers*
◆ **Formal word adorable** *an adorable puppy*

low [adjective]
1 a low wall
    shallow *shallow waters*

Ll

short There was a short hedge in front of the house.

2 Your name is low on the list.
near the bottom teams near the bottom of the league table

3 low lighting
muted Muted lighting gives the restaurant a relaxed atmosphere.
soft a room with cream walls and soft lighting
subdued The subdued lighting made the room feel very cosy.

4 low prices
cheap Get the cheapest prices by booking early.
inexpensive a restaurant with inexpensive prices
reasonable The clothes are a very reasonable price.

5 Supplies are low.
meagre a meagre ration of water
scant the hospital's scant resources

6 feeling a bit low
depressed You seem a bit depressed.
downcast He looked downcast.
gloomy feeling gloomy during the winter
unhappy He's been unhappy for a while now.

7 a low voice
bass the bass tones of a tuba

deep She has a deep voice for a female singer.

luck [noun]
1 trust to luck
chance leave it to chance
fate I put our meeting down to fate.
fortune Through fortune rather than choice, he had been successful.
2 I wish you luck.
good fortune You need to appreciate your own good fortune.
success I wish you every success with your new job.

lucky [adjective]
fortunate I was very fortunate in that I wasn't badly injured.
♦ **Informal word** **jammy** They were pretty jammy to win it.

lump [noun]
1 a lump of sugar • a lump of coal
chunk a chunk of cheese
clod a clod of earth
nugget a nugget of gold
piece a piece of rock
2 a lump on his head
bump There was a big bump on his nose.
growth a growth on her cheek
swelling a swelling on his arm

Ll

machine [noun]
    appliance *kitchen appliances such as microwaves*
    contraption *a strange-looking contraption*
    device *a device for opening tins*
    gadget *electronic gadgets*
    mechanism *the mechanism that starts the engine*

VOCABULARY CHOICES
• To call a machine a **contraption** hints that you think it is a bit ridiculous, either because it is very shoddy or because it is more complicated than it has to be.

mad [adjective]
1 *He went mad with grief.*
    demented *He ran at me like a demented animal.*
    deranged *She looked at me as if I were deranged.*
    insane *Jason became quite insane with jealousy.*
    ♦ **Formal word unbalanced** *She had become temporarily unbalanced.*
    ♦ **Informal phrases mad as a hatter** *I like him, but he's mad as a hatter.*
    out of your mind *If you think that will work, you must be out of your mind.*
    ♦ **Technical term psychotic** *The man was dangerously psychotic.*
2 (informal) *She got really mad.*
    angry *The teacher could get really angry.*

fuming *Tony was fuming when he saw the mess.*
    furious *I was furious with her for forgetting.*
    raging *He could fly into a raging temper at any moment.*
3 *a mad idea*
    absurd *The whole idea is pretty absurd.*
    foolish *It was a foolish thing to think.*
    silly *That's a silly suggestion.*
    ♦ **Formal word preposterous** *The plan was quite preposterous.*
    ♦ **Informal word daft** *Whose daft idea was that?*
4 *mad about cars • mad about football*
    enthusiastic *We thought they'd be more enthusiastic about going.*
    ♦ **Formal word fanatical** *a fanatical follower of football*
    ♦ **Informal words barmy** *I'd been barmy about her since we were at school.*
    crazy *She's crazy about animals of all kinds.*
    nuts *He wants to marry you. He's nuts about you.*

VOCABULARY CHOICES
[meaning 1]
• **Mad as a hatter** is a **simile**. It is also a phrase that has been used so often that it has very little impact – a **cliché**. It is now also used in a joking and affectionate way

about someone who behaves in a silly way, rather than someone who is really mad.

magic [noun]

1 black magic

sorcery *tales of sorcery*

witchcraft *She says that she practises witchcraft.*

2 He performs magic.

conjuring *She taught me some basic conjuring.*

illusion *His interest in illusion began at the age of nine.*

sleight of hand *card tricks done with sleight of hand*

main [adjective]

central *the film's central idea*

chief *Our chief concern is safety.*

essential *This is the essential point he is making.*

primary *Money is not my primary concern.*

prime *The daughter is still the police's prime suspect.*

principal *The telephone is our principal method of communication.*

◆ **Formal word paramount** *Good behaviour is of paramount importance.*

make¹ [verb]

1 a factory making cars

build *They're building a new runway at the airport.*

construct *The frame is constructed of steel.*

create *a new perfume created by Dior*

manufacture *Where will the new car be manufactured?*

produce *The engines are produced in Britain.*

put together *I'm trying to put this wardrobe together.*

2 make trouble • I made a mistake.

bring about *We need to bring these changes about quickly.*

cause *I didn't mean to cause you any bother.*

◆ **Formal word generate** *The programme generated a lot of complaints.*

3 They made him do it.

force *Harris forced me to pay the money.*

press-gang *I had been press-ganged into helping them out.*

pressurize *We felt pressurized into inviting them.*

push *Arthur had been pushed into retiring.*

◆ **Formal words coerce** *She felt she had been coerced into doing it.*

compel *I did feel compelled to apologize.*

oblige *The law obliges you to pay tax.*

4 They made her a partner in the firm.

appoint *She was appointed director in 1999.*

elect *a meeting to elect a new secretary*

◆ **Formal word install** *She was safely installed in her new job.*

5 make money • make a profit

earn *How much did she earn last year?*

gain *His fortune has been gained over a period of years.*

◆ **Formal words acquire** *How was all this wealth acquired?*

obtain *The money was obtained illegally.*

6 Two plus two makes four.

add up to *What do these numbers add up to?*

amount to *Two jars only amounts to just over a litre.*

VOCABULARY CHOICES

[meaning 1]

• The word **create** suggests that a lot of skill and thought has gone into making something. It can be a good word to use in job applications and CVs.

make² [noun]

We have the same make of motorbike.

brand *a more expensive brand of ice cream*

sort *What sort of car does she drive?*

Mm

male [adjective]
boyish *She has a rather boyish face.*
manly *We think of physical strength as a manly characteristic.*
masculine *Anne had slightly masculine features.*

man¹ [noun]
1 I don't know that man.
fellow *Archie was rather an odd fellow.*
gentleman *Would you serve this gentleman here?*
◆ **Informal words bloke** *He's quite a friendly bloke.*
chap *I like Sanjit. He's a nice chap.*
guy *one of those guys who never does washing–up*
2 All men are equal.
human being *All human beings have the same rights.*
individual *Each individual will react differently.*
person *The disease is passed from person to person.*
3 the evolution of man
humanity *What would humanity do with this knowledge?*
human race *The book is the story of the human race.*
mankind *All mankind could be wiped out.*
◆ **Formal word humankind** *Such a disaster would mean the end of mankind.*

man² [verb]
man the lifeboats
crew *The ship is crewed entirely by women.*
operate *Who operates the big guns?*
staff *Our offices are staffed round the clock.*

VOCABULARY CHOICES
• You can use the word **crew** when a big group of people are running something, especially a ship, plane or other large vehicle.
• You usually use the word **operate** when

someone is working a machine of some kind.
• A place is **staffed** by the people who work in it.
• Many people avoid using the word **man** in this way because it might suggest that only men are doing the work.

manage [verb]
1 We managed to do it.
succeed *Firefighters succeeded in controlling the blaze.*
◆ **Formal word accomplish** *Have you accomplished everything you set out to do?*
2 *managing a small company* • *manage a major project*
direct *Who directed the rescue operation?*
govern *No single party will govern the country.*
oversee *Frank will oversee the closure of the Leeds factory.*
run *Jan runs things while I'm away.*
supervise *The job involves supervising staff.*
3 We can't manage on less than two hundred pounds per week.
cope *He couldn't cope without an assistant.*
get by *They don't have much but they get by.*
make do *If we can't afford new clothes, we just make do with what we've got.*
survive *I don't know how they survive without running water.*
◆ **Formal word fare** *How did you fare in that heat?*

VOCABULARY CHOICES
[meaning 3]
• If you say someone can **cope**, you are suggesting that they are calm or organized enough to deal with something.
• If someone **gets by** or **makes do**, they

Mm

manage to do something by using things they already have. These phrases give the impression that someone is trying very hard and doesn't have very much.

• You use the word **survive** to emphasize that someone's situation is very difficult, and they have to work very hard or be very lucky just to stay alive.

manager [noun]
director the director of a local company
executive a note from the chief executive
governor The minister spoke to the prison governor.
head Which teacher is the head of the English Department?
supervisor Ask the supervisor if you can have the afternoon off.
♦ **Informal word boss** Sharon is a very strict boss.

Mm

manners [noun]
behaviour We'll expect good behaviour from the children.
conduct Your conduct has been appalling.
♦ **Formal word etiquette** They don't know the rules of etiquette.

many [adjective]
countless There were countless reasons why it wouldn't work.
numerous The same thing has happened on numerous occasions.
several There are several differences between them.
various We had letters of support from various people.
♦ **Informal terms lots of** Lots of people disagreed.
umpteen I've told you umpteen times not to do that.

mark¹ [noun]
1 The wax left marks on the table. • marks on her skin
blemish The powder covers up blemishes on your face.

smudge a few ink smudges on the page
speck specks of dirt on the tablecloth
spot spots of paint on the mirror
stain There's a stain on this shirt.
2 a mark of good quality
badge A scar on the cheek is seen as a badge of honour.
emblem The crown is an emblem of royalty.
indication Five stars is an indication that a hotel is of a high standard.
sign The black belt is a sign that you have reached the highest level.
symbol A gift is given as a symbol of friendship.

mark² [verb]
1 marked the paintwork
stain Red wine will stain the carpet.
2 marked with a kite symbol
identify The drink is identified by its pear-shaped bottle.
label foods labelled 'organic'
stamp documents stamped 'Top Secret'

marriage [noun]
wedding We celebrate the wedding of Joanna and Mark.
♦ **Formal words matrimony** These two are considering matrimony.
wedlock a couple joined in wedlock

marry [verb]
get married She got married to Andrew the following spring.
♦ **Formal word wed** The royal couple will wed at the abbey.
♦ **Informal terms get hitched** We hear you're getting hitched!
tie the knot We're in no hurry to tie the knot.

VOCABULARY CHOICES
• **Wed** is an old-fashioned word that is sometimes used in poems and stories. It is also often used in newspapers. However, it is not often used in speaking.

• The informal terms **get hitched** and **tie the knot** are quite light-hearted and humorous in tone.

match[1] [verb]

These colours don't match.

agree *The totals should agree.*

correspond *Each number in the first set should correspond with one in the second set.*

go together *These socks don't go together.*

match[2] [noun]

a rugby match

contest *an exciting contest between two top players*

game *a game of football*

tie *a cup tie between two local teams*

mate [noun]

1 my best mate

companion *She became a close companion of mine.*

friend *one of her school friends*

partner *Hold hands with your partner.*

♦ **Formal words colleague** *a present from a colleague at work*

comrade *Because you're comrades, you stick up for each other.*

♦ **Informal words buddy** *Frank and I were bosom buddies.*

pal *going to the pub with a few pals*

2 find a mate for life

partner *Do you live with your partner?*

♦ **Formal word spouse** *Your spouse would receive the money if you died.*

3 a carpenter's mate

assistant *the manager's assistant*

helper *She works as a classroom helper.*

matter[1] [noun]

1 a very serious matter

affair *the embarrassing affair with the lost key*

business *Have you heard about this business with Tom and the manager?*

incident *the number of violent incidents in the area*

subject *The subject of money never came up.*

2 What's the matter?

difficulty *There's some difficulty with old passports.*

problem *Is there a problem with my credit card?*

trouble *This new motor shouldn't give you any trouble.*

worry *The worry is that there won't be enough money.*

3 plant matter

material *printed material such as newspapers and magazines*

stuff *The silk she showed us was really nice stuff.*

matter[2] [verb]

It doesn't matter what people think.

be important *If they've got your size, is the colour important?*

count *My opinions count for something too.*

make a difference *A single vote can make a difference.*

mean something *She sent you a reply and that means something.*

mature[1] [adjective]

1 a mature young man • a mature attitude

adult *She has a very adult approach to homework.*

grown-up *He's been very grown-up about the whole business.*

2 mature trees

full-grown *A full-grown tiger can weigh up to 500 pounds.*

fully grown *When fully grown, the plant will be about three feet tall.*

mature[2] [verb]

1 The cheese improves as it matures.

age *The wine hasn't aged very well.*

mellow *The flavour will mellow slightly.*

ripen *Give the fruit time to ripen.*

Mm

Types of meal:

Everyday meals:	supper	picnic	snack
breakfast	tea	takeaway	**Formal meals:**
dinner	**Informal meals:**	TV dinner	banquet
evening meal	barbecue	**Light meals:**	luncheon
lunch	buffet	brunch	tea party

2 He's matured into a fine young man.
come of age Your daughter has really come of age.
develop Janice is developing into a beautiful young woman.
grow up I can't believe how much Kevin has grown up.

meal [noun]
See the box above.

mean¹ [adjective]
1 He's too mean to spend the money.
miserly the miserly Scrooge
penny-pinching his penny-pinching attitude
stingy He didn't want to appear stingy.
♦ **Informal words tight** He's too tight to buy a round of drinks.
tight-fisted her tight-fisted friend
2 a mean thing to say
cruel She's very cruel to her dog.
nasty There's a nasty side to her character.
unkind It's an unkind thing to do to a friend.
unpleasant Some of the teachers are a bit unpleasant.

mean² [verb]
1 A red light means 'stop'.
indicate The sign indicates that there are low-flying aircraft.
represent A white dove represents peace.
signify What does the skull and crossbones signify?
stand for St. stands for 'street'.
2 What do you mean to do?
intend I didn't intend to upset you.
plan He planned to cause trouble all along.

measure [verb]
assess The damage was assessed at thousands of pounds.
calculate She calculated the distance as ten miles.
determine Can you determine how long the work will take?
gauge The device gauges the amount of rain that has fallen.
quantify We tried to quantify the cost of running a car.

medicine [noun]
drug The drug has already saved lives.
medication The doctor changed my medication.
prescription Pick up your prescription at the pharmacy.
remedy a clinic specializing in natural remedies
♦ **Technical term pharmaceutical** the pharmaceutical industry

VOCABULARY CHOICES
• **Medication** is quite a formal word that doctors often use to mean medicines of any kind.
• You use the word **pharmaceutical** when you are talking about medicines as things that companies make, rather than as things that people take.

medium [adjective]
average beer of average strength
middle players of middle ability
♦ **Formal word intermediate** classes for intermediate students

meet [verb]
1 I met him in the street.

Mm

164

come across I came across Tim at the meeting.
run across Guess who I ran across at the station?
run into She's always running into old boyfriends.
♦ **Formal word** **encounter** the last time Holmes had encountered the professor
♦ **Informal term** **bump into** I bumped into her at the farmers' market.
2 We'll all meet at the station.
assemble We'll assemble in the playground.
congregate Fans were congregating round the stage door.
gather Protesters gathered outside the factory.
♦ **Formal word** **convene** The clubs convene here tonight for a special meeting.
3 meet in the middle
come together The two rivers come together a few miles further south.
connect This is where the tubes connect.
join The legs of the table have to join under the top.
touch The two ends of the rods must be touching.
♦ **Formal word** **converge** The two motorways then converge.
4 It is difficult to meet the demands that everyone makes.
answer A bigger house would answer the family's needs.
fill a product that fills a gap in the market
fulfil The day fulfilled our expectations.
satisfy The answer satisfied his curiosity.
suit products to suit the needs of different customers

meeting [noun]
assembly the General Assembly of the Church of Scotland
conference the Labour Party conference
gathering a gathering of parents in the school hall

get-together Some old school friends have organized a get-together.
rally a mass rally of striking miners
♦ **Formal word** **convention** a StarTrek fans' convention

VOCABULARY CHOICES

- A **gathering** is any occasion when people come together in order to do something. It is a slightly formal word.
- **Get-together** is a more informal word for an occasion when people come together, especially a small group of friends coming together to have a nice time. You might use the word when talking to friends, or in an invitation.

---

mend [verb]
fix How much will it cost to fix the TV?
repair A man came to repair the cooker.

mess [noun]
1 It took a long time to clear up the mess after the party.
chaos The bar was in chaos after the fight.
clutter Get rid of all that clutter in your room.
untidiness My dad can't stand untidiness.
2 He got himself into a mess with money.
difficulty If you get into difficulty, call for help.
disorder The government was in a state of complete disorder.
predicament This is an awkward predicament to be in.
shambles The applications procedure is a shambles.
trouble We got a signal that a ship was in trouble.
♦ **Formal word** **disarray** The whole system is in disarray.
♦ **Informal word** **fix** I'm in a bit of a fix.

messy [adjective]
chaotic Because there was no chairman, the meeting was a bit chaotic.
cluttered Their house is so cluttered!

Mm

disorganized She's quite a disorganized person.
grubby The dog put his grubby paws on my clean shirt.
untidy Why is your room so untidy?
♦ **Formal words dishevelled** She arrived looking wet and dishevelled.
unkempt Employers will be put off by his unkempt appearance.

middle[1] [adjective]
the middle section of the film
central the central area of the target
halfway the halfway point in the journey

middle[2] [noun]
a pole in the middle of the garden
centre a table in the centre of the room
core the Earth's core
heart a country in the heart of Europe
mid-point the mid-point in the process

mild [adjective]
1 mild manners
gentle He's a very gentle animal.
placid Sean has a very placid temperament.
soft a soft voice
2 mild weather
fair more fair weather to come
pleasant very pleasant temperatures for the time of year
warm It's quite warm for an autumn day.

mind[1] [noun]
1 My mind wasn't on the task.
attention Keep your attention focused on the job.
concentration Young children don't have much concentration.
head My body's here but my head is elsewhere.
thoughts Our thoughts are with the families of the victims.
2 Asha has a brilliant mind.
intelligence We were impressed by her intelligence.

♦ **Formal word intellect** a man of great intellect
♦ **Informal word brains** Frank doesn't have the brains to think up such a plan.

mind[2] [verb]
1 He didn't mind the noise.
object to Local people objected to the mast.
resent We resent the money other clubs receive.
take offence at We took offence at being called foreigners.
2 mind the step
be careful of Be careful of low branches.
look out for Look out for holes in the road.
watch Watch the traffic when you're crossing.
watch out for If you're using the bathroom, watch out for spiders.
3 Who is minding the shop?
guard Who was guarding the bags while you were away?
look after A neighbour can look after the kids.
take care of We need someone to take care of the cat.
♦ **Informal phrase keep an eye on** Joan keeps an eye on things while the manager is away.

miserable [adjective]
1 The news made him miserable.
crushed After he heard the news, Tim looked crushed.
dejected We left the meeting feeling very dejected.
heartbroken She left him and he was heartbroken.
sad Why do she look so sad?
unhappy He's feeling pretty unhappy today.
♦ **Formal word despondent** The team are despondent after yet another defeat.
2 a miserable, wet day
depressing a depressing result

dismal *the dismal news that our bid had failed*
dreary *grey dreary weather*
gloomy *The school's future looks gloomy.*

miss [verb]

1 He missed his chance.
  let slip *She had let her opportunity slip.*
  lose *You might lose the right to keep the money.*
  pass up *I didn't want to pass up the chance of seeing her again.*
2 The car just missed a tree.
  avoid *They stayed behind the wall to avoid attack.*
  dodge *I ran across the drive, dodging puddles.*
  evade *Our group managed to evade capture.*
3 He is missing his family.
  long to *I was longing to hear her voice again.*
  pine for *The dog sits by the door and pines for her.*

missing [adjective]

  absent *How many children are absent today?*
  lost *Let's face it — the key is lost.*
  ♦ **Formal term unaccounted for** *Five soldiers were unaccounted for.*

mistake [noun]

  blunder *Forgetting her birthday was an embarrassing blunder.*
  error *There's an error in the calculation.*
  fault *There's a fault in the fabric.*
  slip *Sorry. That was a slip of the tongue.*
  ♦ **Formal word oversight** *The date is wrong. That was an oversight on my part.*
  ♦ **Informal words clanger** *I was nervous about the kids dropping a clanger.*
  gaffe *an enormous gaffe, like calling the Queen 'love'*
  howler *TV presenters are worried about making a howler in front of millions of people.*

mix [verb]

1 Mix the ingredients in a bowl. • The flavours mix well.
  blend *Blend the sugar with the butter.*
  combine *If you combine blue and yellow, you get green.*
  merge *Three companies merged to form Global plc.*
  mingle *The paints mingle to produce a strange colour.*
  ♦ **Formal word fuse** *The two teams fused to form a single team.*
2 He doesn't mix with the locals much.
  associate *Jules was associating with criminals.*
  mingle *Helen went off to mingle with the guests.*
  socialize *We haven't been out for months — we don't socialize much.*
  ♦ **Formal word fraternize** *Soldiers were not allowed to fraternize with the enemy.*
  ♦ **Informal word hobnob** *He got the chance to hobnob with Hollywood actors.*

mixed [adjective]

1 a dog of mixed breed
  blended *a blended whisky*
  ♦ **Formal word hybrid** *The plant is a hybrid variety.*
2 mixed biscuits
  assorted *kitchens available in assorted styles*
  diverse *a diverse bunch of people*
  miscellaneous *boxes of miscellaneous items for sale*
  varied *a varied collection of CDs*

mixture [noun]

  blend *The colour is a blend of blue and pink.*
  combination *You need a combination of patience and skill.*
  mix *Add water to the sand and cement mix.*
  ♦ **Formal words assortment** *She had an assortment of pens in her pocket.*

Mm

concoction *Stella had made punch. It was an evil-looking concoction.*
fusion *The music is a fusion of African and Latin American styles.*
◆ **Informal terms** **hotchpotch** *a hotchpotch of nationalities: Scots, Irish and Italians*
mixed bag *The show is a mixed bag of music, comedy and dance.*
◆ **Technical terms** **alloy** *Brass is an alloy of copper and zinc.*
compound *poisonous chemical compounds*

moan [verb]
1 *People were crying and moaning.*
groan *Hughes groaned with the effort of lifting the box.*
howl *patients howling in pain*
wail *Women stood at the graveside and wailed.*
whimper *You could hear the dog whimpering outside.*
2 (informal) *She's always moaning about something or other.*
complain *He always finds something to complain about.*
grumble *Dad grumbled about the slow service.*
whine *There's no use whining — we'll just have to wait.*
◆ **Informal words** **gripe** *What's she been griping about now?*
whinge *I'm fed up of you lot whingeing.*

modern [adjective]
current *Current experts have a different opinion.*
fashionable *shops selling fashionable furniture*
latest *the latest technology*
new *It's not a very new idea.*
state-of-the-art *a kitchen with a state-of-the-art cooker*
◆ **Formal words** **contemporary** *contemporary styles*

innovative *innovative designs*
◆ **Informal words** **hip** *She always wears such hip clothes.*
newfangled *I don't like these newfangled mobile phones.*
trendy *We met in some trendy bar.*

modest [adjective]
1 *a modest man*
humble *She's very humble about her achievements.*
quiet *The professor was a quiet character.*
reserved *Andrew was very reserved in company.*
◆ **Formal words** **self-effacing** *Although she seemed self-effacing, she could be strong-willed.*
unassuming *Most of the actors were very unassuming people.*
2 *a modest lifestyle*
ordinary *They live in an ordinary little house.*
small *He had a small amount of money to invest.*

moisture [noun]
condensation *She wiped the condensation off the window.*
damp *the smell of damp in the cellar*
humidity *the humidity of a Florida summer*
water *Water was running down the walls.*
water vapour *Steam is just water vapour.*

moment [noun]
minute *Dinner will be ready in a minute.*
second *A few seconds later, we heard another noise.*
split second *For a split second, I thought he was going to cry.*
◆ **Formal word** **instant** *In an instant, the police had arrived.*
◆ **Informal words** **sec** *Hang on a sec. I can't find the key.*
tick *I'll be back in a tick.*

money [noun]
banknotes *a suitcase full of banknotes*

cash How much cash do you have on you?
currency We changed our pounds for local currency.
wealth a woman of great wealth
◆ **Formal word funds** You don't have enough funds in your account.
◆ **Informal words dosh** Today's players earn loads of dosh.
readies Have you brought the readies?
◆ **Technical word capital** We raised enough capital to buy the land.

monster [noun]
brute Only a complete brute could say something like that.
fiend He was the fiend who gave the order for the killings.
ogre We imagined he'd be some sort of ogre.
villain The kids thought of him as a right villain.

mood [noun]
1 the mood of the country
frame of mind We were in a relaxed frame of mind.
state of mind a state of mind I would describe as 'depressed'
◆ **Formal word disposition** her cheerful disposition
2 in one of his moods
bad mood She's been in a bad mood all morning.
temper We'd never seen her in a temper.
the sulks Charlie was having a fit of the sulks.
◆ **Informal terms the blues** She's really got the blues this morning.
the dumps Why are you looking so down in the dumps?

moody [adjective]
irritable Is he normally this irritable?
morose They teased her and she became morose.

short-tempered It's no fun having a short-tempered boss.
sulky Sarah could be very sulky at times.
sullen a sullen expression on her face
temperamental He was often a temperamental actor.
touchy He's a bit touchy about his baldness.
unpredictable Ben is unpredictable — he might not be able to take the joke.
◆ **Informal words crabby** As he got older, he became crabby.
crotchety a crotchety old aunt

more [adjective]
added cereals with added vitamins
additional You pay an additional two pounds if you book over the phone.
extra They'll pay me £100 extra if I finish the job early.
further It took a further three weeks to build the garage.
increased She sang the second song with increased energy.
◆ **Formal word supplementary** Are there any supplementary charges?

mother[1] [noun]
a young mother and her child
◆ **Formal words matriarch** She was the matriarch ruling the family.
matron a plump, middle-aged matron
◆ **Informal words ma** I'll tell my ma!
mama I was delighted when my baby called me 'mama'.
mum I have to call my mum.
mummy Give the sweets to mummy.

VOCABULARY CHOICES
• The formal word **matron** is often used to emphasize the physical appearance of a mother, but it also suggests the power a mother can have in the home.
• **Matriarch** particularly suggests this power, especially if the mother, rather than a father figure, is in charge of the home.
• The words **mama** and **mummy** suggest

Mm

childish dependency on your mother when they are used in the context of adults.

---

mother² [verb]
He's left home, but she still mothers him.
baby She tends to baby all the children.
fuss over I don't want my parents fussing over me.
pamper If they're pampered, they'll grow up soft.
spoil He must have been spoiled as a child.
◆ **Formal word indulge** You indulge that boy too much.

mouth [noun]
1 open your mouth to speak
jaws His hand was in the animal's jaws.
lips Not a sound came from his lips.
2 the mouth of the cave
entrance The entrance to the tunnel was blocked.
opening The children went through an opening in the wall.

move¹ [verb]
1 move suddenly • move forward
budge The rock wouldn't budge an inch.
go The wagons were going forward.
◆ **Formal words proceed** The car was proceeding along High Road.
progress The little van progressed slowly along the track.
2 moving goods
carry A mule carried our belongings.
transfer The crates will be transferred by helicopter.
transport They transported the boat to the other coast.
◆ **Formal word convey** The coffin was conveyed through the streets by a horse and carriage.
3 They're moving to London.
go away She's going away at the end of the month.
leave It sounds like they're leaving for good.

move house I hate the thought of moving house.
relocate The company has relocated to Bristol.
4 The speech moved her to tears.
affect I was deeply affected by the poem.
touch Her speech touched everyone in the room.
◆ **Formal word stir** We are stirred by the sound of singing in harmony.

move² [noun]
1 work out what the next move should be
action a series of actions that led to war
step Our first step is to get more support.
2 a move to the city
relocation the company's relocation to Glasgow
transfer Keith managed to get a transfer to the York office.

much¹ [adverb]
1 He's feeling much better.
a lot I slept a lot better last night.
considerably The second house was considerably larger.
greatly Her marks have improved greatly.
2 I don't get out much.
a lot Do you go to the cinema a lot?
frequently The toilets are frequently out of order.
often I often miss this bus.

much² [adjective]
I haven't had much luck.
a lot of We didn't have a lot of time for sightseeing.

muddy [adjective]
1 muddy ground
boggy boggy patches on the pitch
marshy These birds live in marshy parts.
swampy Rice grows best in swampy areas.
2 muddy boots
dirty Put those dirty overalls in the wash.
grimy By the end of a game, the strips are grimy.

Types of music:

Modern music:		bebop	operatic
bhangra	pop	blues	orchestral
disco	punk	boogie-woogie	**Country types:**
electronic	rap	honky-tonk	bluegrass
funk	reggae	jazz	country
garage	rock	ragtime	country-and-
grunge	rock 'n' roll	rhythm and blues	western
heavy metal	salsa	swing	**Other types:**
hip-hop	ska	**Classical types:**	folk
house	soul	chamber	gospel
indie	techno	choral	skiffle
nu-metal	trance	classical	world music
	Jazz types:		

mucky Don't put your mucky shoes on the table!

murder[1] [noun]
a vicious murder

assassination the assassination of President Kennedy

killing the killing of innocent people

massacre the massacre of villagers by government forces

◆ **Technical terms homicide** He's been charged with homicide.

manslaughter the crime of manslaughter

VOCABULARY CHOICES
• The word **assassination** is used when someone kills a famous person, especially a politician or leader.

• **Homicide** and **manslaughter** are terms used in the context of the law and in criminal trials.

murder[2] [verb]
the maniac who murdered five women

assassinate Leaders are assassinated and civil wars break out.

butcher He had butchered his own people.

kill Evans killed the man in cold blood.

massacre Over five thousand people were massacred in one day.

slaughter All infected animals were slaughtered.

◆ **Formal word slay** Saint George is pictured slaying a dragon.

VOCABULARY CHOICES
• The words **massacre** and **slaughter** are used when someone kills a lot of people on one occasion. These words have a lot of impact and are often used in newspaper reports.

• **Butcher** is also used in newspaper stories, to increase the sense of horror.

• **Slay** is an old-fashioned word that is sometimes used in stories and poems.

muscular [adjective]
brawny You don't have to be big and brawny to be tough.

burly The officer was a burly man.

hefty He looks heftier now he is training.

powerful An athlete needs a powerful build.

strapping a strapping lad for just sixteen

strong He has such strong arms.

◆ **Informal word beefy** a couple of beefy rugby players

music [noun]
See the box above.

mysterious [adjective]
cryptic a cryptic message that none of us understood

Mm

obscure For some obscure reason, she refused.

odd That's odd – I'm sure I left my keys here.

puzzling These numbers are puzzling. What do they mean?

strange We saw a strange shape in the shadows.

weird A weird noise was coming from the bathroom.

mystery [noun]

conundrum students struggling with a mathematical conundrum

puzzle It was a puzzle how he had got the job.

riddle We had to solve the riddle of where the money had gone.

◆ **Formal word** **enigma** Her past remains an enigma.

Mm

N

nag [verb]
  criticize My boyfriend continually criticized me and destroyed my self-confidence.
  goad She goaded me into joining her although I didn't want to.
  harass constantly harassed by an interfering sister
  pester Jimmy pestered me to buy him a bike.
  plague Children often plague you with constant questions.
  scold My wife often scolds me about hogging the remote control.
  ♦ **Formal word upbraid** I was often upbraided by my boss for carelessness.
  ♦ **Informal word henpeck** Your partner may henpeck you about changing your bad habits.

naked [adjective]
  bare If you leave your shoulders bare they may burn.
  nude nude sunbathing
  stark naked She came into the changing room when I was stark naked.
  stripped I got stripped and changed into my tracksuit.
  unclothed He painted unclothed figures.
  uncovered uncovered arms
  undressed She got undressed and stepped into the bath.
  ♦ **Informal phrase in the altogether** I opened the curtains, forgetting I was in the altogether!

name[1] [noun]
  1 What's the cat's name?
  label I resent the label 'housewife'.
  term the scientific term for 'chalk'
  title Her title is Office Manager.
  2 They have a good name for service.
  renown a hotel of great renown, where the rich and famous stay
  reputation He has the reputation of being a hard player. • The report damaged the company's good reputation.
  repute a singer of some repute who has performed all over the world

name[2] [verb]
  1 name the baby
  baptize They baptized the baby 'Robert'.
  call I called her Annie after her aunt. • a village called Stockton
  christen She was christened Sarah, but prefers to be called Sadie.
  dub Edinburgh was dubbed 'festival city'.
  label I object to being labelled a coward.
  term They were termed temporary workers.
  2 name the culprit
  cite He cited his smoking as the cause of his illness.
  identify Marco refused to identify the ringleader to the police.
  specify She did not specify her reasons for not coming.

Nn

narrow [adjective]

1 a narrow passage
confined stuck in a confined space
constricted a constricted cell with no room to move
tight a tight space • a tight gap

2 a narrow waist • a narrow margin
slender The goal gave them a slender advantage.
slim slim hips
thin a thin book of poems

3 a narrow outlook
bigoted bigoted views against other religions
narrow-minded He's narrow-minded, and hostile to other cultures.

nasty [adjective]

1 a nasty smell
disgusting That fish smells disgusting.
foul The milk was off and tasted foul.
noxious noxious fumes
offensive The medicine has an offensive smell.
sickening The story was so sickening I actually felt ill.

♦ **Formal words objectionable** the objectionable job of cleaning the toilets
repellent The idea of his company was repellent, so I did not meet him.
repulsive picking his toenails, and other repulsive habits

2 a nasty thing to happen
horrible The accident was a horrible sight.
unpleasant The fall must have been an unpleasant experience for you.

3 a nasty remark
malicious She was malicious and intended to cause trouble. • a malicious attempt to put the blame on me
mean It was mean of you to steal gran's money.
spiteful His spiteful remarks hurt everyone's feelings.

vicious a vicious temper

natural [adjective]

1 He spoke in his natural voice.
normal Fear is a normal response to a threat.
ordinary an ordinary young boy, with ordinary hobbies
regular a child's regular reaction to strangers
typical typical Scottish weather
usual It's not usual for winter to be so warm.

2 a natural ability
inborn an inborn sense of self-esteem
instinctive Parents have an instinctive urge to protect their children.
intuitive an intuitive understanding of how people think
native His native wit helped him through his difficulties.

♦ **Formal words inherent** He thinks badness is inherent in people.
innate innate footballing skills which can't be learned

3 natural materials
pure pure honey, straight from the hive
unprocessed Try to eat more unprocessed foods.
unrefined Unrefined rice is brown in colour.

4 She's always so natural.
genuine He's always genuine and never puts on an act.
open open and honest with everyone she meets
sincere She's very sincere, always means what she says.
unaffected Despite his fame, he remains unaffected, with no airs and graces.

naughty [adjective]

1 a naughty child
bad Tommy was so bad today we sent him to bed.
badly behaved When she is badly

Nn

behaved she disrupts the whole class.
disobedient *a disobedient little boy, never doing as he's told*
mischievous *always up to no good, playing mischievous pranks*
wayward *a wayward child, always getting into trouble*
2 a naughty word
indecent *He made an indecent gesture.*
obscene *The book was so obscene it was banned.*
smutty *a smutty magazine*

near [adjective]
1 near neighbours
adjacent *adjacent rooms in the hotel • the house adjacent to mine*
adjoining *the adjoining property • the office adjoining ours*
alongside *the car alongside mine in the car park*
close *These houses are close to each other.*
nearby *a nearby town*
neighbouring *the neighbouring village*
2 The exams are near.
approaching *the approaching end of the century*
coming *this coming Wednesday*
forthcoming *forthcoming events in the town*
imminent *A general election is imminent.*
impending *an impending war*
not far away *Hallowe'en is not far away.*

nearby[1] [adjective]
They ran down a nearby alley.
accessible *Local schools are accessible.*
adjacent *adjacent rooms in the hotel • the house adjacent to mine*
adjoining *the adjoining property • the office adjoining ours*
close by *The shops are close by.*
convenient *Keep this in a convenient place. • a house convenient for schools*
handy *I keep my diary handy. • The house*

is handy for the shops.
near *The railway station is near.*
neighbouring *the neighbouring village*

VOCABULARY CHOICES
- If you use the word **accessible** to describe something, you suggest that it is easy to reach. The words **convenient** and **handy** suggest that because something is near, it makes life easier.
- Estate agents often use all these words when they describe the location of a house, to make it sound appealing.

nearby[2] [adverb]
Find out if there's a station nearby.
at close quarters *The sides were fighting at close quarters.*
close at hand *My mother lives close at hand.*
near *My birthday is coming near.*
within reach *The finishing line came within reach.*

nearly [adverb]
almost *almost five years old*
as good as *The job is as good as done.*
just about *We have just about enough time.*
more or less *They've more or less finished the job.*
practically *The room was practically full.*
virtually *He was virtually penniless.*
well-nigh *It was well-nigh six o'clock when we arrived.*

neat [adjective]
clean *Cats are very clean animals.*
orderly *an orderly room*
shipshape *She left all her files shipshape when she retired.*
smart *a smart suit*
spruce *a spruce young man • You're looking very spruce!*
tidy *a tidy room • a tidy person*
trim *a trim moustache and beard*
♦ **Informal word spick-and-span** *She*

Nn

175

made the whole house spick-and-span.

necessary [adjective]

1 Give only the necessary details.
crucial *It is crucial that you remember to switch the machine off.*
essential *Strong boots are essential for hillwalking.*
needed *Our funds were given a needed boost.*
required *the required standards of hygiene*
vital *vital food supplies • Speed is vital to our plan.*
◆ **Formal word indispensable** *Our first aid team provides indispensable help.*
2 It is necessary that you attend.
compulsory *Attendance at school is compulsory.*
◆ **Formal words imperative** *It is imperative that you contact us by Friday.*
obligatory *National service is obligatory in some countries.*

VOCABULARY CHOICES
[meaning 1]
• Words such as **crucial** and **vital** might be used to emphasize strongly that something is necessary, and to persuade others that this is the case: *It is vital that we raise more funds to do this crucial work.*

necessity [noun]
essential *Is a television an essential?*
need *Food is one of our basic needs.*
obligation *You are under no obligation to buy this.*
requirement *It is a legal requirement that your brakes work properly.*
◆ **Formal word prerequisite** *An interest in people is a prerequisite for a writer.*

need¹ [verb]
We don't need anyone interfering.
call for *Your rudeness was not called for.*
demand *This puzzle demands careful thought.*

have need of *I have need of your help.*
necessitate *Rebuilding the castle will necessitate a lot of money.*
require *Is there anything else you require, sir?*
want *This wall wants a coat of paint.*

need² [noun]
1 a need for caution
call *There is no call for shepherds nowadays.*
demand *There is a demand for more modern mobile phones.*
requirement *Our company will supply all your requirements.*
2 the family's needs
essential *Is a television an essential?*
necessity *A warm coat is a necessity in this weather.*
◆ **Formal words prerequisite** *An interest in people is a prerequisite for a writer.*
requisite *bathroom requisites*
3 a need for equipment
lack *a lack in funds*
shortage *a water shortage*
◆ **Formal word insufficiency** *an insufficiency in food supplies*

needy [adjective]
deprived *deprived areas of the city*
destitute *They were left destitute when he died.*
impoverished *His betting left him impoverished.*
poor *the poor nations of the world*
poverty-stricken *Her family are poverty-stricken.*
◆ **Formal words disadvantaged** *government aid for disadvantaged families*
underprivileged *raising funds for underprivileged children*

VOCABULARY CHOICES
• The words **destitute** and **impoverished** have a lot of impact, as they suggest that someone or something is extremely needy.

- The word **poverty-stricken** also suggests this, and it is often used to stir people's emotions. It is sometimes used in newspaper reports, or in leaflets from charities.
- The words **disadvantaged** and **underprivileged** are more often used in formal writing such as government reports.

neglect[1] [verb]
1 He neglects his family.
ignore She ignored all my advice.
leave alone The couple left the children alone to fend for themselves.
pass over Did she resent being passed over for promotion again?
◆ **Formal word** **disregard** He keeps disregarding my warnings.
2 Don't neglect your duty.
fail He failed to inform the police of the accident.
forget I forgot to feed the cat.
shirk shirking the responsibility of making a decision
◆ **Informal term** **let slide** I let my chores slide during the holidays.

VOCABULARY CHOICES
[meaning 1]
- The term **pass over** is frequently used when a candidate for a job has been overlooked, especially for a better job in the same company. The term can hint that this is unfair, and that the person is good enough for the job.

neglect[2] [noun]
children in danger of serious neglect
carelessness His carelessness when driving could cause an accident.
disregard utter disregard for my feelings
indifference His inattention to his studies meant he failed his exam.
negligence They did not look after the children and were found guilty of negligence.
slackness slackness of discipline at home

- slackness in getting things done
◆ **Technical term** **dereliction of duty** The sergeant was accused of dereliction of duty.

negotiate [verb]
bargain We bargained with management and won a pay rise.
confer Staff conferred with the headmaster about plans for the school.
consult He consulted with me about what he had to do next.
deal I have dealt with this company for years.
discuss a meeting to discuss future plans
settle Have you settled with the builders when the work will start?
work out We worked out an agreement among ourselves.
◆ **Formal words** **arbitrate** asked to arbitrate in the dispute between workers and management
mediate The USA is trying to mediate between the two countries.

negotiation [noun]
bargaining bargaining between unions and management
conference a conference of surgeons
consultation The law will be passed after public consultation.
dealings We have not mentioned money in our dealings.
discussion discussion between heads of state
◆ **Formal word** **arbitration** The dispute has gone to arbitration.

nerve [noun]
1 I lost my nerve.
courage He hadn't the courage to tell his mother he'd failed.
daring We feared for her safety but couldn't help admiring her daring.
fearlessness great fearlessness in battle
mettle He is obviously a man of mettle.

Nn

nerve-racking ➡ net

pluck *She showed a lot of pluck in taking part.*
spirit *He reacted with spirit and improved his game.*
♦ **Informal word guts** *He's got a lot of guts, fighting his illness like that.*
2 What a nerve he's got!
boldness *the boldness of their plan of attack*
cheek *He had the cheek to refuse me entrance.*
impertinence *The child was scolded for her impertinence.*
impudence *The impudence of the child!*
insolence *The pupils showed laziness and insolence.*
♦ **Formal word audacity** *They had the audacity to ignore my letter.*

VOCABULARY CHOICES
[meaning 1]
• The words **mettle** and **pluck** are rather old-fashioned words, and they are usually used in an admiring way. You may come across these words in stories.

Nn

nerve-racking [adjective]
frightening *a frightening fairground ride*
stressful *Waiting for exam results can be stressful.*
tense *a tense situation in which neither side will give in*
trying *It's a trying time, what with dad being in hospital.*
worrying *His reckless behaviour is worrying for his mother.*

nerves [noun]
anxiety *She was filled with anxiety about her child's health.*
fretfulness *Your father's fretfulness is down to your behaviour.*
nervousness *her nervousness at travelling by air*
strain *the strain she felt looking after her mother*

stress *suffering from exam stress*
tension *his tension at waiting to discover if he had won*
worry *a face marked by worry*

nervous [adjective]
1 I'm nervous about the exam.
agitated *She felt agitated in his presence.*
anxious *I'm anxious about the future.*
apprehensive *He is rather apprehensive about his interview.*
jumpy *Deepak has been jumpy and irritable recently.*
on edge *She was on edge waiting for her results.*
tense *The crowd was tense with excitement.*
uneasy *They spent an uneasy day waiting for news.*
worried *He gave me a worried look.*
♦ **Informal word jittery** *She gets jittery alone in the house at night.*
2 a nervous type of person
excitable *a very excitable dog that would often bite*
highly-strung *He was so highly-strung he jumped at the slightest noise.*
neurotic *I hate working with him — he's so neurotic about being late.*
tense *She is a very tense person.*
♦ **Informal word nervy** *The horse is rather nervy.*

VOCABULARY CHOICES
[meaning 2]
• The word **highly-strung** is often used to describe someone who is easily upset, without saying so bluntly or hurtfully.
• You have to be careful if you use the word **neurotic** to describe someone, as you are suggesting that they are mentally ill and so the word can offend people.

net¹ [noun]
fishing net
lace *a shawl of lace*

lattice *a lattice of wood for the roses to climb up*
mesh *tights with a very fine mesh*
netting *Wire netting keeps the chickens in the yard.*
network *a network of roads*
web *a web of lacy material*

net² [adjective]
net pay
after tax *I earn £200 per week after tax.*
clear *She made a clear profit on the sale.*
final *He made a final loss in his share dealings.*

new [adjective]
1 *new ideas*
different *Get me a different book.*
fresh *a fresh look at the problem*
original *Some original thinking will solve the puzzle.*
unfamiliar *an unfamiliar face in the school*
♦ **Formal words** **innovative** *He is full of innovative ideas.*
novel *a novel approach to cooking*
2 *new clothes*
brand-new *He has a brand-new car.*
mint *a coat in mint condition*
unused *an unused wedding dress for sale*
3 *new technology*
advanced *the most advanced computer software available*
latest *the latest ideas in fashion*
modern *a kitchen with all modern appliances*
recent *recent developments in science*
up-to-date *Is this the most up-to-date phone book we have?*
up-to-the-minute *I want an up-to-the-minute mobile phone.*
♦ **Informal word** **newfangled** *I hate these newfangled gadgets.*

VOCABULARY CHOICES
[meaning 1]
• **Fresh**, **innovative**, **novel** and **original**

are all used in a complimentary way to describe something new that is quite clever, or that seems to work well.
• **Unfamiliar** is less complimentary, as it hints that you are unsure of this new thing.

news [noun]
1 *news in the local paper*
bulletin *a bulletin on the radio*
release *There will be an official release on the prince's health later.*
report *a report on today's sports events*
statement *The Prime Minister will make a statement shortly.*
story *scandalous stories in the tabloids*
♦ **Technical term** **dispatch** *Dispatches came in from the front line of the battle.*
2 *Any news on how John is feeling?* • *Tell me all your news.*
gossip *What's the gossip from work?*
information *I get the latest information from television.*
latest *Have you heard the latest about Diana?*
word *I haven't had any word about how she got on.*
♦ **Formal words** **intelligence** *intelligence about the enemy's movements*
tidings *We bring good tidings from the east.*
♦ **Informal words** **gen** *the latest showbiz gen*
lowdown *What's the lowdown on the party?*

next¹ [adjective]
1 *the next street*
adjacent *adjacent rooms in the hotel* • *the house adjacent to mine*
adjoining *the adjoining property* • *the office adjoining ours*
closest *The closest school is in Norwich.*
nearest *The nearest town is two miles away.*
neighbouring *the neighbouring district*
2 *the next day*

Nn

following *I called her the following morning.*
later *We met again a year later.*
succeeding *We enjoyed the succeeding months after our wedding.*
◆ **Formal words ensuing** *A challenge was made, and people were hurt in the ensuing fight.*
subsequent *We'll discuss the matter in subsequent meetings.*

next[2] [adverb]
What happened next?
afterwards *I was a bit rude, but apologized afterwards.*
later *I'll wash these clothes now, and I'll do the others later.*
subsequently *He was arrested and subsequently released.*
then *I decided to go, then changed my mind.*

nice [adjective]

Nn

1 *a nice person • a nice gesture*
charming *I thought she was a charming woman.*
friendly *I was trying to be friendly towards her.*
kind *It is kind of you to help me.*
likeable *Tom is a friendly and likeable child.*
pleasant *He wasn't very pleasant to me today.*
polite *It is polite to say 'please' and 'thank you'.*
respectable *She comes from a very respectable family.*
2 *a nice place to live*
attractive *an attractive view of the sea*
charming *a charming little village*
pleasant *The city centre isn't very pleasant.*
◆ **Formal word enchanting** *The little island is enchanting.*
3 *We had a nice time.*
delightful *The children put on a delightful show.*

enjoyable *It was an enjoyable evening.*
lovely *It had been a lovely day.*
pleasant *a pleasant chat about our schooldays*
◆ **Formal word agreeable** *It was a good holiday and the weather was agreeable.*

night [noun]
dark *Please come home before dark.*
darkness *He returned home as darkness fell.*
dead of night *She crept out of the house in the dead of night.*
night-time *I find it hard to sleep, even at night-time.*

nip [verb]
bite *The little dog bit at his ankle.*
clip *Clip the older flowers from the plant.*
pinch *She pinched her baby brother and he screamed.*
squeeze *Stop squeezing your spots!*
tweak *She went to the window and tweaked the curtain.*

noise [noun]
1 *a loud noise*
blare *the blare of a trumpet*
clash *the clash of the cymbals*
clatter *the clatter of pots and pans being washed*
cry *He heard a cry in the dark.*
sound *What's that strange sound?*
2 *Stop that constant noise!*
clamour *the clamour of children's voices in the playground*
commotion *There was some commotion in the classroom.*
din *the din of the radio*
hubbub *The tutor came in and the hubbub died down.*
racket *The drums made a terrible racket.*
row *We could hear a row in the street outside.*
uproar *There was uproar in the parliament when the plan was announced.*

noisy [adjective]
boisterous *a house full of boisterous children*
deafening *a deafening clap of thunder*
loud *The party got louder as the night wore on.*
rowdy *The more they drank, the rowdier they became.*
✦ **Formal words clamorous** *the clamorous sound of the bells*
vociferous *a vociferous group of protesters*

VOCABULARY CHOICES
• The word **boisterous** suggests noisy good fun, while **rowdy** suggests rough behaviour and hints at possible trouble.
• **Vociferous** is sometimes used in news reports to describe people who are speaking out to complain about something or to support a cause. It suggests they are doing this in a very loud or forceful way.

nonsense [noun]
1 *You're talking nonsense.*
drivel *How can you believe such drivel?*
gibberish *He was drunk and talking gibberish.*
gobbledegook *The document was in legal gobbledegook and took a bit of working out.*
rubbish *I don't believe any of that rubbish.*
✦ **Informal words claptrap** *What's all this claptrap about a party?*
garbage *He talks a load of garbage.*
rot *Don't talk such rot!*
twaddle *The plot of the book is romantic twaddle.*
✦ **Slang word cobblers** *I thought her speech was a load of cobblers.*
2 *Please stop this nonsense now.*
antics *the silly antics of cartoon characters*
foolishness *Enough of this foolishness!*
silliness *I giggled at the silliness of the situation.*

tomfoolery *the mischief and tomfoolery of children*

VOCABULARY CHOICES
[meaning 1]
• The word **gibberish** is not quite so critical as the others, as it is used when someone is talking in words that don't make sense perhaps because they are drunk or ill.
• **Gobbledegook** is similar in a way — it is used about words or sentences that do not make sense because, for instance, they are in jargon or they are over-complicated. However, it is a critical word which suggests that you find this unnecessary and annoying.
• All the other words are mocking in tone, and they attack the ideas a person has rather than the words they are using.

normal [adjective]
1 *a normal day*
average *How much do you earn in an average week?*
conventional *a conventional dinner suit*
ordinary *It started out as an ordinary day.*
regular *My regular dentist is on holiday.*
routine *routine health checks*
standard *The shirts are available in standard sizes.*
typical *typical British weather*
usual *the usual treatment for the illness*
2 *That girl is not normal.*
natural *His reaction to the news was not natural.*
rational *a rational, sane human being*
reasonable *Any reasonable person would have done the same thing.*
well-adjusted *We all want happy, well-adjusted children.*

nosy, nosey [adjective]
curious *curious onlookers at the scene of the accident*
inquisitive *I'm sorry to sound inquisitive, but I need to know.*

Nn

interfering *I'm an interfering parent, always asking what is going on.*
meddling *I don't want meddling children seeing my papers.*
prying *a pack of prying journalists*
snooping *A snooping bank manager found out what was going on.*

note¹ [noun]

1 a note of absence
communication *a communication from the government*
letter *a letter about council tax increases*
line *Drop a line to Aunt Jane to say 'thank you'.*
memo *a memo from the boss about coming in late*
message *Are there any new messages on the board?*
record *We have no record of your payment.*
reminder *I left him a reminder to feed the cat.*

♦ **Formal word   memorandum** *a memorandum to the President*
2 a note in the margin
annotation *Annotations in the text explain things to the reader.*
comment *He scribbled comments on my exercise book.*
gloss *There are glosses in the margins to define difficult words.*
remark *She wrote her remarks at the end of my essay.*
3 Take note of what I say.
attention *Pay attention to your tutor's advice.*
heed *Take heed of my warnings.*
notice *He took no notice of what I told him.*
regard *You have no regard for my feelings.*

note² [verb]

1 *Your absence was noted.* • *Note what I have to say.*

heed *heed warnings*
mark *Mark what I have to say to you.*
notice *I noticed that she always wore red.*
perceive *We perceived there was a problem.*
see *I saw that you were behind with your payments.*
witness *The incident was witnessed by at least five people.*

♦ **Formal word   observe** *The policeman observed the suspect's movements.*
2 *The police officer noted down the details.*
enter *He entered the figures in the cash book.*
put down *Just put down that we're pleased.*
record *The events were recorded in his diary.*
register *Her arrival was registered in the guest book.*
write down *The journalist wrote down what was said.*

nothing [noun]

nought *an increase of nought point two per cent*
zero *It goes from zero to fifty miles per hour in seconds.*

♦ **Informal word   zilch** *I expected a present but he brought me zilch.*

VOCABULARY CHOICES

• The informal word **zilch** is usually used in a humorous way. Sometimes it hints at a feeling of disappointment or failure: *This record will do zilch in the charts.*

notice¹ [verb]

Do you notice anything different about me today?
detect *I detected a feeling of nervousness about her.*
distinguish *He distinguished an animal in the darkness.*
note *I noted that she wore red all the time.*

Nn

perceive We perceived a change in her attitude.
see He didn't see her come in.
spot I hadn't spotted the mistake.
◆ **Formal words** **discern** I discerned a shape in the fog.
observe I observed him sneaking out the door.

notice² [noun]
1 Did you read the notice about tax cuts?
announcement a government announcement about welfare benefits
communication We received a communication from the general informing us of progress.
declaration a declaration of human rights
information the latest travel information
instruction The instruction came that we were to go ahead.
◆ **Formal word** **notification** notification of gas and electricity charges
2 a notice on the board
advertisement advertisements in the paper
poster a poster advertising a pop concert
sign The sign said 'No entry'.
3 take some notice
attention Pay no attention to what he says.
consideration He drives with no consideration for other motorists.
note I took note of your advice.
◆ **Formal word** **heed** Take heed of my warnings.
4 Give us plenty of notice if you are coming.
warning He arrived without warning on our doorstep.

now [adverb]
1 Do it now!
at once We'll leave at once.
directly I'll move on directly to the matter of your behaviour.
immediately Send back your form immediately.

instantly Get dressed instantly, we have to go.
promptly We'll have to leave promptly if we want to arrive before dark.
straight away I'll do it straight away.
◆ **Formal term** **this instant** I insist on speaking to the manager this instant!
2 You can't get those sweets now.
at present There is no-one here at present.
in the here and now The film is set not in the past but in the here and now.
nowadays Children nowadays have no respect.
these days Everything seems so noisy these days.

nudge [verb]
bump He bumped my arm to get my attention.
elbow She elbowed me out of the way.
jog He jogged my desk and I spilled my coffee.
jolt He jolted my arm and I dropped the tray.
poke She poked him in the ribs.
prod The cat prodded her with its paw.
push He pushed me towards the door.
shove He shoved me gently in the back.

nuisance [noun]
annoyance The loud music was another annoyance.
bother It's a bit of a bother having to do it twice.
inconvenience The delay was an inconvenience.
irritation late trains and other irritations
pest You are a real pest with all these questions.
◆ **Informal words** **drag** Most of us find housework a drag.
pain Walking all the way into town was a real pain.

VOCABULARY CHOICES
• The word **inconvenience** is slightly more

Nn

formal than the others, and can be used to be polite, for example in a letter of complaint.

---

numb [1] [adjective]

Her face was numb with the cold.

deadened My arm became deadened to the pain.

frozen My fingers were white and frozen.

insensitive The coat was so heavy I was insensitive to cold.

♦ **Formal word insensible** The tablets made me insensible to my fear.

numb [2] [verb]

an anaesthetic to numb the area

deaden He took an aspirin to deaden the pain.

dull She drank to dull the feelings of grief.

freeze We'll freeze the gum before we remove the tooth.

paralyse Nerve damage paralysed his right leg.

stun The animals are stunned and then killed.

♦ **Technical term anaesthetize** Your gum will be anaesthetized before the extraction.

number [noun]

1 a list of numbers

digit a seven-digit telephone number

figure a six-figure sum of money

numeral Roman numerals

unit Divide the numbers into hundreds, tens and units.

2 a large number of things

amount Add the totals to give you a final amount.

collection a collection of strange objects

quantity a quantity of stolen goods

sum a six-figure sum of money

total thirty people in total

nurse [1] [verb]

1 nurse the sick

care for She cares for her ill son as well as her two other children.

look after He looks after his sick mother.

tend nurses tending their patients

treat He is being treated for the illness in hospital.

2 a mother nursing her baby

breastfeed These days, women often breastfeed babies in public.

feed She looked for a private place to feed the baby.

nurture Children must be carefully nurtured in their early years.

suckle My child was given to me to suckle straight away.

nurse [2] [noun]

1 a nurse at the hospital

matron The matron did her rounds.

sister The ward sister is very nice.

2 a nurse at the children's nursery

nanny It is expensive to hire a nanny.

nursemaid Rich people had nursemaids for their children.

Nn

obey [verb]
   comply *Fines are issued for failing to comply.*
   follow *He didn't even try to follow my instructions.*
   ◆ **Formal terms abide by** *You must abide by the rules of the competition.*
   adhere to *adhere to a strict set of rules*
   observe *observe the law*

obvious [adjective]
   apparent *The reason for the problem is immediately apparent.*
   clear *The advantages soon became clear.*
   evident *His fear was evident.*
   noticeable *The differences between them were very noticeable.*
   plain *It was plain that she was not happy.*
   ◆ **Formal words conspicuous** *a conspicuous lack of affection*
   overt *overt criticism of the government*

occasion [noun]
1 *on each occasion*
   instance *the instances when it is necessary to complain*
   time *Do you remember the time when we met in Brighton?*
2 *It was quite an occasion.*
   affair *a posh affair at the Town Hall*
   celebration *a big celebration*
   event *special events*
   function *We do catering for parties and other functions.*

party *a party to celebrate their engagement*

occasional [adjective]
   infrequent *infrequent visits to her mother's home*
   odd *I enjoy the odd beer.*
   ◆ **Formal words intermittent** *intermittent bouts of illness*
   sporadic *sporadic bursts of energy*

odd [adjective]
1 *an odd smell • odd behaviour*
   bizarre *What a bizarre thing to say!*
   curious *I had a curious feeling that I'd been there before.*
   peculiar *peculiar behaviour*
   queer *A queer thing happened to me.*
   strange *a strange smell*
   unusual *people with unusual hobbies*
   weird *I had a weird dream last night.*
   ◆ **Formal word abnormal** *changes in mood and abnormal behaviour*
2 *a few odd bits of paper*
   leftover *leftover pieces of cheese*
   spare *You can make the bag from any spare pieces of material.*
   various *various bits of equipment*

VOCABULARY CHOICES
[meaning 1]
• The word **queer** is slightly old-fashioned.
• The word **abnormal** is often used in the context of health, when someone's behaviour or body function is odd.

Oo

off [adjective]

1 This milk is off.
bad The fish went bad before we'd eaten it.
mouldy mouldy bread
rancid rancid butter
rotten rotten vegetables
sour sour milk

2 The match is off.
cancelled The game is cancelled.
postponed The wedding is postponed until June.

3 He's off somewhere.
absent children who are frequently absent from school
away I'm going to be away tomorrow.
gone He's gone already.

office [noun]
workplace She arrived at her workplace earlier than usual.

often [adverb]
again and again I've warned you again and again.
frequently I check my e-mail frequently.
repeatedly He has repeatedly refused to comment.
time after time He made the same mistake time after time.
time and again a question that has come up time and again

Oo

VOCABULARY CHOICES
• The phrases **again and again**, **time after time** and **time and again** are often used to suggest it is annoying that something has happened or been done so often.

OK¹ [adjective]
Is it OK if I come along?
acceptable Racist behaviour is not acceptable.
all right Are you all right? You look very pale.
fine I'm fine, thanks.
not bad The meal wasn't bad actually.

satisfactory The work they did was satisfactory but not brilliant.

OK² [interjection]
'I'll see you at six.' 'OK, that suits me.'
all right 'Let's go for a meal.' 'All right, That would be nice.'
fine 'I'll be there in an hour.' 'Fine, see you later.'
right Right, who wants to come with me?
very well Very well then, I'll come.
yes 'Let's meet at eight.' 'Yes, I'll see you then.'

VOCABULARY CHOICES
• The term **very well** is slightly old-fashioned, and it also suggests that someone is agreeing to something unwillingly.

old [adjective]

1 an old person
aged people looking after aged parents
elderly an elderly gentleman

2 an old manuscript
ancient ancient churches

3 an old friend
long-established a long-established tradition
long-standing their long-standing friendship
time-honoured a cheese made by time-honoured methods
traditional wine produced in the traditional way

4 an old girlfriend
ex- my ex-husband
former a former boyfriend
one-time his friend and one-time lover
previous a previous girlfriend

VOCABULARY CHOICES
[meaning 1]
• The word **elderly** is a tactful word to use when you want to be polite and avoid saying the word 'old'.

old-fashioned [adjective]
antiquated *antiquated medical equipment*
behind the times *She's behind the times and needs to catch up with the fashions.*
dated *a style that is beginning to look dated*
outdated *outdated ideas*
◆ **Formal word outmoded** *outmoded attitudes*

VOCABULARY CHOICES
• The word **old-fashioned** can sometimes be used in a positive, complimentary way, for example *lovely old-fashioned quilts.* However, the synonyms are all quite negative in tone.
• **Antiquated** is sometimes used to put extra emphasis on how old something is, and how it is no longer as useful as it should be.

once [adverb]
at one time *At one time, they lived in Spain.*
formerly *The house was formerly a nursing home.*
in the past *In the past, she worked for an engineering firm.*
previously *He was previously a teacher at Woodlands School.*

only¹ [adverb]
I was only kidding.
just *He was just joking.*
merely *It was merely an accident.*
purely *It was purely a business arrangement.*
simply *It's simply a matter of time before he finds out.*

only² [adjective]
the only remedy that works
lone *Their lone cup final appearance was in 1970.*
one and only *This is the one and only time of day I get any peace.*

single *He wrote the poems in a single week.*
sole *the sole survivor of the plane crash*
solitary *A solitary tree stood in the middle of the field.*

VOCABULARY CHOICES
• **One and only** means the same as 'only' but has much more emphasis.

open¹ [adjective]
1 *an open door*
ajar *The window was slightly ajar.*
unlocked *The door was unlocked so she went in.*
2 *She was very open about her problems.*
candid *He was very candid about his love life.*
frank *He was remarkably frank about his failures.*
honest *She's being honest about her feelings.*
truthful *She gave truthful answers in the interview.*

open² [verb]
1 *open the window*
undo *She got the key and undid the lock.*
unfasten *She unfastened her trousers.*
unlock *He unlocked the door and went in.*
2 *open the meeting*
begin *Now's the right time to begin the debate.*
launch *They launched the campaign in August.*
start *I'd like to start by welcoming our visitors.*
◆ **Formal word commence** *Fighting could not commence until a declaration of war had been made.*

operate [verb]
function *Oil keeps everything functioning smoothly.*
run *All the machines are now running normally.*
work *How does this television work?*

Oo

operation [noun]

1 He is to have an operation on his heart.
surgery She's having surgery to remove a lump in her breast.

2 operation of the controls
handling High winds affected the handling of the car.

◆ **Formal word manipulation** a design that offers easier manipulation

3 a military operation
action military action in Iraq
campaign a bombing campaign
exercise an defensive army exercise
manoeuvre a tactical manoeuvre

opinion [noun]

attitude Our attitudes were too different for us to be friends.
feeling What are your feelings on the subject?
idea He has some strange ideas.
mind We are of the same mind on this issue.
point of view We'd like to hear your points of view.
stance the government's stance on global warming
view her views on smoking
way of thinking a book which changed my way of thinking on a lot of things

---

VOCABULARY CHOICES

• The word **stance** is usually the official opinion that an organization or person has, especially on a political subject.

---

opposite [adjective]

1 on the opposite bank
facing the facing wall

2 opposite views
conflicting conflicting demands
contradictory contradictory answers
different people with different opinions
differing They had differing ideas on how things should be done.
opposed two opposed versions of 'the truth'

opposite [noun]

Whatever I say, he'll do the opposite.
reverse He was not hopeful, in fact, quite the reverse.

◆ **Formal word converse** The converse is also true.

orange [noun]

Shades of orange:

amber	peach
apricot	tangerine
coral	

order [noun]

1 an order of the court • obey orders
command commands to the soldiers
decree A decree ordered all weapons to be given up.
instruction He ignored her instructions.

◆ **Technical term injunction** A court injunction banned him from contacting her.

2 We will deal with your order immediately.
request a request for a copy of our new catalogue

3 change the order of events
pattern the normal pattern of sleeping and waking
sequence We're trying to piece together the exact sequence of events.

4 restore order
calm Police have appealed for calm following yesterday's riot.
law and order the failure of the army to maintain law and order
peace efforts to restore peace in the area

order [verb]

1 He ordered them to go.
command The troops were commanded to fire.
decree The government decreed that student numbers should be cut.
instruct I delivered the letters as instructed.
tell She told us to leave.

Oo

2 I have ordered a taxi.
book *I'll book the tickets.*
request *I've requested a copy of the catalogue.*
reserve *I've reserved a table at the restaurant.*

3 Order the books according to author.
arrange *Arrange the letters in alphabetical order.*
classify *They were classified according to age.*
group *Group the children according to ability.*

ordinary [adjective]
average *So, what do you do on an average day?*
everyday *everyday experiences*
normal *It had been a normal day until then.*
routine *routine medical checks*
run-of-the-mill *people doing run-of-the-mill jobs*
typical *On a typical morning, I get up around 6am.*
usual *the usual way of doing things*

VOCABULARY CHOICES
• The word **run-of-the-mill** suggests that something is so ordinary that it is boring.

organize [verb]
1 organize the information
arrange *She arranged the list alphabetically.*
structure *You need to structure the essay a little better.*
2 organize a party
arrange *I'm arranging a surprise party for him.*
co-ordinate *Tim will co-ordinate the timetable of events.*
set up *I'm trying to set up a meeting.*

original¹ [adjective]
1 the original version
earliest *the earliest form of the language*

first *This book is a first edition.*
♦ **Formal word** **initial** *The initial design was very different.*
2 a very original piece of work
creative *creative solutions*
fresh *a fresh approach to the problem*
imaginative *an imaginative design*
inventive *a restaurant serving inventive meals*
♦ **Formal words** **innovative** *an innovative business*
novel *a novel combination of flavours*

original² [noun]
Not even an expert can tell this copy from the original.
master *make a copy of the film from the master*
prototype *a prototype of a camera phone*

out [adjective]
1 He's out at the moment.
not at home *He's not at home right now. Can I take a message?*
unavailable *I'm afraid the manager is unavailable at the moment.*
2 Their secret was out.
disclosed *The girl's name was not disclosed.*
public *I didn't want the information to become public.*
revealed *His real identity was revealed.*

VOCABULARY CHOICES
[meaning 1]
• The word **unavailable** suggests that someone is there but you cannot speak to them. It is often used to be polite when refusing a request to see someone.

outfit [noun]
clothes *She took a spare set of clothes for the baby.*
costume *He was wearing a pirate's costume.*
♦ **Formal word** **ensemble** *She was*

Oo

wearing an elegant silk ensemble.
♦ **Informal word get-up** *a woman in a strange get-up*

VOCABULARY CHOICES
• The word **get-up** suggests you think someone looks a bit ridiculous in their outfit.

outside¹ [adjective]
1 the outside wall of the house
exterior *the exterior paintwork of the building*
external *external doors*
outer *the outer gates of the castle*
2 an outside chance
faint *a faint hope of victory*
remote *We've only a remote possibility of winning.*
slight *a slight chance of sunshine in the west*
slim *a project with only a slim likelihood of success*

outside² [adverb]
Let's have our coffee outside.
outdoors *Why don't you go and play outdoors?*

outside³ [noun]
Work is needed on the outside of the house.
exterior *the exterior of the building*

over¹ [adjective]
I'll be glad when this is all over.
ended *when the war is ended*
finished *once the work is finished*
gone *My football-playing days are gone.*

past *Put the plant outside when any danger of frost is past.*

over² [adverb]
1 Two birds flew over.
above *planes flying above*
overhead *A helicopter circled overhead.*
2 There were six left over.
left *There were two cakes left.*
remaining *If there's any money remaining, we could buy some flowers.*

over³ [preposition]
1 the roof over our heads
above *the sky above us*
2 She spent over £400 on that coat.
in excess of *people earning in excess of £500 000 a year*
more than *There must have been more than 100 people there.*

overdue [adjective]
delayed *their delayed arrival*
late *late payments*

own¹ [adjective]
I'd love to have my own business.
individual *We can organize a holiday to suit your individual taste.*
particular *a course which is relevant to your particular needs*
personal *from my personal experience*

own² [verb]
Do you own a car?
have *She has a Mercedes.*
♦ **Formal word possess** *The law allowed him to possess four guns.*

P

packet [noun]
box a box of matches
pack a pack of cigarettes
package She was carrying a package under her arm.
parcel She untied the parcel.

pain [noun]
1 a pain in his stomach • feel pain
ache an ache in her hip
agony He died in great agony.
cramp stomach cramps
discomfort You will experience some discomfort after the operation.
throb I had a nagging throb in my head.
twinge He felt a twinge in his back.
2 the pain of losing someone you love
agony couples going through the agony of not being able to have a baby
anguish People trapped in the rubble cried out in anguish.
distress the distress caused by burglary
hurt I regret the hurt I have caused to my family.
suffering the suffering caused by divorce
torment the torment of being forced to live apart from her daughter
3 (informal) It's a real pain.
nuisance I don't want to be a nuisance but is it all right if I stay?
♦ **Informal word headache** Keeping children entertained in the school holidays can be a real headache.

VOCABULARY CHOICES
[meaning 1]
• The word **discomfort** suggests that the pain is not very bad. It is often used in medical advice instead of the direct word 'pain', which could be more upsetting.
[meaning 2]
• The words **agony**, **anguish** and **torment** have a lot of emotional impact, as they suggest extreme mental pain.

painful [adjective]
1 a painful wound
aching his aching legs
agonizing suffer an agonizing death
excruciating an excruciating pain in his side
sore My leg is really sore.
tender Her glands were swollen and tender.
2 a painful experience
agonizing They made the agonizing decision to turn off her life-support machine.
distressing distressing pictures of starving children
harrowing The kidnap has been a very harrowing experience for the family.
traumatic the traumatic year in which her marriage ended
upsetting the upsetting experience of losing your job

Pp

191

Pp

VOCABULARY CHOICES
[meaning 1]
• The words **agonizing** and **excruciating** are very powerful, as they suggest that something is almost more painful than you can bear.

pair [noun]
We must have looked like a right pair of idiots.
couple *They're a strange couple.*
duo *the famous comedy duo, Laurel and Hardy*
twosome *The twosome have been asked to present the programme.*

pair [verb]
I was paired with him for the next game.
match *Each client is matched with a trained volunteer.*
match up *How are kidney donors and recipients matched up?*
team *a pair of grey trousers teamed with a cream shirt*

pale [adjective]
1 She went pale. • You look pale.
pasty *a young man with a pasty complexion*
pasty-faced *pasty-faced teenagers*
white *She went white when she heard the news.*
♦ **Formal words** **ashen** *His face was ashen and his skin shiny with sweat.*
pallid *her pallid face*
2 pale blue
light *light green*
pastel *pastel pink*

VOCABULARY CHOICES
[meaning 1]
• The words **pasty** and **pasty-faced** suggest that someone looks pale in a way that is unpleasant to look at.
• The words **ashen** and **white** tend to be used to emphasize that someone is ill or very shocked.

panic [noun]
The horses were in a complete panic.
fear *people fleeing the scene in fear*
fright *She woke up in a terrible fright.*
hysteria *There was a touch of hysteria in his voice.*
terror *The children screamed in terror.*
♦ **Informal word** **flap** *She was in a complete flap when I got there.*

panic [verb]
Don't panic, everything's going to be all right.
go to pieces *I just went to pieces when I got on stage.*
lose your nerve *I lost my nerve at the last minute.*

paper [noun]
1 the Sunday papers
broadsheet *broadsheets like 'The Times' and 'The Daily Telegraph'*
newspaper *She was reading a newspaper.*
tabloid *tabloids such as 'The Sun' and 'The Mirror'*
♦ **Informal word** **rag** *The local rag did an article on him.*
2 personal papers • legal papers
document *Keep your travel documents in a safe place.*

VOCABULARY CHOICES
[meaning 1]
• When people speak of the **broadsheets**, they are speaking about larger-sized newspapers, usually in terms of their quality and seriousness.
• Describing a newspaper as a **tabloid** sets up a contrast with a 'broadsheet', as this word is often used to emphasize the less serious content and sensational stories in a smaller, popular newspaper.
• **Rag** is a very uncomplimentary word for a paper. The word suggests it has no worthwhile content, perhaps because it is full of extreme opinions or scandalous stories.

Types of party:

barbecue	dinner party	hen party	sleepover
birthday party	fancy-dress party	housewarming	soirée
ceilidh	garden party	pyjama party	stag party
cocktail party	Hallowe'en party	shindig	tea party

part¹ [noun]

1 The jigsaw has some parts missing.
bit put all the bits back together again
element a key element of the plan
piece The desk came in three pieces.
portion the upper portion of the chimney
section Business Class is in the front section of the plane.
♦ **Formal word component** engine components

2 a different part of the organization • southern parts of the country
branch a separate branch of government
department an organization divided into three departments
district the industrial districts of France
division the sales division of the company
region people from different regions of the world
sector the poorer sectors of society

3 get a part in a film
appearance Her acting credits include several film appearances.
role He played the role of the teacher in the movie.

part² [verb]

1 By 1997, the couple had parted.
break up They broke up after a year together.
separate Her parents have separated.
split up They split up after a furious row.

2 The crowd parted to let them through.
divide The search party divided into three.
separate The crowd separated to make way for the car.

partner [noun]

1 my partner in crime
accomplice The robber and his accomplice have not been found.
associate a known associate of the drug dealer
♦ **Formal word collaborator** She was arrested as a collaborator.
♦ **Informal word sidekick** Batman and his sidekick, Robin

2 my life partner
boyfriend I live with my boyfriend.
girlfriend He's been with his girlfriend for ten years.
husband Bring your husband too.
significant other people looking for a significant other
wife This is my wife, Clare.
♦ **Formal word spouse** people who have cheated on their spouse
♦ **Informal terms better half** I don't believe you, so I'll ask your better half.
other half What's your other half doing tonight?

VOCABULARY CHOICES
[meaning 2]
• The terms **partner** or **significant other** are used to be tactful when you do not want to be specific about which sex the partner is, or whether they are married or not.
• The terms **better half** and **other half** are humorous, and used when you want to be funny.

party [noun]

1 a birthday party
celebration She has asked him to her 21st birthday celebration.
function an official function at the Town Hall
gathering family gatherings

Pp

reception *a wedding reception*
social *rugby club socials*
◆ **Informal words** **bash** *her 18th birthday bash*
do *We've been invited to a do at the golf club.*
See also the box on the previous page.
2 a search party
group *There is a discount for groups of ten or more.*
team *a mountain rescue team*
3 a political party
association *political associations*

pass [verb]
1 She passed the other runners and went on to win the race.
overtake *The car overtook us.*
2 passing the day
fill *How do you fill your evenings?*
occupy *He doesn't have enough to occupy his time.*
spend *He spends several hours a day reading.*
while away *whiling away sunny afternoons on the beach*
3 Time passes slowly.
go *The time went in a flash.*
go by *Time seemed to go by much faster than usual.*
go past *The months went past very quickly.*
◆ **Formal word** **elapse** *Eight months have elapsed since the accident.*
4 I passed him the butter.
give *Could you give me the salt, please?*
hand *She reached across and handed the letter to him.*
5 pass an exam
get through *Do you think you'll get through your driving test?*

VOCABULARY CHOICES
[meaning 2]
• The term **while away** suggests you are spending time doing something very nice and relaxing.

past[1] [adjective]
1 Those days are past now.
done *Thank goodness that job's done.*
ended *when the war is ended*
gone *My football-playing days are gone.*
over *I felt that my life was over.*
2 past experiences
former *her former life in Japan*
previous *He's had no previous experience of looking after children.*
3 past times
bygone *fading photos of bygone days*
former *memories of former glories*
olden *People had few luxuries in olden times.*

VOCABULARY CHOICES
[meaning 3]
• The word **bygone** suggests a romantic view of the past, and that you consider the past times to be very pleasant.

past[2] [noun]
1 in the past
former times *In former times, the cottage was known as 'Hollyhock House'.*
history *a way of life that belongs to history*
olden days *In the olden days, people only had outside toilets.*
2 I know nothing about her past.
background *His background is in sales and marketing.*
experience *What's her experience?*
life *She started to tell him all about her life.*

pat[1] [verb]
I patted the dog on the head.
slap *I slapped him gently on the back.*
tap *He tapped her on the shoulder.*
touch *He touched her on her knee.*

pat[2] [noun]
a reassuring pat on the arm
slap *a gentle slap on the back*
tap *a tap on her shoulder*

patch [noun]
  area an area of mould on the wall
  spot a bird with black spots on its wings
pathetic [adjective]
1 a pathetic sight
  distressing the distressing sight of children begging for money
  heartbreaking the heartbreaking sight of her struggling to breathe
  pitiful a woman in a pitiful state
  sad We were a sad spectacle when we finally got off the boat.
  sorry the sorry sight of starving animals
2 (informal) a pathetic attempt at humour
  feeble a feeble joke • Don't be so feeble!
  hopeless a hopeless effort at karaoke
patience [noun]
1 You need to have patience with children.
  calmness He displayed calmness while all this was going on.
  self-control I needed self-control to stop myself hitting him.
  tolerance Children need to learn tolerance when playing with other children.
2 If you play with patience you'll eventually get a goal.
  perseverance His perseverance has finally paid off.
  persistence Her persistence was admirable.
◆ **Formal word** **tenacity** She stuck to the task with tenacity.
patient [adjective]
You need to be patient when training animals.
  calm She's very calm with the children.
  long-suffering His long-suffering wife put up with his drinking for years.
  tolerant She's very tolerant of others.
  uncomplaining his uncomplaining support for her
patient [noun]
a ward full of elderly patients

  case We're treating three new cases of skin cancer every week.
  invalid Invalids should be given plenty of water to drink.
  sufferer AIDS sufferers

VOCABULARY CHOICES
• The word **case** is a very impersonal-sounding word, and it is usually used by people in medical situations.

pay [verb]
1 pay £30 • pay the bill
  pay out The company has paid out compensation to all victims.
  settle We need to settle the account.
  spend I spent a fortune on that coat.
2 You'll pay for your mistakes.
  pay the price He was careless and he paid the price.
  suffer You'll suffer for eating all those cakes.
pay [noun]
a take-home pay of £200 a week
  earnings an increase in earnings
  income people on high incomes
  salary a job with a starting salary of £19,000 a year
  wages You will receive your wages at the end of the week.

peace [noun]
1 I enjoy the peace of the countryside.
  calm Little disturbs the calm of the village.
  calmness Guests can relax in the calmness of the hotel grounds.
  quiet She enjoyed the cool and quiet of the cathedral.
  tranquillity The tranquillity of the island lures many holidaymakers.
2 After years of war, the two countries are trying to achieve peace.
  ceasefire There have been calls for a ceasefire.
  truce The two sides agreed on a truce.

Pp

people [noun]

folk *a meeting place for old folk*
human beings *the difference between human beings and other animals*
humans *The disease doesn't affect humans.*
individuals *the use of nicknames to identify individuals*
mankind *Space travel is one of mankind's greatest achievements.*
the general public *Is the general public ever asked about these matters?*
the public *The palace is not open to the public.*
♦ **Formal word persons** *The cottages each sleep ten persons.*

perfect [adjective]

1 *a perfect performance*
faultless *a faultless display of goalkeeping*
flawless *the team's flawless record*
immaculate *His timing was immaculate.*
impeccable *his impeccable behaviour*
2 *He would make a perfect partner for her.*
ideal *the ideal car for a family*
model *They had been model parents.*

Pp

person [noun]

character *He's an odd character.*
human *She wanted to feel like a normal human again.*
human being *It's no way to treat another human being.*
individual *Each individual has a role in the project.*
soul *I won't tell a soul, I promise.*

personal [adjective]

1 *We all have our personal memories of the special day.*
individual *We can organize a holiday to suit your individual taste.*
own *My own experience of hospital was different from yours.*
particular *a course which is relevant to your particular needs*

2 *I can't tell you what the letter said because it's personal.*
confidential *confidential records about employees*
private *I like to keep my family life private.*

pest [noun]

annoyance *The loud music was another annoyance.*
bother *It's a bit of a bother having to do it twice.*
inconvenience *The delay was an inconvenience.*
irritation *late trains and other irritations*
nuisance *You are a complete nuisance with all these questions.*
♦ **Informal words drag** *Most of us find housework a drag.*
pain *Walking all the way into town was a real pain.*

phone [verb]

call *I'll call you next week.*
call up *Just call me up if you need me.*
dial *I dialled his number.* • *She grabbed the phone and dialled the police.*
ring *Just ring us if you need a lift.*
ring up *Ring him up and ask him when he's coming over.*
telephone *He telephoned his mother to say he'd be late.*
♦ **Informal phrases give a buzz** *I'll give you a buzz tomorrow.*
give a tinkle *Give me a tinkle when you're ready to set off.*

pick[1] [verb]

1 *Pick a number.*
choose *Choose what you like from the menu.*
decide on *I was trying to decide on something wear.*
opt for *We opted for the leather sofa in the end.*
select *Select the option you want.*
2 *picking strawberries*
harvest *farmers harvesting their crops*

pluck He plucked an apple from the tree.

pick [superscript]2[/superscript] [noun]
1 Take your pick.
choice Indicate your choice.
preference My preference is for the red shirt rather than the blue one.
selection Make your selection.
2 the pick of the crop
best the best of the group
cream the cream of the local sporting talent

picture [superscript]1[/superscript] [noun]
1 I hung pictures on the wall.
drawing drawings by children
illustration The illustrations in the book are beautiful.
image television images of starving children
painting There were paintings hung on the walls.
photograph a photograph of her on the beach
portrait a portrait of the Queen
print prints by famous artists
2 Give me a picture of the overall situation.
description The book gives a good description of life during the war.
impression I couldn't really get an impression of what had happened.

picture [superscript]2[/superscript] [verb]
1 I can picture the scene.
imagine I can just imagine him complaining about that.
see Can't you just see us lying there on that beach?
visualize He visualized a romantic dinner by candlelight.
♦ **Formal word envisage** She had never envisaged herself winning an Olympic medal.
2 He was pictured sitting on a wall.
photograph The singer was photographed leaving a nightclub.

show The painting showed her lying on the sofa.

piece [noun]
bit an interesting bit of news
fragment Fragments of glass lay everywhere.
part a shop selling spare parts for motorbikes
particle a particle of dust
portion She handed me a large portion of the cake.
scrap a scrap of fabric
segment orange segments
♦ **Formal word component** The company supplies components for aircraft.

pile [superscript]1[/superscript] [noun]
a pile of compost at the bottom of the garden
heap a heap of clothes on the floor
mound a mound of rubbish
stack the stack of books on her desk

VOCABULARY CHOICES
• The word **heap** suggests that the pile is untidy whereas the word **stack** suggests that the pile is neat and tidy.

pile [superscript]2[/superscript] [verb]
He started piling the dishes on to a tray.
heap sitting on the floor with her belongings heaped around her
stack She stacked the boxes by the wall.

pill [noun]
capsule Swallow the capsule with water.
tablet medicine in tablet form

pinch [verb]
clip Clip the older flowers from the plant.
nip She nipped the skin of my arm.
squeeze Stop squeezing your spots!
tweak Dad tweaked my ear playfully.

pink [noun]

Shades of pink:

coral	rose
fuchsia	salmon

Pp

pity¹ [noun]

1 I feel some pity for them.

compassion *He showed a lot of compassion and love for other people.*

sympathy *sympathy for the victims of the earthquake*

2 What a pity!

shame *It's a shame you can't come.*

pity² [verb]

I pity anyone who has to go out in this weather.

feel for *I really feel for him because he lost a lot of money.*

feel sorry for *I feel sorry for anyone who has to live with him.*

sympathize with *Every parent would sympathize with them.*

place¹ [noun]

1 The statue is broken in several places. • Find a place to sit down.

location *a beautiful location for a wedding*

point *the point where the river meets the sea*

position *the radar showing the plane's position*

site *the site where the crash happened*

spot *a lovely spot for a picnic*

2 a place on the map

area *one of the industrial areas*

city *Birmingham is a big city.*

district *people living in country districts*

region *one of the most popular holiday regions of France*

town *Belper is a small town in Derbyshire.*

village *a village in the Yorkshire Dales*

place² [verb]

The body was placed in a tomb.

lay *Lay the map on the table.*

position *She positioned the hat neatly on her head.*

put *He put the books carefully on the desk.*

set *Jean set the tray down on the table.*

plain [adjective]

1 good plain cooking

basic *a recipe for a basic sponge cake*

ordinary *just an ordinary house*

simple *a lovely simple dress*

2 It was plain to see he was upset.

apparent *It was apparent that things were not right between them.*

clear *She made it clear that we weren't wanted.*

evident *His lack of interest was evident.*

obvious *He made his feelings very obvious.*

♦ Formal word **conspicuous** *a conspicuous lack of affection*

3 a plain face

ordinary *a very ordinary-looking man*

ugly *She felt fat and ugly.*

unattractive *an unattractive woman in a red cardigan*

4 plain fabric

unpatterned *unpatterned material*

plan¹ [noun]

1 Look at the plans for the extension.

blueprint *The blueprint may be amended before building starts.*

design *the designs for the new hospital*

diagram *a diagram showing where all the parts would go*

drawing *architect's drawings*

2 I have a cunning plan.

idea *I've got an idea how we could do it.*

plot *a plot to kill the President*

scheme *coming up with money-making schemes*

strategy *the company's marketing strategy*

VOCABULARY CHOICES

[meaning 2]

• The word **plot** is used when the plan is to do something bad.

plan² [verb]

1 plan the attack

Pp

Types of plant:

algae	fern	hybrid	tree
bush	flower	lichen	vegetable
cactus	fungus	moss	vine
cereal	grass	pot plant	weed
climber	herb	shrub	

arrange *trying to arrange a meeting*
organize *organizing a wedding*
plot *plotting to kill the President*
◆ **Formal word formulate** *formulate a strategy to deal with the problem*
2 plan to be a lawyer
aim *He aims to retire next year.*
intend *I intended to leave early.*

VOCABULARY CHOICES

[meaning 1]
• The word **organize**, as well as the word **plan** itself, can make a good impression if used in CVs and job applications. It suggests to employers that you can think things through in an organized way.

plant [noun]
See the box above.
plant [verb]
1 plant seeds
sow *Sow the seeds in autumn.*
2 plant an idea in his head
put *putting ideas into impressionable young minds*
play [verb]
1 children playing in the garden
enjoy oneself *children enjoying themselves on the swings*
have fun *They were having fun in the paddling pool.*
2 Play tennis with us.
join in *Come and join in.*
take part *He didn't want to take part in the game.*
3 France played Italy.
take on *Scotland took on Wales in the final.*

4 He played Hamlet on stage.
act *He acted the part of Macbeth.*
perform *perform the role of King Lear*
play [noun]
1 all work and no play
entertainment *looking for entertainment*
fun *You need some fun in your life.*
leisure *People have less time for leisure.*
◆ **Formal word recreation** *recreation facilities*
2 a part in a play
drama *a TV drama about family life*
performance *a theatre performance*
show *going to a show in the West End*
pleasant [adjective]
delightful *The hotel is set in delightful gardens.*
enjoyable *It was an enjoyable evening.*
lovely *It had been a lovely day.*
nice *What a nice surprise!*
◆ **Formal word agreeable** *an agreeable companion*
please [verb]
You can't please everybody.
delight *The singer delighted fans with the concert.*
satisfy *It satisfied him to see his paintings on display.*
please [interjection]
Please don't smoke in here.
kindly *Would you kindly close the door?*
would you mind *Would you mind turning the TV down?*
◆ **Formal phrases could I trouble you to** *Could I trouble you to lend me some sugar?*
I would appreciate it if *I would*

Pp

appreciate it if you could give me a call.
I would be grateful if I would be
grateful if you would send me a copy.
would you be so kind Would you be so
kind as to open the window for me?

VOCABULARY CHOICES

• Although apparently polite, the terms
kindly and **would you mind** often add a
hint of impatience or annoyance to the
request.
• The formal phrases **I would appreciate it
if** and **I would be grateful if** are often
used in writing to be polite, for example in
business letters when just saying 'please'
might sound curt. Such phrases can be used
instead of writing 'please' over and over
again.

pleased [adjective]
content I feel content with what I've
achieved.
delighted We're delighted you've come.
glad I'm glad to hear Michael has
recovered.
happy He's happy with the way things
have turned out.
satisfied I am very satisfied with my new
cooker.

plenty [noun]
a good deal Being a mum takes a good
deal of patience.
enough There's enough for everyone.
♦ **Informal words heaps** We've got
heaps of time.
loads There's loads of milk in the fridge.
lots We had lots to talk about.
masses There is masses of space.

point¹ [noun]
1 the point of a dart
end The cat's tail is white at the end.
nib The pen's nib is broken.
spike a metal ball covered with spikes
tip a pencil with a sharp tip
top the top of the mountain

2 At that point, we burst out laughing.
moment This would be a good moment to
reflect on what happened.
stage By that stage we had completely
lost the place.
♦ **Formal words instant** At that instant,
the police arrived.
juncture We will take no further action at
this juncture.
3 the highest point in the area
location the town's location on the map
place Find a place to sit down.
site the site where the crash happened
situation Put the plants in a sunny
situation, away from draughts.
spot a lovely spot for a picnic
4 He has a lot of good points.
aspect the pleasant aspects of his
personality
characteristic the characteristics of a
good nurse
feature The house has many attractive
features.
quality He can be bad-tempered, but he
has some good qualities.
trait The test is supposed to reveal your
character traits, such as shyness.
♦ **Formal word attribute** She has all the
attributes of a good leader.
5 I hope I have made my point clear.
drift I couldn't hear every word she said,
but I got the drift.
gist The gist of the letter is that we have
been refused permission.
meaning He used a lot of jargon but the
meaning was clear.
significance I didn't understand the
significance of what he said.
6 What's the point of doing that?
aim Our aim is to improve things.
purpose I need to see the purpose of
what I am doing.
reason There was a reason behind our
decision.
sense There's no sense in forcing him to go

Pp

if he doesn't want to.
use There's no use in getting upset now.
7 Deal with each point in turn.
   detail the details of the contract
   issue I will raise the issue at the meeting.
   item the next item on the agenda
   matter We have another matter to discuss.
   question Next we will deal with the question of money.
   subject The debate will cover many subjects.
   topic a new topic for discussion

point² [verb]
1 point a gun
   aim He aimed the rifle at me.
   direct She directed the arrow towards the centre of the target.
   level He levelled the gun at the captive's head.
   train She trained the gun on the thief.
2 She pointed at the suspect.
   gesture She invited me to sit down and gestured towards the empty seat.
   indicate I indicated the direction they should go.
   signal The police officer signalled that I should go left.

poison¹ [noun]
a deadly poison
   toxin the toxins found in cigarettes
   venom a snake's venom

poison² [verb]
gases which are poisoning the atmosphere
   contaminate The drinking water had been contaminated by lead.
   pollute water polluted by oil

poisonous [adjective]
   deadly deadly chemicals
   lethal lethal fumes
   noxious noxious substances
   toxic toxic chemicals

poke¹ [verb]
Stop poking me with your elbow!

jab He jabbed me in the eye with his thumb.
prod She prodded me playfully in the arm.
stab Karl stabbed the table with his finger.

poke² [noun]
a poke in the eye with a stick
   dig He gave me a dig in the ribs.
   jab I felt a jab in my back.
   prod a prod in the stomach

police [noun]
   constabulary a spokesperson for Cheshire Constabulary
   police force She wants to join the police force.
 ◆ **Informal word cops** He was worried the cops would find him.

polite [adjective]
   civil He didn't even try to be civil. • He didn't have a civil word to say about her.
   respectful She was always so respectful.
   well-mannered a well-mannered young man
 ◆ **Formal word courteous** She was courteous to everyone. • a courteous reply

poor [adjective]
1 a poor country
   badly off We were badly off when we first married.
   destitute destitute children
   hard-up We were hard-up in those days.
   impoverished impoverished families
   penniless The divorce had left him penniless.
   poverty-stricken Ethiopia and other poverty-stricken countries
 ◆ **Formal words disadvantaged** a scheme to help disadvantaged children
   underprivileged doctors working in underprivileged areas
 ◆ **Informal word broke** Can you lend me some money? I'm broke.
 ◆ **Slang word skint** I'm skint until the weekend.

2 a poor mark
   bad a bad score in a test
   inferior inferior accommodation
   second-rate companies offering a second-rate service
   shoddy shoddy workmanship
   substandard substandard housing
   unsatisfactory work of an unsatisfactory standard
3 The poor souls!
   unfortunate the unfortunate people caught up in the storm
   unlucky the unlucky few who didn't make it

VOCABULARY CHOICES

[meaning 1]
- The words **destitute** and **impoverished** have a lot of impact, as they suggest someone or something is extremely poor.
- The word **poverty-stricken** also suggests this, and is often used to stir people's emotions. It is sometimes used in newspaper reports or in leaflets from charities.
- The words **disadvantaged** and **underprivileged** are more often used in formal writing such as government reports.
- The words **broke** and **skint** tend to be used in less serious contexts, for example when talking to friends.

---

popular [adjective]
   fashionable Long skirts are fashionable at the moment.
   in demand products that are in great demand
   in vogue Bright colours are in vogue at the moment.
   sought-after The house is in a sought-after area.
   ◆ **Informal word trendy** a trendy area to live

posh [adjective]
   de luxe a de luxe hotel
   exclusive exclusive apartments

lavish a lavish wedding
luxury a luxury apartment overlooking the sea
smart smart restaurants
up-market up-market shops
◆ **Informal words classy** a classy venue for the party
swish He bought a swish new car.

position [noun]
1 the radar showing the plane's position
   location the town's location on the map
   place Find a place to sit down.
   point the point where the river meets the sea
   site the site where the crash happened
   situation Put the plants in a sunny situation, away from draughts.
   spot a lovely spot for a picnic
   whereabouts Can you inform us of your whereabouts?
2 She holds a senior position in the company.
   grade members of staff at managerial grade
   job civil servants in top jobs
   office The Home Secretary holds high office in the government.
   post a teaching post in London
   rank an army officer of junior rank
3 the government's position on crime
   attitude He had a poor attitude to work.
   line What's the official line on overtime pay?
   policy They have a different policy towards education.

power [noun]
1 political power
   authority a challenge to the Prime Minister's authority
   control political control
   influence He has a lot of influence in the organization.
2 the power to arrest people
   authorization authorization to proceed with the sale

Pp

right *Police had the right to search the house.*

3 The engine is losing power.
energy *The wind can be used to produce energy.*
force *the force of the bomb blast*

powerful [adjective]

1 a powerful argument
compelling *compelling proof of her guilt*
convincing *a convincing case for changing the law*
persuasive *persuasive proof that ghosts exist*
strong *There is no strong evidence that mobile phones are dangerous.*
2 powerful political leaders
high-powered *high-powered people in business*
influential *an influential group of politicians*
3 a car with a powerful engine
high-powered *high-powered vehicles*

practise [verb]
rehearse *They were rehearsing for the concert.*
run through *I ran through my lines before I went on stage.*
train *training for the race*

praise¹ [noun]
Most of the praise should go to the director.
recognition *He deserves some recognition for his work.*
♦ **Formal words acclaim** *The film won great acclaim.*
commendation *He received a letter of commendation for his courage.*

praise² [verb]
The police praised her quick thinking.
pay tribute to *The President paid tribute to the rescue workers.*
recognize *The painting has been recognized as one of the greatest of the last century.*
♦ **Formal words acclaim** *The artist's work*

was widely acclaimed.
applaud *The decision has been applauded by staff.*
commend *The company should be commended for its decision.*

precious [adjective]
1 my precious daughter
beloved *my beloved son*
cherished *my cherished grandmother*
darling *She won't leave her darling cats.*
dear *John has been a dear friend in difficult times.*
prized *his prized pet birds*
treasured *This ring is my most treasured possession.*
valued *Kate is a valued companion of mine.*
2 precious jewels
expensive *expensive gold bracelets*
fine *fine fabrics*
priceless *Priceless objects were stolen from the museum.*
rare *rare diamonds*
valuable *She owned expensive clothes and valuable furs.*

prefer [verb]
favour *She favours the Labour Party candidate.*
like better *I like strong colours better.*
would rather *I'd rather stay in if you don't mind.*
would sooner *I'd sooner we didn't go.*

pregnant [adjective]
expecting *She's expecting again.*
♦ **Formal word expectant** *expectant mothers*
♦ **Informal phrase in the club** *I hear your sister's in the club.*

Pp

VOCABULARY CHOICES
• An informal phrase such as **in the club** can sound humorous when you use it with friends, but it might sound mocking or offensive to people you don't know so well.

prepare [verb]
1 prepare for a meeting
  get ready We're busy getting ready for the conference.
  organize organizing a wedding
2 prepare a meal
  cook He was cooking dinner.
  make She was busy making lunch.
  produce She produced a wonderful feast.

present[1] [adjective]
1 present at the meeting
  here How many people are here?
  there All the old crowd will be there.
  ◆ **Formal term in attendance** Armed police were in attendance.
2 at the present time
  current your current job
  existing the existing situation

present[2] [verb]
1 He was presented with a trophy.
  award The prizes will be awarded at a special ceremony.
  give They gave her a medal for her bravery.
2 The children presented a play.
  mount The gallery is mounting an exhibition of her work next week.
  put on The school is putting on a show.
  stage staging an event

present[3] [noun]
a wedding present
  favour party favours
  gift a shop selling cards and gifts
  ◆ **Informal word prezzie** Have you bought my birthday prezzie yet?

press[1] [verb]
1 Press the button.
  push Push the lever to start the machine.
  ◆ **Formal word depress** Depress the pedal with your foot.
2 She pressed him for an answer.
  pressure He was pressured into resigning from his job.
  push I had to push him into taking all his holidays.
  urge urged him not to leave

press[2] [noun]
Let's hope the press don't get hold of this story.
  Fleet Street one of Fleet Street's finest writers
  journalists He refused to speak to journalists.
  newspapers She sold her story to the newspapers.
  papers The papers published stories about his love life.
  reporters She gave an interview to reporters.
  the media The story first appeared in the media last week.

pretend [verb]
1 Pretend to be pleased.
  fake More and more workers are faking illness.
  put on He can't really think that — I'm sure he's just putting it on.
  ◆ **Formal word feign** Christina feigned interest.
2 Pretend this is a castle.
  imagine Imagine you're on holiday.
  make believe a game that allows you to make believe you are famous

pretty[1] [adjective]
She was very pretty as a child.
  attractive an attractive woman
  beautiful She looked beautiful with her hair done.
  bonny a bonny baby
  good-looking She's a good-looking girl.

pretty[2] [adverb]
I'm pretty certain I locked the door.
  fairly They're fairly rich.
  quite It's quite dangerous.
  rather He felt rather tired.

Pp

prevent [verb]
avoid You must take action to avoid an accident.
foil The robbery was foiled when the police were called.
halt A fallen tree halted our progress.
stave off He is taking vitamins to stave off colds.
stop I tried to stop him from leaving.
thwart A last-minute goal thwarted our chances of winning.
ward off Some herbs can ward off certain illnesses.
♦ **Formal words arrest** ways of arresting the spread of AIDS
avert last-minute talks to avert a strike by firefighters

VOCABULARY CHOICES
• **Stave off** and **ward off** are used for keeping something which is threatening at bay, especially illnesses.
• **Foil** and **thwart** suggest plans have been prevented in a very definite or even deliberate way.

previous [adjective]
earlier as described in earlier chapters
preceding an issue referred to in the preceding paragraph
prior He had been involved in prior research.

price [noun]
charge There is a small charge for hiring the equipment.
cost the cost of petrol
fee The fee for the lesson is £25.

pride [noun]
1 Pride goes before a fall.
arrogance There is an unpleasant arrogance about him.
bigheadedness His bigheadedness lost him a few friends.
self-importance a great show of self-importance

smugness Her smugness is irritating.
2 She kept going for the sake of her pride.
dignity a loss of dignity
self-esteem ways of building up self-esteem
self-respect This job gives him back some of his self-respect.

prison [noun]
jail He was put in jail for 15 years.
♦ **Informal word nick** He's just got out of the nick.
♦ **Slang word clink** I've spent seven years in clink.

prisoner [noun]
convict escaped convicts
inmate inmates at Barlinnie jail
♦ **Informal word jailbird** a former jailbird
♦ **Slang word con** a gangster and ex-con

private [adjective]
1 a private discussion
confidential confidential talks
secret a secret meeting
2 my private life
intimate intimate details of their relationship
personal I won't comment on my personal life.
3 a private place
isolated The cottage is quite isolated.
quiet a quiet spot for a picnic
secluded The villa was large and secluded.

prize[1] [noun]
first prize in an art competition
award an award for best hotel
honour actors winning the top honours at the Academy Awards
jackpot this week's lottery jackpot
winnings She shared her winnings with the rest of the family.

prize[2] [verb]
He prizes honesty above all other virtues.
cherish She cherished her independence.
treasure her treasured possessions

Pp

value I value my freedom too much to have children.

problem [noun]

1 problems with the machine

complication There are a few complications to be sorted out.

difficulty difficulties at work

snag The only snag is that John won't be able to come with us.

trouble We've had a lot of trouble with this car.

2 He has personal problems.

care A child should not have a care in the world.

concern our concerns about money

difficulty My husband's illness was just another difficulty to deal with.

trouble Feel free to come to me with your troubles.

worry Their teenage daughter is a real worry for them.

VOCABULARY CHOICES

[meaning 1]

• The word **snag** suggests that the problem is only a small one in an otherwise good situation.

product [noun]

goods a drop in demand for British goods

produce dairy produce

◆ **Formal words commodity** basic commodities such as bread, gas and sugar

merchandise football club merchandise

profit¹ [noun]

He made a good profit on the deal.

gain Their only interest is financial gain.

proceeds The proceeds from the event will go to a charity.

return He got a return of 10% on his investment.

profit² [verb]

Who will profit from this war?

benefit the people who will benefit from the scheme

gain They will gain from the experience.

programme [noun]

1 a radio programme

broadcast a live broadcast

show a new show on Channel 4

◆ **Formal word transmission** the first television transmissions in colour

2 the programme of events for the day

agenda the agenda for the meeting

line-up What's the line-up for this evening?

schedule What's on his schedule today?

timetable the timetable for the introduction of the new laws

promise¹ [verb]

Promise me you'll be home by midnight.

assure He assured me he wouldn't tell anyone.

give your word He gave his word that he'd be here.

guarantee They guaranteed that we would receive the money.

pledge The Prime Minister pledged that taxes would not go up.

swear She swore she'd never tell anyone.

vow He vowed never to drink alcohol again.

promise² [noun]

make a promise

assurance He gave an assurance that he would look into the matter.

commitment She'd made a commitment to help them.

guarantee a guarantee that no jobs will be lost

pledge the party's pledge to ban smoking in public places

vow We made a vow to avenge his death.

◆ **Formal word undertaking** a written undertaking not to make the details public

VOCABULARY CHOICES

• The words **pledge** and **vow** are quite old-fashioned and formal-sounding but they

Pp

are often used in newspapers about a promise that someone has made publicly, to help convey how serious it is.

proof [noun]
confirmation Their red faces were confirmation of their guilt.
evidence Your success is evidence that you worked hard.

VOCABULARY CHOICES
• If you are asked in a job application to write about something good that you have done, you can say that it is **evidence** of a particular skill or quality you have.

property [noun]
1 I could fit all my property in two cases.
belongings Remember to pick up your belongings before leaving the train.
goods At our wedding, we vowed to share all our goods.
possessions He doesn't have much in the way of possessions.
things Get your things together and go.
♦ **Formal word effects** Her personal effects were sold after her death.
♦ **Informal word gear** I picked up my gear and left.
2 They own property all over the country.
buildings beautiful buildings beside the river
estate the Duke of Devonshire's estate
houses The estate agent has a number of attractive houses for sale.
land He owns land in Scotland.
premises The company is looking for new premises.

protect [verb]
conserve a charity that helps conserve gorillas in the wild
defend the right to defend yourself when being attacked
preserve efforts to preserve old buildings
safeguard tighter laws to safeguard animals

shield He put out a hand to shield her from attack.

protection [noun]
conservation the conservation of the panda
preservation the preservation of old buildings
safeguard safeguards for the future of the industry

proud [adjective]
1 He's too proud to admit he was wrong.
arrogant an arrogant young man
bigheaded I don't want to sound bigheaded but I knew I was pretty.
cocky a couple of cocky lads
conceited He was conceited enough to think that he was always right.
high and mighty She's too high and mighty to speak to someone like me.
self-important a self-important young businessman
2 proud of his achievements
delighted He was delighted at his success.
pleased She was pleased at her work.
satisfied I'm very satisfied at the way my kids have turned out.

prove [verb]
Your passport proves your nationality.
bear out Her behaviour bears out her guilt.
confirm This just confirms what I thought.
demonstrate The study demonstrates that children are affected by violence on TV.
show It shows you can't be too careful.
♦ **Formal word verify** We were unable to verify his claims.

prove wrong [verb]
The results proved his theory wrong.
debunk Has the theory about the Loch Ness monster now been debunked?
disprove This fact disproves Allen's story that he was at home at the time.
explode The research could explode the

Pp

myths about passive smoking.

give the lie to *Thatcher gave the lie to the notion that women can't be leaders.*

pry [verb]

nose *She's always nosing into other people's business.*

snoop *journalists snooping into the lives of celebrities*

♦ **Informal phrase poke your nose in** *I don't want to poke my nose in where I'm not wanted.*

pull¹ [verb]

1 pull a caravan

drag *She dragged the suitcase along the ground.*

draw *a carriage drawn by horses*

haul *He hauled her out of the water.*

jerk *She jerked the horse's reins.*

tow *a car towing a trailer*

tug *He tugged the rope.*

♦ **Informal word yank** *He grabbed my hair and yanked my head back.*

2 pull a tooth

pull out *pull out a tooth*

remove *He's having a wisdom tooth removed.*

take out *I've had two teeth taken out.*

♦ **Formal word extract** *He's having a front tooth extracted.*

3 pull the crowds

attract *a place that attracts visitors from all over the world*

draw *The concert is expected to draw large crowds.*

entice *ways of enticing customers into the shop*

lure *We were lured by the promise of big prizes.*

4 pull a muscle

sprain *He sprained his wrist.*

strain *She strained a ligament in her shoulder.*

wrench *She slipped and wrenched her ankle.*

Pp

VOCABULARY CHOICES

[meaning 3]

• The words **entice** and **lure** sometimes suggest that something is being used to attract people but it may be disappointing, or they may not actually get it.

pull² [noun]

1 Give the rope a pull.

jerk *She gave the handle a jerk.*

tug *She felt a tug on her sleeve.*

♦ **Informal word yank** *He gave the door a yank.*

2 the pull of London

attraction *the attraction of life in the city*

lure *the lure of more money*

punch¹ [verb]

He punched me on the arm.

bash *Someone bashed him on the back of the head.*

hit *He had hit her on the nose.*

thump *He thumped her in the face.*

♦ **Informal word wallop** *He walloped me on the cheek.*

♦ **Slang word sock** *He'd sock me if I said that.*

punch² [noun]

a punch on the nose

bash *a bash on the head*

blow *a blow to the skull*

thump *I gave him a thump.*

♦ **Informal word wallop** *a wallop on the arm*

♦ **Slang word sock** *a sock in the eye*

punish [verb]

discipline *They will have to be disciplined for their disobedience.*

penalize *The team was penalized for foul play.*

♦ **Formal word chastise** *The boys were chastised for not doing their homework.*

♦ **Informal phrase teach someone a lesson** *If he is rude to me again, I'll teach him a lesson!*

punishment [noun]
   penalty *We need harsher penalties for drug offences.*
   revenge *The bombs were revenge for the country's support of the war.*
◆ **Formal word** **retribution** *People fear retribution for their crimes.*

pure [adjective]
1 *pure gold*
   genuine *genuine leather goods*
   one hundred per cent *one hundred per cent cotton*
   real *a scarf of real silk*
   solid *solid silver*
   undiluted *undiluted orange juice*
   unmixed *unmixed fabrics*
◆ **Formal word** **unadulterated** *unadulterated chemicals*
2 *pure greed*
   absolute *That's an absolute lie!*
   complete *I felt a complete fool.*
   downright *a downright disgrace*
   sheer *sheer joy*
   thorough *It was a thorough waste of time.*
   total *a total lack of regard for others*
   utter *To my utter amazement, he agreed.*
3 *pure water*
   clean *clean drinking water*
   clear *a clear stream*
   natural *natural ingredients*
   spotless *a spotless kitchen*
   sterile *a sterile hospital environment*
   uncontaminated *uncontaminated foods*
   unpolluted *unpolluted sea water*
4 *a pure person*
   innocent *innocent children*
   virginal *a virginal young woman*
◆ **Formal word** **chaste** *chaste thoughts*

VOCABULARY CHOICES
[meaning 2]
• The word **downright** is used to emphasize something that is bad or offensive: *That is downright insulting.*

purple [noun]

Shades of purple:
lavender   plum
lilac   violet
mauve

purpose [noun]
1 *You need a purpose in life.*
   aim *the aim of the project*
   goal *achieve your goals*
   intention *the intention of the scheme*
   objective *his political objectives*
2 *He couldn't see any purpose in it.*
   benefit *I can't see any benefit to it at all.*
   good *What's the good in loving someone you can never have?*
   use *What's the use in saying anything? He never listens.*

push [verb]
1 *Push the button.*
   press *Press the lever to start the machine.*
◆ **Formal word** **depress** *Depress the pedal with your foot.*
2 *She pushed him out of her way.*
   jostle *People in the queue were jostling each other.*
   ram *She rammed her shopping into her bag.*
   shove *He shoved her against the wall.*
   thrust *She thrust her way through the crowds.*
3 *The company is pushing its products.*
   advertise *advertising new brands*
   promote *She was on the show promoting her latest book.*
   publicize *They want to publicize the event with posters.*
◆ **Informal word** **plug** *He's always plugging that restaurant he owns.*

Pp

VOCABULARY CHOICES
[meaning 2]
• **Shove** and **thrust** both suggest the use of a lot of force, as does **ram**, which also

suggests the action is done in an angry way.
- **Jostle** also suggests rough treatment, usually in or by a crowd.

[meaning 3]
- The word **plug** is often used with a little disapproval, for example if you want to suggest something is being publicized too much or in a very obvious way.

push ² [noun]

She gave him a push to make him move.

nudge a gentle nudge on the shoulder
shove I gave him a shove in the back.
thrust He made several thrusts with this sword.

put [verb]

1 Put it over there.

lay She laid flowers on her mother's grave.
place He placed the books on the shelf.
position He positioned the hat on his head.
set Jo set the tray down on the table.
stand You could stand the bookcase in the corner.
◆ **Informal word plonk** He plonked his bag down on the table.

2 You have put me in a difficult situation.

place The decision placed us at a serious disadvantage.

3 How can I put it another way?

express expressed in different terms
phrase I couldn't have phrased it better myself.
state He stated it very clearly.
word It might be better if we worded it differently.

VOCABULARY CHOICES

[meaning 1]
- The word **plonk** suggests that you put something somewhere without thinking about what you are doing.

puzzle ¹ [verb]

1 Their behaviour always puzzled him.

baffle The look on her face baffled him.
confuse Her reply confused me even more.
mystify a disease that has mystified doctors
stump We were all stumped by that question.
◆ **Formal words bewilder** His attitude bewilders me.
perplex Their friends were perplexed by their decision.
◆ **Informal word throw** The message threw me.

2 We puzzled over the problem for a while.

mull over She is mulling over the situation in her mind.
rack your brains I'm racking my brains to think of a solution.
think I need to think carefully about what to do next.
◆ **Formal words deliberate** There's no point in deliberating over what happened.
ponder He was pondering what he should say to her.

puzzle ² [noun]

a crossword puzzle • the puzzle of what to do next

brainteaser a book of brainteasers
conundrum We were faced with a conundrum that was hard to solve.
mystery Women had always been a mystery to him.
poser That crossword clue is a bit of a poser!
problem maths problems
riddle solving riddles

Pp

quarrel¹ [noun]

another quarrel about money

argument She's had an argument with her mum.

clash clashes between the minister and a journalist

disagreement We have disagreements from time to time.

dispute a dispute between workers and management

row They were having a row in the street.

tiff He's had another tiff with his girlfriend.

VOCABULARY CHOICES

• The word **dispute** is slightly formal and is usually used about disagreements between groups of people over a particular issue.

• The word **clash** is used in newspapers to talk about arguments, especially between politicians, to suggest they are very forceful.

quarrel² [verb]

We quarrelled a lot before we split up.

argue Her parents are always arguing.

bicker Why do children bicker so much?

clash She clashed with the Chancellor over income tax.

disagree I disagreed with Frank on one or two things.

fall out Have you two fallen out again?

row They were rowing with each other about something silly.

squabble a noise like two cats squabbling

question¹ [verb]

The detectives questioned him for hours.

ask We asked him about his job.

cross-examine Stop cross-examining the child!

interrogate She was interrogated by enemy troops.

interview The police are interviewing her now.

quiz Why do you keep quizzing me about my past?

♦ **Informal word grill** He was grilled for four hours by the police.

question² [noun]

1 I have a couple of questions.

query Does anyone have any queries?

♦ **Formal word inquiry** Please make all inquiries in writing.

2 That's not the question we're dealing with at the moment.

issue Money is always an awkward issue.

matter Have you discussed the matter of childcare?

point There were arguments on the point of cost.

subject The weather is an interesting subject.

topic books on the topic of politics

queue [noun]

line a long line of fans waiting to meet the star

Qq

211

tailback *a five-mile tailback of traffic on the M8*

quick [adjective]

1 *a quick look • a quick phone call*
brief *I had a brief glance at the letter.*
fleeting *For a fleeting moment, I felt glad.*
2 *a quick reply • quick service*
brisk *walking at a brisk pace*
fast *very fast delivery*
hasty *Alex made a hasty grab for the glass.*
hurried *a hurried journey north*
prompt *Thank you for your prompt reply.*
rapid *a rapid change in the weather*
speedy *a speedy system*
swift *He made a very swift recovery.*
3 *She's very quick at picking things up.*
clever *a very clever student*
sharp *one of the sharpest politicians*
shrewd *a shrewd businessman*
smart *She's too smart to be fooled by that.*

VOCABULARY CHOICES

[meaning 2]
• You use the word **brisk** especially about the quick way someone is doing something, often walking.
• The formal word **prompt** and the rather more informal word **speedy** suggest that you appreciate the speed with which something has been done. **Prompt** can also be used in a polite request to have something done quickly: *a prompt reply would be appreciated.*
• If something is done quickly because you are in a hurry, you can describe it using the word **hasty** or **hurried**, and these words sometimes suggest that something is poor because it is not done in a careful or organized way.

quiet¹ [adjective]

1 *quiet as a mouse • in a quiet voice*
silent *The room was completely silent.*

soft *a soft whisper*
♦ **Formal word hushed** *He spoke in hushed tones.*
2 *quiet surroundings*
calm *Back in the empty house, everything was calm.*
peaceful *a peaceful corner of the garden*
still *the still waters of the lake*
tranquil *The little village has a tranquil atmosphere.*
3 *a quiet person*
introverted *He is outgoing, but his wife is very introverted.*
reserved *She is the quiet, reserved type.*
shy *Alan is quite shy in company.*
♦ **Formal word retiring** *a rather retiring gentleman*
4 *a quiet spot*
isolated *The cottage is quite isolated.*
private *We wanted a room that was more private.*
secluded *a secluded garden*

quiet² [noun]

I longed for some peace and quiet.
calm *the calm after the storm*
peacefulness *the peacefulness of a summer afternoon*
silence *We stood in silence.*
stillness *the stillness of early morning*
tranquillity *the tranquillity of these wild places*

quit [verb]

1 *He quit his job.*
give up *He wants to give up work and move to France.*
leave *She's leaving the company at the end of the month.*
2 *She quit smoking.*
give up *She'd find it hard to give up wine completely.*
stop *They persuaded him to stop drinking altogether.*
♦ **Informal term pack in** *She found it hard to pack in smoking.*

Qq

quite [adverb]

1 quite good

  a bit *I am getting a bit annoyed by your antics.*

  fairly *a fairly posh hotel*

  rather *He looked rather tired.*

  reasonably *You are reasonably healthy for your age.*

2 quite awful

  absolutely *The film was absolutely brilliant.*

  completely *He made a completely stupid suggestion.*

  totally *We were totally shocked.*

  utterly *Most of the children looked utterly bored.*

Qq

R

race [1] [noun]

They made a race for the exit.

dash It will be a mad dash to get there on time.

run We made a run for the bus.

rush a rush for concert tickets

scramble There was a scramble to get the best seats.

sprint a sprint to the finish line

race [2] [verb]

He raced out of the room to be sick.

dash Clara dashed off before we could speak to her.

hurry We hurried inside to get out of the rain.

run I saw a man run out into the road.

rush Hundreds of people were rushing to get their shopping done.

sprint He sprinted across the yard to greet us.

zoom The black car zoomed off in the other direction.

race [3] [noun]

equal treatment for people of all races

people the Asian peoples of India, Pakistan and surrounding countries

rage [1] [noun]

He could barely contain his rage.

anger the force of her anger

fury Pike's face reddened with fury.

tantrum A child was having a tantrum in the shop.

temper We stay away from her when she's in a temper.

VOCABULARY CHOICES

• The word **tantrum** suggests a childish outburst of temper over something trivial. It sounds quite mocking if you use it about the actions of an adult.

rage [2] [verb]

He'll be raging when he finds out.

fume I could see he was fuming inside.

seethe She came off the phone seething.

rain [1] [noun]

I'll go out when this rain stops.

downpour We got soaked in a sudden downpour.

drizzle It's not heavy rain, just drizzle.

rainfall The region had four inches of rainfall in a single day.

shower It's just a shower — the sun will be out again soon.

storm The little boat was tossed about in the storm.

rain [2] [verb]

It's been raining all day.

drizzle It was drizzling a bit when we left.

pour You'll need your coat — it's pouring.

spit It's spitting with rain.

◆ **Informal term bucket down** It's bucketing down outside!

rare [adjective]

unusual It's unusual for him to be late.

◆ **Formal word scarce** *Players as good as her are scarce.*

raw [adjective]
1 raw vegetables
fresh *fresh fruit*
uncooked *The chickens are sold uncooked.*
2 raw cotton
crude *crude oil*
unrefined *unrefined petroleum*
untreated *untreated sewage*
3 The wound is still raw.
sensitive *The surrounding skin is still sensitive.*
tender *The bruise is quite tender.*
4 It's raw outside.
biting *a biting north wind*
bitter *We stood outside in the bitter cold.*
freezing *one of those freezing January mornings*
piercing *chilled to the bone by a piercing wind*

read [verb]
browse through *She's browsed through your report.*
look at *Janice didn't even look at the letter.*
scan *I scanned the newspaper for his photo.*
skim through *I skimmed through the first few pages.*
study *A man was studying his map.*

VOCABULARY CHOICES
• If you **browse through** something or **skim through** something, you read it quickly and not very carefully.
• If you **scan** something, you look at it carefully in order to find a particular word, sentence, or piece of information.
• If you **study** something, you read it very carefully and slowly.

ready [adjective]
1 Everything is ready for the party.

arranged *The hotel and the flights are arranged.*
organized *Is the food organized?*
prepared *The room is prepared for your meeting.*
set *Everything was set for a fun evening.*
2 He's always ready to help.
eager *I'm eager to give it a try.*
happy *She was happy to do any job we gave her.*
keen *The kids are keen to be involved.*
willing *The money is good, if you're willing to work hard.*

real [adjective]
1 real diamonds
actual *It's not actual rabbit fur.*
genuine *genuine leather*
◆ **Formal word authentic** *an authentic signature*
2 His anger was real.
genuine *My shock was genuine.*
heartfelt *a heartfelt apology*
honest *Her tears were an honest expression of sadness.*
sincere *sincere feelings of sympathy*

realize [verb]
become aware *She became aware they planning a party for her.*
catch on *The teachers caught on to our plot and stopped us.*
discover *I discovered what he was up to by accident.*
get *I didn't get the meaning of his words.*
grasp *Eric hadn't grasped the purpose of our visit.*
understand *She doesn't understand how dangerous this is.*
◆ **Informal word twig** *I quickly twigged what was going on.*

reason [noun]
1 the reason for his silence • *What was their reason for leaving?*
cause *What was the cause of his anger?*

Rr

excuse *Alan always has an excuse for being late.*
explanation *Did she give any explanation for her behaviour?*
motive *What motive did he have for stealing the letter?*
purpose *the purpose of our visit*
2 Work it out using reason.
common sense *Sam had the common sense not to walk across the tracks.*
sense *We're glad you had the sense to open a window.*
◆ **Informal word brains** *He didn't have the brains to switch the gas off.*

record¹ [noun]
1 a record of events
account *The book gives a personal account of the incident.*
history *a history of the 20th century*
notes *my notes from the class*
report *reports on the war*
◆ **Formal words chronicle** *a chronicle of the war years in France*
documentation *documentation relating to the new rules*
minutes *the minutes of last month's meeting*
2 a new world record
best performance *the player's best performance this season*
fastest time *She recorded her fastest time over 10,000 metres.*
personal best *The jump is a personal best for the Swedish woman.*
3 This company has a good record in the electronics industry.
background *Despite his impressive background, he didn't get the job.*
history *a department with a long history of failures*
track record *The firm has an excellent track record in customer relations.*

record² [verb]
1 I recorded the time in my notebook.

enter *Enter your name on the top line.*
note down *Giles noted down the address.*
put down *Just put down that we're pleased.*
register *Did you register your name at the front desk?*
write down *I wrote down her number.*
2 I recorded last night's programme.
tape *If you're going out, you could tape it.*
video *My brother videoed the wedding.*

recover [verb]
1 recover from illness
get better *She's still weak, but she's getting better.*
get over *Dad is getting over a nasty bout of flu.*
◆ **Formal word recuperate** *He's recuperating in hospital.*
2 recover stolen goods
get back *It's unlikely you'll get the money back.*
◆ **Formal word retrieve** *Two bottles fell into the water but we managed to retrieve them.*

red¹ [noun]

Shades of red:

burgundy	maroon
cerise	ruby
cherry	scarlet
crimson	vermilion
magenta	

red² [adjective]
1 a red face
flushed *She looked flushed after the long walk.*
rosy *Alison's rosy complexion*
ruddy *His cheeks were ruddy from the cold.*
2 red hair
auburn *her long auburn locks*
chestnut *a chestnut horse*

Rr

ginger *a boy with ginger hair*

reduce [verb]
cut *We're always cutting prices.*
fall *The number of births has fallen.*
lessen *The agreement lessened the tension between the two sides.*
lower *Lower the temperature in the oven.*
shrink *Washing at very high temperatures will shrink your clothes.*
slash *The value of our houses has been slashed.*

VOCABULARY CHOICES
• The word **slash** is used to add impact by suggesting dramatic cuts. It is often used in advertisements for sales to attract attention: *All our prices have been slashed.*

redundant [adjective]
1 *Mina was made redundant.*
out of work *the number of people out of work*
sacked *Unions are supporting the sacked workers.*
unemployed *benefits for unemployed people*
2 *a redundant machine*
unnecessary *After everything that had been said, his comment was unnecessary.*
♦ **Formal word superfluous** *The report contained a lot of superfluous information.*

reference [noun]
1 *He makes no reference to his family in either of his books.*
comment *She passed a pleasant comment about my hat.*
mention *There was no mention of his name in the letter.*
remark *He made unkind remarks about my appearance.*
2 *in reference to your letter*
connection *evidence in connection with a robbery*
relation *questions in relation to my salary*

♦ **Formal words regard** *No changes were made with regard to tax.*
respect *an interesting painting in respect of its colours*

VOCABULARY CHOICES
[meaning 2]
• 'In **reference** to' and 'with **regard** to' are more often used in polite or formal writing such as business letters and reports.

refund [verb]
pay back *If the goods are faulty they should pay you back.*
repay *Has the loan been repaid?*
return *Your deposit will not be returned.*
♦ **Formal word reimburse** *His travelling expenses will be reimbursed.*

refuse [verb]
reject *She rejected our offer of help.*
turn down *Anna was offered the job but turned it down.*
♦ **Formal word decline** *The minister declined our invitation.*

relate [verb]
1 *The two companies are related.*
ally *The countries allied themselves in the war.*
associate *We associate some words with sadness.* • *dangers associated with drinking*
connect *companies connected with the tourist industry* • *The police did not connect him to the crime.*
link *These two ideas are linked.*
2 *letters relating to the issue*
apply *These rules apply to us all.*
be relevant *skills that are relevant to the job*
refer *notes referring to the court case*
♦ **Formal word pertain** *all situations to which the law pertains*
3 *I can't relate to him at all.*
get on with *He doesn't get on with his father.*

Rr

identify with Readers identified with the hero of the book.

sympathize with It's difficult to sympathize with such extreme views.

understand I don't really understand my sister.

♦ **Formal term empathize with** Try to empathize with people from other cultures.

♦ **Informal phrase be on the same wavelength** I am definitely on the same wavelength with my best mate.

relations [noun]

1 all our friends and relations

family aunts, uncles and other members of my family

relatives There are more relatives on my mother's side.

2 friendly relations with other countries

relationship There have been attempts to improve the relationship between the two nations.

terms We were on good terms with the Germans.

relax [verb]

calm down A drink will calm you down.

unwind Listening to music helps me to unwind.

♦ **Informal terms chill out** I like to chill out to dance music.

loosen up You'll have to learn to loosen up.

relaxed [adjective]

a relaxed manner

calm the calm mood inside the meeting room

carefree Sarah has a carefree attitude to most things.

easy an easy life in the country

easy-going We liked his easy-going approach.

informal There's a nice informal atmosphere in the classroom.

natural You want a leader with a natural style.

release [verb]

free We couldn't free him from the animal's grip.

let go The child eventually let go of my hand. • Let the captives go.

let out All the prisoners were pardoned and let out.

♦ **Formal word liberate** He aimed to liberate all people from slavery.

reliable [adjective]

dependable a very dependable colleague

faithful your faithful dog

trustworthy Are the staff trustworthy?

VOCABULARY CHOICES

• Someone who is **dependable** does what they say they will do. You usually use this word about people who you are likely to ask for help, such as friends, or people you normally work with.

• If you say someone is **trustworthy**, you think they are honest and you feel you can trust them to do what you ask them to do.

• You usually use the word **faithful** about people you love, to emphasize that they always give you support or help when you need it. In stories, you sometimes see this word used about animals and servants.

religious [adjective]

religious texts

holy The priest sprinkles holy water.

sacred Mecca is a sacred place for Muslims.

spiritual a discussion of spiritual matters

remember [verb]

1 remember old times

call to mind I called to mind the days gone by.

cast your mind back Cast your mind back to when we met.

look back She looked back to a time when she was happier.

Rr

◆ **Formal words recall** *I don't recall saying that.*
recollect *I can't quite recollect where I have seen him.*
reminisce *We reminisced about the good times.*
2 Remember to put the cat out.
bear in mind *Bear in mind all the things you have to do.*

VOCABULARY CHOICES

[meaning 1]

• If you **reminisce**, you deliberately think about pleasant times in the past. The word has positive connotations, as it means you are enjoying the memories.

remind [verb]

bring to mind *The words brought to mind an old song.*
call to mind *The sweet taste calls to mind roasted chestnuts.*
jog your memory *I carry notes to jog my memory about things to do.*
prompt *She prompted me when I forgot what I had to say.*
put you in mind of *The smell of baking puts me in mind of my grandmother's house.*
refresh your memory *I can't remember which meeting you mean, could you refresh my memory?*
take back *That song takes me back to my schooldays.*
◆ **Formal word evoke** *The taste of ice-cream evokes summer days.*

remove [verb]

1 remove a tooth
cut off *Cut the label off.*
pull off *Pull the top off the bottle.*
pull out *Pull out the plug.*
strip off *Strip all the old paint off.*
take away *Some men came to take the rubbish away.*
take off *Take off your shirt.*

◆ **Formal word detach** *Complete and detach the form at the bottom of the page.*
2 Remove all traces of dirt.
delete *They deleted the file from the hard drive.*
erase *She had erased the incident from her memory.*
get rid of *You should get rid of that idea.*

VOCABULARY CHOICES

[meaning 2]

• **Get rid of** suggests that you are removing something unwanted or unhelpful, sometimes quite forcefully, and that you will be relieved when it is gone.

rent[1] [noun]

We can hardly afford to pay the rent.
hire *Car hire will be around £20 a day.*
rental *a television rental company*

rent[2] [verb]

We can rent a car once we arrive.
charter *Evans had chartered a plane to take us there.*
hire *We hired offices in the city centre.*
lease *They lease a fleet of cars for the business.*

repair [verb]

fix *A man came to fix the washing machine.*
mend *I'll have to mend the broken fence.*
renovate *The whole building is being renovated.*
restore *She restores old furniture.*

VOCABULARY CHOICES

• You usually use the word **renovate** to talk about repairing old buildings that haven't been used for a while or haven't been looked after very well.
• The word **restore** is used especially about old things that no longer look good. When you restore them, you make them look as good as they did when they were new.

Rr

repay [verb]
  pay back *Have you paid back the money you borrowed?*
  refund *If you cancel, your deposit will not be refunded.*
◆ **Formal word reimburse** *Your travelling expenses will be reimbursed.*

repeat [verb]
1 *I don't want to repeat that experience.*
  do again *You'll have to do the sum again until it is correct.*
  redo *I had to redo all the work.*
◆ **Formal word duplicate** *If we plan the job well, we won't duplicate our efforts.*
2 *Repeat these words after me.*
  echo *This statement echoes what I said before.*
  parrot *Don't just parrot the manager's words!*
  quote *Tom quoted exactly what Ramesh had said.*
  say again *Could you say that again, please?*
◆ **Formal words reiterate** *The President reiterated his policy on TV.*
  restate *Can you restate your name, please?*
◆ **Informal word recap** *Let's recap what we promised to do.*

Rr

VOCABULARY CHOICES
[meaning 2]
• The word **parrot** sounds critical, as you are suggesting that someone is just repeating what another person has said and is not really thinking about what the words mean.

reply¹ [verb]
She hasn't replied to any of my e-mails.
  acknowledge *I wrote but he never acknowledged my letter.*
  answer *When I called her name, she didn't answer.*
  respond *How did she respond to that question?*

  retort *'Of course I'm nervous,' he retorted.*

VOCABULARY CHOICES
• The word **retort** itself suggests that the answer is angry, even without an adjective describing it.

reply² [noun]
We've written to them twice but have had no reply.
  acknowledgement *I complained to the company three weeks ago but have had no acknowledgement yet.*
  answer *I asked the question but she gave no answer.*
  reaction *Her reaction was to call me a liar.*
  response *I've had no response to my letter.*
  retort *an angry retort*
◆ **Formal word riposte** *a witty riposte*

report [noun]
  account *The book gives a personal account of the incident.*
  article *a magazine article about the latest fashions*
  bulletin *the most recent news bulletins*
  description *Can you give me a description of the scene?*
  item *an interesting item on the news*
  piece *a newspaper piece about Kennedy*
  story *The story will be covered in our current affairs programme.*
◆ **Formal word chronicle** *a chronicle of the war years in France*

rescue¹ [verb]
He rescued a child from drowning.
  free *Have the hostages been freed?*
  save *Firefighters managed to save the whole family.*
◆ **Formal word liberate** *A week later Paris was liberated by Allied troops.*

rescue² [noun]
the dramatic rescue of three sailors
  release *the release of all hostages*

◆ **Formal word liberation** the liberation
of animals from cruelty

resign [verb]
  leave He's thinking of leaving the
  company.
  quit I've decided to quit my job.
  stand down Alan will be standing down
  as secretary at the end of the year.

respect¹ [noun]
  1 They have respect for their elders.
  admiration He soon won the admiration
  of his students.
  courtesy The junior members treat her
  with courtesy.
  2 excellent in every respect
  aspect You learn all aspects of the game.
  sense He's a gentleman in every sense.
  way It was in every way a lovely holiday.

respect² [verb]
  1 I respect his judgement.
  admire You have to admire his patience.
  value I really value your friendship.
  2 We teach kids to respect the law.
  follow You must follow the instructions.
  obey Soldiers are expected to obey
  orders.
  ◆ **Formal word observe** The game is
  more fun if you observe the rules.

responsible [adjective]
  1 Are you responsible for this mess?
  guilty She was guilty of being too
  confident.
  to blame Who's to blame for that?
  2 a responsible adult
  mature a very mature young woman
  reliable a reliable assistant
  sensible He's a pretty sensible boy.
  trustworthy Are the staff trustworthy?

rest¹ [noun]
  1 Try to get some rest.
  relaxation a busy week with not enough
  relaxation
  2 You need a rest.
  break After hours of marking, all the

teachers needed a break.
  pause There will be a brief pause for
  coffee.
  ◆ **Informal term time out** I think we need
  some time out after all that effort.

rest² [verb]
  1 Just rest for a moment.
  break We'll break there for coffee.
  pause I'll pause now and answer
  questions.
  stop Let's stop there for lunch.
  2 You should rest in bed.
  relax I relaxed on the couch for an hour.
  3 He rested his hand on her shoulder.
  lean The woman was leaning on his
  shoulder.
  prop Just prop your bike up against that
  wall.

rest³ [noun]
Just take what you want and leave the rest.
  balance You can pay the balance in
  instalments.
  leftovers The leftovers will do for
  tomorrow's lunch.
  others Three children had speaking parts.
  The others did singing and dancing.
  remainder Heat the remainder of the
  sauce in a small pan.

result¹ [noun]
What result do you expect from the
meeting?
  effect the effect of the illness on children
  end He started the fire with one end in
  mind.
  outcome the outcome of the police
  investigation
  upshot What was the upshot of your talk
  with the boss?

result² [verb]
  1 Her insecurity results from her background.
  follow the events that followed her arrest
  spring Where did this feeling spring from?
  stem Our problems stem from lack of
  money.

Rr

◆ **Formal word arise** *the dangers arising from that decision*

2 Carelessness results in mistakes.
cause *The decision will cause anger among the workers.*
involve *The task doesn't involve much work.*
mean *Less grant money will mean severe cutbacks.*

return¹ [verb]

1 return home
come back *She's coming back to her home town next month.*
go back *He went back to his native Portugal.*

2 return his belongings
give back *You'll have to give the money back.*
hand back *She handed me back the knife.*
send back *Alison sent back all my letters.*

return² [noun]

1 He will deal with this on his return.
comeback *The 70-year-old singer is ready to make a comeback.*
homecoming *Friends and family gathered for her homecoming.*

2 a good return on their investment
profit *The company failed to make a profit this year.*

reverse¹ [verb]

1 reverse into the garage
back *She backed the car into the drive.*
back up *A truck was backing up.*

2 reverse a decision
cancel *That order has been cancelled.*
overturn *The Appeal Court overturned his conviction.*
quash *The high court quashed an earlier ruling.*
undo *What is done cannot be undone.*

3 A mirror reverses the image.
turn round *If you turn the words round, it makes sense.*

◆ **Formal word invert** *a shape like an inverted letter C*

VOCABULARY CHOICES
[meaning 2]
• The words **quash** and **overturn** are most often used in news reports when a court or other official body reverses a decision that was made earlier. These words suggest dramatic actions, and convey any dramatic effect of the reversal. The word would not be used by the court itself.

reverse² [noun]

the reverse of the card
back *the back of the coin*
opposite side *the opposite side of the paper*

rich [adjective]

1 a rich family
wealthy *the wealthy nations of the world*
well off *Her parents are quite well off.*
well-to-do *a well-to-do neighbourhood*
◆ **Formal words affluent** *Our society is very affluent.*
prosperous *a prosperous lawyer*
◆ **Informal word moneyed** *his moneyed girlfriend*

2 a rich supply of food
abundant *Meat provides an abundant source of protein.*
ample *The hotel offers ample parking.*
◆ **Formal words copious** *copious amounts of alcohol*
plentiful *Fish are plentiful in this river.*

3 rich food
fatty *Cut down on fatty foods.*
heavy *The cake was a little too heavy for me.*

ride [noun]

drive *We went for a drive in the country.*
journey *a two-day journey to France*
lift *I can give you a lift to the station.*

Rr

outing *Parents have to pay for school outings.*
trip *We had planned a trip to the beach.*
♦ **Informal word spin** *Why don't you take the car for a spin?*

VOCABULARY CHOICES

• The words **trip** and **outing** both refer to a short journey that people make for pleasure, although the word **outing** is slightly old-fashioned now.
• **Spin** also suggests a trip taken for pleasure, in a car.

right[1] [adjective]

1 the right answer
accurate *These measurements aren't accurate.*
correct *The correct answer is C.*
2 the right thing to do
appropriate *That wasn't the appropriate thing to say.*
proper *Some of the children didn't have the proper uniform.*
suitable *He wasn't wearing suitable clothes for sailing.*
3 a right decision
fair *a fair judgment*
good *You can feel proud that you've done a good thing.*
just *They have a just claim to the money.*

right[2] [adverb]

1 You've got to do it right.
accurately *Measure the distance accurately.*
correctly *If you've cut it correctly, it should fit.*
properly *You're not holding the knife properly.*
2 The stone sank right to the bottom.
directly *We went directly home.*
straight *The truck drove straight into a wall.*

ring[1] [noun]

1 chairs arranged in a ring

band *a simple gold band on his finger*
circle *We all stand in a circle.*
circuit *The runners do two circuits of the track.*
hoop *a white shirt with green hoops*
loop *The belt goes through these loops.*
2 a drugs ring
band *a band of robbers*
gang *gangs of youths*
group *a terrorist group*
mob *a mob of hooligans*

ring[2] [verb]

1 The doorbell rang.
chime *I heard the town clock chime.*
clang *a busy kitchen with pots and pans clanging*
jingle *His keys jingled as he ran.*
sound *We waited for the bell to sound.*
2 He asked me to ring him back.
call *I'll call back when you're less busy.*
call up *Just call me up if you need me.*
dial *I dialled his number.* • *She grabbed the phone and dialled the police.*
phone *Your mum phoned earlier.*
ring up *Why don't you ring them up and complain?*
telephone *We'll telephone you with the results.*
♦ **Informal phrases give a buzz** *I'll give you a buzz tomorrow.*
give a tinkle *Give me a tinkle when you're ready to set off.*

VOCABULARY CHOICES

[meaning 2]
• The informal phrases **give a buzz** and **give a tinkle** have a friendly, familiar tone. While they might be used with friends and family they would not be used, for example, when speaking to a contact at work.

ring[3] [noun]

1 the ring of a bell
chime *the chimes of a grandfather clock*
clink *the clink of coins*

Rr

tinkle *the tinkle of breaking glass*

2 She promised to give me a ring.
call *I'll give David a call later.*
phone call *Have there been any phone calls for me?*

◆ **Informal words** **bell** *Will you give me a bell when you know?*
buzz *I'll give her a buzz later.*
tinkle *She said she'd give you a tinkle.*

rip¹ [verb]

1 He ripped his sleeve on the wire.
shred *Finely shred the lettuce leaves.*
tear *He tore the photograph to pieces.*

2 She ripped the book out of his hand.
grab *She grabbed the phone from me.*
seize *He got up on stage and seized the microphone from her.*
snatch *He snatched the paper from my hand.*

rip² [noun]

a rip in the page
split *a split in his jeans*
tear *a tear in her T-shirt*

rise¹ [verb]

1 *smoke rising into the sky*
climb *The aircraft continued to climb.*
go up *We went up to two thousand feet.*

2 Temperatures are rising.
increase *The number of unemployed people has increased.*
intensify *The wind intensified.*
jump *The death toll has jumped to 40.*
mount *Pressure is mounting on the Prime Minister.*

3 Living standards are rising.
get better *The nation's health is getting better.*
improve *Has her performance in maths improved?*

4 She rose to her feet.
get up *James got up and walked to the window.*
stand up *Now stand up and stretch your arms up.*

VOCABULARY CHOICES
[meaning 2]
• The word **jump** indicates a sudden and dramatic rise, and is used is news reports.

rise² [noun]

the rise in crime
increase *tax increases*
jump *a jump in house prices*

risk¹ [noun]

1 *a job that involves risk*
danger *Will he be in any danger?*
◆ **Formal word** **peril** *Our lives were in real peril.*

2 There is no risk of flooding.
danger *Is there any danger the road will become blocked?*
possibility *There's the possibility of snow on the hills.*

VOCABULARY CHOICES
[meaning 1]
• The word **peril** is sometimes used when you want to be funny and suggest that something has more dangers than it really does: *the perils of being married to a pop star.*

risk² [verb]

Don't risk your health by taking drugs.
endanger *You wouldn't endanger the lives of your children.*
jeopardize *She didn't want to jeopardize her career.*

road [noun]

roadway *Cyclists should travel on the roadway, not the pavement.*
route *a shorter route to London*
street *a house across the street*
◆ **Formal words** **highway** *Protesters were arrested for obstructing the highway.*
thoroughfare *This is the town's main thoroughfare.*

roar [verb]

1 *'Get out!', he roared.*

Rr

bawl *Rugby fans were bawling out songs in the street.*

bellow *The teacher bellowed at them to stop talking.*

cry *'Shut up!' he cried.*

howl *'Don't dare move!' she howled.*

yell *He yelled at me to help him.*

2 roaring with laughter

guffaw *The audience guffawed.*

hoot *Everyone hooted with mirth.*

howl *She had the children howling at her jokes.*

rob [verb]

burgle *The place had been burgled.*

cheat *She cheated relatives out of their savings.*

defraud *an employee who defrauded the Post Office of £100,000*

hold up *Two men held up the train.*

steal from *He would even steal from his own grandmother.*

swindle *The company had swindled its clients.*

♦ **Informal terms do** *I had the feeling I'd been done.*

rip off *Customers are being ripped off.*

rock [noun]

a mermaid sitting on a rock

boulder *A crane lifted the boulders onto the back of a truck.*

stone *Their house is now just a pile of stones.*

rock² [verb]

The ladder rocked but did not fall.

lurch *The van lurched as the driver took the corner.*

reel *My head is reeling from the noise.*

toss *The little boat is tossed around on the waves.*

roll¹ [verb]

1 *The dice rolled. • He rolled the ball to me.*

rotate *The wheel rotates once only. • Rotate the handle clockwise.*

spin *The blade spins at great speed. • She spun the wheel.*

turn *His car left the road and turned over. • Turn over on to your back.*

twirl *The baton twirled in her hands. • He twirled the drumstick between his fingers.*

2 *The hedgehog rolled up into a ball.*

coil *The snake coils itself around a branch.*

curl *She was curled up under the covers.*

roll² [noun]

1 *a roll of paper*

reel *eight reels of film*

spool *a spool of thread*

2 *the electoral roll*

directory *the telephone directory*

list *a list of all the students on the course*

record *Do you keep a record of what you sell?*

register *Is my name on the register?*

3 *the roll of drums*

clap *a loud clap of thunder*

roar *the roar of a plane overhead*

rumble *the rumble of a passing goods train*

romantic [adjective]

1 *a romantic view of the world*

fairytale *She had imagined a fairytale wedding.*

starry-eyed *He's a bit starry-eyed about love.*

unrealistic *an unrealistic estimate of how long the job would take*

♦ **Formal word idealistic** *an idealistic view of life in the countryside*

2 *He wrote romantic letters.*

loving *a loving husband*

passionate *a passionate lover*

tender *tender words*

♦ **Formal word amorous** *amorous behaviour in public*

♦ **Informal words lovey-dovey** *a card with a lovey-dovey message*

mushy *She was getting all mushy.*

slushy *She gets slushy text messages from her boyfriend.*

soppy *a soppy love story*

Rr

Rooms:

Rooms in houses:		Rooms in other buildings:	
attic	kitchen		foyer
basement	lavatory	boardroom	laboratory
bathroom	living room	changing room	office
bedroom	loft	classroom	staff room
boxroom	lounge	common room	storeroom
cellar	playroom	consulting room	strongroom
conservatory	sitting room	control room	studio
dining room	spare room	courtroom	waiting room
guest room	study	darkroom	
hall	toilet	dormitory	
	utility room		

VOCABULARY CHOICES

[meaning 2]
• The words **mushy**, **slushy** and **soppy** hint at embarrassment: *Those slushy songs make me cringe.*

---

room [noun]
capacity *the stadium's seating capacity*
elbow-room *There isn't much elbow-room in the kitchen.*
legroom *a car with plenty of legroom*
space *Is there space for a table in here?*
volume *Measure the volume of each box.*
See also the box above.

rot [verb]
eat away *rust eating away the metal*
wear away *You can see where part of the rock has been worn away.*
♦ **Technical terms corrode** *Some of the pipes had been corroded.*
erode *Many of our beaches are being eroded.*

rotten [adjective]
1 *rotten wood • rotten fruit*
bad *These pears have gone bad.*
decaying *Her teeth were decaying.*
mouldy *Don't eat the bread if it's mouldy.*
off *Does this milk smell off?*
2 *a rotten job*
bad *The film was really bad.*
poor *a poor standard of service*

terrible *The DJ played some terrible music.*
♦ **Informal words crummy** *a crummy little guest house*
lousy *The room was okay but the food was lousy.*
ropy *ropy advice*

rough [adjective]
1 *a rough surface*
bumpy *bumpy roads*
uneven *uneven ground*
2 *rough treatment*
cruel *a cruel system*
hard *Conditions in prison were hard.*
harsh *a harsh decision*
severe *severe punishment*
3 *a rough guess*
vague *a vague idea of how many people are coming*
♦ **Formal word approximate** *an approximate number*
4 *rough seas*
choppy *The lake looked a bit choppy.*
stormy *stormy weather*
violent *violent storms*
wild *a wild and windy day*

roughly [preposition]
about *There were about 50 people at the meeting.*
approximately *approximately 1.70 metres tall*

Rr

around *There were around one hundred people at the party.*
more or less *He's been here more or less 18 months.*

round [adjective]
circular *a circular table*
curved *a curved line*
rounded *rounded edges*
◆ **Formal word spherical** *The bulb is completely spherical.*

row [superscript 1] [noun]
a classroom filled with rows of desks
column *a column of figures*
file *prisoners walking in single file*
line *a line of cars*
queue *Hundreds of people were already in the queue.*
tier *several tiers of seating*

row [superscript 2] [noun]
1 *I had a row with my husband.*
argument *arguments between friends*
clash *a legal clash over the issue*
disagreement *We had a disagreement over pay.*
dispute *disputes between workers and management*
quarrel *He's had a quarrel with his wife.*
tiff *a lovers' tiff*
◆ **Informal term slanging match** *A difference of opinion turned into a full-scale slanging match.*
2 *Stop that row immediately!*
clamour *the clamour of children's voices in the playground*
commotion *There was some commotion in the classroom.*
din *I shouted above the din.*
noise *Who's making all that noise?*
racket *Where's that racket coming from?*
uproar *There was uproar in parliament when the plan was announced.*

VOCABULARY CHOICES

[meaning 1]
• The word **clash** is usually used in

newspapers and news reports to add impact to the story.
• You might use the word **tiff** to play down an argument and suggest that it is not very serious. It is most often used when the people arguing are boyfriend and girlfriend, or wife and husband.

rowdy [adjective]
boisterous *a house full of boisterous children*
loud *his loud friends*
noisy *The children were being particularly noisy.*
wild *a wild party*
◆ **Formal word unruly** *unruly behaviour*

rub [verb]
1 *These shoes are rubbing my heels.*
chafe *The collar was chafing the dog's neck.*
graze *I grazed my elbow on the wall.*
scrape *She fell and scraped her chin on the ground.*
2 *Rub the cream into your skin.*
buff *Spray on the polish and buff with a clean cloth.*
massage *Massage the lotion into your neck.*

rubbish [noun]
1 *rubbish scattered on the beach*
junk *His bedroom is full of junk.*
litter *streets full of litter*
waste *All the waste is recycled.*
◆ **Formal words debris** *We remove leaves and other debris from the train lines.*
refuse *Refuse collection is organized by the council.*
2 *He's talking rubbish.*
drivel *Don't believe any of that drivel.*
nonsense *What a lot of nonsense!*
◆ **Informal words claptrap** *a speech full of the usual claptrap*
garbage *He talks a load of garbage.*
rot *Don't talk such rot!*

Rr

227

twaddle *The plot of the book is romantic twaddle.*

◆ **Slang word cobblers** *I thought his speech was a load of cobblers.*

rude [adjective]

1 The girl was rude to the teacher.
abusive *The man was very abusive.*
disrespectful *He was drunk and disrespectful towards staff.*
insulting *an insulting remark*
offensive *offensive behaviour*

◆ **Formal words impertinent** *Teachers don't like impertinent children.*
impudent *an impudent pupil*
insolent *insolent behaviour*

◆ **Informal word cheeky** *Don't be cheeky to your mum.*

2 The boy made a rude noise.
coarse *coarse language*
dirty *dirty jokes*
obscene *an obscene gesture*
vulgar *a vulgar expression*

ruin [verb]

destroy *The news destroyed our hopes.*
mar *The event was marred by a few violent incidents.*
shatter *a bomb that shattered the peace of the day*
spoil *This has spoiled my chances of winning.*
undermine *The noise undermined our enjoyment of the holiday.*
wreck *The affair wrecked our marriage.*

◆ **Informal term mess up** *I hope I don't mess up this test.*

rule [noun]

command *commands to the soldiers*
decree *A decree ordered all weapons to be given up.*
guideline *government guidelines on safety in the workplace*
instruction *a set of instructions to be followed*

law *a law banning smoking from public places*
order *a court order*

rumour [noun]

gossip *I don't listen to gossip like that.*
hearsay *He's not leaving. That was just hearsay.*
story *I heard stories that Alan had won the lottery.*
talk *There's been a lot of talk about me resigning.*
word *The word is that Francis has asked her to marry him.*

run¹ [verb]

1 I had to run for the bus.
dash *We dashed in out of the rain.*
hurry *I hurried along to the bank.*
jog *You see dozens of people jogging in the park.*
race *The kids go racing round the playground.*
rush *A middle-aged man came rushing into the room.*
sprint *The boys went sprinting off to catch the bus.*
tear *The car came tearing out of a side street.*
zoom *The black van zoomed off in the other direction.*

2 The route runs through the village.
go *This road goes to Cannock.*
pass *The Edinburgh train passes through York.*

3 Leave the engine running.
function *The computers are functioning normally again.*
operate *The motor can operate at half speed.*
perform *The machines are all performing well.*
work *When the system works, it's fantastic.*

4 Muhammad runs a company.
control *Sarah controls our office in Swindon.*

Rr

head The team is headed by a former lawyer.
lead The project is led by a man in his thirties.
manage Who manages the Claims Department?
oversee Mike oversees the packing process.
5 I can hear water running.
flow The dirty water flows out through this pipe.
gush You expect oil to come gushing out of the ground.
pour Blood was pouring from a wound on his arm.
stream She had tears streaming down her face.

run² [noun]
1 I go for a run every morning.
jog I had a jog round the park before breakfast.
sprint We jog for a hundred yards then do a sprint.
2 She took the family for a run in the car.
drive a drive in the country
ride He gave me a ride in his new Bluebird.
spin Do you fancy going for a spin?
3 a run of bad luck
chain a strange chain of events
series a series of mistakes

string a string of unlucky experiences
runny [adjective]
thin a thin paste
watery The sauce is a bit watery.
rush¹ [verb]
Two policemen rushed into the room.
charge He came charging into my office.
dart A squirrel darted up a tree.
dash Arthur dashed across the road to the pub.
fly A car came flying out of a side street.
hurry Let's hurry or we'll miss the bus.
race She raced home to catch the news.
run I decided to run into town to buy it.
sprint Two young women sprinted up to him.
tear His dog came tearing out of the house.
rush² [noun]
He made a sudden rush for the door.
hurry The letter was written in a hurry.
race the race to be the first country to put a man on the moon
scramble There was a scramble to get the best seats.

VOCABULARY CHOICES
• The word **scramble** is used when people try very hard to get something before others get it, and often treat each other roughly in order to be first.

Rr

S

sack¹ [verb]

He was sacked from his job for stealing.
   fire *They fired him for smoking in the toilets.*
   lay off *Hundreds of workers have been laid off.*
   make redundant *She was made redundant last month.*
   ♦ **Formal word dismiss** *You could be dismissed for doing that.*

sack² [noun]

He got the sack for being rude to customers.
   notice *The company has given him his notice.*
   ♦ **Formal word dismissal** *The slightest mistake resulted in instant dismissal.*
   ♦ **Informal terms the boot** *The bank is giving Sarah the boot.*
   the push *It looks like we're all getting the push.*
   your cards *They'll give you your cards if you're late again.*

sad [adjective]

1 Don't look so sad.
   dejected *We left the meeting feeling very dejected.*
   down *I was feeling quite down until you called.*
   downcast *He was looking very downcast, so I asked what was wrong.*
   gloomy *Why are you looking so gloomy?*
   glum *There's no need to be glum.*
   heartbroken *She left him and he was heartbroken.*
   miserable *Why is she always so miserable?*
   unhappy *He's feeling pretty unhappy today.*
   upset *She was so upset when her father died.*
   ♦ **Formal words despondent** *The team are despondent after yet another defeat.*
   sorrowful *a dog with large, sorrowful eyes*

2 That is sad news. • *a sad story*
   depressing *a depressing result*
   distressing *I have some distressing facts to report.*
   painful *I had the painful task of telling them about the accident.*
   tragic *a tragic case of neglect*
   unfortunate *an unfortunate injury*
   upsetting *This is a very upsetting film.*
   ♦ **Formal words heart-rending** *the heart-rending plight of starving children*
   poignant *a poignant love story*

VOCABULARY CHOICES

[meaning 1]
- **Glum** and **downcast** suggest that someone looks sad on the outside as well as feeling sad inside.
- The word **heartbroken** is sometimes used to stir the emotions, by suggesting someone

is extremely upset by something that has happened to them.
[meaning 2]
• The word **tragic** is often used to add impact and emotion to newspaper stories, even if the event was not as bad as the word suggests: *If Jones retires, it will be a tragic loss to football.*

sadness [noun]
gloom *She told a joke to try to lift the gloom.*
grief *He felt terrible grief when she died.*
heartbreak *the heartbreak of divorce*
misery *the misery suffered by the people of the town*
unhappiness *She tried to smile, but her unhappiness was obvious.*
♦ **Formal words despondency** *There was an air of despondency in the dressing room.*
sorrow *She tried to comfort him in his sorrow.*

safe [adjective]
1 *Is the water safe to drink?*
harmless *fertilizers that are harmless to the environment*
non-toxic *Many of these chemicals are non-toxic.*
uncontaminated *They delivered uncontaminated milk to the villages.*
2 *Make your property safe from burglars.*
protected *The palace was protected against attack.*
secure *a secure place to store the money*
3 *They were found safe and well.*
all right *I heard you fall — are you all right?*
unharmed *The prisoners were released unharmed.*
unhurt *I'm glad you're all unhurt.*
uninjured *The driver of the other car was uninjured.*
unscathed *We survived the experience unscathed.*

♦ **Informal word OK** *Don't worry, I'm OK.*

safety [noun]
protection *The witnesses were given police protection.*
security *the security of the country*
shelter *a place of shelter for the refugees*

sail [verb]
1 *We sail for France tomorrow.*
set sail *They set sail for Greece.*
♦ **Formal terms embark** *The ship embarks from Liverpool next week.*
put to sea *We put to sea for a day's fishing.*
2 *She sailed the yacht around the world.*
skipper *She skippered the boat to Paros.*
steer *I steered the little tug into the harbour.*
3 *The kite sailed over our heads.*
float *The balloons float up into the sky.*
glide *Clouds glide across the sky on a gentle breeze.*

salary [noun]
earnings *What were your earnings for the year?*
income *the tax we pay on our income*
pay *a higher rate of pay*
wages *She got an extra £50 in her wages this week.*

same [adjective]
1 *You gave the same excuse yesterday.*
identical *Your jacket is identical to one I had.*
selfsame *The selfsame thing happened last week.*
2 *These words have the same meaning.*
equivalent *It is much cheaper in the USA for the equivalent amount of fuel.*
matching *curtains in a matching fabric*
similar *This car is similar but smaller.*

save [verb]
1 *save money • save time*
cut back *We're cutting back on the amount of sugar we eat.*
♦ **Formal word economize** *I managed to*

Ss

save over £100 just by economizing.

2 I'm saving money for my holidays.
keep Keep some of the juice to use in the sauce.
put by I have a little money put by.
set aside Set aside ten minutes during the day for relaxation.

3 The wall will save the village from floods.
defend The hedgehog's spikes defend it from attack.
protect The shelter was supposed to protect us from fallout.
shield The mountains shield us from the worst of the wind.

say [verb]

1 Say the words aloud.
read Please read the name on the label.
speak She refuses to speak his name.
♦ **Formal word recite** We had to recite these poems in class.

2 She says she's innocent.
claim He claims he's never seen her before.
maintain The police maintain that no gun was found.

3 I'd say it was about two o'clock. • We can't say yet how much it will be.
estimate Billy estimated the job would take three weeks.
guess I guessed there were fifty or sixty people in the hall.
imagine I imagine they've already arrived.
presume We presumed you'd be coming too.
reckon I reckon it's about five o'clock.

scare [verb]

frighten Did the darkness frighten you?
startle A loud noise startled the horse.
terrorize The youths were terrorizing the entire neighbourhood.
threaten She threatened me with a knife.
♦ **Formal word intimidate** They were intimidated into paying more money.

scared [adjective]

frightened a frightened look
nervous I was nervous about the test.
shaken She looked shaken after her experience.
startled eyes wide like a startled rabbit
terrified He had a gun — we were terrified.
worried a worried expression on his face

VOCABULARY CHOICES

• All these words could be used to create a fearful mood in a piece of text.
• The word **terrified** has a lot of impact, as it suggests that someone is very afraid.

scary [adjective]

chilling There was a chilling silence in the hotel.
creepy a room at the end of a creepy corridor
eerie eerie shadows
frightening Getting stuck in a lift was a frightening thought.
hair-raising a hair-raising scream
spine-chilling a spine-chilling ghost story
terrifying the terrifying violence of the wind
♦ **Informal word spooky** The room was dark and spooky.

VOCABULARY CHOICES

• All these words can be used to create a mood of suspense or fear in a piece of text.
• The words **creepy**, **eerie** and **spooky** can create a tense atmosphere where you feel frightening things could happen.
• The words **chilling**, **hair-raising**, **spine-chilling** and **terrifying** in particular suggest something is extremely frightening, and are used for more impact.

scatter [verb]

diffuse a device that diffuses light
disperse The mob dispersed when the police arrived.

Ss

shower *Guests showered confetti over the happy couple.*

spread *Spread the seeds over a wide area.*

sprinkle *She sprinkled the chocolate over the cake.*

strew *We strewed the path with rose petals.*

scruffy [adjective]

messy *You're such a messy dresser.*

ragged *a ragged little boy*

shabby *a shabby old tramp*

tatty *I keep some tatty clothes for working in the garden.*

untidy *She arranged her untidy hair.*

worn-out *an old, worn-out sofa*

◆ **Formal words dishevelled** *She came in from the garden looking hot and dishevelled.*

unkempt *His tie was not straight and his hair was unkempt.*

search[1] [verb]

a mother searching for her lost child

comb *Police combed the area for the weapon.*

hunt *detectives hunting for the killer*

look *We looked everywhere but couldn't find the keys.*

scour *Volunteers scoured the countryside for clues.*

search[2] [noun]

a nationwide search for the killers

hunt *the hunt for the kidnapper*

◆ **Formal word quest** *the quest for knowledge*

second [noun]

flash *In a flash, he was gone.*

minute *Just a minute — I think I've left my phone behind.*

moment *Wait a moment while I check.*

◆ **Formal word instant** *The meal is ready in an instant.*

◆ **Informal words jiffy** *I'll be back in a jiffy.*

tick *Hang on a tick.*

secret [adjective]

1 *They kept everything secret.*

concealed *She kept her real identity concealed.*

hidden *They kept the affair hidden from the public.*

private *It's a private matter I won't discuss.*

2 *a secret mission • a file marked 'secret'*

confidential *confidential information about a patient*

inside *He has inside knowledge of what is going on.*

◆ **Formal word classified** *The precise location of the base is classified.*

3 *a secret message*

cryptic *a cryptic remark*

mysterious *written in some sort of mysterious code*

see [verb]

1 *I can see it in the distance.*

distinguish *He distinguished an animal in the darkness.*

make out *I could make out a figure in the shadows.*

sight *After three days at sea, we finally sighted land.*

spot *We spotted her going into a pub.*

◆ **Formal words discern** *I discerned a shape in the fog.*

observe *I observed him sneaking out the door.*

2 *She could see it in her mind's eye.*

imagine *Try to imagine you're on a beach.*

picture *I can just picture his face when you told him.*

visualize *I tried to visualize the lost map.*

3 *I see your point.*

appreciate *I appreciate the problem you have.*

follow *We don't quite follow what you mean.*

get *I didn't get the meaning of his words.*

grasp *She grasped the situation immediately.*

Ss

realize *I didn't realize you were coming.*
understand *I do understand that this is difficult for you.*
4 See them into the study.
escort *A man with a torch escorts you to your seat.*
show *A student showed us round the campus.*
usher *Troublemakers were quickly ushered out of the building.*
5 He's seeing another woman.
date *He started dating his secretary.*
go out with *Did you know he was going out with Amy?*
6 We're going to see his family.
meet *We're meeting her for lunch.*
spend time with *How much time does he spend with the kids?*
visit *She's visiting a cousin in Glasgow.*

selfish [adjective]
greedy *a greedy attitude*
self-centred *He's quite a self-centred person.*
self-interested *I've never met anyone so self-interested.*

sell [verb]
peddle *the sort of rubbish these shops peddle*
retail *The shirt normally retails for around £15.*
traffic *involved in trafficking heroin*

Ss

VOCABULARY CHOICES
• You use the word **peddle** if you don't like the things that someone is selling, for example because they are of bad quality.
• The word **traffic** is used especially about selling illegal drugs.
• **Retail** is quite a formal way of saying 'sell', and you use it especially about companies or shops.

seller [noun]
dealer *arms dealers*
merchant *a wine merchant*

retailer *high-street retailers*
supplier *We ordered more from our supplier.*

VOCABULARY CHOICES
• The word **dealer** is quite a general word and can be used to describe a person who buys and sells any kind of product. It is also used about someone who sells things illegally, for example drugs or arms.
• A **supplier** is a person or company who sells things to a shop.
• The word **retailer** is quite a formal word and it means a shop or shopkeeper.
• The word **merchant** is also quite formal and is usually used about people or companies who sell expensive things or things of good quality.

sense¹ [noun]
1 a sense of longing
feeling *a feeling of not belonging to the group*
impression *He gives the impression he's an expert.*
sensation *a spinning sensation in my head*
2 He had the sense to realize his mistake.
intelligence *He wouldn't have the intelligence to think up a plan like that.*
wisdom *I'm glad you had the wisdom not to get involved.*
♦ **Informal word brains** *At least you had the brains to switch the electricity off.*
3 the sense of a word
definition *What's the definition of 'wicked'?*
meaning *There are several meanings of that word.*

sense² [verb]
I sensed that I was not alone.
feel *She felt that someone was watching her.*
realize *I realized he was standing behind me.*

sensible [adjective]
  commonsense *a commonsense approach to the problem*
  level-headed *She stays level-headed in a crisis.*
  rational *He'd lost his mind. He wasn't rational any more.*
  sane *Any sane person would think the same.*
  wise *a wise decision*

sensitive [adjective]
1 *sensitive to criticism*
  temperamental *Be careful what you say. She can be temperamental.*
  touchy *He's a bit touchy about his lack of hair.*
2 *sensitive instruments*
  precise *a precise piece of equipment*

sentimental [adjective]
  emotional *He's quite an emotional person.*
  nostalgic *She gets very nostalgic about her childhood.*
  romantic *a romantic film*
  schmaltzy *schmaltzy music*
  ◆ **Informal words** **gushy** *gushy praise for his new book*
  mushy *a card with a mushy message*
  slushy *She gets slushy text messages from her boyfriend.*
  soppy *Don't be so soppy — I've only been away a few hours!*
  weepy *a weepy film*

VOCABULARY CHOICES
• A few of these synonyms are disapproving in tone. **Gushy**, for instance, hints that the feeling is insincere.
• The terms **mushy**, **slushy** and **soppy** are also negative, and hint at embarrassment: *Soppy love songs make me cringe.*
• Some of the words do not suggest criticism: **nostalgic** simply suggests being sentimental about the past, while **romantic** suggests being sentimental about love.

separate[1] [verb]
My parents separated when I was nine.
  divorce *The couple divorced a year later.*
  part *At least we parted as friends.*
  part company *We decided it was time to part company.*
  split up *She's split up with her boyfriend.*

separate[2] [adjective]
We all have separate rooms.
  apart *Keep the cows and the bulls apart.*
  detached *Is the house detached?*
  distinct *Leopards and jaguars are two distinct animals.*
  independent *These are two independent parts of the motor.*
  individual *Each guest has their own individual bathroom.*
  unconnected *a completely unconnected incident*
  unrelated *These two events are unrelated.*

serious [adjective]
1 *a serious error*
  crucial *a crucial mistake*
  important *an important decision*
2 *a serious accident* • *a serious illness*
  dangerous *Is the virus dangerous?*
  severe *a severe headache*
3 *a serious expression on her face*
  earnest *She always looks so earnest.*
  solemn *a solemn handshake*

serve [verb]
1 *Someone will serve you shortly.*
  assist *How can I assist you?*
  attend to *Attend to this lady, please.*
  help *We try our best to help our customers.*
  wait on *I had to wait on seven tables in the restaurant.*
2 *serve food*
  dish out *Help me dish out the potatoes.*
  dish up *She dished up a fabulous meal.*
  give out *I'll give out the peas, you give out the carrots.*

Ss

Shapes:

circle	diamond	prism	sphere
cone	hexagon	pyramid	square
crescent	oval	rectangle	trapezium
cube	parallelogram	rhombus	triangle
cylinder	pentagon	semicircle	

set [noun]
 batch a batch of papers
 bunch a bunch of keys
 collection a collection of objects
 group Sort the toys into groups.
shake [verb]
1 The wind was shaking the branches.
 jerk The noise jerked me from my sleep.
 jog She jogged my elbow and I spilled my drink.
 jolt The train jolted to a halt.
2 The earth shook. • He shook with fear.
 quake Her loud voice made them quake in their boots.
 quiver She could feel her lip begin to quiver.
 tremble The children were trembling with excitement.
 vibrate The whole house vibrates when a train goes past.
3 The news shook him.
 distress The report distressed me.
 disturb We were disturbed to discover he was missing.
 shock We were all shocked by this announcement.
 unsettle He was unsettled by his opponent.
 upset Her comments had upset me.
 ◆ **Formal word unnerve** What unnerved me was how easy it had been to break in.
shaky [adjective]
 rickety a rickety bridge
 unsteady He's a bit unsteady on his legs.
 wobbly a wobbly tooth
shame [noun]
 disgrace She had brought disgrace on

the whole family.
 embarrassment the embarrassment of another failure
 humiliation the humiliation of being beaten by a child
 ◆ **Formal words dishonour** He brings dishonour on the entire nation.
 disrepute Her conduct brings the whole game into disrepute.
shape¹ [noun]
1 I could see the shape of a ship in the fog.
 contours the contours of her body
 outline the outline of the skyscrapers on the horizon
2 Dad's in good shape for his age.
 condition The animal is in excellent condition.
 form He'll be on top form for next week's game.
 health We hope you'll soon be back in good health.
 state What sort of state was he in after the party?
See also the box above.
shape² [verb]
a machine that shapes the pasta
 form Form the clay into a ball.
 mould Take the dough and mould it into a disc shape.
share¹ [verb]
I'll share my winnings with my family.
 distribute Distribute your chores rather than doing them all yourself.
 divide These three rulers divided the country up between them.
 share out Share these sweets out among your friends.

Ss

split *We'll split the money fifty-fifty.*

share² [noun]

He took more than his fair share.

part *I've done my part of the work.*

portion *Each person is given a portion of the pie.*

quota *The gallery gets its quota of ten per cent of the picture's sale price.*

ration *We'd used the day's ration of food by lunchtime.*

◆ **Informal word cut** *An actor's agent takes a 15 per cent cut of the fee.*

sharp¹ [adjective]

1 a sharp needle

pointed *pointed teeth*

2 a sharp rise

clear *a clear change in the weather*

distinct *There is a distinct possibility that you're wrong.*

◆ **Formal word well-defined** *well-defined limits*

3 sharp practice

clever *a clever manager of money*

crafty *a crafty lawyer*

cunning *a cunning plan*

shrewd *a shrewd businessman*

◆ **Formal word astute** *Astute investors take no chances.*

4 sharp pain

acute *Is the pain acute or dull?*

extreme *extreme anger*

intense *intense fear*

piercing *a piercing scream*

stabbing *a stabbing pain*

5 sharp-tasting

acid *an acid taste*

bitter *a bitter flavour*

sour *sour like a lemon*

tart *quite a tart sauce*

6 sharp wit

cutting *a cutting remark*

scathing *scathing comments*

◆ **Formal words caustic** *his caustic wit*

incisive *incisive criticism*

sharp² [adverb]

1 Arrive at 8 o'clock sharp.

exactly *She left exactly when she said she would.*

precisely *It is now one o'clock precisely.*

promptly *We expect you to turn up promptly for the meeting.*

punctually *The guests arrived punctually at 7.30.*

◆ **Informal phrase on the dot** *Be here at six on the dot.*

2 The horses were pulled up sharp.

abruptly *The laughter stopped abruptly.*

suddenly *The train suddenly came to a halt.*

shift [noun]

a shift towards working from home

change *the change to digital television*

movement *a movement away from traditional methods*

swing *a swing towards Labour in the polls*

switch *a switch in government policy*

shine [verb]

1 sun shining on the sea

gleam *Her eyes gleamed with affection.*

glint *The paintwork glinted in the sunshine.*

glisten *In the lane, snow is glistening.*

glow *His cigarette glows in the dark.*

sparkle *The fairy lights sparkled like diamonds.*

twinkle *Thousands of stars twinkle overhead.*

2 shine shoes

buff *Buff the surface to a shine with a clean cloth.*

polish *She polishes the boots every day.*

3 shine at athletics

stand out *Mark stands out in a class of excellent students.*

◆ **Formal word excel** *Zoe excels at music.*

shiny [adjective]

bright *bright eyes*

gleaming *gleaming teeth*

Ss

Types of shop:

baker	charity shop	greengrocer	stationer
barber	chemist	grocer	supermarket
betting shop	corner shop	hairdresser	superstore
bookmakers or	delicatessen or	health-food shop	sweet shop
bookies	deli	ironmonger	takeaway
bookshop	department store	jeweller	tobacconist
boutique	fish and chip shop	newsagent	toy shop
butcher	fishmonger	pharmacy	video shop
cash-and-carry	florist	shoe shop	

glossy *glossy hair*
sleek *the horse's sleek coat*

shiver [verb]

quake *Collins quaked with fear.*
shudder *I shuddered at the thought of touching it.*
tremble *I could see her lip beginning to tremble.*

shock¹ [verb]

1 I was shocked to hear of his accident.
astound *The response of the public astounded us.*
stun *I was stunned by their refusal to help.*
2 He was shocked by the things he saw.
disgust *That attitude disgusts me.*
horrify *We were horrified by the cruelty of the system.*
outrage *Daly was outraged by the terrible living conditions.*
sicken *The smell sickened me.*
♦ **Formal word** **scandalize** *I was sent to prison, which scandalized my mother.*

VOCABULARY CHOICES

[meaning 2]
• These words are very strong, and they express a feeling of disgust or anger as well as shock.

shock² [noun]

I had a brandy to help me get over the shock.
blow *It was a blow to hear about the accident.*
bombshell *She dropped the bombshell*

that she was leaving me.
start *The news gave me a real start.*
trauma *She never recovered from the trauma of losing him.*

shocking [adjective]

appalling *They were treated in an appalling way.*
offensive *offensive language*
outrageous *outrageous behaviour*
scandalous *a scandalous price*
sickening *a sickening lack of sympathy for the victims*

shoot [verb]

1 shooting a gun
fire *Had the gun been fired?*
launch *They launched missiles on Moscow.*
2 The car shot out of a side street.
dart *The rabbit darted back into its burrow.*
dash *I dashed up to the library before it closed.*
hurtle *An express train came hurtling through the station.*
rush *Stella was always rushing off somewhere.*
sprint *He came sprinting across the road towards us.*
3 The prisoners were shot.
gun down *They gunned him down in the street.*
kill *The police had killed an unarmed man.*
♦ **Informal term** **pick off** *A sniper in a tree*

Ss

was picking our men off one by one.

shop [noun]
See the box on the previous page.

short [adjective]
1 a short stay • a short story
brief a few brief comments
fleeting just a fleeting visit
quick That was a quick conversation.
short-lived Luckily, her anger was only short-lived.
2 a short person
little a little dog
petite clothes for petite women
small His wife is very small.
3 He was rather short with me.
blunt She was blunt to the point of being rude.
curt a curt reply
gruff a rather gruff old man
sharp Alison could be a bit sharp with customers.

VOCABULARY CHOICES
[meaning 2]
• The word **petite** describes someone who is both short and slim and it is almost always used to describe women. It is more tactful and complimentary than the word 'short'.

shortage [noun]
lack There's no lack of talent in this team.
need There's a need for experienced teachers.
shortfall a shortfall of around £5,000

shout [verb]
bawl Rugby fans were bawling out songs in the street.
bellow The teacher bellowed at them to stop talking.
call She called for help.
cry 'Shut up!' he cried.
howl 'Don't dare move!' she howled.
roar 'Get out!' he roared.
yell He yelled at me to help him.

show¹ [noun]
1 He just did it for show.
appearance He's only interested in appearances.
impression She gives the impression of being confident.
pose His look of interest was just a pose.
pretence Deepak made a pretence of liking him.
2 a show of strength
demonstration The play is a demonstration of the college's acting talent.
display a terrible display of rudeness
parade a parade of military firepower
3 a West End show
exhibition an art exhibition
performance We're doing five performances in three days.
presentation the school's presentation of this popular musical
production the National Theatre's production of Shakespeare plays
spectacle a dazzling Hollywood spectacle

show² [verb]
1 Show him how it is done. • show good judgement
demonstrate I'll demonstrate how to operate the pump.
display She displayed a talent for working with children.
reveal Clive revealed that he has great patience.
2 Please show him out.
escort We were escorted to our seats.
guide A young woman guided us through the maze of corridors.
lead He led us through to the garden.
usher They quickly ushered the protesters out of the hall.
♦ **Formal word conduct** We were conducted round the castle by a guide.

Ss

show off [verb]
boast *Avoid boasting about your success.*
brag *He brags about his children's achievements.*
flaunt *a woman who flaunts her wealth*
parade *The students get annoyed when she parades her knowledge in class.*

shut [verb]
close *Close the door behind you.*
fasten *Make sure you fasten the lid on properly.*
seal *We seal each container.*

shy [adjective]
bashful *He was too bashful to ask her to dance.*
coy *She plays at being coy.*
nervous *She gets a bit nervous in company.*
reserved *He's very reserved about his achievements.*
self-conscious *a self-conscious young man who finds public speaking difficult*
timid *The dogs are quite timid at first.*
♦ **Formal words** **retiring** *a retiring man who tends not to get involved*
withdrawn *a quiet, withdrawn little girl*

VOCABULARY CHOICES
• The word **timid** suggests that someone is shy because they are a bit afraid as well, while **bashful** suggests that they are shy because they are quite modest. **Coy** can sometimes hint that a person is not really as shy as they make out, and are pretending a little.
• **Reserved** and **withdrawn** emphasize that a person cannot, or does not want to, speak to others. The word **retiring** is similar, and emphasizes how someone is deliberately staying in the background.

sick [adjective]
1 *a sick child*
ill *He looks really ill.*

laid up *Dad's been laid up in bed for days.*
off-colour *He's been a bit off-colour recently.*
poorly *She told her dad she was feeling poorly.*
unwell *She complained of feeling unwell.*
♦ **Informal phrase** **under the weather** *I'm still a bit under the weather.*
2 *I feel sick.*
nauseous *The smell made me nauseous.*
queasy *Some of the passengers felt queasy.*
3 *He's sick of waiting.*
tired *I'm tired of doing the dirty jobs.*
♦ **Informal term** **fed up** *I'm fed up with the rotten pay.*

VOCABULARY CHOICES
[meaning 1]
• **Off-colour** and **under the weather** suggest someone is feeling slightly sick, and these terms help to make it sound less serious.

sickness [noun]
1 *She's recovering from a long sickness.*
complaint *a stomach complaint*
condition *a rare medical condition*
disease *heart disease*
illness *mental illness*
♦ **Formal word** **ailment** *patients with all sorts of ailments*
2 *The symptoms are sickness and dizziness.*
nausea *A wave of nausea came over me.*
queasiness *Some queasiness is to be expected.*
vomiting *The illness can cause headaches and vomiting.*

sign [noun]
1 *a sign of peace*
emblem *For Russians, the bird is an emblem of long life.*
logo *the company logo*

Ss

symbol *The heart has always been a symbol of love.*
token *A handshake is a token of friendship.*
2 He gave a sign of annoyance.
  gesture *He made a rude gesture with his finger.*
  signal *She made a signal to turn left.*
3 The sign said 'Keep off the grass'.
  notice *There's a notice on the board about it.*

silence¹ [noun]
They sat in complete silence.
  hush *the hush of a summer's afternoon*
  quiet *the quiet of the library*

silence² [verb]
He silenced us with a stern glance.
  muffle *a device that muffles the noise of the engine*
  quieten down *Turning on the TV usually quietens them down.*

silent [adjective]
  quiet *The house was deathly quiet.*
  still *the still night*
♦ **Formal word hushed** *She spoke in a hushed whisper.*

silly [adjective]
  childish *a childish joke*
  foolish *a foolish young man*
  idiotic *What an idiotic suggestion!*
  immature *She's too immature for that job.*
  irresponsible *It was an irresponsible thing to do.*
  ridiculous *It's ridiculous to expect them to work for nothing.*
  stupid *a stupid idea*
♦ **Formal words ludicrous** *It's ludicrous to expect a three-year-old to know that.*
  senseless *a senseless crime*
♦ **Informal word daft** *Don't be daft! That would never work.*

simple [adjective]
1 a simple question
  easy *an easy task*

straightforward *a straightforward thing to explain*
uncomplicated *Fixing it is an uncomplicated job.*
2 He has a simple nature.
  innocent *These are innocent children.*
  naive *He was naive enough to believe her.*

VOCABULARY CHOICES
[meaning 2]
• If you describe someone as **naive**, you may be criticizing them for being a bit too innocent, and not realizing that they were being fooled or treated badly by someone.

sit [verb]
  perch *A robin perched on the fence.*
  rest *The thrush rested on a windowsill for a few seconds.*
  settle *A bee settled on his hand.*

situation [noun]
  case *It was a bad case of neglect.*
  circumstances *He behaved quite politely given the circumstances.*
  condition *What is the patient's current condition?*
  predicament *I found myself in a difficult predicament.*
  state *The drought was so severe that a state of emergency was declared.*
  state of affairs *What an awful state of affairs this is!*

size [noun]
  extent *the extent of the problem*
  height *the height of the fence*
  length *Measure the length of the table.*
  measurements *You'll need the measurements of the floor.*
  scale *the scale of the disaster*
  volume *What's the volume of the water tank?*
♦ **Formal words dimensions** *the dimensions of the Earth*

Ss

proportions *a scandal of huge proportions*

skill [noun]
ability *He has excellent athletic ability.*
expertise *We need your expertise in computers.*
talent *She has a great talent for music.*
◆ **Formal word proficiency** *the student's proficiency in English*

skip [verb]
1 *Children skipped around the playground.*
bounce *The kids bounced about with excitement.*
dance *We danced around happily.*
hop *Sparrows hopped across the lawn.*
jump *We walked along, jumping over puddles.*
prance *prancing around like a ballet dancer*
◆ **Formal word gambol** *lambs gambolling in the field*
2 *Skip that section of the book.*
jump *The book was boring so I jumped a chapter.*
leave out *I'd leave that bit of the letter out.*
miss out *Miss out the introduction and just go straight to chapter one.*
◆ **Formal word omit** *You omitted the last verse of the song.*

slap¹ [noun]
a slap on the cheek
clip *a clip round the ear*
smack *a smack on the bottom*

slap² [verb]
1 *slap someone's face*
hit *She hit him on the back of the head.*
smack *He smacked me in the mouth.*
◆ **Formal word strike** *The blow struck Jenkins square on the chin.*
◆ **Informal word clout** *I'll clout you if you do that again!*
2 *slap on paint*
daub *Graffiti had been daubed on the walls.*

plaster *She had plastered her face with make-up.*

sleep¹ [verb]
I can't sleep with all that noise going on.
doze *She was dozing in a chair.*
snooze *I snoozed for a couple of hours.*
◆ **Informal terms drop off** *I must have dropped off for a few minutes.*
nod off *The room was so warm I kept nodding off.*

sleep² [noun]
She never gets enough sleep now the baby's here.
doze *He had a doze in front of the fire.*
nap *Get your head down for a nap.*
snooze *I managed a snooze for half an hour.*
◆ **Formal word slumber** *He was deep in slumber when I called.*
◆ **Informal term forty winks** *I decided to have another forty winks.*

slide [verb]
glide *We watched the skaters glide across the ice.*
skid *A car skidded off the road.*
skim *skimming stones across the water*
slip *I stood on a banana skin and slipped along the pavement.*
slither *The snake slithered quietly towards them.*

slight [adjective]
little *a little misunderstanding*
minor *a few minor injuries, but nothing serious*
small *a small problem*
trivial *a trivial complaint*

slim [adjective]
1 *a slim waist*
lean *He looked lean and fit.*
slender *a slender young woman*
thin *thin arms*
trim *a trim figure*
2 *a slim chance of success*

Ss

faint *There's a faint hope that he'll come back.*
remote *There's a remote possibility that we've made a mistake.*
slight *There's a slight chance we'll find it.*

VOCABULARY CHOICES
[meaning 1]
• The words **slender** and **trim** are approving words that suggest someone is slim in an attractive-looking way.
• The word **lean** is associated more with looking healthy.

slip¹ [verb]
1 She slipped on the snow.
fall *She fell and sprained her wrist.*
skid *The car skidded to a halt.*
slide *The skate slides over the ice.*
stumble *I stumbled over a large stone.*
trip *Watch you don't trip.*
2 I slipped into the room without being seen.
creep *I crept upstairs.*
slink *He slinks away before anyone notices.*
sneak *We managed to sneak into the meeting.*
◆ **Formal word steal** *Celia stole into his room while he was away.*

slip² [noun]
a slip of the tongue
error *a serious error*
mistake *Everyone makes mistakes.*
◆ **Formal word oversight** *an oversight on my part*

slippery [adjective]
greasy *a greasy surface*
icy *Be careful — the roads are icy.*
treacherous *With all the snow, the pavements were treacherous.*

slow [adjective]
1 a slow pace
gradual *a gradual change*
leisurely *He walked at a leisurely pace.*

slow-moving *Traffic is slow-moving on the A34.*
sluggish *They made sluggish progress.*
unhurried *Your voice should be calm and unhurried.*
2 a slow film
boring *a boring book*
dull *The speech was so dull we fell asleep.*
long-drawn-out *a long-drawn-out meeting*
tedious *I'm sick of listening to his tedious jokes.*
uneventful *I've had a fairly uneventful day.*
uninteresting *an uninteresting story*

VOCABULARY CHOICES
[meaning 1]
• The words **leisurely** and **unhurried** suggest taking your time in a relaxed way.
• **Sluggish** suggests a more unwanted or annoying slowness.

slowly [adverb]
gradually *The clouds gradually disappeared.*
lazily *I got out of bed and moved lazily to the bathroom.*
sluggishly *We walked sluggishly in the heat.*

sly [adjective]
artful *an artful plan to avoid paying tax*
crafty *He came up with a crafty ploy to make us change our minds.*
cunning *She was both charming and cunning enough to influence the judges.*
devious *devious politicians*
furtive *He gave me a furtive wink.*
shrewd *A shrewd businesswoman can make a lot of money.*
wily *a wily old man*

smack¹ [verb]
She smacked the back of the boy's legs.
hit *The cupboard door hit me in the face.*
slap *men slapping each other on the back*

Ss

spank *The teacher would spank you if you misbehaved.*
- ◆ **Formal word** **strike** *He struck me in the face.*

smack² [noun]
a smack in the mouth
- **blow** *a powerful blow to the chin*
- **pat** *a pat on the back*
- **slap** *He'd never even had a slap from his parents.*

small [adjective]
1 a small man • a small house
- **little** *a little child*
- **minute** *minute fragments of glass*
- **petite** *clothes for petite women*
- **short** *He's very short for a basketball player.*
- **tiny** *these tiny insects*

2 a small fee • a small mistake
- **minor** *minor details*
- **petty** *a petty crime*
- **trivial** *a trivial matter*
- ◆ **Formal word** **insignificant** *an insignificant amount of money*

VOCABULARY CHOICES
[meaning 1]
- The word **petite** describes someone who is both short and slim and it is almost always used to describe women. It is more tactful and complimentary than the word 'small'.

Ss

smart¹ [adjective]
1 smart clothes • a smart appearance
- **chic** *French women are so chic.*
- **elegant** *a very elegant suit*
- **fashionable** *a very fashionable dress*
- **stylish** *She always looks stylish.*

2 a smart player • a smart move
- **bright** *a very bright student*
- **clever** *a clever thing to do*
- **intelligent** *She's a very intelligent person.*
- **sharp** *The sharper members of the audience will notice.*
- **shrewd** *a shrewd manager*

- ◆ **Formal word** **astute** *an astute politician*

smart² [verb]
My cheek still smarted from the slap.
- **sting** *It stings where I grazed my arm.*
- **twinge** *My ankle still twinges when I put weight on it.*

smell¹ [noun]
the smell of burning rubber
- **aroma** *mouthwatering aromas from the kitchen*
- **fragrance** *the fragrance of spring flowers*
- **odour** *unpleasant body odour*
- **perfume** *The flower has a lovely perfume.*
- **scent** *These candles give off a pleasant scent.*
- **stench** *the stench of rotting flesh*
- **stink** *the stink of fish*
- ◆ **Formal word** **bouquet** *a wine with a fruity bouquet*
- ◆ **Informal words** **pong** *There's a pong coming from your socks.*
- **whiff** *a whiff of cigar smoke*

VOCABULARY CHOICES
- Some of these words are very suggestive of pleasant smells, for example, **aroma**, which is used of delicious food or cooking smells.
- **Fragrance** and **perfume** also convey the idea of very pleasant smells, but these words suggest the smell of flowers.
- **Stench** and **stink**, however, are highly suggestive of nasty smells, as is the informal word **pong**, but this is often used with humour.
- The formal term **bouquet** is most often used by people discussing the smell and taste of wine.

smell² [verb]
1 Your breath smells. • The room smells strongly of spices.
- **reek** *The hall reeked of sweat.*
- **stink** *The whole place stank of fish.*

◆ **Informal word pong** *Those socks don't half pong!*
2 I smell gas.
 nose out *He nosed out the rich odours of the food.*
 scent *The wolf scented the deer in the forest.*

smelly [adjective]
 foul *a foul stench*
 stinking *Your feet are stinking!*

smile [verb]
 beam *The children beamed with pleasure.*
 grin *Alistair was grinning from ear to ear.*
 smirk *He stepped forward, smirking with confidence.*

VOCABULARY CHOICES

• **Grin** suggests a very wide smile, while **beam** suggests a sincere and very enthusiastic smile.
• **Smirk**, however, makes the negative suggestion that the smile is unpleasant because it is a bit smug: *He smirked in triumph.*

smooth [adjective]
1 a nice smooth surface
 even *You want a nice even edge.*
 flat *Spread the map out flat.*
 level *The concrete should be level.*
2 He's a smooth talker.
 slick *a slick advertising campaign*
 smarmy *I don't want to deal with some smarmy young salesman.*
 smooth-talking *the kind of smooth-talking guy that women love*

sneak [verb]
 creep *She crept down the stairs and into the kitchen.*
 lurk *someone lurking in the trees*
 prowl *a fox prowling around the garden*
 skulk *He was discovered skulking in the bushes.*
 slink *He was embarrassed and slunk out of the room.*

 slip *If we slip in quietly then no one will see us.*

snobbish [adjective]
 haughty *She gave me a haughty stare, then looked away.*
 superior *He has a superior attitude towards the workers.*
◆ **Informal words snooty** *the posh house of some snooty little girl*
 stuck-up *His parents are a bit stuck-up.*
 toffee-nosed *I didn't want to be with his toffee-nosed friends.*

soft [adjective]
1 a soft bed
 spongy *mossy ground that was spongy to walk on*
 tender *tender carrots and green beans*
2 soft colours
 delicate *a delicate shade of blue*
 muted *She always dresses in muted shades.*
 pale *pale pink*
 pastel *a room decorated in pastel colours*
3 soft fur • soft skin
 furry *a coat with a furry collar*
 silky *the dog's silky coat*
 smooth *She has skin that is beautifully smooth.*
 velvety *a rabbit's velvety ears*
4 You're too soft with that boy.
 gentle *Be gentle with the dog.*
 kind *She can be a bit too kind for her own good.*
 lax *The standards of discipline are a bit lax.*
 lenient *He's too lenient with troublemakers.*
 soft-hearted *He's a soft-hearted fool.*
 tolerant *a tolerant attitude towards bad behaviour*
◆ **Formal word indulgent** *Grandparents are sometimes too indulgent with their grandchildren.*
5 Don't go soft on us now!

Ss

Types of soldier:

cadet	guardsman	non-commissioned	rifleman
cavalryman	guerilla	officer (NCO)	sapper
commando	gunner	officer	sentry
dragoon	hussar	orderly	serviceman
ensign	infantryman	paratrooper	Territorial
fusilier	lancer	private	trooper
GI	marine	regular	

cowardly *They would be too cowardly to say that to your face.*
spineless *The management were spineless and agreed too easily.*
weak *Most bullies are very weak people.*

soggy [adjective]
   boggy *boggy ground*
   pulpy *The bread was a bit pulpy.*
   waterlogged *The pitch was still waterlogged.*

soldier [noun]
See the box above.

solve [verb]
   answer *I don't know how to answer this sum.*
   clear up *The famous detective cleared up another mystery.*
   crack *He cracked the secret code.*
   figure out *I can't figure out why she left so suddenly.*
   puzzle out *I tried to puzzle out what the weird noise could be.*
   settle *Could you settle this point for us?*
   work out *Can you work out the area of the floor?*
   ◆ **Formal word** **decipher** *The language was strange and hard to decipher.*

sometimes [adverb]
   from time to time *We still see them from time to time.*
   now and again *Now and again, a plane screams down the valley.*
   now and then *We all need to smile now and then.*

occasionally *She occasionally misses the target.*
once in a while *The grandchildren visit once in a while.*

song [noun]
   number *He sings old Frank Sinatra numbers.*
   tune *They played some familiar tunes.*

soon [adverb]
   before long *Before long, the whole street was flooded.*
   in a minute *I'll speak to her in a minute.*
   in the near future *We won't be buying a new car in the near future.*
   presently *The report will be available presently.*
   shortly *She'll be arriving shortly.*

sore [adjective]
   aching *my aching legs*
   inflamed *The skin becomes inflamed.*
   painful *a painful cut*
   raw *The wound was still raw.*
   sensitive *the sensitive area around the sprain*
   tender *The bruises are still tender.*

sorry[1] [interjection]
Sorry! I made a mistake.
   excuse me *Excuse me — I didn't mean to interrupt.*
   forgive me *Forgive me, but I've forgotten your name.*
   I apologize *I apologize for being so rude on the phone.*
   ◆ **Formal phrase** **I beg your pardon** *I*

Ss

beg your pardon, I didn't realize this was your seat.

VOCABULARY CHOICES
• All of these terms are more formal and polite ways of saying 'sorry'.

sorry² [adjective]

1 He said he was sorry for what he'd done.
apologetic Considering all the trouble he's caused, he wasn't very apologetic.
regretful He was regretful that he hadn't asked her to marry him.
2 The house is in a sorry state.
miserable the miserable conditions in the hospital
pitiful The children were in a pitiful state of health.
poor a car in poor condition
sad the sad state of the buildings
3 I was sorry to hear the sad news.
concerned She listened with a concerned expression on her face.
sad He had a good time, and he was sad to leave.
◆ **Formal word saddened** I was deeply saddened to hear of your loss.
4 I feel sorry for her.
sympathetic Most of the people he spoke to were sympathetic.

VOCABULARY CHOICES
[meaning 2]
• The word **pitiful** suggests a state that makes you sorry for any person living through it, so it is often used to stir people's emotions. It is sometimes used in newspaper reports, or in leaflets from charities.
[meaning 3]
• **Saddened** is a formal-sounding word that you might use, for example, in notes of sympathy when someone has died.

sort¹ [noun]
What sort of questions did they ask?
brand Which brand of washing powder do you use?

breed What breed is their dog?
kind This is the kind of holiday I like.
make She drives a different make of car from me.
type Choose a different type of wallpaper.
variety They have every variety of birthday cake.

sort² [verb]
Sort the clothes into white and coloured and wash separately.
arrange Arrange these events in the order they happened.
classify The film is classified a U, which means anyone can see it.
grade The eggs are graded according to size.
group The students are grouped into adults and teenagers.

sound¹ [noun]
the sound of gun fire
noise the noise of a helicopter going overhead

sound² [verb]
The siren sounded.
chime Has the clock chimed yet?
◆ **Formal term ring out** Cheers rang out from around the ground.

sound³ [adjective]
1 in sound condition
healthy The grass is looking very healthy.
solid The house looks solid enough.
sturdy a pair of sturdy walking shoes
2 a sound argument
good That's not a good reason for doing it.
logical That's the logical conclusion we reached.
rational a rational decision
reasonable The points you make are all reasonable.
valid a valid argument for killing these animals

sour [adjective]
bitter a bitter aftertaste

Ss

sharp *a sharp taste like lemon juice*
tart *The wine was quite tart.*

space [noun]

1 space to grow • space to move
capacity *The aeroplane has capacity for five hundred passengers.*
elbow-room *There's no elbow-room on the train.*
room *There isn't much room on the back seat.*
volume *Measure the volume of each box.*

2 an empty space
blank *Fill in the blanks on the form.*
gap *a gap in the fence*
opening *She looked for an opening in the rock.*

spare [adjective]

additional *Any additional money is given back to the school.*
extra *Are there any extra sheets of paper?*
leftover *They give the leftover food to the dog.*
remaining *Use the remaining herbs in the sauce.*
reserve *several gallons of reserve fuel*
surplus *The surplus grain is fed to the animals.*

speak [verb]

1 We sat speaking about different things.
communicate *This message isn't being communicated to parents.*
discuss *The children discuss their favourite food.*
say *You have to say your name.*
talk *I'll talk to the manager about it.*
tell *He was telling me his whole life story.*
♦ Formal word express *She expressed an interest in the course.*
2 She was invited to speak about her work with deaf children.
address *He addressed a crowd of schoolteachers.*

lecture *Maggie will be lecturing on history.*

special [adjective]

1 a special occasion
important *The hall is used for all important ceremonies.*
significant *a very significant event in his life*
♦ Formal word momentous *This is a momentous occasion for the country.*
2 She has her own special way of doing things.
characteristic *her characteristic way of walking*
distinctive *The pub has a very distinctive character.*
individual *The restaurants each have their own individual atmosphere.*
particular *We can build a computer to suit your particular needs.*
peculiar *The town has its own peculiar sense of style.*
unique *Each town on the lake has a unique charm.*

speed¹ [noun]

1 Cameras measure the speed of the cars.
pace *We were walking at a leisurely pace.*
rate *measure your heart rate*
2 With surprising speed, he raced away.
haste *He ate the cake with haste.*
quickness *the quickness of her movements*

speed² [verb]

The thieves sped off in the getaway car.
career *The stolen vehicle careered on followed by police.*
hurry *He hurried off in the direction of the shops.*
race *She came racing round the corner.*
rush *Ambulances rushed to the scene of the accident.*
tear *I didn't want children tearing around the house.*

Ss

zoom *The taxi zoomed off before I could get in.*

◆ **Informal word belt** *They were belting down the motorway at 100 miles per hour.*

VOCABULARY CHOICES
• The word **career** suggests that something is going so fast that it is out of control.

spend [verb]
1 spend money
lay out *The company has laid out a lot of money on new computers.*
pay out *We'd paid out £80 on tickets we couldn't use.*

◆ **Informal terms fork out** *The meal was £100 then we had to fork out extra for the drinks.*
shell out *Parents will shell out thousands of pounds on their children.*
splash out *They have just splashed out two million pounds on a mansion.*

2 spend time • spend the day
devote *He devotes most of his time to charity work.*
fill *He didn't know how he'd fill the day.*
occupy *How do you occupy your time?*
pass *a good way to pass an hour or two*

VOCABULARY CHOICES
[meaning 1]
• **Fork out** and **shell out** hint that you are unhappy as you do not really want to spend the money.
• The term **splash out** suggests someone is being extravagant, and spending a lot of money in order to treat themselves or another person.

spicy [adjective]
fiery *the fiery taste of chilli*
hot *hot curries*
nippy *a nippy sauce*

spill [verb]
overflow *The bath water overflowed onto the floor.*

pour *The water main burst and water poured down the road.*
slop *Tea was slopping over the edge of the cup.*

split¹ [noun]
1 a split in the rock
crack *cracks in the ice*
crevice *a crevice in the castle wall*
slit *She was peeping through a slit in the curtains.*
tear *a tear in his jeans*
2 a split in the party
division *the division between members of the party*

split² [verb]
1 Split the money between you.
divide *Divide the cake between you.*
share *We shared the profits.*
2 He'd split his jeans.
rip *I ripped my T-shirt.*
tear *She tore her skirt on a nail.*

spoil [verb]
1 Bad weather spoiled the holiday.
mar *The game was marred by violence.*
ruin *The rain ruined our plans for a walk.*
upset *He didn't want to do anything that would upset their friendship.*
wreck *an injury which wrecked her chances of being picked for the team*
2 Don't spoil the child.
mollycoddle *I think many young people have been mollycoddled.*

◆ **Formal word indulge** *His doting mother indulged him.*

sport [noun]
See the box on the next page.

spot¹ [noun]
1 spots of blood
dot *Red dots on the map marked where each house was.*
fleck *brown eyes with flecks of green*
speck *specks of paint*
2 a spot on her chin
pimple *a young man with pimples*

Ss

Sports:

Animal sports:	croquet	**Gym sports:**	speedway racing
greyhound racing	football	fencing	**Water sports:**
horse-racing	golf	gymnastics	canoeing
showjumping	handball	weightlifting	diving
Athletics:	hockey	**Racket sports:**	rowing
cross-country	hurling	badminton	sailing
hurdling	netball	lacrosse	swimming
javelin	polo	squash	water polo
running	rugby	table-tennis	water-skiing
shot put	snooker	tennis	**Winter sports:**
Ball games:	soccer	**Target sports:**	bobsleigh
American	volleyball	archery	curling
football	**Combat sports:**	darts	ice hockey
baseball	boxing	shooting	ice-skating
basketball	judo	**Vehicle racing:**	skiing
bowls	karate	cycle racing	snowboarding
cricket	wrestling	motor racing	tobogganing

♦ **Slang word** **zit** *a zit on his nose*

3 Find a quiet spot.

location *a beautiful location for a wedding*

place *a good place to have a picnic*

position *From his position on the roof, he could see everything.*

site *the site where the crash happened*

situation *Put the plants in a sunny situation, away from draughts.*

spot² [verb]

Can you spot the difference between them?

detect *The system can detect weapons hidden in luggage.*

notice *I hope he didn't notice that I was late.*

see *I saw him in the crowd.*

VOCABULARY CHOICES

• The word **detect** suggests that you spot something that has been difficult to see or hear.

spread¹ [verb]

1 spreading outwards

expand *The town centre has expanded over the years.*

extend *an area extending from the coast to the mountains*

sprawl *New buildings are sprawling across the countryside.*

stretch *The desert stretched for miles in front of them.*

2 The eagle spread its wings.

open *He opened his arms and put them around her.*

unfold *She unfolded the map.*

unfurl *They unfurled a banner.*

3 spreading disease

pass on *Colds can be passed on quite easily.*

♦ **Formal word** **transmit** *Mosquitoes can transmit malaria.*

VOCABULARY CHOICES

[meaning 1]

• The word **sprawl** suggests that you do not approve because something is spreading too far or in an untidy way.

spread² [noun]

1 the spread of its wings

span *the span of the bridge*

Ss

2 the spread of the disease
advance Doctors are trying to halt the advance of flu.
expansion an expansion of health care for poorer people

squash [verb]
crush The car was crushed by a falling tree.
mash Thoroughly mash the potatoes.
pound The ship was pounded against the rocks.
press Press the soil down firmly.
pulp Raspberries are pulped to make jam.
squeeze We squeezed into the crowded lift.
♦ **Formal word compress** Petrol and air are compressed in the cylinder.

squeak[1] [verb]
The mice squeaked in terror.
cheep Birds were cheeping in the nest.
peep I heard the chick peeping.
squeal 'Stop tickling me!' she squealed.

squeak[2] [noun]
squeaks of laughter from the children
cheep the cheep of baby birds
peep peeps of protest
squeal squeals of delight

squeeze[1] [verb]
1 squeeze a tube of toothpaste
crush He crushed the paper in his hand.
press He pressed her hand tightly.
2 squeeze into a corner
cram More than 500 people crammed into the church.
jam People are jammed into overcrowded airports.
pack A thousand people packed into the hall.
squash We all squashed into his car.

squeeze[2] [noun]
It was a tight squeeze, but I got through the window.
crush the crush of Christmas shoppers

squash We all got in the car but it was a bit of a squash.

stab[1] [verb]
stabbed with a dagger
jab He jabbed me with the tip of a pencil.
knife The man was knifed to death.

stab[2] [noun]
a stab of toothache
prick He felt a sharp prick in his arm.
twinge a twinge of pain in his back

staff [noun]
employees a company with over 200 employees
workers Workers demanded a pay increase.
workforce The company sacked a third of its workforce.
♦ **Formal word personnel** military personnel

stagger [verb]
1 The horse staggered to its feet.
lurch He lurched into the bedroom holding his stomach.
reel She reeled and collapsed on the road.
teeter She was teetering about in a pair of high heels.
totter The men came tottering out of a bar.
2 The price staggered me.
amaze His reaction amazed me.
astonish It astonishes me that she lets him get away with it.
astound His lack of concern astounds me.
stun Her answer stunned everyone in the room.

stain[1] [verb]
1 The grease stained the tablecloth.
mark The wine had marked the carpet.
2 I stained the wood green.
colour special substances that colour hair
paint You can paint the table.
tint lenses tinted red
varnish Varnish the floor.

Ss

stain² [noun]
grass stains on my skirt
mark There was a mark on her dress.
smear smears of blood on the cloth
smudge smudges of ink all over the paper
spot a grease spot on his trousers

stale [adjective]
1 stale bread
dry The cake was dry.
old old crackers
2 a stale smell in the room
fusty a fusty odour in the wardrobe
musty musty air

stammer [verb]
falter 'I ... I'm sorry', he faltered.
splutter 'This is private', she spluttered.
stutter 'S ... sell my car?' he stuttered.

VOCABULARY CHOICES
• The word **falter** is mainly used in stories rather than in everyday speech.
• The word **splutter** suggests that someone is angry or shocked, and that is why they cannot speak well.

stand [verb]
1 Stand the table in the corner.
place You could place a plant in that corner.
position Position the lamp where light is needed most.
put Put the bookcase next to the table.
2 I can't stand it.
bear I can't bear all this tension in the house.
tolerate I can't tolerate all this noise.
3 Stand for the national anthem.
get up He got up from the floor.
stand up Everyone stood up and started singing.
♦ **Formal word rise** He rose from his chair and walked to the window.

star [noun]
celebrity television celebrities
lead He's the lead in the school play.

megastar The singer is a megastar in Japan.
superstar sports superstars
♦ **Informal word celeb** I like to read about top celebs.

start¹ [verb]
1 start walking
begin He began seeing her two months ago.
♦ **Formal word commence** The meeting will commence at 10am.
♦ **Informal term kick off** The annual beer festival kicked off last week.
2 start a business
establish The company was established in 1973.
found a school founded in 1898
launch The group will launch a campaign to save our forests.
open She opened the shop in 1985.
3 I started at the sudden noise.
flinch She flinched when he touched her.
jump Someone shouted and he jumped.

start² [noun]
1 the start of the meeting
beginning the beginning of the day
outset He made his views clear at the outset.
♦ **Formal word commencement** the commencement of building works
2 She gave a start.
jerk I sat up with a jerk.
jump He gave a jump when he heard her voice.

stay¹ [verb]
Please stay in your seats.
remain He remained where he was.

stay² [noun]
We hope you enjoy your stay with us.
holiday a short holiday in Venice
stopover a two-night stopover in Vancouver
visit It was a long visit.

steady [adjective]
1 The chair must be steady.
firm Make sure the ladder is firm before you climb.
stable The table wasn't very stable.
2 a steady income
consistent His moods were never consistent.
constant Love is constant.
regular We don't have a regular amount of money coming in.
unchanging an unchanging pattern of work

steal [verb]
embezzle He embezzled thousands of pounds from the bank where he worked.
pilfer Hotel towels are pilfered by guests.
shoplift She hid the goods she'd shoplifted in the pram.
snatch The woman had her bag snatched in the street.
swipe The bike was swiped from outside a shop.
take Someone had been taking money from the till.
♦ **Informal words nick** He was done for nicking cars.
pinch Someone's pinched my pen.

VOCABULARY CHOICES
• The word **embezzle** is used when someone steals money from the company they work for over a long period of time.
• The word **pilfer** suggests that someone is stealing something small, or something that they do not think is valuable or important.

steep [adjective]
sheer a journey across sheer mountain passes

step [noun]
1 Take a step back.
pace She took a few paces backwards.
stride He took three strides and was outside the room.

2 She heard his step on the stairs.
footstep She heard footsteps outside the door.
tread the heavy tread of his feet
3 What's the next step?
move a move towards improving the situation
stage the next stage of the process
4 the first step on the ladder
rung the top rung of the ladder
stair the bottom stair

step [verb]
stepping carefully on the ice
stamp She stamped on my foot.
tread Be careful not to tread in the mud.
walk They walked out of the room.

stick [verb]
1 He was sticking his head through the window.
poke He poked his head round the door.
thrust She thrust her head into the water.
2 Stick the two edges together.
cement rocks cemented by ice
glue Joe glued the picture onto the card.
♦ **Formal word affix** Affix the stickers to the boxes.
3 mud sticking to his clothes
cling dirt clinging to her shoes

stick [noun]
a walking stick
baton an orchestra conductor's baton
branch He was waving a branch.
cane Tie the plants to the cane.
rod a rod for fishing
twig twigs and leaves on the ground

sticky [adjective]
gluey The rice was in gluey lumps.
tacky The worktop was tacky with treacle.
♦ **Formal word glutinous** a thick glutinous jelly
♦ **Informal word gooey** gooey chocolate cake

Ss

253

stiff [adjective]
1 stiff cardboard
  firm *a firm dough*
  hard *The bread was hard.*
  rigid *rigid metal frames*
2 His manner was very stiff.
  cold *He was cold and unwelcoming.*
  formal *a very formal person*
  standoffish *She was rather standoffish.*
3 a stiff test
  difficult *a difficult task*
  hard *a hard job*
  rigorous *the rigorous demands of parenthood*
  tough *a tough test of his ability*

still¹ [adjective]
The water was still and dark.
  motionless *He stood motionless and listened.*
  stationary *stationary traffic*

VOCABULARY CHOICES
• The word **motionless** is usually used in stories rather than in everyday speech.

still² [adverb]
That's better, but it's still not right.
  even so *Even so, you'd think he'd have rung.*
  however *They arrived late. However they weren't the last.*
  nevertheless *I know he's busy but nevertheless he could have called.*
  nonetheless *It wasn't a bad flat. Nonetheless it wasn't what we'd had in mind.*

sting¹ [verb]
1 A bee stung him on the nose.
  bite *A mosquito bit him.*
  nip *The crab nipped him in the ankle.*
2 My eyes were stinging with the smoke.
  burn *She was sick until her throat was burning.*
  smart *My cheek was smarting from the slap.*

sting² [noun]
a wasp sting
  bite *insect bites*
  nip *The crab gave me a nip in the ankle.*

stomach¹ [noun]
cramps in my stomach
  belly *His belly was full.*
  gut *pains in his gut*
• **Technical term abdomen** *She had chest and abdomen injuries.*
• **Informal word tummy** *You need some food in your tummy.*

stomach² [verb]
I can't stomach her smugness.
  bear *I can't bear those TV programmes.*
  stand *I can't stand things like that.*
  take *I can't take much more of his behaviour.*
  tolerate *I find your attitude difficult to tolerate.*

stop¹ [verb]
1 Please stop shouting.
  end *pleas to end the fighting*
  halt *The council halted plans to build a sports centre.*
  quit *He was told to quit playing football.*
• **Formal words cease** *He ceased writing around 1850.*
  terminate *The interview was terminated abruptly.*
• **Informal term pack in** *Pack in fighting, you two!*
2 The car stopped at the traffic lights.
  halt *He walked briskly to the door then halted.*
  pull up *I heard a car pull up outside.*
3 Stop him entering.
  bar *The golfer was barred from playing in the competition.*
  prevent *She tried to prevent him from hurting himself.*
  thwart *A last-minute goal thwarted our chances of winning.*
• **Formal word arrest** *ways of arresting the spread of AIDS*

Types of story:

adventure story	folk tale	myth	spy story
comedy	ghost story	parable	thriller
crime story	historical novel	romance	western
detective story	horror story	saga	whodunnit
fable	legend	science fiction	
fairy tale	love story	short story	
fantasy	mystery	spine-chiller	

stop² [noun]

1 Get off at the next stop.

station *I'm getting off at the next station.*

2 a short stop

break *Have a little break and then carry on.*

pause *There was a long pause.*

rest *I had a short rest before continuing.*

3 The taxi came to a stop.

halt *The car came to a halt outside a large house.*

standstill *Traffic was brought to a standstill.*

store [noun]

1 a good store of food for the winter

cache *Police found a cache of drugs and guns.*

hoard *a hoard of gold coins*

reserve *reserves of money*

stock *the village's grain stock*

stockpile *the country's stockpile of nuclear weapons*

supply *Food supplies are low.*

◆ **Informal word stash** *a stash of money under the bed*

2 We keep all the boxes in a store.

storehouse *a former grain storehouse*

storeroom *The room was being used as a storeroom for boxes.*

warehouse *goods in the warehouse*

VOCABULARY CHOICES

[meaning 1]

• The words **cache**, **hoard**, and **stash** suggest that someone keeps things in a secret place because they don't want them to be found.

storm [noun]

1 winter storms

blizzard *Blizzards are affecting the north.*

gale *gales and heavy rain*

hurricane *The south coast of the USA was hit by a hurricane.*

thunderstorm *We got caught in a thunderstorm.*

2 a storm of protest

outburst *an outburst of anger*

outcry *an outcry over plans to build a new road*

uproar *His remarks provoked an uproar.*

stormy [adjective]

blustery *a blustery day*

gusty *gusty conditions*

rough *rough seas*

windy *a windy night*

story [noun]

1 Tell us a story.

anecdote *He told us amusing anecdotes about his life in the army.*

tale *wonderful tales of adventure*

yarn *old-fashioned yarns about pirates*

See also the box above.

2 He accused her of telling stories.

fib *She's telling fibs again.*

lie *I'm sure it was a lie.*

VOCABULARY CHOICES

[meaning 1]

• If you call a story an **anecdote**, you are

saying that it is, or is meant to be, entertaining and quite funny.

• The words **tale** and **yarn** suggest a story that is made up, or has elements that are made up or exaggerated. **Yarn** also gives the impression of a long, rambling story.

straight [adjective]

1 a straight line
level The picture isn't level.
2 Keep your things straight.
neat making the room neat
orderly Please form an orderly queue.
organized an organized pile of papers on her desk
tidy The children never keep their bedrooms tidy.
3 Give me a straight answer.
blunt I asked what she thought of me, and got a blunt reply.
candid He was very candid about his own feelings.
direct His message was pretty clear and direct.
frank He was very frank about the chances of success.
honest Just give me an honest answer.
open I want you to be very open with me.
truthful a truthful account of the war
♦ **Formal word forthright** a forthright statement of his opinion
4 straight whisky
neat a glass of neat gin

VOCABULARY CHOICES

[meaning 3]
• You use the word **frank** to emphasize that someone is telling the truth even though it might offend or upset other people. If you want to suggest you disapprove of this, you might use the word **blunt**.

strain¹ [verb]

1 strain a muscle
pull I think I've pulled a muscle in my leg.
sprain I sprained my wrist.

twist I've twisted my ankle.
wrench She slipped and wrenched her knee.
2 strain the gravy
filter filtered water
sieve Sieve the flour into a bowl.
sift sifting the dust for bits of pottery
3 strain yourself
exert Don't exert yourself too much.
overtax He didn't want to overtax her.
overwork We don't overwork the horses.
tire I don't want to tire you.

strain² [noun]

1 His drinking put a strain on the friendship.
burden This tax will put a burden on poor families.
pressure the pressure of his job
2 I have a shoulder strain.
sprain an ankle sprain

strange [adjective]

bizarre a bizarre situation
curious Then a curious thing happened.
funny I had a funny feeling I'd been there before.
odd What an odd thing to say!
peculiar a peculiar little man
weird The weird thing is I don't even miss him.

stranger [noun]

newcomer We welcome newcomers to the club.
outsider She felt she would always be an outsider in the town.

strength [noun]

1 physical strength
brawn a task that needs brains rather than brawn
force the force of the wind
might He pushed with all his might.
muscle It will take a lot of muscle to lift that.
power the power of the explosion
2 He has regained his strength slowly after the illness.

Ss

fitness *It will be a while before he's back to full fitness.*

health *You need to rest to allow you to regain your health.*

stamina *A lack of stamina following flu is very common.*

3 *He has great inner strength.*

courage *She has courage and determination.*

toughness *a woman known for her mental toughness*

4 *the strength of the wood*

robustness *the robustness of the truck's body*

sturdiness *a car known for its sturdiness*

toughness *the toughness of the materials used*

VOCABULARY CHOICES

[meaning 1]

• The word **brawn** is often used when you are setting physical strength against intelligence, and suggesting a comparison of the two.

stress [noun]

1 *I suffer a lot from stress.*

pressure *The pressure of the job was almost unbearable.*

strain *She's been under a lot of strain recently.*

tension *headaches caused by tension*

worry *We were living with the worry of not having enough money.*

◆ **Informal word hassle** *I don't want all this hassle.*

2 *She puts great stress on being polite.*

emphasis *The emphasis is on quality.*

importance *We should place more importance on education.*

stress [verb]

I can't stress enough the significance of this discovery.

emphasize *I will emphasize that point to them.*

highlight *He highlighted the need for more money to be spent.*

impress *We must impress on them the importance of this.*

underline *I'd like to underline that last point I made.*

stretch [verb]

The material stretches to fit all sizes.

expand *As the sea warms, it expands and rises.*

lengthen *The muscles in your face lengthen as you age.*

stretch [noun]

1 *a stretch of water*

area *a large area of land*

expanse *a broad expanse of beach*

sweep *the sweep of moorland*

tract *vast tracts of forest*

2 *a short stretch in prison*

period *We lived in Canada for a brief period.*

spell *a long spell away from home*

stint *a twelve-year stint in the army*

term *lengthy prison terms*

time *his short time as director*

strict [adjective]

1 *a strict teacher*

firm *You need to be firm with children.*

harsh *harsh treatment of prisoners*

no-nonsense *her no-nonsense approach to management*

severe *I thought the head teacher was too severe with her pupils.*

stern *He was very stern with them.*

2 *strict controls on spending*

harsh *harsh laws*

rigorous *rigorous safety checks*

severe *severe spending cuts*

stringent *stringent rules about pollution*

tough *tough new measures to reduce crime*

VOCABULARY CHOICES

[meaning 1]

• The words **harsh** and **severe** often hint that

Ss

you think something is unfair as well as strict.
- **No-nonsense**, however, is slightly more positive as it suggests someone is sensible. [meaning 2]
- The words **harsh** and **severe** often hint that you think something is unfair as well as strict.
- **Rigorous**, however, is more positive in tone, as it suggests being thorough.

strike¹ [noun]

1 go on strike
industrial action *industrial action by firefighters*
sit-in *Workers staged a sit-in at the company's head office.*
stoppage *a 24-hour stoppage in protest at job cuts*
walkout *an unofficial walkout by 100 staff*
2 strikes against enemy targets
attack *aerial attacks on the city*
raid *air raids*

strike² [verb]

1 They are striking because of poor pay.
down tools *Workers downed tools in support of the sacked men.*
walk out *Fifty staff walked out in a dispute over pay.*
2 strike a gong
hit *She hit him in the stomach.*
slap *I slapped him on the back.*
smack *He smacked her across the face.*
thump *I thumped him on the arm.*
3 His behaviour struck me as odd.
seem *It seemed a bit strange to me.*

stripe [noun]

band *The bird's beak has a yellow band across it.*
line *paper with pink and black lines on it*
streak *brown hair with blond streaks*

strong [adjective]

1 strong shoes
hard-wearing *hard-wearing fabrics*
heavy-duty *heavy-duty rubber gloves*

robust *a plant with a long robust stem*
sturdy *sturdy boots*
tough *The material is very tough.*
- ◆ **Formal word durable** *The material is lightweight but durable.*

2 strong arms
brawny *a brawny chap*
burly *a burly man of average height*
muscular *his muscular legs*
strapping *a strapping young man*
strong as an ox *Sonny was tall and strong as an ox.*
- ◆ **Informal word beefy** *a big, beefy security guard*

3 strong feelings • strong support
deep *the deep anger he felt*
fierce *her fierce determination to lead a normal life*
intense *intense feelings of hate*
- ◆ **Formal word fervent** *a fervent belief that things would get better*

4 strong colours
intense *the intense blue of her eyes*
vivid *a room painted in vivid colours*

5 a strong argument
compelling *compelling evidence*
convincing *I didn't find his reasons very convincing.*
forceful *a forceful criticism of the plan*
persuasive *a persuasive speech to support the theory*

VOCABULARY CHOICES

[meaning 2]
- **Strapping** creates a picture of someone tall with a strong build.
- **Strong as an ox** is a **simile**. It is also a phrase that has been used so often that it has very little impact – a **cliché**. A similar phrase is **strong as a horse**.

stubborn [adjective]

headstrong *He was headstrong and always ignored advice.*
obstinate *his obstinate refusal to do what she asked*

Ss

pigheaded *She was too pigheaded to listen.*

VOCABULARY CHOICES

• **Headstrong** creates a picture of someone who is determined to get what they want, but this might be because they have a strong will rather than because they are being deliberately difficult.
• However, **obstinate** and, especially, **pigheaded** more clearly make a criticism, and suggest that someone is being unreasonable.

stuck [adjective]
1 The door is stuck.
jammed *The drawer was jammed.*
2 I was stuck for an answer.
baffled *I was baffled and didn't know what to say.*
stumped *For a while I was stumped.*

student [noun]
learner *learners of English*
pupil *a school with 200 pupils*
trainee *hairdressing trainees*
undergraduate *university undergraduates*

study¹ [verb]
The laboratory will study the samples.
analyse *analyse the results*
examine *We need to examine the case in more detail.*
read *He read the report before speaking.*
scrutinize *The results will be scrutinized by officials.*

VOCABULARY CHOICES

• The word **scrutinize** suggests you are looking at something carefully in order to find faults.

study² [noun]
1 The subject needs further study.
analysis *The results need further analysis.*
examination *examination of the findings*
research *More research is needed.*

scrutiny *He is facing scrutiny from the media.*
2 We're turning the spare room into a study.
office *the desk in his office*

VOCABULARY CHOICES

[meaning 1]
• The word **scrutiny** suggests you are looking at something carefully so you can find faults.

stuff¹ [verb]
1 Stuff some clothes into a bag.
cram *Raj crammed all the clothes back into the suitcase.*
jam *He jammed his fingers into his ears.*
push *She pushed the handkerchief into her pocket.*
ram *He rammed the cake into his mouth.*
shove *She quickly shoved the letter into her bag.*
2 (informal) The kids stuff themselves with too many sweets.
gorge *She gorged herself on popcorn.*
♦ **Formal word overindulge** *a remedy for those who have overindulged in beer and wine*

stuff² [noun]
1 What's this stuff for?
substance *a stain-removing substance*
2 (informal) Don't touch my stuff.
belongings *He left, taking his belongings with him.*
possessions *The fire destroyed all her possessions.*
things *He'd left his things all over the floor.*
♦ **Informal word gear** *They packed all their camping gear.*
♦ **Slang word clobber** *You have to take a lot of clobber with you when you have young children.*

stuffy [adjective]
airless *a tiny airless room*
stifling *a stifling and crowded train*

Ss

stunt [noun]
  feat *amazing feats of skill and bravery*
  trick *performing tricks*

stupid [adjective]
  brainless *brainless idiots*
  dumb *How can anyone be that dumb? •
  dumb questions*
  foolish *a foolish idea • He'd been made
  to look foolish.*
  idiotic *idiotic comments • a few idiotic
  students*
  ridiculous *a ridiculous idea • You look
  ridiculous in that hat.*
  silly *What a silly thing to do! • Don't be so
  silly.*
  ◆ Informal word thick *Are you thick or
  what?*

VOCABULARY CHOICES
• The informal word **thick** may be all right to
use with friends and can sound humorous,
but in formal company it can sound rather
offensive.

style [noun]
1 *a style of jacket • a style of painting*
  design *The tiles come in a range of colours
  and designs.*
  form *an unusual form of art*
  kind *different kinds of dresses and skirts*
  sort *A different sort of jacket might suit you
  better.*
  type *different types of writing*
2 *She has great style.*
  chic *the casual chic that she had achieved*
  elegance *She dressed with great
  elegance.*
  flair *He displays a great deal of skill and
  flair.*
  sophistication *her air of sophistication*
  stylishness *the stylishness of the design*
  taste *He dresses with taste.*
  ◆ Formal word panache *He dressed
  with typical panache.*
3 *a style of management*

approach *a new approach to teaching*
method *a different method of dealing
with problems*
technique *business techniques*
way *different ways of dealing with stress*

subject [noun]
1 *the subject of the conversation*
  issue *They are discussing pay and other
  issues.*
  matter *They were talking over important
  matters.*
  theme *The main theme of the book is love.*
  topic *an interesting topic of conversation*
2 *French, science and other subjects*
  field *She's an expert in the field of art
  history.*
  study *the study of chemistry*

success [noun]
1 *She owes her success to hard work.*
  fame *people seeking fame*
  triumph *They deserve their triumph.*
  victory *the team's World Cup victory*
2 *He was a success. • The book was a huge
success.*
  hit *The film was a hit in France.*
  winner *The comedian's style was a
  winner with audiences.*

successful [adjective]
1 *a successful business*
  booming *a booming economy*
  flourishing *a flourishing mail-order
  company*
  thriving *a thriving market town*
2 *We've had a very successful day.*
  fruitful *a fruitful meeting*
  productive *a productive discussion*
3 *a successful writer*
  bestselling *a bestselling author*
  famous *a famous actor*
  leading *one of the world's leading
  players*
  popular *a popular artist*
  top *one of the country's top athletes*

Ss

sudden [adjective]
   abrupt His career came to an abrupt end.
   hasty Don't make any hasty decisions.
suddenly [adverb]
   abruptly The concert ended abruptly.
   hurriedly She hurriedly said goodbye and left.
   sharply The car pulled up sharply and a man got out.
suffer [verb]
1 suffer in silence
   hurt I hate to see anyone hurting like that.
2 suffer humiliation
   endure He has endured years of pain.
   experience people experiencing depression
   go through He's going through a bad time at the moment.
suggest [verb]
1 Can you suggest a solution?
   put forward ideas that have already been put forward
   recommend Can you recommend somewhere we could eat?
 ◆ **Formal word propose** I propose that we discuss this at the next meeting.
2 The survey suggests that more people are shopping online.
   imply What are you implying?
   indicate The results indicate that most people do not exercise enough.
suit [verb]
1 products to suit the needs of different customers
   be appropriate for Make sure your clothes are appropriate for the interview.
   be convenient for What day would be convenient for us to meet?
   be relevant to skills that are relevant to the job
 ◆ **Informal phrase fit the bill** It's a tough job, but I think you will fit the bill.
2 That shirt suits you.
   flatter The dress flatters your figure.

   go well with Fresh cream goes well with pudding.
   look good on Jeans look good on you.
   match His scarf matched his brown eyes.
suitable [adjective]
   appropriate The film is not appropriate for young children.
   fit a meal fit for a king
sunny [adjective]
   bright It was bright and breezy outside.
   clear On a clear day you can see for miles.
   fine a period of fine weather
supervise [verb]
   control She controls sales.
   manage She manages a team of ten people.
   oversee He will oversee the building work.
supervisor [noun]
   foreman a foreman in charge of a team of ten bricklayers
   manager office managers
   overseer an overseer of government policy
 ◆ **Informal word boss** Speak to your boss.
support[1] [verb]
1 support your team • support local charities
   back The proposals have been backed by officials.
   promote an organization that promotes recycling
2 beams supporting the roof
   carry Can the barrow carry the weight of the bricks?
   hold up the pillars holding up the porch
3 She works hard to support her family.
   feed He barely earned enough to feed us all.
   provide for I just want to be able to provide for my children.
support[2] [noun]
1 the support of many people

Ss

approval *His plans won the approval of people in the area.*

backing *The policy has the backing of the Prime Minister.*

2 a roof support

prop *roof props*

sure [adjective]

certain *Are you certain about that?*

confident *I'm confident he'll agree.*

convinced *I'm not convinced that he really understood.*

definite *He was very definite about his plans.*

positive *I'm positive I've seen him before somewhere.*

surprise¹ [verb]

I was surprised when she told me her age.

amaze *It amazes me that he still feels that way.*

astonish *It astonishes me that the book has been so successful.*

astound *She astounded friends by announcing she was getting married.*

stagger *They were staggered by the distance he'd covered.*

startle *The deer were startled by a sudden noise • I was startled to hear he had never driven before.*

stun *He was stunned into silence.*

VOCABULARY CHOICES

- The words **astonish** and **astound** have a lot of impact and convey the idea of extreme surprise.
- **Stagger** and **stun** are even stronger, and suggest that you are overwhelmed by surprise.
- **Startle** suggests that the surprise is sudden, or that gives you a bit of a fright.

surprise² [noun]

1 *She expressed surprise at the news.*

amazement *To my amazement he walked out without paying.*

astonishment *a look of astonishment on her face*

2 *The news came as a surprise.*

bombshell *the bombshell that he was leaving*

shock *His death came as a complete shock.*

surprised [adjective]

amazed *I'm amazed he's still alive.*

astonished *She was astonished to find that he was already married.*

astounded *I was just astounded that this could happen.*

shocked *I was shocked to see how much weight he'd lost.*

staggered *He was staggered and speechless when he was given the award.*

♦ **Informal word flabbergasted** *I was completely flabbergasted when she told me.*

surrender [verb]

give in *He decided to give in.*

give up *We can't give up now.*

surround [verb]

enclose *The garden is enclosed by a hedge.*

ring *The President was ringed by bodyguards.*

♦ **Formal word encircle** *a field encircled by barbed wire*

suspect¹ [verb]

1 *I don't suspect the truth of what he says.*

distrust *He distrusted his doctor's diagnosis.*

doubt *I had no reason to doubt what he said.*

2 *I suspect she's not happy.*

believe *Police believe he murdered many more people.*

guess *I guess he may have already left.*

suspect² [adjective]

a suspect insurance claim

dubious *The results seem a little dubious.*

Ss

questionable *His motives are questionable.*
suspicious *She died in suspicious circumstances.*
♦ **Informal words dodgy** *dodgy deals*
fishy *There's something fishy going on.*

suspense [noun]
anticipation *We waited with a feeling of anticipation.*
apprehension *He felt some apprehension before he went on stage.*
excitement *a feeling of excitement before the game*
tension *the tension of waiting for the results*

suspicious [adjective]
1 *a suspicious look*
distrustful *people who are distrustful of each other*
doubtful *She gave me a doubtful look.*
mistrustful *I became mistrustful of everyone.*
wary *wary of strangers*
♦ **Formal word sceptical** *Scientists are sceptical about these claims.*
2 *a suspicious character*
dubious *dubious business practices*
shifty *a shifty-looking man*
suspect *Police removed a suspect package.*
♦ **Informal words dodgy** *dodgy characters*
fishy *There's something fishy going on.*

swap [verb]
exchange *They exchanged addresses.*
switch *The two women switched places.*

swear [verb]
1 *He swore he'd never leave.*
insist *He insisted he had not meant to hurt her.*
promise *He promised he'd be there.*
vow *Emma vowed she'd never smoke again.*

2 *swearing at the top of his voice*
curse *Jim was cursing under his breath.*

VOCABULARY CHOICES
[meaning 1]
• The word **vow** is quite old-fashioned and formal-sounding but it is often used in newspapers about a promise that someone has made publicly, to help convey how serious it is.

swear-word [noun]
curse *He muttered something which sounded like a curse.*
four-letter word *She shouted a four-letter word at journalists.*
♦ **Formal words expletive** *He hurled a string of expletives at the referee.*
obscenity *Vandals wrote obscenities all over the wall.*

sweat[1] [noun]
Sweat was dripping down his face.
♦ **Formal word perspiration** *a bead of perspiration on his brow*

sweat[2] [verb]
We all sweat when we exercise.
swelter *I'm sweltering in this heat.*
♦ **Formal word perspire** *people who perspire heavily*

sweet[1] [adjective]
1 *a sweet taste*
sugary *sugary snacks*
2 *a sweet nature*
kind *A very kind young man offered to help.*
likeable *a likeable personality*
lovely *She's a lovely person.*
3 *a sweet little dog*
cute *Isn't their baby cute?*
4 *a sweet smell*
fragrant *the fragrant scent of roses*

sweet[2] [noun]
Sorbet makes a refreshing sweet.
dessert *cold desserts such as trifle and fruit salad*

Ss

pudding *What's for pudding?*

♦ **Informal word afters** *For afters we had apple pie and custard.*

swelling [noun]

bulge *the bulge in her pocket*

bump *There was a large bump on his head.*

lump *She found a lump in her breast.*

swing [verb]

1 *clothes swinging on the line*

sway *trees swaying in the breeze*

wave *hair waving in the wind*

2 *He swung the bag over his head.*

wave *She was waving the paper in the air.*

♦ **Formal word brandish** *He ran into the shop brandishing a knife.*

VOCABULARY CHOICES

[meaning 2]

• The word **brandish** is usually used when someone has a weapon. When it is used about something else it can hint, often in a humorous way, that it is troublesome: *We were cornered by a girl brandishing a questionnaire.*

switch¹ [verb]

We can switch the dates if you like.

change *He's changed courses.*

swap *Do you want to swap places?*

switch² [noun]

a switch to another Internet provider

change *the change to digital television*

swap *We did a straight swap.*

swollen [adjective]

bloated *bloated bodies*

enlarged *enlarged glands*

inflamed *inflamed tonsils*

puffy *puffy ankles*

♦ **Formal word distended** *a distended stomach*

VOCABULARY CHOICES

• The word **distended** sounds impersonal, and might be used by people working in

medicine to describe swelling in a part of the body.

• The words **enlarged** and **inflamed** are also more formal-sounding than **bloated** or **puffy**, and might be used by doctors.

• **Puffy** is a more informal way of describing something swollen.

swot [verb] (informal)

cram *He spent the day cramming for his exam.*

revise *I need to revise for the French test.*

study *He spends most of his time studying.*

♦ **Informal term bone up** *I need to bone up on the subject before I talk about it.*

sympathetic [adjective]

caring *She's a very caring person.*

kind *He was very kind when my Mum died.*

supportive *She was very supportive while I was having problems.*

understanding *Thanks for being so understanding.*

♦ **Formal word compassionate** *her soft, compassionate voice*

sympathize [verb]

feel for *I really feel for her having to work so many hours.*

identify with *I can identify with that feeling.*

pity *I pity those who have to work with him.*

understand *I understand how you feel.*

sympathy [noun]

compassion *She has compassion for her fellow human beings.*

pity *He felt pity for the poor little dog.*

understanding *He treated her with kindness and understanding.*

symptom [noun]

characteristic *One characteristic of depression is to feel completely hopeless.*

indication *an indication of a deeper problem*

sign *The player showed no signs of injury.*

Ss

T

take [verb]

1 I passed him the letter and he took it.

get *The baby was trying to get the cups from the table.*

grab *He grabbed the rope.*

grasp *She reached out and grasped his hand.*

seize *He seized her arm and turned her round.*

snatch *She snatched the paper from his hand.*

2 Take five from ten.

deduct *Your earnings before tax are deducted.*

subtract *Subtract five from fifteen.*

take away *Take away ten from thirty.*

3 It takes courage to be a fireman.

demand *The work demands a huge amount of energy.*

require *Looking after young children requires a lot of patience.*

4 Take me home.

bring *He brought me back last night.*

escort *She escorted me to the exit.*

ferry *Ambulances ferried the injured to hospital.*

5 I can't take pain.

bear *She couldn't bear the suspense any longer.*

stand *I can't stand much more of this.*

tolerate *people who can't tolerate noise*

VOCABULARY CHOICES

[meaning 1]

• The words **grab**, **seize** and **snatch** suggest you take something very forcefully and quickly.

take part [verb]

be involved *Jim is involved with charity events.*

contribute *We are all expected to contribute to society.*

join in *Why don't you join in the fun?*

participate *I like to participate in team sports.*

VOCABULARY CHOICES

• Terms such as **be involved** and **participate** can make a good impression if they are used in CVs and job applications. They let employers know that you are prepared to take part in working life and make a contribution.

talent [noun]

ability *a child with a lot of ability*

flair *He had a flair for languages.*

gift *her gift for acting*

skill *her skill at managing people*

strength *a project which helps young people recognize their strengths*

♦ **Formal word** **aptitude** *children with an aptitude for art*

talk¹ [verb]

She's nice enough, but she talks too much.

Tt

chat *I was chatting to my friends.*
chatter *He chattered excitedly during the journey.*
gossip *She's always gossiping about the neighbours.*
speak *I was speaking to Joshua yesterday. • She was so upset she could barely speak.*
♦ **Informal word natter** *He was nattering away on the phone.*

VOCABULARY CHOICES
• The words **chatter**, **chat** and **natter** suggest you talk for a long time about things that are not very important.
• The word **gossip** suggests you are talking about things that are none of your business, for example about other people's private lives.

talk² [noun]
1 We had a long talk.
chat *I just called for a chat.*
conversation *I had a long conversation with him yesterday.*
discussion *After a lengthy discussion, he decided to leave.*
♦ **Informal word natter** *He phoned me up just for a natter.*
2 She gave a talk about her travels.
lecture *He gave a lecture on history.*
sermon *The vicar's sermon was about forgiveness.*
speech *I've got to give a speech at the conference.*

talk about [verb]
confer *Staff conferred with the headmaster about plans for the school.*
debate *We will debate the advantages and disadvantages of the scheme.*
discuss *a meeting to discuss the future of the factory*
negotiate *We negotiated a pay rise with management.*

tall [adjective]
big *a boy who is very big for his age*
high *one of the highest mountains in the world*
soaring *The cathedral has a soaring spire.*
towering *Duncan is a towering six feet seven inches tall. • the towering cliffs of Gibraltar*
♦ **Formal word lofty** *the lofty peaks of the Alps*

VOCABULARY CHOICES
• The words **lofty** and **soaring** are mainly used in stories and other types of writing rather than speaking.
• The word **towering** suggests that someone or something is so tall that they seem impressive or a little frightening.

tame [adjective]
1 a tame owl
domesticated *domesticated horses*
2 The party was pretty tame.
bland *The interviewer asked bland questions.*
boring *her boring life*
dull *The restaurant's menu is pretty dull.*
unadventurous *an unadventurous meal of beans on toast*

tangle¹ [noun]
a tangle of roots
jumble *a jumble of cables behind the computer*
knot *the knots in her hair*

tangle² [verb]
Dolphins get tangled in the nets.
catch *Her necklace had got caught in her hair.*
knot *The wires kept on getting knotted.*
snarl *Her scarf got snarled in a bramble bush.*

tap¹ [verb]
A branch was tapping the window.
drum *He was drumming his fingers impatiently on the steering wheel.*

Ways of describing taste:

acid	fruity	salty	sweet
acrid	hot	savoury	tangy
bitter	meaty	sharp	tart
bittersweet	peppery	sour	vinegary
citrus	piquant	spicy	
creamy	pungent	sugary	

knock *Someone knocked on the door.*
pat *He patted her gently on the back.*
rap *James rapped angrily on the door.*

tap² [noun]
a tap on the shoulder
knock *There was a knock on the door.*
pat *a pat on the back*
rap *They were interrupted by a rap on the door.*

taste¹ [noun]
1 a taste of garlic
flavour *a stew with a spicy flavour*
savour *This salt has lost its savour.*
tang *the sharp tang of lemons*
See also the box above.
2 Have a taste of this cake.
bit *Do you want to try a bit of this pie?*
bite *Just try a bite – it's lovely!*
dash *Add a dash of whisky to the mixture.*
drop *'Would you like some wine?' 'Just a drop, please.'*
mouthful *I'll just have a mouthful.*
3 The museum gives us a taste of life in the Middle Ages.
experience *My first experience of France was on a school visit.*
flavour *The film gives a flavour of life on the island.*
4 a taste for adventure
appetite *He has never lost his appetite for women.*
fondness *She developed a fondness for jazz music.*
liking *a liking for poetry*
5 You have very good taste. • Her clothes show taste.

elegance *The shoes combine comfort with elegance.*
style *He has a lot of style.*

taste² [verb]
Taste the soup before adding seasoning.
sample *Come in and sample our delicious chocolates.*
try *Just try this ice cream.*

tasty [adjective]
appetizing *a large appetizing meal*
delicious *delicious home-made cakes*
luscious *a bowl of luscious strawberries*
mouthwatering *a range of mouthwatering desserts*
succulent *a succulent pear*
♦ **Formal word flavoursome**
flavoursome tomatoes
♦ **Informal words moreish** *I picked a bag of moreish-looking chocolates.*
scrumptious *a scrumptious meal*
yummy *all kinds of yummy snacks*

VOCABULARY CHOICES
• The word **yummy** is quite childish in tone, and is often used about the foods children like.

teach [verb]
coach *He coaches young rugby players.*
educate *We need to educate people about health.*
instruct *a book which instructs you how to use the computer*
train *a building used for training police officers*
tutor *He had been tutored at home by his mother.*

teacher [noun]
  coach *a basketball coach*
  instructor *a driving instructor*
  lecturer *college lecturers*
  professor *He's a professor at a university.*
  schoolteacher *a rise in pay for schoolteachers*
  trainer *a fitness trainer*
  tutor *an English tutor*

tear¹ [verb]
1 He tore his sleeve on the wire. • He tore the letter into shreds.
  rip *He ripped the photograph to pieces.*
  shred *Finely shred the lettuce leaves.*
2 She tore the book out of his hand.
  grab *She grabbed the phone from me.*
  seize *He got up on stage and seized the microphone from her.*
  snatch *He snatched the paper from my hand.*
3 She tore down the street.
  charge *He came charging past me.*
  dash *She dashed down to London to help her mother.*
  fly *She came flying out of the front door.*
  race *Three ambulances came racing past.*
  rush *He rushed off up the corridor.*
  shoot *Ann shot out of the room and down the stairs.*
  speed *The train sped through the countryside.*
  ◆ **Informal word** **belt** *The car was belting down the road at high speed.*

tear² [noun]
a tear in the curtain
  rip *a rip in her T-shirt*
  split *a split in his jeans*

tease [verb]
  ridicule *He was ridiculed by his colleagues.*
  taunt *She was taunted at school about her weight.*
  ◆ **Informal word** **rib** *The boys enjoyed ribbing their little sister.*

tell [verb]
1 Tell him the news.
  advise *The staff can advise you about money.*
  brief *I will brief you on what you have to do.*
  explain *Let me explain the situation to you.*
  inform *Police have not yet informed relatives of the deaths.*
  let know *Let me know when you're ready.*
  ◆ **Formal word** **notify** *You must notify your employer if you are pregnant.*
  ◆ **Informal term** **fill in** *Can you fill me in on what's been happening?*
2 tell a story
  report *reporting the events of the day*
  ◆ **Formal words** **recount** *She recounted word for word what was said.*
  relate *He became upset while relating the incident.*
3 She told them to wait.
  command *Police commanded him to drop his gun.*
  instruct *He was instructed to say nothing.*
  order *They ordered us to wait outside.*
  ◆ **Formal word** **direct** *Take the medicine as directed by your doctor.*
4 I can't tell the brothers apart. • Can you tell which is which?
  differentiate *Children can differentiate between right and wrong.*
  distinguish *The fake coins can easily be distinguished from real ones.*

VOCABULARY CHOICES
[meaning 1]
• The words **inform** and **notify** are usually used in official situations, such as letters and notices.

tell off [verb] (informal)
  scold *My wife often scolds me about hogging the remote control.*
  ◆ **Formal words** **rebuke** *The doctors were sharply rebuked for their conduct.*

Tt

reprimand He was sent to the head teacher to be reprimanded.

reproach The company was reproached for failing to keep its employees safe.

♦ **Informal terms give someone a piece of your mind** I'll give him a piece of my mind when I catch him!

rap someone's knuckles Anyone who disobeyed the rules had their knuckles rapped.

tick off The tutor ticked me off for being late.

temporary [adjective]
interim an interim government
makeshift a makeshift bed of chairs pushed together
stopgap It's a stopgap measure until a new system is in place.

tempt [verb]
attract We are often attracted into shops by 'Sale' signs.
entice Buyers were enticed by low prices.
interest It was the location and salary which interested me.
lure Top players are lured by fame and money.
seduce seduced by a very tempting offer

VOCABULARY CLUES

• The words **lure** or **seduce** can hint that someone is tempted by something they should not be, or by something that appeals to emotions such as greed or selfishness.

• Along with the word **entice**, these words are sometimes used when the thing you are tempted by might be disappointing or might not be as promising it looks.

tense [adjective]
1 My muscles were tense.
stiff a stiff neck
strained strained muscles
tight His shoulders felt tight.
2 I feel tense.
anxious He was anxious about the results.

apprehensive He is rather apprehensive about his interview.
edgy She looked a little edgy.
jumpy Sit down! You're making me jumpy.
keyed up She was so keyed up with everything that had happened.
nervous It's normal to feel nervous before an exam.
on edge She was on edge waiting for her results.
3 a tense moment
fraught The atmosphere in the room was fraught.
stressful Pregnancy can be a stressful time for many women.
worrying a worrying few weeks waiting for the test results

tension [noun]
1 Increase the tension on the rope.
tautness He tugged on the rope and felt the tautness.
tightness Massage your neck to ease the tightness in the muscles.
2 Mum is suffering from nervous tension.
anxiety anxiety in her voice
edginess Signs of edginess were showing in his face.
nervousness Her nervousness was obvious.
worry feelings of worry about her son

terrible [adjective]
appalling appalling weather conditions
awful We've had an awful journey.
disgusting a disgusting smell
dreadful a dreadful mistake
horrible Then something horrible happened.
horrific horrific injuries from the accident
revolting The smell in the flat was revolting.

test[1] [verb]
I was tested for allergies.
analyse Scientists analysed samples of the water.

Tt

269

assess *questions to assess your abilities*
check *The doctor will check iron levels in your blood.*
examine *You should have your eyes examined once a year.*

test [noun]
The doctors are running tests on him.
analysis *an analysis of the soil*
assessment *an assessment of his fitness*
check *tyre checks*
examination *an eye examination*
trial *trials of new drugs*

thank [verb]
express thanks *She expressed her thanks to all those who had helped her.*
say thank you *Have you said thank you to John for the present?*
show appreciation *He showed his appreciation by offering to buy me a drink.*

thanks [interjection]
Thanks for covering for me.
many thanks *Many thanks for getting us the tickets.*
thank you *He showed his appreciation by offering to buy me a drink.*
that's very kind of you *'Let me get your coat.' 'That's very kind of you.'*
you shouldn't have *'I brought you a little gift.' 'Oh, you shouldn't have.'*
◆ **Formal term much obliged** *I'm much obliged to you for all your help.* • *Thank you Sir, much obliged.*
◆ **Informal words cheers** *'Here's your change.' 'Cheers!'*
ta *Ta for waiting.*

VOCABULARY CHOICES
• **Thank you** is a slightly more formal way of saying 'thanks'.
• The phrase **you shouldn't have** is often used when receiving a gift to suggest it was unnecessary, although it can be said just to be polite when the gift was expected.
• The term **much obliged** might be used in writing so as to sound more formal or polite,

for example in letters to people you do not know so well.
• The informal words **cheers** and **ta**, on the other hand, are very friendly in tone and would not be used in formal or business situations.

thanks [noun]
My manuscript was returned with thanks.
acknowledgement *Has Pauline sent an acknowledgement of your gift?*
appreciation *He showed his appreciation by offering to buy me a drink.*
credit *She doesn't get the credit she deserves.*
gratitude *She expressed her gratitude to all those who had helped her.*
recognition *I got no recognition for the fact that I had been working all day.*

theft [noun]
robbery *Robbery is a serious crime.*
shoplifting *Stores lose a lot of money through shoplifting.*
stealing *He was accused of stealing.*
thieving *There are many different forms of thieving.*

thick [adjective]
1 thick slices of bread
broad *broad bands of colour*
fat *fat legs*
2 thick forest
dense *dense woodland*
3 (informal) You can be thick sometimes.
brainless *brainless idiots*
dim-witted *He's too dim-witted to understand.*
slow *She's a bit slow.*
stupid *Are you stupid or what?*

thief [noun]
burglar *Burglars stole jewellery and CDs from the house.*
mugger *The mugger held a knife to her throat and demanded money.*

pickpocket *Beware of pickpockets when you're shopping.*
robber *bank robbers*
shoplifter *The store's security guards stopped the shoplifter.*

thin [adjective]
1 thin arms • a thin man
lean *his lean powerful body*
scrawny *her scrawny arms*
skeletal *At one point the woman was a skeletal five stone.*
skinny *a skinny young boy • skinny legs*
slender *a slender figure*
slim *She was tall and slim.*
◆ **Formal word emaciated** *She was emaciated from drug use.*
2 thin fabric
fine *a fine cotton nightdress*
flimsy *a flimsy cotton skirt*
light *a light summer jacket*
3 thin soup
runny *runny honey*
watery *watery paint*

VOCABULARY CHOICES
[meaning 1]
• The words **emaciated** and **skeletal** suggest that someone is dangerously thin, for example because they are very ill or do not eat enough.
• The word **scrawny** suggests that someone or something is thin in a way that is not attractive, so it is a very uncomplimentary word to use.
• The words **slender** and **slim** are far more complimentary, as they suggest that someone or something is thin in an attractive way.
• The word **lean** is also quite complimentary, as it suggests that someone is thin and very fit.

thing [noun]
1 He makes things out of wood.
object *a strange-looking object*
◆ **Formal word article** *articles belonging to the missing person*
2 the things we need to discuss
detail *I need to check a few details with you.*
factor *a factor worth considering*
item *deal with the next item on the list*
point *the main points of the discussion*
3 the thing that turns the wheels
device *a device for measuring blood pressure*
gadget *gadgets used in the kitchen*
machine *a machine that prints labels*
tool *a tool for removing nails*
4 I have too many things to do.
job *jobs around the house*
task *daily tasks*
5 A strange thing happened.
event *the events of the previous day*
incident *One incident sticks in my mind.*
occurrence *Crime is a rare occurrence on the island.*

VOCABULARY CHOICES
[meaning 5]
• The word **incident** suggests that the thing that has happened is strange or bad.

things [noun]
belongings *personal belongings*
bits and pieces *I've got to go and pick up a few bits and pieces in town.*
equipment *camping equipment*
possessions *He tried to rescue his possessions from the flood.*
◆ **Informal words gear** *climbing gear*
stuff *I'll just go and get my stuff.*
◆ **Slang word clobber** *Can you move your clobber from the hall, please?*

VOCABULARY CHOICES
• The word **clobber** often suggests that someone has too many things that are not necessary.

think [verb]
1 I think the story was true.

Tt

believe *I believe he lives in London now.*
guess *I guess you're right.*
reckon *I reckon he was lying.*
suppose *Dave supposed we'd got lost.*
2 Think of the consequences.
imagine *Imagine what would happen.*
♦ **Formal word envisage** *He couldn't envisage what life would be like without her.*
3 Think over my offer.
chew over *I'll chew it over and let you know.*
mull over *I was mulling over what she'd said.*
reflect *We were reflecting on the day's events.*
♦ **Formal words contemplate** *He contemplated the reasons for his failed marriage.*
ponder *They are pondering what to do next.*

thirsty [adjective]
dry *I'll just get some water, I'm a bit dry.*
♦ **Informal words gasping** *Is the kettle on? I'm gasping.*
parched *I needed that drink, I was parched.*

thorough [adjective]
full *a full investigation*
in-depth *an in-depth inquiry into the affair*
intensive *intensive cleaning*
meticulous *a meticulous piece of work*
painstaking *After a painstaking search, he found his brother.*

threaten [verb]
bully *She'd bullied other children.*
terrorize *The young boy had terrorized people living nearby.*
♦ **Formal word intimidate** *He intimidated people who refused to give him money.*

through¹ [preposition]
1 The new road goes through the village.

by *Let's go by Durham and see the cathedral.*
via *They went to Aberdeen via Edinburgh.* • *She sent me a message via my brother.*
2 all through the night
during *During the war, he was based in Somerset.*
in *She'd been awake a lot in the night.*
throughout *He'd been ill throughout much of the year.*
3 The plan was a success through his efforts.
as a result of *He passed the exam as a result of hard work.*
because of *late because of roadworks*
thanks to *She's here today thanks to the effort of doctors.*

through² [adjective]
the through service to Bournemouth
direct *a direct train to Edinburgh*
express *an express bus to Nottingham*
non-stop *a non-stop train to Cambridge*

throw [verb]
fling *She flung a log on the fire.* • *He was flung to the ground by the force of the explosion.*
hurl *I hurled a brick through the window.*
launch *Hand grenades were launched at the enemy.*
lob *Bottles were lobbed at police.*
toss *She tossed the can into the bin.*
♦ **Informal words chuck** *I ripped the letter up and chucked it in the bin.*
sling *He slung the bags into the back of the lorry.*

VOCABULARY CHOICES
• The words **hurl** and **launch** suggest a forceful, fairly violent action.
• **Fling**, **toss**, **chuck** and **sling** suggest a much more casual or even careless action.

throw away [verb]
dump *The factory had dumped its waste in the river.*

Tt

Periods of time:

age	fortnight	millennium	season
century	generation	minute	second
day	hour	moment	week
epoch	instant	month	weekend
era	lifetime	period	year
eternity	long weekend	quarter	

Times of day:

afternoon	evening	night-time	the early hours
bedtime	midday	noon	twilight
dawn	morning	sunrise	
daytime	night	sunset	
dusk	nightfall	teatime	

scrap You'll have to scrap all those old comics.

throw out I'm going to throw out all these useless ornaments.

♦ **Formal terms discard** Discard the orange pips before chopping.

dispose of Dispose of old paints carefully.

♦ **Informal word ditch** I ditched my old typewriter and bought a computer.

tidy¹ [adjective]
trying to keep the house tidy

neat neat piles of clothes

orderly orderly stacks of papers on his desk

uncluttered Keep your desk uncluttered and clean.

tidy² [verb]
Tidy the kitchen when you've finished cooking.

neaten Trim the ends to neaten them.

straighten Tim was trying to straighten the house before his parents got back.

tie¹ [verb]
hair tied back with a ribbon

bind Her hands had been bound with a rope.

knot Knot the two ends together.

tether horses tethered to a post

tie² [noun]
1 He had broken all his family ties.

bond attempts to strengthen bonds between the two countries

link The school wants to strengthen its links with the community.

2 The match ended in a tie.

dead heat The race finished in a dead heat.

draw a 1–1 draw

tight [adjective]
1 Keep the line tight.

stretched stretched canvas

taut a taut rope

tense tense muscles

2 tight clothes

close-fitting a close-fitting T-shirt

snug a snug black dress

3 a tight grip

firm a firm hold

strong a strong grasp

4 tight security

rigorous a rigorous budget

strict strict controls on spending

stringent stringent checks on passports

time [noun]
1 You can stay for a short time.

interval the interval between the two events

Tt

273

period *the period when he was President*
spell *a brief spell in the army*
while *I haven't seen her for a while.*
2 He was happy at that time in his life.
moment *At that moment he realized he no longer loved her.*
point *at that point in my career*
stage *a stage in my youth when I didn't have much money*
3 in Roman times • in the time of Nelson
age *We live in an age where most households have a television.*
era *an era of great change*
See also the box on the previous page.

tip[1] [noun]
1 He gave us a few useful tips.
clue *For clues on how to do this, see the handbook.*
hint *handy hints on preparing a family meal*
pointer *Here are a few pointers on what to look for.*
2 She gave the waiter a tip.
♦ **Formal word gratuity** *a small gratuity*

tip[2] [verb]
A friend tipped us off.
inform *Please inform the police if you see him.*
tell *Someone told police where he was.*
warn *We were warned about the dangers ahead.*
♦ **Formal word forewarn** *They were forewarned of the dangers.*

tired [adjective]
1 I felt very tired.
drained *She felt quite drained by the whole experience.*
exhausted *I'm exhausted from looking after the children all day.*
sleepy *I'm feeling a bit sleepy.*
weary *She gave a weary sigh.*
worn out *I'm completely worn out by the end of the day.*

♦ **Informal words bushed** *I'm bushed.*
knackered *By the end of the day I was absolutely knackered.*
shattered *I'm off to bed. I'm shattered.*
whacked *I'm whacked.*
2 I'm tired of waiting.
bored *I am bored of sitting here doing nothing.*
sick *I'm sick of being told what to do.*
♦ **Informal term fed up** *I'm fed up of her whining.*

VOCABULARY CHOICES
[meaning 1]
• **Worn out** and **exhausted** are strong terms that convey the idea that you have used up your strength completely, as are the informal words **knackered** and **shattered**.
• **Drained** suggests you are emotionally or mentally tired as well.

tiring [adjective]
exhausting *an exhausting day at the office*
wearing *Looking after elderly relatives can be very wearing.*

together [adverb]
1 They all arrived together.
all at once *They came all at once.*
at the same time *Everyone arrived at the same time.*
simultaneously *The two aircraft took off simultaneously.*
2 We worked together in London.
side by side *They worked side by side for many years.*

tolerate [verb]
accept *The teachers refused to accept bad behaviour.*
put up with *I'm not putting up with this any longer.*

tool [noun]
apparatus *an apparatus for measuring rainfall*

Tt

appliance *kitchen appliances such as microwaves*
device *a set of gardening tools*
instrument *instruments used by surgeons*
◆ **Formal words implement** *spades and other garden implements*
utensil *cooking utensils*

top¹ [noun]

1 the top of the hill
crest *the crest of a wave*
head *the head of the ladder*
summit *the summit of a mountain*
tip *the tip of his finger*
2 Put the top back on the toothpaste.
cap *Make sure the cap is screwed on tightly.*
lid *Put the lid back on the box.*
stopper *Replace the bottle stopper.*

top² [adjective]

Britain's top chefs
best *one of the best players in the game*
finest *London's finest hotel*
greatest *He was one of the greatest artists of his time.*
highest *the highest award possible*
leading *a leading expert in children's health*
◆ **Formal word foremost** *one of the country's foremost centres for cancer research*

top³ [verb]

1 ice cream topped with raspberry sauce
cap *mountains capped with snow*
cover *cake covered with cream*
2 That tops everything!
beat *This beats his previous record.*
exceed *The results exceeded all our expectations.*
surpass *His achievements surpassed those of his brother.*

total¹ [noun]

Add them up to get a total.
sum *the sum of the four numbers*

total² [adjective]

1 the total amount
entire *the entire contents of her bag*
full *pay the full price*
whole *It has been upsetting for the whole family.*
2 I was in total shock.
absolute *The party was an absolute disaster.*
complete *The journey was a complete nightmare.*
downright *I knew it was a downright lie.*
sheer *That's sheer nonsense!*
utter *a look of utter amazement on her face*

total³ [verb]

We total the scores to work out your grade.
• His debts totalled over £100,000.
add *Add all the figures in the left-hand column.*
add up *Their gas and electricity bills added up to more than £2,000 a year.*
amount to *Their earnings amount to more than £50,000.*
come to *The bill came to more than £500.*

touch¹ [noun]

1 the touch of her hand
brush *She felt the brush of his lips on her cheek.*
caress *his gentle caresses*
2 a touch of garlic
dash *Add a dash of cream.*
hint *fruit tea with a hint of ginger*

touch² [verb]

1 I touched his face.
brush *The branch brushed against his arm.*
feel *She felt his forehead to see if he was hot.*
handle *You should wash your hands before handling food.*
2 The edges are touching on either side.
come together *The two rivers come together a few miles further south.*
meet *the place where the two paths meet*

Tt

Ways of travelling:

cruise	hike	ride	ski
cycle	hitch–hike	row	swim
drive	motor	sail	trek
fly	pilot	skate	walk

3 The story touched her heart.
affect *She was affected by the events of that day.*
move *His comments really moved me.*

tough [adjective]
1 a tough material
strong *strong fabric*
sturdy *sturdy boots*
♦ **Formal word durable** *durable plastics*
2 a tough regime
harsh *harsh penalties*
severe *severe punishments*
strict *strict rules*
3 They had to be pretty tough to survive.
determined *a determined young woman*
4 a tough job
difficult *a difficult task*
hard *I've had a hard day at the office.*
♦ **Formal word arduous** *an arduous journey*

train [verb]
1 You have to train hard to be an athlete.
exercise *He spent every morning exercising.*
practise *You have to practise every day as a swimmer.*
work out *He was working out in the gym.*
2 He trains boxers.
coach *She coaches a football team.*
prepare *preparing footballers for the game*
3 She's training to be a hairdresser.
learn *He's learning how to drive a bus.*
study *She's studying to be a doctor.*

training [noun]
instruction *instruction in basic child care*
tuition *Staff will receive tuition in using the new computer system.*

trap [verb]
catch *He'd caught a fox.*
corner *They cornered him as he was leaving the building.*
snare *Police finally snared the thief.*

travel[1] [verb]
1 He spends a lot of time travelling.
go *He'd been to Japan many times.*
tour *We met them while we were touring in Australia.*
♦ **Formal word journey** *They journeyed south in search of a better life.*
See also the box above.
2 a car travelling at 50 miles per hour
go *The van was going too fast.*
move *a bus moving slowly down the road*
♦ **Formal word proceed** *The vehicle was proceeding in a westerly direction.*

travel[2] [noun]
They say travel broadens the mind.
globetrotting *She returned home after three years of globetrotting.*
touring *The hotel is a perfect base for walking or touring.*
travelling *He enjoyed travelling.*

treat[1] [noun]
1 He bought her some wine as a treat.
gift *She's always buying him little gifts.*
♦ **Formal word indulgence** *Chocolate is my biggest indulgence.*
2 It was a real treat to see him in concert.
delight *It was a delight to see her again.*
thrill *It's a thrill to see her work.*

treat[2] [verb]
1 How will you treat this question?
deal with *The book deals with the subject in a sympathetic way.*

Tt

276

Types of tree:

acacia	Dutch elm	lime	rowan
alder	ebony	linden	rubber tree
almond	elder	mahogany	sandalwood
apple	elm	maple	silver birch
ash	eucalyptus	monkey puzzle	spruce
bay	fig	oak	sycamore
beech	fir	palm	teak
birch	gum	pear	walnut
box	hawthorn	pine	weeping willow
cedar	hazel	plane	willow
cherry	horse chestnut	plum	yew
chestnut	larch	poplar	
cypress	laurel	redwood	

handle *She handled the situation very well.*

2 the best way to treat the patient
  care for *doctors caring for patients*
  nurse *nursing patients with infectious diseases*

3 I will treat you to lunch.
  buy *He bought me a drink.*
  pay for *Let me pay for dinner.*
  stand *Let me at least stand you a pint.*

tree [noun]
See the box above.

trick¹ [noun]
I think someone's played a trick on you.
  hoax *The whole thing could be a hoax.*
  practical joke *He's always playing practical jokes on his friends.*
  prank *The bus had been stolen for a prank.*

trick² [verb]
tricked into revealing his bank details
  cheat *cheated her out of her life savings*
  deceive *He had been deceived about how many miles the car had done.*
  defraud *a man who defrauded the bank out of millions of pounds*
  dupe *She'd been duped into believing he was a wealthy businessman.*
  fool *She fooled me into thinking she would marry me.*

hoodwink *People are hoodwinked into buying products that don't work.*

trip¹ [noun]
a trip to the Lake District
  drive *a drive in the car*
  expedition *a shopping expedition • an expedition to Mount Everest*
  journey *the journey into town*
  outing *an outing to the zoo*
  ride *a long bus ride*
  tour *a ten-day tour around Italy*
  ◆ **Formal word excursion** *The holiday includes an excursion to Barcelona.*

VOCABULARY CHOICES
• The word **expedition** is either used about a trip to a place a long way away in which you may face dangers, or humorously, about a trip close to home in which you may face problems.

trip² [verb]
She tripped and fell flat on her face.
  lose your footing *I lost my footing and fell down the hill.*
  stumble *He stumbled over a book on the floor.*

trouble¹ [noun]
1 We have a lot of trouble with our son. • He told her his troubles.

Tt

bother *We used it without any bother.*
difficulty *We had a lot of difficulty parking the car.* • *financial difficulties*
inconvenience *The company hopes that customers will not be caused any inconvenience.*
problem *We've had a lot of problems finding good staff.* • *It helps to talk about your problems.*
upset *She didn't want to cause any more upset.*
♦ **Informal words aggravation** *I don't need this aggravation.*
hassle *She's had a bit of hassle with bullies.*
2 trouble in the streets
disorder *violence and disorder caused by drinking*
disturbance *disturbances in the prison*
3 back trouble
complaint *a heart complaint*
disorder *a stomach disorder*
problem *people with skin problems*
4 It's too much trouble to do it.
effort *It's not worth the effort of going all that way.*

trouble² [verb]
Are you troubled by nightmares?
bother *Something was obviously bothering him.*
haunt *a problem which had haunted him for a long time*
plague *a man plagued by health problems*
worry *Something seemed to be worrying her.*

true [adjective]
1 the true facts
accurate *accurate information*
correct *I don't think what he said is correct.*
real *I don't think we'll ever find out the real story.*
2 a true friend

devoted *her devoted companion*
faithful *a faithful servant*
loyal *a loyal ally*

trust¹ [noun]
I have complete trust in your judgement.
belief *her belief in his honesty*
confidence *Public confidence in the government is very low.*
faith *He'd put all his faith in her.*

trust² [verb]
You can trust me not to tell anyone.
count on *You can count on him. He's very reliable.*
depend on *I knew I could depend on her.*
rely on *Jamal can be relied on to do a good job.*

truth [noun]
1 There's some truth in the comments.
accuracy *The accuracy of the report is in question.*
♦ **Formal word validity** *There are doubts about the validity of what he said.*
2 I had to discover the truth.
facts *We found out the facts about the accident.*
reality *The reality was a little different.*

try¹ [verb]
1 They tried to escape.
attempt *Thieves attempted to break into the garage.*
♦ **Formal words endeavour** *He lay down and endeavoured to sleep.*
seek *He sought to reassure me.*
strive *striving to achieve better results*
2 Try a piece of this cake.
sample *She sampled all the goods on offer.*
taste *Taste this cheese. It's lovely.*
test *Test the perfume on your wrist.*

VOCABULARY CHOICES
[meaning 1]
• The word **strive** suggests that you are working very hard to try to do something.

Tt

try² [noun]

1 Have another try.
  attempt *He made several attempts to start the car.*
  effort *His last shot was a poor effort.*
♦ **Informal words bash** *I had a bash at windsurfing while I was on holiday.*
  go *Why don't you have a go at skiing?*
  shot *her first shot at decorating a cake*
  stab *I think I'll have a stab at making a dress myself.*
2 Give this cake a try.
  taste *Have a taste of this wine.*

tune [noun]

  melody *a beautiful melody*
  song *songs from the 1980s*
  theme *a CD with themes from TV programmes*

turn¹ [verb]

1 The wheels were turning.
  revolve *The planets revolve around the sun.*
  rotate *The Earth rotates.*
  spin *The wheels were spinning in the mud.*
  swivel *Ann swivelled round in her chair.*
  twirl *She was twirling around on the dance floor.*
  twist *Twist the seat round a little.*
2 Caterpillars turn into butterflies.
  change *Love changed into a feeling of hate.*
  convert *The mill will be converted into flats.*
  transform *The former hospital has been transformed into a luxury hotel.*
3 It will turn frosty this weekend.
  become *He became angry.*
  go *It suddenly went very cold.*

VOCABULARY CHOICES

[meaning 2]
• The word **transform** usually suggests a change that makes something much better.

turn² [noun]

1 Give it a couple of turns.
  spin *He gave the wheel a spin.*
  twirl *She did a twirl in front of the mirror.*
  twist *Give the lid a twist.*
2 a turn in the road
  bend *a bend in the river*
  curve *a curve in the path*
3 It's your turn.
  go *Can I have a go now?*
♦ **Informal word shot** *It's my shot to roll the dice.*

tutor [noun]

  coach *a football coach*
  instructor *a driving instructor*
  teacher *a French teacher*

twist¹ [verb]

1 He twisted round in his chair.
  spin *He span round to look at her.*
  swivel *She swivelled round in her seat.*
  turn *She turned round to see what was going on.*
2 He was twisting his hair round his finger.
  bend *Bend the rubber around the pipe.*
  coil *She coiled the rope around the post.*
  curl *She curled her fingers tightly around his wrist.*
  wind *She wound the cable around the iron.*
3 She has twisted her ankle.
  rick *I nearly ricked my neck.*
  sprain *I sprained my wrist.*
  strain *I've strained a muscle.*
  wrench *He's wrenched his shoulder.*
4 You are twisting my words.
  distort *You're distorting the truth.*
  misquote *The paper misquoted what I actually said.*

twist² [noun]

1 The plumber gave the tap a twist.
  turn *a quick turn of the dial*
2 twists in the road
  bend *a sharp bend in the river*
  curve *a curve in the line*

Tt

turn a turn in the direction of the path

type [noun]

brand What brand of washing powder do you use?

breed a new breed of mobile phone • a rare breed of dog

category This book falls into the category of 'romance'.

class There are different classes of drug.

form a very nasty form of flu

kind I don't like this kind of chocolate.

sort a different sort of problem

variety a new variety of rose

typical [adjective]

average an average woman

common It's a common problem among older people.

conventional He's tried aromatherapy and conventional treatments.

normal This isn't my normal train.

ordinary It was just an ordinary day.

regular Shaving is part of his regular routine.

standard This bed isn't the standard size.

usual He gave me all the usual excuses for being late.

Tt

U

ugly [adjective]
1 an ugly face
plain *a rather plain woman*
unattractive *I think he's very unattractive.*
◆ **Formal word unsightly** *He was left with an unsightly scar.*
2 an ugly scene
nasty *a nasty incident on the train*
unpleasant *an unpleasant argument over money*

VOCABULARY CHOICES
[meaning 1]
• People use the word **plain** to describe a person who is not good-looking when they are being tactful, and they want to avoid using the word 'ugly' because it is not a very kind word.

unbelievable [adjective]
1 His tales of bravery are unbelievable.
far-fetched *He had some far-fetched ideas about his family history.*
impossible *It seems impossible that she could have run so far.*
improbable *That's a highly improbable excuse.*
incredible *She told some incredible story about getting lost.*
unconvincing *The film's plot is unconvincing.*
unlikely *The theory is unlikely for many reasons.*

2 It's been an unbelievable day.
astonishing *He got there with astonishing speed.*
extraordinary *My aunt is an extraordinary character.*
incredible *He walked an incredible distance to raise money for charity.*

uncertain [adjective]
doubtful *I was doubtful about going abroad. • The project has a doubtful future.*
hesitant *She felt hesitant about joining them for dinner.*
unconvinced *I liked the idea, but Bob was unconvinced.*
undecided *I'm undecided about taking that job.*
unsure *I was unsure about the correct address.*

uncomfortable [adjective]
1 uncomfortable shoes
hard *a hard bed*
painful *These shoes are painful to walk in.*
◆ **Formal word ill-fitting** *She squeezed into an ill-fitting dress.*
2 an uncomfortable silence
awkward *There was an awkward moment when nobody said anything.*
embarrassed *We all felt pretty embarrassed.*
uneasy *There was an uneasy hush when he stopped speaking.*

Uu

unconscious [adjective]

1 I was unconscious for five minutes.
out *How long was she out?*
out cold *He's out cold.*
senseless *I hit a branch, which knocked me senseless.*
◆ **Informal phrase out for the count**
Both men were out for the count.
◆ **Technical term comatose** *The patient is in a comatose state.*
2 He was unconscious of his surroundings.
ignorant *I was ignorant of what had happened.*
unaware *She was unaware that he was in the next room.*
◆ **Formal word oblivious** *Alec seemed oblivious to the noise.*
3 an unconscious reaction
automatic *If you see something fall it's automatic to put your hand out to catch it.*
instinctive *We have an instinctive dislike of insects.*
involuntary *an involuntary jerk of the knee*
subconscious *You don't realize you have the feeling — it's subconscious.*
◆ **Formal word unwitting** *She gave unwitting help to the criminals.*
◆ **Informal word knee-jerk** *The knee-jerk reaction is to look for revenge.*

under [preposition]

1 the cupboard under the stairs • a nursery for children under five
below *a scar just below his eye*
beneath *flowers growing beneath the trees*
underneath *a hole in the floor underneath the carpet*
2 The staff are under my command.
junior to *I was junior to Baba in my last job.*
◆ **Formal term subordinate to** *A lieutenant is subordinate to a captain.*
3 The meal cost under £20 for four of us.

less than *great gifts for less than £10*

understand [verb]

1 I understand what you mean.
follow *I can't follow these instructions.*
grasp *She couldn't grasp what Myles was saying.*
make out *From what I could make out, that's his father.*
see *Can you see what I'm getting at?*
take in *It was too much to take in.*
◆ **Formal word comprehend** *I couldn't comprehend why she was angry.*
2 I understand their distress.
identify with *I can identify with that feeling.*
sympathize *It's a difficult situation for you — we do sympathize.*
◆ **Formal term empathize with** *Try to empathize with people from other cultures.*
3 I understood everyone was invited.
assume *I assumed she was his daughter.*
believe *The police believe the thieves may come back.*
gather *I gather you're not coming.*
presume *I presume I should give this to you.*
suppose *I suppose Ted will be there.*
think *We thought the money had already been paid.*

undo [verb]

open *I can't open this jar.*
unbutton *It was so hot, I had to unbutton my shirt.*
unlock *Somebody came and unlocked the door.*
untie *Untie their hands.*
unzip *She unzipped her sleeping bag and climbed out.*

unemployed [adjective]

out of work *I am currently out of work.* • *an out-of-work mechanic*
redundant *She's been made redundant.*
◆ **Formal words jobless** *getting jobless people back into work*

Uu

unwaged The course costs £20, or £10 unwaged.

◆ **Informal phrase on the dole** Irene's been on the dole for eight months.

VOCABULARY CHOICES

• The words **jobless** and **unwaged** are formal words that you often see in newspapers or hear on the news. **Jobless** is often used when talking about the number of people who are unemployed.

• The word **unwaged** is also used on signs or in leaflets for talking about the cost of doing something when it is cheaper for unemployed people.

unfair [adjective]
   biased a biased decision
   prejudiced She's prejudiced against the British.
   unjust Many people thought the ruling was unjust.
◆ **Formal words discriminatory** a rule that is discriminatory against women
   wrongful The police admitted wrongful arrest.

unfriendly [adjective]
   cold her cold manner
   hostile He got a hostile stare from the woman behind the counter.
   standoffish Her friends are a bit standoffish.
   surly The manager was a surly middle-aged man.
   unwelcoming The tone of his voice was unwelcoming.
◆ **Formal words inhospitable** Am I being inhospitable if I leave you for a while?
   unsociable He's pretty unsociable — you'll never see him at parties.

unhappy [adjective]
   dejected We left the meeting feeling very dejected.
   depressed I feel a bit depressed today.
   down I was feeling quite down until you called.
   downcast He was looking very downcast, so I asked what was wrong.
   glum There's no need to look so glum.
   heartbroken She left him and he was heartbroken.
   miserable She looks miserable — what's the matter?
   sad a sad face
   upset She was so upset when her father died.
◆ **Formal word sorrowful** a dog with large, sorrowful eyes

VOCABULARY CHOICES

• **Downcast** and **glum** suggest that someone looks sad on the outside as well as feeling sad inside.

• The word **heartbroken** is sometimes used to stir the emotions, by suggesting someone is extremely upset by something that has happened to them.

unkind [adjective]
   cruel a cruel thing to say
   malicious malicious gossip
   mean Don't be so mean to her!
   nasty a nasty little girl
   spiteful He has a spiteful nature.
◆ **Formal word uncharitable** She had uncharitable thoughts about her teacher.

unknown [adjective]
1 an unknown actor
   obscure She reads books by osbscure writers.
   undiscovered an undiscovered talent for painting
   unfamiliar I was surrounded by unfamiliar faces.
2 The man's identity is unknown.
   anonymous They received money from an anonymous well-wisher.
   nameless A friend of mine, who will remain nameless, was found with no clothes on.

Uu

unidentified An unidentified donor paid for the trip.

unnamed For their protection, witnesses will stay unnamed.

unlucky [adjective]

luckless The luckless owner came out to find his car was stolen.

unfortunate an unfortunate mistake

◆ **Formal words** **ill-fated** The ill-fated flight took off as normal from the airport.

unhappy an unhappy coincidence

VOCABULARY CHOICES

• The formal word **ill-fated** creates a sense of doom, and is often used in newspaper stories.

• **Unhappy** is often used in stories.

unnecessary [adjective]

dispensable These items are just dispensable extras.

needless a needless waste of food

non-essential non-essential luxuries such as satellite television

redundant a redundant machine • redundant comments

uncalled-for He made nasty, uncalled-for remarks.

◆ **Formal word** **superfluous** The report contained a lot of superfluous information.

unusual [adjective]

bizarre a bizarre situation

curious a curious shape in the shadows

odd That was an odd thing to say!

rare a rare type of butterfly

strange We heard a strange noise in the kitchen.

unconventional very unconventional clothes

◆ **Formal word** **abnormal** The test result is abnormal.

upset¹ [adjective]

You're obviously upset about something.

distressed He was clearly distressed.

disturbed I was disturbed to hear about the accident.

hurt She was feeling hurt.

shaken She was shaken but not injured.

sore I still felt sore that I hadn't been asked to the party.

troubled Troubled teenagers can do silly things.

upset² [verb]

Don't let them upset you.

distress It distresses me to see her like that.

trouble What's troubling you?

worry His poor health was worrying everyone.

◆ **Formal word** **unnerve** He was unnerved by the whole experience.

upset³ [noun]

a stomach upset

complaint skin complaints

illness patients with illnesses of all sorts

◆ **Formal word** **ailment** a kidney ailment

◆ **Informal word** **bug** a tummy bug

urgent [adjective]

dire He was in dire need of help.

important It's important that you do it now.

pressing This is a pressing problem for councils.

◆ **Formal word** **immediate** There's an immediate need for clean water.

use¹ [verb]

1 Use your common sense.

employ They employ very clever methods.

make use of Visitors are welcome to make use of the garden.

utilize Feel free to utilize the facilities.

◆ **Formal word** **exercise** You should exercise your right to refuse.

2 We've used all our fuel.

finish I see you've finished all the bread.

spend He spends all his time watching TV.

use up Has the milk all been used up?

Uu

◆ **Formal words exhaust** *They had exhausted their supplies of food.*
expend *Don't expend all your energy at the beginning of the game.*

use ² [noun]
It's no use to me now it's broken.
benefit *What benefit is that to us?*
good *It's no good crying about it.*
point *Is there any point complaining?*
purpose *I need to see the purpose of what I am doing.*

useful [adjective]
convenient *a convenient place for a bin*
effective *an effective way of dealing with the problem*
handy *a handy tool*
helpful *helpful hints*
practical *some practical suggestions*
valuable *very valuable advice*
worthwhile *a worthwhile way to spend time*
◆ **Formal word beneficial** *the beneficial effects of the treatment*

useless [adjective]
1 *We tried to save her, but it was useless.*
fruitless *We had hours of fruitless discussion.*
futile *It's futile to try to persuade her.*
hopeless *It's hopeless trying to find the thief now.*
ineffective *Attempts to make peace were ineffective.*
pointless *It would be pointless to go on searching in the dark.*
unproductive *an unproductive round of meetings*
vain *a vain attempt to cheer him up*
2 *a useless piece of machinery*

broken-down *an old, broken-down car*
inefficient *inefficient working methods*
unusable *These machines are so old they are unusable.*
worthless *He got involved in some worthless scheme.*
◆ **Informal word clapped-out** *a clapped-out typewriter*
3 *I'm useless at maths.*
hopeless *I used to be hopeless at spelling.*
incompetent *an incompetent worker*
weak *He is weak when it comes to remembering things.*

usual [adjective]
common *It's a common problem among older people.*
conventional *He's tried aromatherapy and conventional treatments.*
normal *This isn't my normal train.*
ordinary *It was just an ordinary day.*
regular *Shaving is part of his regular routine.*
standard *This bed isn't the standard size.*
typical *He's a typical teenager.*
◆ **Formal word customary** *It's customary to give the waiter a tip.*

usually [adverb]
generally *We generally have dinner at eight.*
mainly *Our customers are mainly people in business.*
mostly *We mostly stay in and watch television.*
normally *Normally I would catch an earlier train.*
typically *An insect typically has six legs and two pairs of wings.*

Uu

vain [adjective]

1 a vain attempt
pointless *Complaining is pointless — nobody listens.*
useless *useless advice*
◆ **Formal word futile** *Giving the victims money is a futile gesture.*
2 a vain little man
conceited *He was conceited about his appearance.*
self-important *a bunch of self-important film stars*

valuable [adjective]

1 This necklace is very valuable.
dear *The photos are very dear to me.*
precious *precious jewels*
prized *his most prized possessions*
treasured *This ring is my most treasured heirloom.*
2 valuable advice
helpful *some helpful hints*

useful *useful information*
◆ **Formal word beneficial** *Was the treatment beneficial?*

VOCABULARY CHOICES

[meaning 1]
• The words **dear**, **prized** and **treasured** describe something that someone likes very much and would not want to lose, although the thing may not be worth a lot of money.

---

value¹ [noun]

What is the value of the car?
cost *the cost of a modern wedding*
price *a rise in the price of oil*
worth *Most people are not aware of their own worth.*

value² [verb]

1 I value your friendship.
cherish *She cherishes memories of her son.*
prize *the possessions you prize the most*

Types of vegetable:

artichoke	cauliflower	lettuce	radish
asparagus	celery	marrow	shallot
aubergine	courgette	mushroom	spinach
bean	cress	onion	spring onion
beetroot	cucumber	parsnip	swede
broccoli	fennel	pea	sweetcorn
Brussels sprout	kale	pepper	sweet potato
cabbage	leek	potato	turnip
carrot	lentil	pumpkin	watercress

Vv

Types of vehicle:

bicycle	helicopter	scooter	tractor
boat	lorry	ship	train
bus	minibus	sled	tram
camper	moped	sleigh	truck
car	motorbike	tank	van
caravan	plane	taxi	
coach	rickshaw	toboggan	

respect I really respect your opinion.
treasure He treasured the good times they had.
◆ **Formal term hold dear** These are the beliefs we hold dear.
2 I had my bracelet valued.
assess The damage was assessed at thousands of pounds.
evaluate Real talent is difficult to evaluate.
price The watch was priced at £100.
survey Our house surveyed at five thousand pounds more than we paid for it.

vanish [verb]
disappear The stain has disappeared completely.
go away He had unpleasant memories that wouldn't go away.

vegetable [noun]
See the box on the previous page.

vehicle [noun]
See the box above.

very [adverb]
deeply They were deeply shocked at the news.
extremely We were all extremely tired.
greatly The town was not greatly different from how I remembered it.
highly a highly intelligent child
particularly a particularly unpleasant smell
really I'm really thirsty.
terribly I'm not terribly impressed.
◆ **Formal word most** We are all most grateful for your help.

victim [noun]
casualty casualties of the war
sufferer migraine sufferers

view[1] [noun]
What's your view on this subject?
attitude I didn't like her casual attitude.
belief It's the doctor's belief that there's nothing wrong with me.
feeling She shares my feeling that computers are dangerous.
mind We're of the same mind on this matter.
opinion Dad and I have different opinions.
point of view Other people might have a different point of view.

view[2] [verb]
1 I viewed things in a different light.
consider He was considered the best player in the team.
regard Sam was regarded as a troublemaker.
think about I didn't think of her as a girlfriend.
2 We viewed the scene.
look at Residents weren't allowed to look at the plans.
see An estate agent let us see the house.
◆ **Formal word survey** The captain surveyed the horizon, looking for land.

violent [adjective]
1 a violent attack • a violent person
aggressive The customer became aggressive.
brutal a brutal killing

Vv

savage Bears can be savage animals.
vicious a vicious dog • a vicious attack on an elderly lady
2 a violent storm
fierce a fierce tempest
powerful the bomb's powerful blast
severe severe winds

VOCABULARY CHOICES

[meaning 1]
• The words **brutal**, **savage** and **vicious** have a lot of impact, and suggest a frightening level of violence. They are often used in news stories to stir feelings of disgust at violent acts.

visit [verb]
He didn't even visit her when she was in hospital.
call in I'll call in later to see how you're feeling.
call on We could call on Jeremy while we're in London.
look up She said she'd look you up when she's in Edinburgh.
see My parents are coming to see us at New Year.
stay with We usually stay with friends on the island.
◆ **Informal terms drop in on** It's nice to drop in on old friends.
pop in We could pop in later, if you like.
stop by Why don't you stop by and have a coffee?

visit [noun]
He came for a visit in the summer.
call a doctor making his calls • I wanted more information, so I paid Dad a call.
stay a short stay with Maggie's parents
stop We'll make a stop at Paul's when we go to Peter's.

VOCABULARY CHOICES

• A **call** tends to suggest a very short visit, made perhaps because it is your job, or because you have a particular reason.
• A **stop** also suggests a short visit, this time because you are on your way to another place.

voluntary [adjective]
unpaid The work she does is entirely unpaid.

vote [noun]
a campaign to give women the vote
ballot The class is holding a ballot to elect two speakers.
election the election to choose a new party leader
polls The country goes to the polls next week.

vote [verb]
Which candidate did you vote for?
cast a vote I haven't cast my vote yet.
elect The American people will elect a new president.

Vv

W

wages [noun]
  earnings *You are taxed on your earnings.*
  pay *an increase in your pay*
  salary *managers on very high salaries*

wait[1] [verb]
1 *Don't wait — do it now.*
  hesitate *She hesitated, then picked up the money.*
  pause *Alan paused for a drink before continuing.*
  ♦ **Formal word delay** *Don't delay — this offer must end on Saturday.*
  ♦ **Informal terms hang around** *If you hang around, there will be none left.*
  hang fire *Let's hang fire until they get back.*
2 *I waited to speak to the teacher.*
  stay behind *If you have any questions, stay behind at the end.*

wait[2] [noun]
We had a long wait before he agreed to see us.
  delay *a half-hour delay while the signals changed*
  hold-up *If there are no hold-ups, we'll be there in five hours.*

walk[1] [verb]
We walked down the hill to the village pub.
  amble *The cows amble along at their own pace.*
  march *She marched into the room and started shouting at me.*

  pace *Davies paced up and down, waiting for news.*
  saunter *He sauntered in half an hour late.*
  stride *We watched her striding confidently down the street.*
  stroll *He strolled along as if he had all the time in the world.*
  tread *You can see where someone has trodden on the flowers.*
  trek *I had to trek all the way back to the hotel.*
  trudge *They trudged around in the rain for hours.*

VOCABULARY CHOICES

- If you **march** or **stride**, you walk quite quickly and in a confident or angry way, or in a way that shows you have decided to do something.
- If you **amble**, **saunter** or **stroll**, you walk in a slow and relaxed way that suggests you are not anxious about anything.
- If you **pace**, however, you walk up and down a room because you are worried and cannot sit still.
- The words **trek** and **trudge** suggest you are walking with effort, and that you are not enjoying the walk.

Ww

walk[2] [noun]
1 *go for a walk*
  hike *a five-mile hike along the coast*
  stroll *a stroll round the park*
2 *a tree-lined walk*

lane *a narrow lane between the houses*
path *a path through the woods*
want [verb]
1 She wants something to eat. • They
wanted peace.
　crave *politicians who crave power*
　desire *the money to buy everything
　you've ever desired*
　long for *The people are longing for an
　end to the war.*
　wish for *Be careful what you wish for —
　you might get it.*
　◆ **Informal word fancy** *Do you fancy a
　cup of tea?*
2 The door wants a lick of paint.
　need *The fence needs mending.*
　◆ **Formal word require** *Does your car
　require a service?*

VOCABULARY CHOICES
[meaning 1]
• The terms **crave** and **long for** convey
strong feelings of wanting something very
much.

war [noun]
　combat *soldiers killed in combat*
　conflict *the danger of conflict in the region*
　fighting *fighting between rebels and
　government forces*
　struggle *an armed struggle for
　independence*
　warfare *a history of modern warfare*
　◆ **Formal word hostilities** *the end of
　hostilities*

VOCABULARY CHOICES
• **Conflict** is slightly formal and is used in
news reports instead of the word 'war'.
• The word **struggle** is often used by political
groups who use weapons as a way of
trying to change the way their country is run.
The word suggests fighting for a cause, for
example against injustice, whereas a word
such as 'conflict' does not give this same
impression.

Ww

warm[1] [adjective]
1 warm water
　lukewarm *The soup was only lukewarm.*
　tepid *Bath the baby in tepid water.*
2 a warm welcome
　friendly *a friendly atmosphere at the
　party*
　◆ **Formal word cordial** *cordial relations
　between the two countries*
3 a warm climate
　fine *more fine weather to come*
　sunny *a sunny Mediterranean day*
warm[2] [verb]
Warm the plates in the oven.
　heat up *I could heat up some soup for
　you.*
　reheat *Reheat the rice in the microwave.*
warn [verb]
　advise *We were advised to stay indoors.*
　alert *The police alerted us of the danger.*
warning [noun]
　alarm *When we saw he'd escaped, we
　raised the alarm.*
　alert *The police have issued an alert to all
　residents.*
　hint *There was no hint of the danger
　ahead.*
　◆ **Formal word notification** *They've
　given us notification that they intend to sue
　us.*
wash [verb]
　clean *I haven't cleaned the windows for
　weeks.*
　cleanse *Cleanse the wound thoroughly.*
　rinse *Rinse the soap off your hands.*
　scrub *We had to scrub the carpet to get
　the mark off.*
waste[1] [verb]
I wasted a fortune on presents for her.
　fritter away *Don't fritter your money
　away on that rubbish.*
　misuse *She had misused her clients'
　money.* • *The local council was accused of
　misusing funds.*

squander *I don't like to see him squandering his talents.*
throw away *We've thrown away all our chances.*

VOCABULARY CHOICES

• The term **fritter away** conveys the idea of something being wasted gradually, in a way that you might not notice at the time.
• **Misuse** is a slightly more formal term, and it is often used in official contexts.
• The term **squander** has a stronger tone of criticism than the others, and emphasizes that the waste is needless.

waste² [noun]

sorting waste out for recycling
leftovers *You can eat the leftovers the following day.*
litter *streets covered in litter*
rubbish *We put all the rubbish in black bags.*
scrap *Badly damaged cars are sold for scrap.*
◆ **Formal words** **debris** *The road is showered in debris from the bomb.*
refuse *The council is responsible for refuse collection.*

watch [verb]

1 *She watched the children playing.*
look at *Colin was looking at the girls at the other table.*
scan *I scanned the newspaper of the man next to me.*
scrutinize *His every move was scrutinized by reporters.*
see *Have you seen her new film?*
stare at *Don't stare at him when he's concentrating.*
◆ **Formal words** **observe** *The police observed him coming out of the bar.*
survey *Landis surveyed the scene in front of him.*
2 *Watch my bag, would you?*
look after *A neighbour is looking after the house while we're away.*
mind *Who's minding the children?*
take care of *We'll take good care of your dog.*
◆ **Informal phrase** **keep an eye on** *Will you keep an eye on the pasta while I make the sauce?*
3 *Watch for those holes in the road.*
be careful of *Be careful of the ice.*
look out for *Look out for cars as you cross.*

wave [verb]

1 *He waved to his parents.*
signal *She signalled for the race to start.*
2 *He was waving a stick.*
shake *The man shook his fist at us.*
◆ **Formal word** **brandish** *The hero brandishes his sword.*

way [noun]

1 *the usual way*
means *Try to solve the problem by a different means.*
method *This wasn't a good method of dealing with complaints.*
technique *techniques for learning maths*
2 *a study of their ways • It's just his way.*
custom *the customs of people in different countries*
habit *disgusting habits*
nature *It's not in his nature to fight back.*
3 *the way home*
course *The new road follows a course along the coast.*
direction *Is this the direction for York?*
route *They returned by a different route.*

weak [adjective]

1 *She is still feeling weak after the illness.*
delicate *As a girl I was delicate and missed a lot of school.*
feeble *a feeble movement of her arm*
frail *Now he looked old and frail.*
puny *a puny little guy with no strength*
◆ **Formal word** **infirm** *Although Gran is infirm, she has a sharp mind.*
2 *The economy is weak.*

Ww

Types of weather:

breeze	gale	monsoon	thaw
cloud	hail	rain	thunder
cyclone	heatwave	shower	tornado
drizzle	hurricane	sleet	typhoon
drought	ice	snow	whirlwind
fog	lightning	storm	wind
frost	mist	sunshine	

flimsy The flimsy homes could not withstand the earthquake.
fragile thin, fragile glass
shaky Business is a bit shaky these days.
3 a weak position
exposed Small companies are in an exposed position.
unguarded an unguarded part of the castle
unprotected If you don't take the medicine, you leave your body unprotected.
vulnerable The new law leaves workers in a vulnerable situation.
4 a weak argument
feeble an feeble excuse
lame a lame joke
poor the poor quality of the research
puny a puny gesture of defiance
◆ **Formal word unconvincing** The conclusions of the report are unconvincing.
5 a weak signal
faint a faint voice at the end of the line
slight a slight breeze
6 weak tea
tasteless a fairly tasteless wine
watery watery beer
◆ **Formal word insipid** a cup of insipid coffee

VOCABULARY CHOICES

[meaning 1]
• **Puny** is a little mocking in tone, and sounds like you are criticizing someone or something for their weakness.
• A less critical word is **delicate**, which

suggests something dainty.
• The word **frail** suggests someone is old or ill, and it is sometimes used to stir people's emotions, as in a frail old lady.

wear[1] [verb]
1 wearing green • wearing a hat
dress in Everyone was dressed in black.
have on She had on the most beautiful dress.
2 wear away • wear down
fray The cuffs were beginning to fray.
rub The elbows of the jacket are shiny where they've been rubbed.
◆ **Technical terms corrode** Rust gradually corrodes the metal.
erode Beaches are eroded by the action of the sea.

wear[2] [noun]
elegant evening wear
clothes ordinary work clothes
clothing women's clothing
dress All the men were wearing highland dress.
◆ **Formal word attire** formal attire for men

weather [noun]
climate She would like to live in a warmer climate.
conditions Conditions are not good for hillwalking.
temperature What's the temperature like outside? Is it warm?
See also the box above.

Ww

wedding [noun]
  marriage the marriage of Ben and Elizabeth
  ◆ **Formal word nuptials** She changed her mind a week before the nuptials.

weird [adjective]
  bizarre a bizarre coincidence
  creepy The house was dark and creepy.
  eerie An eerie silence fell over the house.
  mysterious I saw a mysterious shape in the garden.
  strange strange noises coming from the attic
  ◆ **Formal word supernatural** ghosts and other supernatural beings
  ◆ **Informal word spooky** It's spooky how she knows what you're going to say.

well¹ [adverb]
1 He plays the piano well.
  skilfully He passes the ball so skilfully.
  ◆ **Formal word expertly** She handles these situations expertly.
2 Everything went well.
  successfully The party had gone successfully.
3 Stir the mixture well.
  thoroughly Make sure the meat is thoroughly cooked.

well² [adjective]
1 I don't feel well.
  fit Wait until you're feeling fit again.
  healthy The dog's coat looks healthy.
  in good health She's happy and in good health.
  strong I'm feeling much stronger today.
2 All is well.
  all right Don't worry — everything will be all right.
  fine There are no problems — everything's fine.
  good Life is good at the moment.
  right It turned out right in the end.

wet¹ [adjective]
1 wet clothes • wet ground

  damp The walls felt damp.
  drenched You'll get drenched in that rain.
  moist Keep the soil moist.
  soaked We got soaked on the way home.
  soaking Your socks are soaking.
  waterlogged The game had to be cancelled because the pitch was waterlogged.
2 a wet day
  miserable It's too miserable to go out.
  rainy a rainy afternoon

VOCABULARY CHOICES

[meaning 1]
• The word **drenched** creates a strong image of someone or something being soaked through, and gives the impression of its being very unpleasant and uncomfortable.

[meaning 2]
• If your describe weather as **miserable** rather than just 'wet' or 'rainy' you are adding the suggestion that it is making you a bit unhappy.

wet² [verb]
Wet the edges of the pastry and seal by pressing.
  dampen Dampen the hair before applying the shampoo.
  moisten Moisten the sponge first.
  soak Soak the beans in salt water.
  water Make sure the grass is watered regularly.

white [noun]

Shades of white:	
ecru	off–white
magnolia	

Ww

whole [adjective]
  complete I have a complete set of the coins.
  entire Davies read the entire report.

full *The course runs for a full day.*
wide [adjective]
a wide avenue
  broad *broad tree-lined streets*
wide [adverb]
The shot went wide of the goal.
  off target *The missile drifted off target.*
  wide of the mark *The second shot went wide of the mark.*

wild [adjective]
1 *a wild horse*
  ferocious *a ferocious lion*
  fierce *The dog looked fierce.*
  savage *a savage wolf*
  untamed *untamed horses living in the plains*
2 *wild country*
  barren *a barren desert*
  desolate *a desolate place where nothing much grew*
3 *wild behaviour*
  boisterous *very boisterous children*
  riotous *riotous behaviour*
  rowdy *a rowdy atmosphere in the pub*
  ♦ **Formal words disorderly** *They were arrested for being drunk and disorderly.*
  unruly *The crowd became an unruly mob.*
4 *a wild night*
  blustery *blustery conditions*
  stormy *a stormy Channel crossing*

win [verb]
1 *win a race*
  come first *He came first in a cookery contest.*
  finish first *She finished first in the sprint.*
  triumph *We triumphed over our biggest rivals.*
2 *win a prize*
  achieve *He achieved third place in the national finals.*
  carry off *She carried off first prize in a poetry competition.*
  gain *She has gained the respect of us all.*

  secure *The company have secured a new deal.*
win [noun]
a fantastic win for the team
  conquest *City added United to their list of conquests.*
  success *The runner achieved success in the 500 metres.*
  triumph *It was a personal triumph for her.*
  victory *the British victory at the Battle of Trafalgar*

wind [noun]
The wind howled in the trees.
  air *a still day with no air at all*
  breeze *a pleasant cool breeze*
  draught *If there's a draught, close the door.*
  gale *We had to put the tent up in a gale.*
  gust *A sudden gust blew the paper out of my hand.*

VOCABULARY CHOICES
- The words **air** and **breeze** are positive, as they give the impression of a very gentle and pleasant wind.
- **Draught**, however, suggests cold air that makes you feel uncomfortable.

wind [verb]
a path winding down the side of the cliff
  bend *The road bends sharply to the left.*
  curl *You can see the river curling through the valley.*
  loop *Loop the rope round your waist twice.*
  twist and turn *The track twists and turns its way through the forest.*

windy [adjective]
  blowy *a blowy day*
  blustery *blustery conditions*
  breezy *It's a bit breezy now.*

wise [adjective]
1 *a wise old man*
  clever *The champion was too clever for her.*

experienced She's very experienced in business.
shrewd a shrewd judge of character
2 a wise decision
sensible a sensible choice
sound sound investments
◆ **Formal word prudent** Would it be prudent to stop now?

wish [verb]
1 wishing for success • wishing for rain
desire The job had everything he desired.
hope We're hoping for good weather tomorrow.
want She had everything she'd ever wanted.
yearn People are yearning for peace in the region.
◆ **Formal word aspire** She aspired to be party leader.
2 Do as she wishes.
ask We've done everything you asked.
order He ordered an investigation to be carried out.

witness [noun]
eyewitness The police took statements from eyewitnesses.
onlooker Terrified onlookers saw the fight take place.

wobble [verb]
rock The boat rocked form side to side.
shake We heard the bomb then felt the ground shake.
totter She tottered along on high heels.
tremble The man's hands trembled as he spoke.

wood [noun]
1 Cut the wood into strips.
timber trucks stacked high with timber
2 an oak wood
forest We went walking in the forest.
trees Then the animal disappeared into the trees.
woodland an area of woodland
woods They built a hut in the woods.

word [noun]
1 What does this word mean?
expression It's an old Jewish expression.
term Are you familiar with the term 'irony'?
2 I'll have a word with him later.
chat Could we have a quiet chat?
conversation We had a conversation about it this morning.
discussion discussions between management and workers
talk We need to have a talk about money.
3 Get word to his family that he is ill.
message I didn't get the message.
news We don't know where they are — there's been no news of them.
4 I give you my word.
assurance You gave us an assurance that everything would be fine.
guarantee Our manager gave us his guarantee that we would not lose our jobs.
pledge I made a pledge not to drink alcohol.
promise The school has broken its promise.
word of honour Give me your word of honour that this will not happen again.

work¹ [noun]
1 What sort of work do you do?
business She's in the music business.
line of business What line of business is his father in?
profession the legal profession
trade the building trade
2 She is doing important work for the government.
assignment Our best people are needed for a difficult assignment.
task Getting them to help would not be an easy task.
3 It takes a lot of hard work to be successful.
drudgery the constant drudgery of housework
effort Becoming a champion requires a lot of effort.

Ww

◆ **Formal words** **labour** the product of your own labour

toil Clearing the garden took a lot of toil on Dad's part.

VOCABULARY CHOICES
[meaning 3]
• **Drudgery** is a very negative term for work that is always the same and bores you.
• The word **toil** is a strong word that suggests something is exhausting and difficult to do.

work² [verb]
1 I'm not working at the moment.
be employed He's employed as a nurse.
earn a living He earns a living as a waiter.
have a job Alan had a job in a bakery.
2 The air conditioning isn't working.
function The system won't function properly.
go Without petrol, the engine won't go.
operate The computers are operating at high speeds.
perform The machines are all performing well.
run How are the servers running?

worker [noun]
employee Employees get a say in how the company is run.
labourer He worked as a labourer on a building site.

world [noun]
earth the biggest creature on earth
globe people from all corners of the globe
planet She's the most famous person on the planet.

worn-out [adjective]
1 worn-out slippers
decrepit That decrepit old car of yours is dangerous.
frayed a frayed rope
on its last legs Most of our furniture is on its last legs.

ragged I've worn this dress so often it's ragged.
shabby a shabby old sofa
tatty I keep some tatty clothes for working in the garden.
threadbare He wears a threadbare old suit.
2 worn out by work
drained She felt quite drained by the whole experience.
exhausted What have you been doing? You look exhausted.
tired out We were tired out after our long walk.
weary She gave a weary sigh.

worried [adjective]
anxious anxious hours waiting for news
apprehensive I was apprehensive about speaking in front of others.
concerned letters from concerned parents
nervous feeling nervous about the test
on edge Relax. You've been on edge all day.
uneasy I have an uneasy feeling about this.

worry¹ [noun]
1 I know you have a lot of worries.
concern Local people have several concerns.
problem Every family has its problems.
2 Worry showed on her face.
anxiety anxiety about the children's safety
apprehension a look of apprehension on his face

worry² [verb]
Don't worry, everything's fine.
bother Something was obviously bothering him.
concern I'm concerned about her safety.
fret There's no use fretting about the past.
haunt a problem which had haunted him for a long time

Ww

plague *a man plagued by health problems*

wound[1] [noun]

bleeding from a wound on his head

cut *a bad cut on his leg*

gash *a gash on her hand*

injury *A first-aider can treat minor injuries.*

wound[2] [verb]

1 *He wounded his leg.*

hurt *She hurt her elbow in the fall.*

injure *Be careful you don't injure your back.*

2 *The remark wounded them deeply.*

hurt *What she said really hurt me.*

upset *We were upset at the remark.*

wrap [verb]

cover *Cover each sausage with a bacon slice.*

pack *The fish are packed in ice.*

package *These products are packaged in recyclable materials.*

write [verb]

draft *The committee drafted a new set of rules.*

draw up *A lawyer is drawing up my will.*

jot down *I'll just jot down a few details.*

scribble *I quickly scribbled the number in my diary.*

set down *You should set these ideas down on paper.*

take down *The officer took down my name.*

writer [noun]

author *the children's author, Enid Blyton*

columnist *He's a columnist for 'The Mirror'.*

diarist *the famous diarist, Samuel Pepys*

dramatist *dramatists such as Shakespeare*

novelist *books by British novelists*

playwright *The playwright himself will direct the play.*

VOCABULARY CHOICES

- The different words for writer often tell you exactly what kind of writing they do. For example, someone who writes plays is a **playwright** or a **dramatist**.
- **Dramatist** is a slightly more formal word than **playwright**, and it is also a slightly old-fashioned word.

wrong [adjective]

1 *the wrong answer* • *I got the wrong idea about him.*

false *a false accusation*

inaccurate *Our calculations were inaccurate.*

incorrect *incorrect spelling*

mistaken *You must be mistaken; Abu does not live here.*

untrue *We know the story is untrue.*

2 *the wrong thing to say* • *We brought the wrong tools for the job.*

inappropriate *Her remarks were inappropriate at a funeral.*

unsuitable *Your clothes are unsuitable for this weather.*

◆ **Formal word   improper** *Her laughter seemed improper at the time.*

3 *Stealing is wrong.*

bad *bad behaviour*

dishonest *It would be dishonest of me to call in sick today.*

illegal *the illegal sale of drugs*

immoral *It is immoral to tax old people in this way.*

unfair *It's unfair to talk about her when she isn't here.*

unjust *People feel the new laws are unjust.*

unlawful *He is involved in many unlawful activities.*

Ww

Y

yell [verb]

bawl *Football fans bawled out their songs.*

bellow *The officer bellowed commands to the troops.*

call *He called for help.*

cry *'Leave me alone!' she cried.*

roar *'Get out!' he roared.*

scream *She screamed at me to help her.*

shout *I wish you would all stop shouting.*

yellow [noun]

Shades of yellow:	
canary	lemon
gold	saffron

young¹ [adjective]

1 *young lambs • young people*

adolescent *She has two adolescent sons.*

baby *baby birds*

fledgling *fledgling sparrows • a fledgling journalist*

immature *An immature tiger already has the instinct to hunt.*

infant *an infant daughter*

junior *the junior pupils of the school*

teenage *the latest teenage fashions • teenage girls*

youthful *He was an adviser to the youthful king.*

♦ **Formal word** **juvenile** *juvenile crime*

2 *young leaves*

early *early shoots*

immature *immature buds on the trees*

new *new leaves on the plant*

recent *recent growth*

VOCABULARY CHOICES

[meaning 1]

• The word **immature** carries the suggestion of not knowing exactly what to do or how to behave because you are young.

• **Juvenile** is a term used in law, so it tends to be have negative associations with bad behaviour and crime.

young² [noun]

parents and their young

babies *a mother and her babies*

brood *a lively brood of ducklings*

children *They have no children.*

family *a family of five*

litter *a litter of four puppies*

offspring *A rabbit can have up to thirty offspring.*

youth [noun]

1 *Police have arrested a youth.*

adolescent *Many adolescents are too shy to talk about their problems.*

boy *a normal boy, getting into scrapes*

teenager *Teenagers can look and feel awkward.*

young man *a very fashionable young man*

youngster *We are trying to get more*

youngsters to play tennis.

◆ **Formal word juvenile** murders committed by juveniles

◆ **Informal word kid** He's quite a tough kid.

2 the youth of today

the young music and fashion for the young

younger generation The younger generation still have some respect for their elders.

young people Young people need jobs and security.

3 in her youth • in his youth

adolescence the problems of adolescence

boyhood He spent his boyhood in Orkney.

childhood an unhappy childhood

girlhood She would talk about her girlhood in Sheffield.

immaturity His carelessness is down to his immaturity.

Yy

Z

zero [noun]

nil *a nil–nil draw*

nothing *It goes from nothing to fifty miles per hour in seconds.*

nought *an increase of nought point two per cent*

♦ **Informal word** **zilch** *a grand score of zilch*

VOCABULARY CHOICES

• The informal word **zilch** is usually used in a humorous way. Sometimes it hints at a feeling of disappointment or failure: *This record will do zilch in the charts.*

Index of synonyms

Index

Index

Index

Index

Index

Index

Index

Index

Index

Index

Index

Index

Index

Index

Index

Index

321

Index

Index

Index

Index

Index

Index

Index

Index

Index

Index

Index

Index

Index

Index

Index

Index

Index

Index

I

Index

Index

Index

Index

Index

Index

Index

Index

Index

Index

Index

Index

Index

Index

Index

Index

Index

Index

367

Index

Index

Index

Index

Index

Index

Index

Index

Index

Index

Index

Index

Index

Index

Index

Index

Index

Index

Index

Index

Index

Index

Index

Index

Index

Index

Index